The American President in Film and Television

The American President in Film and Television

Myth, Politics and Representation

Gregory Frame

PETER LANG
Oxford • Bern • Berlin • Bruxelles • Frankfurt am Main • New York • Wien

Bibliographic information published by Die Deutsche Nationalbibliothek
Die Deutsche Nationalbibliothek lists this publication in the Deutsche Nationalbibliografie; detailed bibliographic data is available on the Internet at http://dnb.d-nb.de.

A catalogue record for this book is available from the British Library.

Library of Congress Control Number: 2017957162

Cover picture: Martin Sheen in *The West Wing* (2001).
Reproduced with permission from Warner Brothers TV / Kobal Collection.

Cover design by Peter Lang Ltd.

ISBN 978-1-78874-143-9 (print) • ISBN 978-1-78874-263-4 (ePDF)
ISBN 978-1-78874-264-1 (ePub) • ISBN 978-1-78874-265-8 (mobi)

This is a revised version of *The American President in Film and Television*, 2014, ISBN 978-3-0343-0951-6 by the same author.

This paperback edition first published in 2018.

Wabernstrasse 40, CH-3007 Bern, Switzerland
info@peterlang.com, www.peterlang.com, www.peterlang.net

Printed in Germany

For Hannah and Elliott

Contents

Illustrations

Preface to the Second Edition

Many people were shocked and dismayed by Donald Trump's victory in November 2016. I was one of them. While this book argued claims that the United States had entered a 'post-racial' era following President Obama's victories in 2008 and 2012 were premature given the rise of populist, right-wing forces against his administration, it did not seem even when this book was originally published in 2014 that there was any chance Trump could win the Republican nomination, let alone the election itself. As was noted on Election Night 2016 by author and political commentator Van Jones, Trump's win could be construed as a racist 'whitelash' against the demographic changes in the United States and the country's first black president.[1]

However, in many respects the election victory of a reality television star running on a populist platform reinforced the argument of this book that, however seemingly trivial films and television programmes featuring fictional presidents in prominent roles appear to be, they play a vital and significant role in articulating what characteristics people look for in a commander in chief: like many of his fictional counterparts, Trump ran for president as a crusader from outside politics, claiming he wanted to clean up a corrupt system and return power to the people. He fulfilled the desire for a return (if, indeed, such a figure has ever existed) of the authentic politician: not afraid to speak his mind, willing to abandon his predetermined talking points and depart from the teleprompter, and refusing to apply the varnish of a focus group or listen to media polls.[2] Unblemished

1 Josiah Ryan, '"This was a whitelash": Van Jones' take on the election results', November 9th, 2016, <http://edition.cnn.com/2016/11/09/politics/van-jones-results-disappointment-cnntv/index.html>, accessed September 2017.

2 Gregory Frame, '"The Real Thing": Election Campaigns and the Question of Authenticity in American Film and Television', *Journal of American Studies* 50/3 (August 2016), 755-77.

by association with the crooked, dishonest politicians that have engineered the system to work only for them and their rich friends, the populist hero rides into town to 'drain the swamp'. Sound familiar? Think Jefferson Smith (Jimmy Stewart) in *Mr Smith Goes to Washington* (Frank Capra, 1939), Dave Kovic (Kevin Klein) in *Dave* (Ivan Reitman, 1993), or Tom Dobbs in *Man of the Year (*Barry Levinson, 2006). Having said this, a crucial aspect of my argument was that the function of such representations is primarily cathartic. However disenchanted people are with the political system, they will resist the temptation to vote for a figure like this because: firstly, they recognise that reality is much more complicated and the solutions being offered are bunkum; secondly, their yearning for this hero has been reasonably sated by fiction. Donald Trump's victory flipped this equation on its head. He is, to some degree, a fictional character blundering around in the 'real world' of American politics.

So, to a large extent, I should not have been so surprised by Trump's victory. As I argued of *Abraham Lincoln: Vampire Hunter* at the conclusion of this book, 'there remains the desire for a presidential strongman in a period in which the dominant attitude towards politicians and presidents appears to be one of cynicism and disdain, and that such a representation performs a psychological function, simplifying complex issues [and] providing comforting explanations'. To some extent, we can be thankful that Trump believed this fiction, perpetuated by many of the portrayals of the office in film and television, that the presidency enjoys unchallenged power and can bend the world to its will. For all of his bravura posturing on Twitter, Tolkienesque rhetoric in relation to North Korea, and apparent determination to use his presidency simply to undo whatever President Barack Obama did, he has been largely unable to achieve anything thanks to the checks and balances of the American democratic system. Congressional recalcitrance and judicial independence have, thus far, proved their worth and demonstrated that the reality is considerably stickier (however, this is unlikely to provide much comfort to those groups of people who have been, or will be, victims of the racism, misogyny, homophobia and hatred that has been given license to operate by Trump's election). Indeed, it is a reality representations of the presidency since the original publication of this book have been keen to explore: *Scandal* (Shonda Rhimes, 2012–18) and *House of Cards* (Beau Willimon, 2012–), while different in many ways, share in their portrayal of the presidency a sense that it is a frustrating, almost thankless, role. The tiresome bargaining, compromise, shady deals and questionable allies one has to make are here for all to see, rendering the president a weak, impotent, frustrated individual who would either happily give up the job for love (*Scandal*) or resort to extraordinary levels of corruption to inject it with some power (*House of Cards*).[3]

Premiering on ABC the month before Trump's victory, *Designated Survivor* (David Guggenheim, 2016–) tells the story of Tom Kirkman (Kiefer Sutherland), the Secretary of Housing and Development, who suddenly becomes President of the United States when the Capitol Building is blown up in a terrorist attack during the State of the Union. As the 'designated survivor' (the government official asked to remain in a secure location during this setpiece occasion in American political life who will become president should the unthinkable happen) he has the constitutional duty to assume the presidency after the attack. However, he has no experience of high office, let alone the ability to provide a response to the biggest ever terrorist incident on American soil. He is perceived as illegitimate, as weak, as intellectual rather than decisive (because – and, believe it or not, this is a common trope in presidential fiction – he wears glasses). However, unlike the recent, hyperviolent revenge fantasies *Olympus Has Fallen* (Antoine Fuqua, 2013) and *White House Down* (Roland Emmerich, 2013), *Designated Survivor* prescribes a sober, measured and careful response to the attacks. In many ways it appears to be a recalibration of the national 'home invasion' narrative that deliver fantasies of swift and uncompromising retribution: Kirkman is restrained, thoughtful and unwilling to act until he is *absolutely* sure of who has done this and why.

As with all film and television that in some way attempts to mirror reality, it is tempting to read *Designated Survivor* as a 'comment' on Donald

3 Gregory Frame, 'The Leader of the Free World? Representing the declining presidency in television drama', in Betty Kaklamanidou and Margaret J. Tally, eds, *Politics and Politicians in Contemporary US Television: Washington as Fiction* (Abingdon: Routledge, 2017), 61-74.

Trump's conduct in office. The only obvious similarity between Kirkman and Trump is that Kirkman is not a politician. Although he worked in government as Secretary for Housing and Development, he did so for altruistic reasons. He is not a 'Beltway' politician: he has no ambitions to climb the political ladder. He has only become president because of completely unforeseen, tragic circumstances. He is a public servant and assures us that he only got into this game to help people (further completing this picture is the fact that his wife is an immigration lawyer). The show is also at pains to reaffirm his status as a family man: a neat motif throughout is that Kirkman plays with his wedding ring while in the process of making life-or-death decisions in response to the terrorist attack. He refuses to endorse torture as a tactic of catching the people responsible and stands up for the rights of refugees when an immigration ban is proposed (the ban is successful, but he makes sure the refugees make it to Canada, rather than abandon them entirely). Despite safety fears, and a ricin attack, Kirkman refuses to allow elections to be cancelled or postponed, as electing a new Congress is considered the highest priority. Ensuring the stability and continuity of the Republic is his overriding aim. Kirkman deliberates, considers and ponders decisions before acting. He valorises the Constitution above all else, calling in the National Guard when a State Governor starts targeting Muslims shortly after the attack. He does not show off, grandstand; he is dignified, responsible, measured and moderate. The fact that Kirkman is played by Kiefer Sutherland speaks to a rather radical shift in the fictional presidential imaginary – Sutherland is perhaps best known in recent years for his portrayal of counterterrorism agent Jack Bauer in *24* (Joel Surnow, 2001–10), the television show that captured the post-9/11 *zeitgeist* and arguably provided popular cultural justification for the extreme policies pursued by the Bush administration. In *Designated Survivor*, Jack Bauer is president, but one who appears to have learned the lessons of his predecessors. He has the temperament necessary to defend the nation in turbulent times, and he will protect the constitution, liberal values and the rule of law.

This stands in in stark contrast, it must be said, to his real-life counterpart, who spent his first month in office undermining the judiciary over his ill-considered ban on travel from particular countries in the Middle East and North Africa, attacking celebrities like Arnold Schwarzenegger, and making laughably overblown statements as though he was a character in a Hollywood movie (tweeting all in caps when his travel ban was struck down, 'SEE YOU IN COURT, THE SECURITY OF OUR NATION IS AT STAKE!'). Trump's status as a TV character who became president was confirmed by the fact that he fired the director of the FBI, James Comey, live on television. Kirkman's characterisation suggests that fictional models of presidential heroism are becoming considerably more reliant upon people that have occupied the office in reality: Kirkman fancies himself a Kennedy, a Lincoln, or even an Obama, in his measured, thoughtful and liberal responses to national and international conflict. On the other hand, Trump appears more concerned with sharpening his reality TV persona for the political stage. Aggressive, arrogant and loud, Trump is a popular culture president occupying the Oval Office, whereas Kirkman is a real president occupying a fictional television show. It says much about the state of the real presidency that someone as ordinary and unflashy as Kirkman is the new 'fantasy' in which audiences can escape.

Escaping from the reality of Donald Trump's presidency is perhaps the defining factor in the continued nostalgia for *The West Wing* (Aaron Sorkin, 1999–2006), which has enjoyed renewed interest as a result of its availability on US Netflix.[4] *The West Wing Weekly*, a podcast featuring Hrishikesh Hirway and former star Joshua Malina, recaps each episode, commenting on how much politics has changed (largely for the worse) and interviews prominent figures from the show. As this book argued, at the time of its broadcast *The West Wing* was engaged in these processes, positioning the intellectual President Josiah Bartlet (Martin Sheen) as a fictional antidote to the apparently impetuous President George W. Bush. In so doing it offered a fantasy alternative to Bush's 'war on terror' and suggested how the United States' response to 9/11 might have been conducted in a more reasonable and measured way. Now added to this fantasy

4 Jacob Stolworthy, 'Donald Trump presidency sparks rise in *The West Wing* viewership', *The Independent*, 16th February 2017, <http://www.independent.co.uk/arts-entertainment/tv/news/donald-trump-the-west-wing-where-to-watch-aaron-sorkin-a7583516.html>, accessed March 2017.

are generous helpings of nostalgia, which could be viewed as problematic in a number of ways. Whereas previous retreats into presidential fiction could be viewed as necessary catharsis, the existential threat Trump poses to democracy renders such nostalgia at best a dangerous indulgence, a child-like inability to face up to political reality. *The West Wing* is, perhaps, a comfort blanket that one can ill-afford.

Furthermore, *The West Wing* bears many of the qualities to which Trump supporters are opposed: both celebrated and derided for its left-wing slant, it nonetheless has an often haughty, hectoring tone; its stars, members of the Hollywood elite, moonlight as political activists and their relationship with real politics was often uncomfortably close; it was (and is) celebrated by broadsheet critics and watched by the affluent, liberal middle-class. Rather than resort to the lazy, journalistic assertion that shows like *The West Wing* are 'the reason Trump won', it is possible to suggest that it speaks to a division within American society: it cannot be said that Aaron Sorkin's vision of a liberal, intellectual presidency was designed to speak to the nation's heartlands. That said, *The West Wing Weekly* is not unthinking in its look back at the programme, reserving particular criticism for the show's often problematic gender politics, and offers a primer on ways in which it can be a functional tool in the ongoing processes of civic education. Looking at some of the real-world issues that the show explored in a contemporary light – like the Equal Rights Amendment, the death penalty and the racial problematics of the US census – *The West Wing Weekly* attempts to operate as an addendum to the new activism and an education in the processes of government. It cannot help but comment on contemporary politics, with Hiraway and Malina using the phrase 'Trump Ay yay ay!' whenever the politics of the show become eerily reminiscent of reality. In this, *The West Wing* nostalgia appears to yearn for a figure as responsible, intelligent and reassuring as President Bartlet, and for a time when politics was more 'civil'.

While the previous iteration of this book argued that representations of women as occupants of the office are the 'unfinished business' of presidential fiction, there has been a relative boom in this area of late: President Elizabeth Keane (Elizabeth Marvel) in *Homeland* (Howard Gordon and Alex Gansa, 2011–), President Claire Underwood (Robin Wright) in *House of Cards*, President Claire Haas (Marcia Cross) in *Quantico* (Joshua Safran, 2015–) and President Selena Meyer in *Veep* (Armando Iannucci, 2012–18) are all recent examples of the fictional female presidency on television. Further work remains to be done on these iterations of the archetype, although it must be noted that *House of Cards*, *Quantico* and *Veep* perpetuate the tendency to position the female president as an 'accidental' leader, ascending to the highest office as the result of a constitutional manoeuvre rather than popular election. It is difficult to determine what impact Hillary Clinton's defeat in 2016 will have on this aspect of the imaginary, and there are myriad factors as to why Trump won, but it would appear to confirm the notion that the presidency remains an office saturated in unreconstructed masculine ideology. Indeed, it is very depressing that the misogyny Clinton faced during her campaign in 2008 (explored in Chapter 6) was, if anything, worse in 2016.

During the administration of Ronald Reagan, the last time the orbits of celebrity and politics were this proximate, film and television rather retreated from fictional representations of the presidency. It is quite possible that a similar fate will befall the archetype in the Trump years: with a man taken from the screen occupying the real office, there will be perhaps little need to explore the presidential imaginary further until he is gone. Indeed, Trump's victory spoke of a revulsion with politicians in general, and Washington, DC, in particular, and perhaps the widespread disgust with politics will make itself felt in fictional realms too. But we can no longer pretend that revelling in James Marshall's (Harrison Ford) fisticuffs with Kazakh nationalists in *Air Force One* (Wolfgang Petersen, 1997), or cheering Josiah Bartlet as he issues a dressing down to a right-wing radio host in *The West Wing*, or laughing as James Sawyer (Jamie Foxx) struggles to master the use of a rocket launcher while being chased by terrorists across the White House lawn in *White House Down*, is inconsequential. What were once film and television's improbable fantasies of what the President of the United States could, should and can be, have, with the election of Donald Trump, arguably become reality. Popular culture has metastisised in the political bloodstream: the discourses of celebrity, the gaudy sheen of reality television, the infantile longing for the strongman to rescue us, all filtered through the language and imagery of white, male supremacy to which film and television have long been willing contributors. While those of us with the privilege to critique what seemed to be such an unlikely eventuality – identifying the fictional antecedents of such a figure in popular culture, and discussing and debating Trump's impact on the films and television shows yet to be made – will do so, I expect those without such privileges will be content merely to survive it.

Gregory Frame
September 2017

Acknowledgements

I owe as much for the second edition to the people who supported me in the completion of the first. The bulk of the research for this book was conducted while studying for a PhD at the University of Warwick, which I began in October 2009 under the supervision of Professor Stella Bruzzi. Thank you to Stella for her guidance, suggestions and constructive feedback throughout the process, as well as her support since. In addition, much of the intellectual confidence that I developed over the course of my doctorate is down to her, and for this I will always be thankful. This book would not have been possible without the grant I received from the Arts and Humanities Research Council.

I am also grateful to the Institute of Advanced Study at the University of Warwick: the first edition of this book was commissioned for publication while I was an Early Career Fellow. Great appreciation goes to the University of Warwick's Humanities Research Fund, which provided financial support throughout this process, enabling me to present aspects of this research at national and international conferences. Enormous appreciation is due to colleagues and peers in the Department of Film and Television Studies at the University of Warwick, especially my friends Hayley Merchant, Owen Weetch, Nicolas Pillai, Derilene Marco, Lauren Jade Thompson, Richard Wallace, Santiago Oyarzabal, Adam Gallimore, Joseph Oldham, Anna Cooper, Mike Riding, Charlotte Stevens and Celia Nicholls. Your support was invaluable throughout this process. I also want to offer thanks to Helen Wheatley, José Arroyo, Ed Gallafent, Catherine Constable, Alastair Phillips and Rachel Moseley, for the help, advice and encouragement you gave me, as well as the many opportunities to develop as a scholar and teacher.

I will always be indebted to Tracey McVey and Anne Birchall at the University of Warwick, for their assistance and kind words of reassurance throughout. To Richard Perkins, thank you for responding to my every whim by tracking down some long-forgotten films from the dark recesses of the library. Thank you to Ed Braman at the University of York, for his vital help in the final stages of the process, and Laurel Plapp at Peter Lang, who has made the journey from proposal to publication as smooth as it possibly could have been.

Since joining Bangor University in January 2016, I have been fortunate to work with very supportive and helpful colleagues. Thank you to all of you, particularly Nathan Abrams, for his advice and encouragement regarding my research, and Eben Muse, Steffan Thomas, Jamie Sherry, Stephanie Marriott, Huw Powell, Geraint Ellis, Emma Thomas and Ifan Jones for your support and guidance. The dissemination of the ideas in this book at conferences and research seminars would also not have been possible without the support of Bangor, in both practical and intellectual terms.

The continued support and love of my family has played a huge role in the success of this book. Thank you to my mother, father and sister for their love and encouragement in all things, and to my family all over the world; and to my wife, Hannah, I will never be able to thank you enough.

CHAPTER 1

Introduction: The American President in History and Criticism

As the *denouement* of the 2008 American presidential election campaign approached in the midst of global economic meltdown, a poll of considerably less international significance took place. AOL's online blog, Moviefone.com, published the results of its survey of the world's favourite movie presidents.[1] President James Marshall (Harrison Ford), the Vietnam veteran tasked with thwarting a motley crew of bloodthirsty Kazakhstani nationalists in action-thriller *Air Force One* (Wolfgang Petersen, 1997), won by a healthy margin, collecting twenty-four per cent of the votes. In second place, a fair distance behind on sixteen per cent, was President Tom Beck (Morgan Freeman), the aged president who offers spiritual guidance as the world faces impending apocalypse at the hands of an asteroid in *Deep Impact* (Mimi Leder, 1998). The compilers of this poll attempted to impose logic upon these results: the interpretation offered for Marshall's victory was that it indicated a manifest desire for a Nietzschean *Übermensch* to guide the nation at a time of geopolitical and economic turmoil. A reasonable analysis, but how might Beck's strong showing be explained, given

1 'Moviefone Poll Suggests Voters Want Nation Run By Fictional Idiots' <http://gawker.com/5068639/moviefone-poll-suggests-voters-want-nation-run-by-fictional-idiot-presidents>, accessed June 2012. Full results as follows: 1. Harrison Ford – *Air Force One* (1997); 2. Morgan Freeman – *Deep Impact* (1998); 3. Michael Douglas – *The American President* (Rob Reiner, 1995); 4. Bill Pullman – *Independence Day* (Roland Emmerich, 1996); 5. Kevin Kline – *Dave* (Ivan Reitman, 1993); 6. Dennis Quaid – *American Dreamz* (Paul Weitz, 2006); 7. Bruce Greenwood – *National Treasure: Book of Secrets* (John Turteltaub, 2007); 8. James Cromwell – *The Sum of All Fears* (Phil Alden Robinson, 2002); 9. Jack Nicholson – *Mars Attacks* (Tim Burton, 1996); 10. Jeff Bridges – *The Contender* (Rod Lurie, 2000).

that he possesses none of these traits? In Beck's case, the fictional leader's blackness is understood as a straightforward precursor to Barack Obama's candidacy, the popularity of Morgan Freeman as a star allegedly indicative of the widespread tolerant attitudes that have delivered the United States' first black presidential nominee.

Perhaps unsurprisingly, there is scant mention of the generic, iconographic and narrative differences between the two films, nor of the Hollywood traditions from which they emerge. There is no engagement with, or even acknowledgment of, the sheer diversity of representations on offer in the poll's results, which is clearly their primary point of interest.[2] With one or two notable exceptions, the real presidency has been characterised by a distinct *lack* of diversity: John F. Kennedy and Barack Obama aside, the position of American president has been the province of white, Protestant men. What does the presence of films as varied as action-thriller *Air Force One*, disaster movie *Deep Impact*, romantic comedies *Dave* (Ivan Reitman, 1993) and *The American President* (Rob Reiner, 1995), anarchic alien invasion spoof *Mars Attacks!* (Tim Burton, 1996) and serious drama *The Contender* (Rod Lurie, 2000) say about Hollywood's attitude towards the presidency? Aside from the inevitable, though somewhat ham-fisted, attempt to discern a legible pattern within the poll's results, there are other issues that arise from it that are altogether more intriguing.

The fact that a poll was conducted *at all* suggests that the fictional presidency has reached critical mass: there are now enough representations of imaginary chief executives to place them in categories, to distinguish and separate the archetype's various manifestations, and thereby establish criteria upon which the fictional president may be theorised. It is not all too dissimilar from the rating and ranking of real-life presidents, which has been a preoccupation in both scholarly and popular cultural circles since the 1940s. However, the presidents that often emerge at the tops of

2 The contemporaneous nature of the films featured, which receives no acknowledgement in the poll, is perhaps reflective of the computer-literate nature of the people who took part, as it was online. A broader survey may have included films that were produced before the 1990s, but the absence of anything prior to the final decade of the twentieth century is intriguing given the focus of this book.

these polls – George Washington (1789–97), Abraham Lincoln (1861–5) and Franklin D. Roosevelt (1933–45) – conform to a particular brand of presidential leadership. Strong, activist leaders who presided over periods of armed conflict are celebrated above all. The diversity of the presidents in the fictional poll suggests that Hollywood's presidency either has little to do with conceptions of the real Commander in Chief, or the relationship between the real and the fictional is an altogether more complex one.

This book will examine the representation of the American president in mainstream film and television, with particular emphasis on the figure's fictional incarnations. Representations of presidents have become somewhat ubiquitous in the past two decades: where once the presidency was treated with overwhelming reverence, the institution has become a rather throwaway archetype in visual culture (this is not to suggest, however, that all vestiges of the aforementioned deference have disappeared). In keeping with this observation, the primary focus of this book is the last two decades (roughly 1992–2012). The rationale behind this demarcation is as follows: for various reasons which will be explored later, this period has seen representations of the presidency proliferate in film and television. All of the films featured in the 2008 poll of favourite fictional chief executives were produced in these two decades. Furthermore, the 1990s represents a crucial shift in the conception of the presidency: with the collapse of the Soviet Union in 1991 and the end of the Cold War, issues surrounding American power were thrown suddenly into flux. The influence of mass media on the 'personalisation' of the presidency arguably reached its culmination during the presidency of Bill Clinton (1993–2001) and the fallout from the Monica Lewinsky scandal. This transformation of the presidency occurred alongside broader debate surrounding new definitions of masculinity in the 'postfeminist' environment, and discussions of gender are central to this book. This will prove particularly pertinent as I move to discuss fictional presidencies of the 2000s, with emphasis on the impact of the terrorist attacks on New York and Washington, DC in September 2001. The ways the representations of the president negotiated issues surrounding masculinity, the appropriate use of American power in the post-9/11 environment, and the policies of George W. Bush's administration (2001–9) are of crucial importance. Whether these issues – cultural, political and historical – resulted in critique or reinforcement of dominant conceptions of the presidency is a fundamental issue with which this book will grapple.

An additional reason for dealing primarily with post-1992 texts is that much of the pre-existing literature in the field is hamstrung by a totalising approach. Addressing the entire history of Hollywood's representation of American politics and politicians – stretching from silent-era films featuring Abraham Lincoln all the way through to the present day – renders much of the analysis within these studies cursory and underdeveloped. The history of the presidency in film and television, in its entirety, would be far too big a project to undertake in this book. As a result, gaps and elisions are inevitable, and difficult choices have had to be made. It is worth acknowledging a few of these gaps here.

The internet survey's narrow focus upon fictional presidencies of the past two decades is indicative of the tendency to ignore the archetype's development over the course of film and television history. Although star images and their relationship with representations of the presidency is a crucial aspect of this book, space constraints have prevented me from addressing in detail the significance of Henry Fonda's roles as president (*Fail-Safe* [Sidney Lumet, 1964] and *Meteor* [Ronald Neame, 1979]), or as Abraham Lincoln (*Young Mr Lincoln* [John Ford, 1939]). Fonda's influence upon representations of politics is vital.[3] Like Frank Capra, mention of whose work is absent from the survey (but the significance of which will be discussed in Chapter 3), Fonda's political roles celebrate the presence of morally upstanding and conscientious figures in the upper echelons of American politics, an attitude hugely significant in the work of Aaron Sorkin (*The American President* [Rob Reiner, 1995] and *The West Wing* [1999–2006]).[4] In essence, Fonda's involvement in films addressing politics and the presidency reaffirms the common conception of the American system as benign (as long as those in control of it have noble intentions).

3 Fonda also portrayed politicians in *Advise and Consent* (Otto Preminger, 1962) and *The Best Man* (Franklin J. Schaffner, 1964).

4 Fonda's star image was predicated upon playing this kind of figure, the most famous of which is perhaps his role as Juror #8 in *12 Angry Men* (Sidney Lumet, 1957).

Lamentably, political films of the 1970s have remained outside the parameters of this book. Their influence upon representations of politics and the presidency cannot be denied: while films like *The Candidate* (Michael Ritchie, 1972), *Executive Action* (David Miller, 1973), *The Parallax View* (Alan J. Pakula, 1974) and *All the President's Men* (Alan J. Pakula, 1976) do not represent the president directly, their scepticism and mistrust of the political system provide important barometers of attitudes towards American politics and society in the period. Furthermore, their influence on more generic thrillers of the 1990s and 2000s that address politics and the presidency is undeniable: films depicting political corruption like *The Pelican Brief* (Alan J. Pakula, 1993), *Clear and Present Danger* (Phillip Noyce, 1994), *Absolute Power* (Clint Eastwood, 1997) and *Murder at 1600* (Dwight H. Little, 1997) owe aesthetic and narrative debt to the films of the 1970s. For example, although its origin lay in the uncovering of the Watergate scandal, one cannot imagine that the underground parking garage would have become cultural shorthand for political espionage and conspiracy were it not for its representation in *All the President's Men*.

Excluded from the Moviefone survey because of its resolutely cinematic focus, the fictional presidency on television is of vital importance to this book. This is not only because of television's enormous influence on the character and constitution of the presidency, but long-form serial dramas like *Commander in Chief* (Rod Lurie, 2005–6), *The West Wing* and *24* (Joel Surnow, 2001–10) demonstrate the medium's ability to develop broad, complex and nuanced portrayals of fictional leaders which the tighter parameters of a feature film do not allow. Consideration of television also enables focus upon the work of Martin Sheen, an actor who looms large over representations of politics and the presidency. Aside from his portrayal of President Bartlet in *The West Wing*, Sheen has also played John F. Kennedy (*Kennedy* [Jim Goddard, 1983]) and Robert F. Kennedy (*The Missiles of October* [Anthony Page, 1974]) in television mini-series. In film, he has played the vice president in *The Dead Zone* (David Cronenberg, 1983) and chief of staff to Michael Douglas's President Shepherd in *The American President*, provided uncredited voiceover narration for *JFK* (Oliver Stone, 1991) and had a small role in *Bobby* (Emilio Estevez, 2006), which explores the impact of Robert Kennedy's assassination on the

American psyche.[5] The 'real' presidency with which Sheen is most readily associated is Kennedy's, and this influence will be addressed in relation to *The West Wing* (Chapter 4).[6]

Therefore, while this book focuses primarily on the last two decades, it will not address its subject in isolation. Nor will it become another exercise in essentialist comparison between Hollywood representation and historical/political reality. While I look to say something *specific* about the contemporary fictional presidency, a central facet of my work is to position the American president as an archetype that operates within *film and television* history: how it has evolved within the generic, iconographic and narrative parameters of mainstream cinema and television. Hence my suggestion that contemporary, fictional representations of the office have their sites of origin in an earlier period: this book encompasses analysis and discussion of films about politics and the presidency stretching back to the administration of Franklin D. Roosevelt. This is not to suggest that there were *no* representations of the president in film and television prior to this date: the silent era featured many representations of Abraham Lincoln, with the most famous incarnation of the period being in *The Birth of a Nation* (D.W. Griffith, 1915). Furthermore, Theodore Roosevelt's performances in

5 Oliver Stone's contribution to contemporary understanding of presidential myth cannot be underestimated – *JFK* courted enormous controversy for its supposedly anti-historical approach to the Kennedy presidency and assassination. The complexities of Stone's political messages are examined in detail by Susan Mackey-Kallis, *Oliver Stone's America: 'Dreaming the Myth Outward'* (Oxford: Westview, 1996) and in Robert Brent Toplin, ed., *Oliver Stone's USA: Film, History and Controversy* (Lawrence: University Press of Kansas, 2000). Despite the controversies, Stone's films about American politics and society provide reinforcement rather than challenge to dominant conceptions of the American political system, and American national identity. The conclusion of *JFK*, for example, in which Jim Garrison (Kevin Costner) confronts the court with evidence of a conspiracy to assassinate Kennedy, has an idealised view of the American system that would not look out of place in *Mr Smith Goes to Washington*.

6 Sheen is also well known for his liberal activism, and has been arrested upwards of sixty times for protesting and civil disobedience. His portrayal of President Bartlet in *The West Wing* inspired a short-lived campaign to get him elected.

newsreels were a vital progenitor to the later saturation of our televisions and computer screens with images of the president.[7] My decision to position Franklin Roosevelt's presidency as the 'origin' of the cinematic and televisual presidencies is manifold: firstly, historians and political scientists have argued that Roosevelt's enormous expansion of the federal bureaucracy to combat the Great Depression inaugurated what has been described as 'The Modern Presidency' (I will discuss this notion in more detail later). Furthermore, Roosevelt was the first president to consider the use of mass media as a vital component to the successful execution of the office. While later presidents and more advanced communications technologies would expand the significance of this relationship enormously, it was Roosevelt who realised the power of broadcast radio to communicate with, and reassure, his people. This cultivation of an intimate relationship with American citizens is an essential facet of the demystification of the presidency, a process which has had significant impact on the office's fictional incarnations.

In Film and Television Studies, this subject occupies something of a curious place. There is a great deal of literature addressing the representation of politics in film, and some burgeoning explorations of the presidency itself, but this research has tended to be conducted by researchers outside the fields of Film and Television Studies proper: historians, political scientists, literary and communications scholars, and academics from the broad church of American Studies appear to have carved out audiovisual representations of the presidency (and American politics more generally) as their preserve. For a film and television scholar, this presents something of a problem. Much of the work that has been done tends towards the treatment of film as historical artefact, with comparative analyses of the 'real' and the 'reel' being of particular concern. What has not emerged in scholarship in this area is the manner in which the *textual* dynamics at work in mainstream cinema and television impact upon representations of the

7 For a detailed exploration of the various cinematic manifestations of Theodore Roosevelt (both fiction and actuality), see Brian Neve, '"The Picture Man": The Cinematic Strife of Theodore Roosevelt', in Iwan W. Morgan, ed., *Presidents in the Movies: American History and Politics on Screen* (New York: Palgrave Macmillan, 2011), 65–86.

presidency. The essence of this book is to expand upon existing work in the field by employing textual analysis as its central method, alongside historical, political and psychological studies of the presidency. What might be established by conducting a generic, aesthetic and narrative examination of the cinematic and televisual presidencies, in conjunction with a wide-ranging historical, political and cultural discussion of the contexts from which these texts emerge? In essence, can one detect an aesthetic reaction to wider cultural shifts – in terms of gender, race, myth and major historical events – in these representations?

The absence of this aesthetic approach to studies of representations of the presidency within Film and Television Studies is indicative possibly of a scholarly anxiety about dealing with a complex institution that already crosses the boundaries of so many different disciplines. There may be the suggestion that to intervene in a field which requires diverse knowledge would be to invite accusations of ignorance or disciplinary 'tourism' (an accusation that could easily be levelled in the opposite direction). I am not pretending to 'know more' about the presidency than a political scientist or a historian who has devoted their academic life to an understanding of a historically, politically and culturally essential institution. I am looking merely to redress the balance: for example, I contend that you cannot discuss President James Marshall (*Air Force One*), the victor in the 'Favourite Fictional Presidents Poll', *without* an understanding of the action genre and its history, how this generic framework impacts upon the film's representation of gender, the importance of Harrison Ford's star image, and the ways in which these issues reinforce or challenge more general attitudes towards the presidency during the period in which the film was produced.

Further, the absence of textual considerations often results in a misremembering of the nuances within Hollywood's representations of politics and the presidency: much like the term 'Capraesque', the connotations of which suggests an ebullience and optimism that overlooks the dark undertones in Capra's work, a lack of appreciation of textual nuance and generic convention leads to suggestions that President Whitmore (Bill Pullman) in *Independence Day* (Roland Emmerich, 1996) is a straightforward 'action hero' president, when in fact he spends much of the film impotent and powerless in the face of the alien threat. Further, it is crucial to revisit *Deep*

Impact's formal and generic structures in order to re-evaluate the notion that the film partially 'predicted' Obama's presidency. Failure to appreciate the manner in which the construction of images functions in relation to the presidency severely impedes understanding of how dominant myths of the office have been cultivated, complicated and re-articulated in films and television. Rigorous understanding of the cinematic and televisual presidencies demands intervention from scholars more comfortable with discussing the dynamics of visual culture. I will emphasise the fictional presidency's continuities with past representations of the office, while remaining acutely aware of the danger of sliding into essentialist comparisons of the real and the fictional. Ultimately, this book looks to reclaim the fictional president in cinema and television as an archetype that operates within an *aesthetic* framework, but one that intersects in complex ways with the historical, cultural and political contexts in which it operates. This book therefore looks to engage fully with the politics of representation in The Representation of Politics.

***

The structure of the book is as follows: as part of this introduction, I offer a brief survey of the literature that has dealt with this subject, outlining examples of some of the problems I have explored above. I will then move to discuss literature with which this book has a more cooperative relationship, particularly work that contends with the ideological ramifications of mainstream cinema and television.

Chapter 2, 'The Symbolic Presidency: Washington and Hollywood (1932–89)', is intended as a bridge between the introduction and Chapter 3. It will chart the history of the presidency in the twentieth century alongside Hollywood's attitudes towards presidents, politics and the political system. This will be a broad and discursive analysis that will establish various issues with which the remainder of the book will contend, present an account for aspects of this subject that have not found their way into the main body of my analysis, as well as provide a microcosm for the book's methodological approach. This chapter will reaffirm my intention to view the cinematic and televisual presidencies within a broader history of representation, as well as provide crucial contextual discussion that will frame my later chapters.

Chapter 3, 'The Post-Cold War Presidency in Hollywood Cinema', will examine the fictional presidency in the immediate aftermath of the Soviet Union's collapse. In order to develop as broad a picture as possible, the chapter is bifurcated: the first half examines the reversion to conventions of the Capra-era political comedy in *Dave* and *The American President*, while the second half explores the president-as-action-hero archetype in *Independence Day* and *Air Force One*. The methodological approach of this chapter is to engage with debates surrounding America's post-Cold War ascendancy and confidence. This will involve discussion of changing expectations of the presidency in this environment, and how the ambivalence towards President Bill Clinton is reflected in the diverse nature of the films produced in the period. In relation to Clinton, this chapter will contend with issues of gender: firstly, taking into account the changes that dominant conceptions of manhood underwent during this decade, how did these films reflect shifting expectations of the president's masculinity in the 1990s? Secondly, considering how Hillary Rodham Clinton's influence on public policy altered understanding of the First Lady's role, how did these films address the increased proximity of women to the presidency, an institution ordinarily defined by a traditional model of masculinity?

Emerging at the end of the Clinton era, *The West Wing* is perhaps the most famous and expansive exploration of a fictional presidency. Chapter 4 will examine two facets of the programme's construction: the first addresses how the programme provided a complex critique of Bush administration policies through its shifting visual dynamics and changing attitudes towards American power in the pre- and post-9/11 periods. The second section emerges out of this discussion, with a particular focus on the psychology of the programme's fictional president, Josiah Bartlet (Martin Sheen). It will explore how, through an eradication of his deceased father's influence upon his character and decision-making, Bartlet learns to accept the responsibilities of the presidency in the post-9/11 environment. This section will engage with Freudian theories surrounding the father/son relationship, arguing that *The West Wing* posits America's former presidents as more adequate paternal figures for a man of Bartlet's intellectual and moral stature. Overall, this chapter looks to reevaluate the pre-existing scholarship on *The West*

Wing, developing a fuller picture of the ways in which the programme's aesthetics and tone changed over the course of its life.

Chapter 5 will interrogate the phenomenon of the fictional black president in cinema and television, reevaluating the suggestion that Hollywood had an influence on the election of Barack Obama. Through analysis of *Deep Impact*, *24* and *2012* (Roland Emmerich, 2009), I will problematise the notion that these films are 'post-racial' and argue that the fictional black president is a logical extension of representations of black men more generally in film and television.[8] My discussions of *Deep Impact* and *2012* will demonstrate the extent to which the black president is confined by conventions of the disaster film, while my analysis of *24* will address the programme's relationship to the 'war on terror', and the ways in which its attitudes towards race and gender are negotiated in relation to this conflict. This chapter will demonstrate that, without a real-life example on which to base its representation, there was inevitable recourse to pre-existing stereotypes of black men in the creation of the fictional black presidency.

Having complicated the origins of Barack Obama's presidential image in Chapter 5, Chapter 6 will turn to representations of fictional female presidents, with particular focus on *Commander in Chief* which, despite being cancelled after only one season, remains the most elaborate and detailed example of this phenomenon. In its focus upon President Mackenzie Allen's (Geena Davis) attempt to balance her family life and her job as president, the programme sits broadly within problematic postfeminist discourses that express doubts about the ability of working women to manage successfully the competing demands of career, marriage and children. This chapter will examine what impact this has upon the programme's representation of presidential power and its relationship with motherhood and

8 Space constraints have prevented me from delving into *The West Wing*'s representation of Latino candidate for president Matt Santos (Jimmy Smits), but the academic and popular criticism of the character raises many similar issues regarding the problematic nature of the term 'post-racial', and the tendency to collapse all non-white presidencies into one, without much concern for the distinctions between the origins and experiences of African Americans and Hispanic Americans.

femininity. Positioning Allen between real-life examples of female politicians like Hillary Rodham Clinton and a broader representational history of women in film and television, this chapter will argue that *Commander in Chief*'s attempt to carve a place for a woman within the conventionally patriarchal and hypermasculine schema of the American presidency results in a complex and contradictory navigation of the terrain surrounding the traditional nuclear family.

Overall, this book looks to reevaluate and reposition the fictional presidency as beholden not only to its relationship with reality and political history, but the ways in which it promiscuously jumps the barriers between history, politics and visual culture to create images that draw from, and elaborate upon, mythological constructions of the president, American politics and, by extension, the identity and purpose of the United States as a whole.

Given the recent ubiquity of the presidency in cinema and television, the relative lack of critical attention paid to the subject is perhaps unexpected. There are plenty of monographs and articles which address the concept of *politics* and film, but discussion surrounding how the presidency is constructed, and what iconographic tropes and narrative templates are employed in its representation, has been given relatively short shrift. Here I will outline briefly the literature that has examined this subject, demonstrating the tendencies towards essentialism, totality, and the discomfort with discussing audiovisual material.

***

The issue of essentialism pervades Peter Rollins and John O'Connor's edited collection, *Hollywood's White House* (2003). The collection is wide-ranging, beginning to tackle questions surrounding the relationship between history and representation, and putting forward the notion that the real-life presidency has now become inextricably involved with the politics of image-making and the seductive nature of the screen (both televisual and cinematic). However, because of its broad approach, the collection raises more questions than it answers and also falls victim to an essentialist attitude toward history and film – namely, that audiovisual texts which address these issues should be held up to history like a mirror, and we should assess their quality based on this set of criteria.[9] This is particularly true of John Shelton Lawrence's intervention, which suggests that the box-office successes of *Air Force One* and *Independence Day* are indicative of a conscious desire on the part of the electorate for more traditionally masculine leaders.[10] It is the contention of this book that it is never quite as simple as that, and more often than not, mainstream cinema is in fact engaged in a more complex dialogue with the culture from which it emanates.

The problems of the totalising approach are in evidence in John Matviko's edited collection *The American President in Popular Culture*, Michael Coyne's *Hollywood Goes to Washington: American Politics on Screen* and Jeff Smith's *The Presidents We Imagine: Two Centuries of White House Fictions On the Page, On the Stage, Onscreen and Online*.[11] Matviko's collection assesses the cultural imagination of the office, and the person who occupies it, through a variety of diverse prisms, ranging from its representation in the media (film, television, radio and newspapers) to more abstract attitudes gleaned from presidential memorabilia, libraries, homes, birthplaces and graves. While the ground covered is admirable and prompts many interesting questions, once again the attempt to totalise damages the depth of the project, many of the ideas remaining perfunctory and undeveloped. Susan Stoddart's short chapter on 'Film', for example, does

9 This is the approach Leonard Quart and Albert Auster have adopted in *American Film and Society Since 1945* (Oxford: Praeger, 2002), now in its fourth edition. Their method is best encapsulated in the introduction, where they assert, 'It is hardly an original point, though it bears repeating, that films have the ability to evoke the mood and tone of a society in a particular era.' (1). I agree to an extent, although I look to complicate this assertion through closer attention to textual detail.

10 John Shelton Lawrence, 'The 100 Millon$ Men: Presidential Action/Adventure Heroes of *Independence Day* and *Air Force One*', in Peter Rollins and John E. O'Connor, eds, *Hollywood's White House: The American Presidency in Film and History* (Lexington: University Press of Kentucky, 2003), 223–33.

11 John W. Matviko, ed., *The American President in Popular Culture* (Westport: Greenwood Press, 2005); Michael Coyne, *Hollywood Goes to Washington: American Politics on Screen* (London: Reaktion Books, 2008); *The Presidents We Imagine: Two Centuries of White House Fictions On the Page, On the Stage, Onscreen and Online* (Madison: University of Wisconsin Press, 2009).

not go beyond casual observations made of biographical films like *Young Mr Lincoln*, *Sunrise at Campobello* (Vincent J. Donehue, 1960) and *Nixon* (Oliver Stone, 1995). However, it does address the crucial element of performance, impersonation and the presidency, and raises interesting notions regarding how the interpretive performance of a president is almost inevitably dictated by images gleaned from both reality *and* representation.[12] I will develop these ideas further through close textual analysis and rigorous engagement with politics, history and ideology.

Coyne covers the representation of the presidency throughout cinema history, from Abraham Lincoln in D.W. Griffith's *The Birth of a Nation*, through Frank Capra's idealistic political comedies of the 1930s, the political thrillers of the 1960s and 1970s, to more recent biopics of real-life presidents and the resurgence of the conspiracy thriller during the George W. Bush administration. When it comes to the representations of *presidents*, Coyne is particularly concerned with addressing the depictions of real-life chief executives, looking particularly at the cinematic portrayals of Lincoln and Kennedy. He appears less concerned with the ideological implications of the fictional presidency and persists with discussing the cinematic presidency in historically essentialist terms. However, one aspect of Coyne's work of particular interest is his brief examination of presidential nostalgia – why certain presidents are revisited in film and some are not, and at which points these cinematic revivals occur. His discussion of *Wilson* (Henry King, 1994) in relation to its propagandistic function during World War II is particularly useful in this regard.

Jeff Smith's monograph *The Presidents We Imagine* differs slightly, charting the evolution of the president's representation in novels, theatre, film, television and on the internet. Smith wide-ranging approach means many of the ideas are only glanced over, but he raises interesting issues regarding the general impressions of the presidency being dictated by technological changes and significant historical events. His work is also most valuable in demonstrating how the president has evolved from its

12 Scott F. Stoddart, 'Film', in Matviko, ed., *The American President in Popular Culture*, 164–5.

early conception as a pseudo-mythical figure into something altogether more vulnerable and human. His approach is, broadly, a technologically determinist one: the advance of communications technologies (radio, television and the internet) created an increasingly intimate relationship between the president and the populace.

According to Smith, the 1960s represent a radical shift in the cultural imaginary regarding the nature of the presidency, mapping the era's fictions onto its real events to create a thought-provoking picture of the Cold War presidency. He contends that the presidency in the 1960s and 1970s is marked by an overriding sense of fragility, preceded perhaps by the physical afflictions of Roosevelt and Eisenhower, and thrust suddenly into the public consciousness by the assassination of John F. Kennedy in November 1963, a national trauma that arguably still informs our understanding of American society today. As Smith suggests of the Kennedy assassination,

> That a presidency, especially one identified with youth and vigor, could be so easily destroyed was too much for many to accept. ... If we must suffer parricide, if our father is to be taken from us, he must be taken by a most powerful, if malignant, counterforce. We cannot lose him to a casual crank.[13]

Such an assertion raises the notion of the president's health being analogous to the mental and physical well-being of the nation as a whole. Furthermore, it might be suggested that the representations of presidents which we digest through popular culture might be indicative of the temperature of American society in that given period. Rather than understanding cinematic or televisual presidents as rough approximations of their real-life counterparts, perhaps we can begin to perceive fictional chief executives as being involved in a more complex relationship with popular culture, articulating the hopes and anxieties that have been generated by the specificities of their social context. However, Smith too has a tendency to essentialise the relationship between history and mainstream cinema. For example, he makes rather simplistic observations of the similarities between President Merkin Muffley (Peter Sellers) in *Dr Strangelove* and

13 Smith, *The Presidents We Imagine*, 166.

twice-defeated presidential candidate Adlai Stevenson, without delving more deeply into the implications of such a representation for the masculine character of the presidency. This book is concerned primarily with these wider themes and considerations.

Two further interventions in the field, Terry Christensen and Peter J. Haas' *Projecting Politics* and Ernest Giglio's *Here's Looking at You: Hollywood, Film and Politics*, are illustrative of a certain discomfort with writing about audiovisual texts, and a dismissive attitude towards mainstream cinema. Christensen and Haas forge a theory of political filmmaking in Hollywood through a model that measures the political content of a film against its political intent. However, they are guilty of making sweeping value judgements regarding the politics of the films they discuss, dismissing *Independence Day* as 'such a cartoon that only the most naïve viewer would confuse its lazy plotting for a political message.'[14] Similarly, Giglio recognises that films such as *Independence Day* and *Air Force One* 'reinforce a macho image' of the presidency, but he decries the credibility of such images and their lack of historical accuracy.[15] Pre-existing studies in this field only appear willing to acknowledge political messages when they are consciously constructed, but just because the message is implicit does not make it any less political.[16] Dismissing films such as these as pure fantasy is to ignore the critical notion that, as Robin Wood argued, the pleasures they offer are 'patently ideological.'[17]

Ian Scott's *American Politics in Hollywood Film* represents a distinct shift in the discussion, examining the representation of politics as both a

14 Terry Christensen and Peter J. Haas, *Projecting Politics: Political Messages in American Films* (London: M.E. Sharpe, 2005), 212.

15 Ernest Giglio, *Here's Looking at You: Hollywood, Film and Politics* (New York: Peter Lang Publishing, 2007), 120.

16 Terry Christensen's earlier monograph, *Reel Politics: American Political Movies from Birth of a Nation to Platoon* (Oxford: Basil Blackwell, 1987) conducts similar analyses, albeit on a broader canvas. He makes similar value judgements about films, frequently deriding the recourse to 'cliché' in political movies when a greater appreciation of generic convention would be potentially more illuminating.

17 Robin Wood, *Hollywood From Vietnam to Reagan … and Beyond* (New York: Columbia University Press, 2003), 146.

genre study and a project in periodisation. Scott's approach is more nuanced than the others discussed here, recognising more explicitly the symbiotic nature of the Hollywood/Washington relationship:

> Hollywood reflects and indeed encourages the kind of mythmaking that American politics itself has constantly engaged in, and for this reason alone its politics have an acute sensibility to the cinematic medium that is worth investigating and deciphering in greater depth.[18]

Where Scott's work differs from previous interventions into the field is that it begins the work of investigating Hollywood not only as a reflective surface for American politics, but a force that has become enormously influential in shaping the nation's political character.[19] This book aims to build upon Scott's rich and wide-ranging analysis, to delve deeper into the ways in which the frameworks of mainstream filmmaking and television production – like genre, for example – are adopted, developed and extended into complex representations of politics, whereby the reality informs the fiction and, perhaps most significantly, vice versa.

Iwan W. Morgan's recent edited collection, *Presidents in the Movies: American History and Politics on Screen*, represents a further evolution in the scholarly treatment of Hollywood's presidency. There are interventions on the screen representations of Abraham Lincoln, Theodore Roosevelt, Woodrow Wilson, Franklin Roosevelt, John F. Kennedy, Andrew Johnson, Richard Nixon and, finally, George W. Bush. Although this corpus indicates the collection remains inevitably wedded to issues of history and representation, many of the arguments pivot on whether Hollywood privileges 'image, message, and myth' in its representations of the president over 'historical accuracy and complexity'.[20] It acknowledges that the vast majority of presidents have been ignored by Hollywood cinema, and only

18 Ian Scott, *American Politics in Hollywood Film* (Edinburgh: Edinburgh University Press, 2000), 6.
An expanded edition of this book was published through Edinburgh University Press in 2011.

19 Ibid., 12.

20 Iwan W. Morgan, 'Introduction', in Morgan, ed., *Presidents in the Movies*, 2.

a few are consistently revisited.[21] Scott raises a notion, fundamental to the concerns of this book, that 'we might contemplate … the degree to which the presidency has finally become an amalgam of historical construction and Hollywood superimposition.'[22] The suggestion that authenticity and accuracy should not be the only criteria of judgement applied to representations of the presidency is, in my estimation, long overdue.[23]

By marked contrast to the limited forays into the discussion of the American presidency and politics in Hollywood film, there have been an excess of studies analysing the political dimensions of Hollywood cinema, and how films might be read as metaphorical analyses of contemporaneous attitudes and anxieties. James Combs' edited collection suggests that films could be studied as

> observable aesthetic artefacts of the unobservable processes of attitude formation and change among populations, constituting the 'climate of opinion' or 'structure of feeling' characteristic of an age.[24]

The invocation of Raymond Williams' theories surrounding artworks as indicative of a 'structure of feeling' or 'spirit of the age' is crucial to this book.[25] In a similar vein, Horace Newcomb and Paul Hirsch's discussion of television as a cultural forum, in which contemporary concerns and dominant ideologies are presented, debated and 'worked out', is an illuminating

21 Ibid., 8–11.

22 Ian Scott, 'Transition: The Making of Screen Presidents', in Morgan, ed., *Presidents in the Movies*, 30.

23 Ibid., 29.
See Patricia F. Phalen, Jennie Kim and Julia Osellame, 'Imagined Presidencies: The Representation of Political Power in Television Fiction', *The Journal of Popular Culture* 45/3 (2012), 532–50, for a recent discussion of the mythological importance of the presidency as a symbol of the United States.

24 James Combs, ed., *Movies and Politics: The Dynamic Relationship* (London: Garland Publishing Inc., 1993), 4.

25 Raymond Williams, *Marxism and Literature* (Oxford: Oxford University Press, 1977), 128–35.

one in relation to the fictional presidency.[26] What representations of the president might have to say regarding contemporary hopes and anxieties regarding the institution, the incumbent's character, or the outlook for American society more generally (in issues of gender, race and national identity), is vital. However, it must be reiterated that this relationship between text and context is nuanced, and not as straightforward as many scholars have suggested. Williams' work is particularly noteworthy because it complicates a notion widespread in scholarly interventions about the presidency that the man in some way defines the era. As suggested by historian E.H. Carr, 'The cult of individualism is one of the most pervasive of modern historical myths', and 'the desire to postulate individual genius as the creative force in history is characteristic of the primitive stages of historical consciousness.'[27] Rather than dismiss this tendency, however, this book looks to explain it. To believe in the agency of the individual, particularly one seemingly as powerful as the President of the United States, is beneficial in a psychological sense, reinforcing the need to believe that the president is in control of the nation's destiny, and providing a necessary buttress to mythological conceptions of leadership and national identity. While this book is concerned primarily with the ways in which the era defines the person, it is concerned too with the reasons why the converse notion is such a compelling fixation.

Most valuable within Combs's collection is Douglas Kellner's work. He suggests that reading a film politically involves situating it within its historical context and exploring how its textual dynamics work to embody specific political and ideological positions.[28] This appears to have been the dominant method in the analysis of the political dimensions of Hollywood film, but it has been traditionally applied to films that do not speak to American politics directly. An excellent example of this method emerges

26 Horace Newcomb and Paul M. Hirsch, 'Television as a Cultural Forum', in Horace Newcomb, ed., *Television: The Critical View* [5th edn], (Oxford: Oxford University Press, 1994), 503–15.

27 E.H. Carr, *What is History?* (Basingstoke: Palgrave, 2001), 27–39.

28 Douglas Kellner, 'Film, Politics and Ideology: Toward a Multiperspectival Film Theory', in Combs, ed., *Movies and Politics*, 55.

in the analyses of Hollywood cinema in the age of Ronald Reagan, with the early *Rambo* (1982–90) films becoming what Yvonne Tasker describes as the 'overdetermined reference point' for a wide variety of discussions surrounding resurgent patriotism, militarism and traditional masculinity in the period.[29] Although Combs and Kellner do occasionally lapse into the essentialism which characterises much writing in this area, and Kellner employs some problematic Kracauer-esque hindsight analysis in his discussion of films that prepared the United States for the Gulf War, it is the fundamental process of their method which is of most use to my discussion of the screen presidency.[30]

However, a crucial facet of my approach is to complicate the notion that films and television programmes straightforwardly reflect the context in which they were produced. Of particular import here is *Cahiers du Cinéma*'s rigorous and comprehensive analysis of *Young Mr Lincoln*. The editors of *Cahiers* argue that 'an artistic product cannot be linked to its socio-historical context according to a linear, expressive, direct causality (unless one falls into a reductionist historical determinism), but that it has a complex, mediated and *decentred* relationship within this context'.[31] This is the very essence of my challenge: this book will complicate the notion that Hollywood films about politics and the president merely regurgitate

29 Yvonne Tasker, *Spectacular Bodies: Gender, Genre and the Action Cinema* (London: Routledge, 1993), 92.
Prominent investigations of Reagan-era cinema include Robin Wood (1986), *Hollywood from Vietnam to Reagan* (with an expanded edition in 2003); and Andrew Britton, 'Blissing Out: The Politics of Reaganite Entertainment', *Movie* 31/32 (1986), 1–42, reprinted in Barry Keith Grant, ed., *Britton on Film: The Complete Film Criticism of Andrew Britton* (Detroit: Wayne State University Press, 2009), 97–154.

30 I refer here to Siegfried Kracauer's seminal work *From Caligari to Hitler: A Psychological History of the German Film,* originally published in 1947, which examines German cinema from the Weimar era in search of harbingers of the rise of Adolf Hitler and Nazism. This hindsight analysis has been challenged and questioned since, with continual attempts to rescue the book's relevance through careful contextualisation. I will investigate Kracauer's methodology more closely in Chapter 5.

31 *Cahiers du Cinéma*, 'John Ford's *Young Mr Lincoln*', in Bill Nichols, ed., *Movies and Methods: An Anthology* (London: University of California Press, 1976), 495.

aspects of the time period in which they were made, but are in fact complicated intersections of genre, iconography, narrative, and social, political and historical context.

This neo-Marxist perspective is central, particularly because so many of the Hollywood films which take the world of American politics as their setting or subject matter try to inculcate the audience with the notion that, as Combs suggests, 'the system is benevolent, wise and just, urging us toward obedience and deference.'[32] The *Cahiers* editors' argument, that Hollywood's dependence on America's political and economic systems implicates it within the maintenance of these dominant structures, is essential in Hollywood's representation of the presidency.[33] While much Marxist film theory is problematic in its reduction of audiences to a homogenous mass of dupes, the notion that Hollywood film cloaks capitalist ideologies within a palatable framework raises significant issues in relation to the criticism which has emerged already within the field.[34] While many of the critics who have written on this subject have identified that mainstream films tend to regard the American political system as an essentially benign one, the proper functioning of which is dependent upon the actions of individuals good and bad, there has not perhaps been the attention given to the precise ways in which this process occurs, often resulting in the dismissal of texts that do not immediately appear to be 'political' in the most manifest sense of the word. While this book will not be as ideologically pointed, I think it is important to take into account the influential discussions which have, by

32 Combs, *Movies and Politics*, 10.

33 *Cahiers du Cinéma*, 'John Ford's *Young Mr Lincoln*', 499.

34 This thinking is heavily indebted to the work of Theodor Adorno and Max Horkheimer, whose influential 'The Culture Industry: Enlightenment as Mass Deception' put forward the notion that the industrialisation of culture (film, radio and magazines) has manipulated the masses into passivity, rendering them docile and content despite their subordinated position in the unequal capitalist system. – Theodor W. Adorno and Max Horkheimer, *Dialectic of Enlightenment* (London: Verso, 1979), originally published as *Dialektik der Aufklarung* (New York: Social Studies Association, Inc., 1944). 120–67.

and large, argued that the American culture industry gives 'overwhelming ideological legitimation to the extant system.'[35]

Much of the criticism regarding American politics and Hollywood film appears to circumvent Jean-Louis Comolli's and Jean Narboni's assertion that *everything* is profoundly ideological, and that 'every film is political, inasmuch as it is determined by the ideology which produces it.'[36] This seminal work constructs an invaluable approach to mainstream films about American politics and the presidency. Comolli and Narboni also emphasise a facet essential to this book – while much of the criticism about American politics and Hollywood film has privileged content over form, they argue that 'the camera reveals nothing but the realm of ideology, and hence political struggle in the cinema must inevitably involve work at the level of form as well as content.'[37] It is perhaps the privileging of content which has caused critics to dismiss many of the films featuring an American president as a central character as somehow apolitical. Through analysis of form, I hope to demonstrate that genre films featuring the presidency as a central character articulate profoundly ideological discourses about the office, the appropriate use of its power, and the United States as a nation.

Therefore, the criticism that has emerged within the field of politics and the presidency in film and television appears to have fallen into a number of traps. An apparent inability to define a manageable corpus has rendered most of the studies here perfunctory and underdeveloped. Methodologically, they tend to replicate many of the problems traditionally associated with historians and film scholarship, treating films as a window into the past, and making a number of value judgements regarding the accuracy of these representations. One of the crucial problems with this method is that it tends to ignore the dynamics of the discrepancies – if films do not conform to dominant conceptions of the politics of the time, they are

35 James Combs, ed., *Movies and Politics: The Dynamic Relationship* (New York and London: Garland Publishing, 1993), 10.

36 Jean-Louis Comolli and Jean Narboni, 'Cinema/Ideology/Criticism', in Nichols, ed., *Movies and Methods,* 24–5.

37 Bill Nichols, Introduction to 'Cinema/Ideology/Criticism', in *Movies and Methods*, 24.

dismissed as either wholly inaccurate, or are simply ignored because they do not fit within this rigid paradigm. Furthermore, perhaps because of this desire to define films as 'good' and 'bad' examples of history, the *fictional* presidencies which have been frequent and varied since the 1990s have been given little close attention. There is also unbalanced consideration of the composition of the films themselves – there is discussion of plot, characterisation and narrative, but virtually nothing regarding the textual dynamics of the films, and how meaning is created through filmic techniques. As the *Cahiers du Cinéma* editors suggest, while American cinema's role is to reproduce the ideologies of capitalism, 'each film ... is inserted into this circuit according to its specificity ... it is the precise articulations (rarely the same from one film to the next) of the film and of the ideology which must be studied'.[38] This book will reclaim these films and television programmes as *audiovisual texts*, demonstrating how fundamental aspects of moving images, like genre, iconography and *mise-en-scène*, function in relation to discourses circulating within popular culture regarding the presidency and politics in general. It is through this process that I will establish a detailed and cogent analysis of the means by which mainstream cinema and television have imagined the President of the United States within the confines of Hollywood genres and conventional narrative structures.

38 *Cahiers du Cinéma*, 'John Ford's *Young Mr Lincoln*', 499.

CHAPTER 2

The Symbolic Presidency: Washington and Hollywood, 1932–1989

Having addressed the methodological approach of this book, and its position in relation to the existing literature in the field, I now turn to the presidency specifically. Although my central focus is the cinematic and televisual presidency, the institution has a symbolic significance that extends beyond Hollywood, and possesses a rich history that has had a manifest impact on its recent, fictional incarnations. I think a simultaneous discussion of the office's evolution alongside its fictional representation is the most illuminating way to address these issues. This is not to replicate the uncomplicated application of the films of the period onto the context in which they were produced, but to demonstrate the extent to which Hollywood's representations of politics and the presidency participate within these structures of feeling. This short chapter is intended to function as a microcosm of the book's overall approach, as well as to map the contours of Hollywood's representations of politics and the presidency. I intend this to be a broad and discursive exploration that will raise crucial questions that I will address throughout the book.

The position of 'President of the United States' has fundamentally transformed since its conception, with the most profound of these changes occurring in the last eighty years. The office was constructed between a series of competing notions. Conceived in opposition to a monarchy, America's Founding Fathers suggested the president should be an ordinary man and not hold the position on the basis of heredity or familial advantage. However, the president should also be *more than a man*, capable of embodying simultaneously the ideals of the republic and the will of the people, and blessed with extraordinary abilities in rhetoric and diplomacy. Maintaining this balance continues to be of crucial importance for presidential candidates: to appear as both man *and* superman. As Melissa Crawley suggests, 'The president is both an image that symbolizes the country and a mythic representation of the nation's history.'[1] Anne Norton concurs with Crawley's assertion, although puts forward an even more tantalising notion: invoking Alexis de Tocqueville's famous study of American democracy, she argues that 'The President's representative function is … *first semiotic*, and only secondarily executive.'[2] James David Barber reaffirms this, suggesting that 'The Presidency is the focus for the most intense and persistent emotions in the American polity. The President is a symbolic leader'.[3] Not merely a human being of flesh and blood, the figure of the president is invested with overwhelming symbolic and mythological significance, which largely relegates any legislative or administrative responsibilities to secondary concerns.[4]

The exact nature and definition of the presidency prompted great debate among America's Founding Fathers, primarily because the United States was established largely in opposition to the rule of a federal government. Benjamin Franklin warned against 'the frightening prospect of an American "Pharaoh"', and fears that such a position would create authoritarian monsters in the mould of Napoleon or Caesar, were widespread.[5] These concerns were articulated by the anti-federalists who predicted that, having ascended to the presidency, men would succumb to 'classical vices of greed and ambition', their corruption violating the very principles upon which the union was founded.[6] Alexander Hamilton, a Founding Father, and primary political aide to George Washington, was a chief proponent

1 Melissa Crawley, 'Television', in Matviko, ed., *The American President in Popular Culture,* 186.

2 Anne Norton, *Republic of Signs: Liberal Theory and American Popular Culture* (Chicago: The University of Chicago Press, 1993), 87. My emphasis.

3 James David Barber, *The Presidential Character: Predicting Performance in the White House* [4th edn] (Upper Saddle River, NJ: Prentice Hall Books, 1992), 2.

4 Clinton Rossiter, *The American Presidency* [2nd edn] (New York: Harcourt, 1960), 108, quoted in Warren G. Rochelle, 'The Literary Presidency', *Presidential Studies Quarterly* 29/2 (1999), 408.

5 Smith, *The Presidents We Imagine,* 21.

6 Ibid., 26.

of the presidency. He subscribed to the view that the office of the presidency would embody the ideals of the nation, imagining the position to be held by ordinary men with extraordinary abilities. In sharp contrast to the anti-federalists, Hamilton imagined the president as 'a character of modestly "novelistic" size', with the usual flaws and foibles of an ordinary man. However, to be a 'Patriot King, a paragon of "liberty and good government", the president must also possess an inherent good nature and wholesomeness of character, reaffirming the basis of political power as the loyal servitude of the people.[7]

To combat the potential for an elected tyrant, the president shares power with two other branches of government: Congress, whose responsibility for the implementation of legislation rendered it the supposed 'true' representative of the people during the republic's formative years, and The Supreme Court. In addition to its symbolic significance, the presidency was originally conceived as a largely administrative position. As Richard Rose argues, 'The traditional Presidency was not a driving force in government; with occasional exceptions, it was a dignified office of state.'[8] The main responsibilities of the federal government were to combat invasion by a foreign foe, ensure the will of Congress was applied correctly, and maintain the nation's finances through economical taxing and spending policies. Presidents who pursued activist projects were controversial because this was 'considered inconsistent with the dignity and nature of the office.'[9] When presidents acted outside this conception of the role as a matter of necessity (as Lincoln did when he circumvented the constitution by signing the Emancipation Proclamation in 1863), the institution's responsibilities retreated to their former, modest parameters once the danger had passed.[10]

7 Ibid., 16.

8 Richard Rose, *The Postmodern President: George Bush Meets the World* [2nd edn] (Chatham, NJ: Chatham House Publishers, 1991), 2.

9 Ibid., 20.

10 Thomas Cronin and Michael Genovese, *The Paradoxes of the American Presidency* [2nd edn] (Oxford: Oxford University Press, 2004), 68.

The Modern Presidency, 1933–1945: Franklin Roosevelt, Frank Capra and Abraham Lincoln Versus the Great Depression

The traditional presidency is different from contemporary understandings and expectations of the office, and if it had remained a largely administrative position it would seem unlikely to have become a popular archetype in mainstream film and television. It is interesting then to note that the presidency's expansion, the ascendance of modern communications technology (radio), and the advent of the sound film and newsreel occurred almost simultaneously. Historians and political scientists broadly agree that the modern presidency was inaugurated by Franklin D. Roosevelt, who undertook extraordinary measures in response to the economic crisis that threatened to engulf the United States when he took office in March 1933. As Fred Greenstein suggests of the Roosevelt administration, 'the Presidency began to undergo not a shift but rather a metamorphosis.'[11] Roosevelt radically expanded the federal bureaucracy, made many more unilateral decisions, and took an active role in legislative affairs, often wielding the presidential veto if he felt Congress was impeding the progress of his agenda. More importantly in relation to this book, however, is Roosevelt's *personalisation* of the presidency. His radio broadcasts to the nation, dubbed 'Fireside Chats', enabled Roosevelt to cultivate an intimate relationship with the people, offering himself as a reassuring presence in the depths of the Great Depression. As Timothy Raphael notes, 'Roosevelt meticulously trained his voice, honed his delivery, and perfected his timing to exploit the new medium', to the point where 'the words most often used to describe FDR's radio voice were intimate, conversational, and informal.'[12] Prior to

11 Fred I. Greenstein, 'Change and Continuity in the Modern Presidency', in Anthony King, ed., *The New American Political System* (Washington, DC: American Enterprise Institute, 1978), 45, quoted in David K. Nichols, *The Myth of the Modern Presidency* (University Park: The Pennsylvania State University Press, 1994), 3.

12 Timothy Raphael, *The President Electric: Ronald Reagan and the Politics of Performance* (Ann Arbor: The University of Michigan Press, 2009), 93–4.

Roosevelt's administration, the president had been a distant national figurehead, but the importance of radio to FDR's administration rendered the presidency more attainable for millions of Americans. As David Nichols suggests, 'use of electronic media clearly made the President a more personal presence in the lives of most Americans.'[13]

Perhaps inevitably given his cultivation of a reassuring media persona, the period over which Roosevelt presided proved fertile ground for fictional representations of politics and the presidency. As Norton argues, the Depression caused a loss of faith in signs: the presidency, and the political and economic systems.[14] Roosevelt partially restored faith, but it would also require the Hollywood dream factory to refurbish America's fragile nationhood. Over the course of the decade, films held in varying degrees of esteem were released: *The Phantom President* (Norman Taurog, 1932), *Washington Merry-Go-Round* (James Cruze, 1932), *Gabriel Over the White House* and *The President Vanishes* (William Wellmann, 1934) all deal with systemic corruption and corrosion, with diverse solutions offered to restore America to its righteous path. Of these, *Gabriel Over the White House* is perhaps most well known: a Depression-era fable that appears to advocate the temporary installation of authoritarian rule in order to rescue the nation from economic calamity. Its fascist overtones are widely noted, as are the eerie similarities between some of fictional President Hammond's (Walter Huston) policies, and Franklin D. Roosevelt's extra-constitutional measures to combat the Great Depression.[15]

More distinguished, and more influential, was the work of Frank Capra. *Mr Deeds Goes to Town* (1936), *Mr Smith Goes to Washington* (1939) and *Meet John Doe* (1941) deal broadly with the encounter between the innocent, naïve individual and the overwhelming, corrupting force of the political/economic machine. Their broadly populist motifs are well-noted:

13 Nichols, *The Myth of the Modern Presidency*, 6.

14 Norton, *Republic of Signs*, 105.

15 For further investigation of the fascist politics of *Gabriel Over the White House*, see John J. Pitney Jr., 'Fascism in *Gabriel Over the White House*', in Beverley Merrill Kelley, John. J. Pitney jr., Craig R. Smith and Herbert E. Gooch III, eds, *Reelpolitik: Political Ideology in 30s and 40s Films* (London: Praeger, 1998), 45–60.

these three films are deeply suspicious of the encroaching influence of modernity upon American society and appear to argue for America's reversion to traditional values located in her agrarian, frontier past. This concern finds perhaps its most famous embodiment in *Mr Smith Goes to Washington* through the figure of Jefferson Smith, Jimmy Stewart's childlike country boy who takes a seat in the Senate to play patsy for the corrupt Washington elite, but refuses to yield to their power. He calls for a restitution of the values of honesty and communitarian spirit as pillars of American society. As Charles Lindholm and John A. Hall argue,

> Capra's depiction of the depraving influences of governmental power appealed to an American public traditionally leery of politicians and official authority; similarly, the story of a lone hero struggling against all odds for what he knows to be right evoked the American myth of the rugged individual, reliant solely on his own moral compass for direction.[16]

Another apparent strain in the representation of politics, politicians and the political system in the 1930s is the consistent rearticulation of the myth of Abraham Lincoln. Memorialised as the president who saved the nation from itself, freed the slaves, and ended the Civil War, nostalgic yearning for the strength of Lincoln in the 1930s appears to have been triggered by the profound uncertainty brought about by the collapse of the economy. As Tony Pipolo argues, Lincoln has become America's cultural shorthand for moral courage, honour, and virtue, 'the figure invoked whenever a politician's higher aspirations are endangered'.[17] In 1930s Hollywood, D.W. Griffith's *Abraham Lincoln* (1930) takes the totalising, biographical approach, offering an episodic treatment of Lincoln's life that culminates in his assassination. *Young Mr Lincoln* (1939) and *Abe Lincoln in Illinois* (John Cromwell, 1940) are both origin stories, dealing with Lincoln's life before he became president. All three, however, showcase a fundamental

16 Charles Lindholm and John A. Hall, 'Frank Capra Meets John Doe: Anti-Politics in American National Identity', in Mette Hjort and Scott Mackenzie, eds, *Cinema and Nation* (London: Routledge, 2000), 34.

17 Tony Pipolo, 'Hero or Demagogue?: Images of Lincoln in American Film', *Cineaste* 35/1 (2009), 14.

aspect of the Lincoln myth: his humble beginnings as an ordinary country boy who, through honesty, integrity and toil, rose to the highest office in the land. The films are less concerned with the complexities of Lincoln's political philosophy and life, and more with invoking his memory as cultural shorthand for the theme of moral strength in the face of adversity. Taken together, all three Lincoln films of the 1930s represent an anxious retelling of a familiar, reassuring national story at a time of national and international turmoil.[18]

All three strains of political film in the 1930s are legible through the prisms of the Great Depression, and concerns surrounding the rise of fascism and the subsequent outbreak of World War II. While films that emerged prior to Roosevelt's election demonstrated Hollywood's worry regarding the efficacy of its formula in the face of economic collapse, later films had a renewed faith in the system.[19] The political films of the 1930s, particularly Capra's interventions, lay the foundations for Hollywood's political film, and its representation of the president. Capra's heroes, the retelling of the Lincoln story, and President Hammond in *Gabriel Over the White House* are all indicative of Hollywood's nostalgic look to America's past for comfort and reassurance. They valorise the innocent individual in opposition to the impersonal, omnipotent (and often corrupt) collusion between politics and capitalism, and yearn for strong leadership to defy enemies both foreign and domestic. Roosevelt's canny use of the radio to reassure Americans of the brilliance of democracy and capitalism existed alongside a challenging, though ultimately celebratory, examination of these systems in Hollywood cinema.

18 See Melvyn Stokes, 'D.W. Griffith's *Abraham Lincoln*', in Morgan, ed., *Presidents in the Movies*, 45–61.

19 For an investigation of these films, see Andrew Bergman, *We're in the Money: Depression America and its Films* (New York: New York University Press, 1971), 92–109.

The 1940s and 1950s: Conformity and Communism in an Era of Anxiety and Prosperity

The expansion of the presidency's bureaucracy, and the influence of modern communications technologies on expectations of the office, continued during the administrations of Harry Truman (1945–53) and Dwight Eisenhower (1953–61). With America's global supremacy confirmed by the Allied victory in World War II, the widespread expectation that the president could bend the world to his will led Greenstein to suggest that 'the expectations for the modern presidency have far exceeded the possible.'[20] Although the powers of the president had expanded, America faced larger, and even graver, challenges. The threat of nuclear annihilation severely hindered the president's ability to act swiftly and decisively in response to threats posed by the Soviet Union and her allies. The United States' supposed global supremacy met stiff challenge with the rise of 'Red China', and the Korean War was a messy, compromised, only partially successful intervention to prevent the march of communism. Fear of communists created irrational hysteria, and the investigations into this invisible threat by the House Committee on Un-American Activities severely undermined many of the principles for which the United States fought in World War II.

Given the apprehension in Hollywood during the McCarthy era, it is perhaps unsurprising that the controversial subject of politics would be marginalised, and the production of political films declined.[21] Although he would produce *State of the Union* (1948), a Spencer Tracy/Katherine Hepburn romantic comedy featuring Tracy as a presidential hopeful, Frank Capra's career faded in this divisive, poisonous political environment. There

20 Fred I. Greenstein, quoted in Nichols, *The Myth of the Modern Presidency*, 4.

21 For an exploration of the decline of the political film during the 1950s, see Brian Neve, 'HUAC, The Blacklist and The Decline of Social Cinema', in Peter Lev, ed., *Transforming the Screen 1950–9* (New York: Charles Scribner's Sons, 2003), 65–86; and Tony Shaw, *Hollywood's Cold War* (Edinburgh: Edinburgh University Press, 2007).

were commercial problems with the political film too: the relative failure of Darryl Zanuck's lavish 1944 biopic of Woodrow Wilson, designed explicitly as propaganda to support the post-war creation of an international organisation along the lines of the earlier League of Nations, did not help the genre's fortunes.[22] Aside from Robert Rossen's adaptation of *All the King's Men* (1949), which chronicles the fortunes of corrupt demagogue Willie Stark (Broderick Crawford), Hollywood's penchant for political subjects remained largely dormant. Concerns regarding the occupant of the Oval Office appeared to dissipate in the conformist, anti-communist Eisenhower era, with contemporary anxieties regarding nuclear war and the threat of the Soviet Union migrating into science-fiction films such as *The Day the Earth Stood Still* (Robert Wise, 1951), *The Thing From Another World* (Christian Nyby, 1951), *Them!* (Gordon Douglas, 1954), *Invasion of the Body Snatchers* (Don Siegel, 1955), and *Earth vs The Flying Saucers* (Fred F. Sears, 1956). The Eisenhower era was the age of consensus, Roosevelt's New Deal settlement surviving into the 1950s. As demonstrated by the absence of explicitly political subjects in Hollywood cinema, there was little appetite to examine the conception of the presidency in fiction, primarily because there was little anxiety surrounding its enormously popular, comforting real-life counterpart in a time of general prosperity and optimism (despite the looming threats from abroad).

22 For an aesthetic appreciation of *Wilson*, as well as differing accounts of its production and reception, see Thomas J. Knock, 'History with Lightning: The Forgotten Film *Wilson* (1944)', in Peter C. Rollins, ed., *Hollywood as Historian* (Lexington: The University Press of Kentucky, 1998), 88–108; Leonard J. Leff and Jerold Simmons, '*Wilson*: Hollywood Propaganda for World Peace', *Historical Journal of Film, Radio and Television* 3/1 (1983), 3–18; Mark Wheeler, 'Darryl F. Zanuck's *Wilson*', in Morgan, ed., *Presidents in the Movies*, 87–104.

The 1960s and 1970s: Losing Faith in the System

However, by the 1960s, the dominance of television had led to a more human impression of the president. This shift somewhat undermined the notion that he possessed superhuman qualities.[23] The tension between the conception of the president as Herculean, and the reality of his human frailty, arguably reached its apotheosis during the administration of John F. Kennedy (1961–3), widely considered 'The First Television President'. Kennedy was a consummate political performer, noted for his ease in front of the camera, and his calm, controlled televised press conferences. Indeed, he has proved an enormous influence on representations of the presidency; his benign spectre lurks at the edges of Sorkin's presidential fictions, and the desire to adapt aspects of his life and death on the big and small screens shows little sign of abating, with assassination-themed drama *Parkland* (Peter Landesman, 2013) following the relatively recent, expansive and controversial four-part History Channel drama *The Kennedys* (2011). The continued obsession with Kennedy has much to do with his shocking death, itself a televised event, because it revealed the fragile, fleshy humanity that existed beneath the carefully constructed presidential façade.[24] The revelation that the presidency was vulnerable was an unwelcome realisation in a period of global tension and possible nuclear conflict.

It was in the middle of the century that the modern presidency began to be undermined. Lyndon Johnson's (1963–9) escalation of the Vietnam War, and Richard Nixon's (1969–74) abuses of presidential power which culminated in the Watergate scandal, led Arthur Schlesinger to argue that 'by the early 1970s the American president had become on issues of war and peace the most absolute monarch … among the great powers of the

23 As suggested in the review of literature, this notion is explored by Jeff Smith in *The Presidents We Imagine*, 161–205.

24 The most shocking footage of Kennedy's death, the infamous Zapruder Film, would not be widely available until 1975.

world'.[25] However, the controversial exercise of executive power with which both Johnson and Nixon are associated, and their inability to prevent the United States' first military defeat in Vietnam, led to the suggestion that the presidency was 'imperilled'.[26] In his lament against the lack of heroic leadership in the presidents that followed Roosevelt, Richard Neustadt argues of the events that beleaguered Jimmy Carter's (1977–81) administration,

> The United States was no longer the overwhelming military power in the world, no longer sure of never losing wars, no longer confident of having learned how to maintain employment and check inflation, no longer revelling in resource independence, technological supremacy, favourable exchange rates, and the privileged life abroad. If there *was* an 'American century', as Henry Luce proclaimed during World War II, it lasted only twice as long as Adolf Hitler's Thousand-Year Reich.[27]

As Nichols suggests, 'The doctrine of the modern Presidency was not a mistake. The office had been transformed to heroic proportions. The problem was that the expectations of the modern Presidency had grown so great that no President could fulfil them.'[28] The presidency and the political system appeared to be in an impossible double-bind: overreaching to impose the will of the United States upon the world had led to accusations that America had become an imperial power (the very thing against which the country was founded), while the complexities of the post-war geopolitical environment meant that faith in the ability of an individual to maintain control over the situation declined.

25 Arthur Schlesinger Jr., *The Imperial Presidency* (New York: Columbia University Press, 1994), ix.

26 Debates surrounding the decline of the office are discussed by George Reedy, *Twilight of the Presidency* (Cleveland: New American Library, 1970); Vincent Davis ed., *The Post-Imperial Presidency* (New Brunswick: Transaction Books, 1980); Harold M. Barger, *The Impossible Presidency* (Glenview: Scott, Foresman, 1984), and Aaron Wildavsky ed., *The Beleaguered Presidency* (New Brunswick: Transaction Publishers, 1991), among many others.

27 Richard Neustadt, *Presidential Power and The Modern Presidents* (New York: The Free Press, 1980), 94.

28 Nichols, *The Myth of the Modern Presidency*, p. 8.

It might be suggested that the political and social turbulence of the 1960s and 1970s brought about a similar erosion of confidence in symbols of American power experienced during the Great Depression. This anxiety is clearly present in Hollywood films of the period which concern the political process. Although now remembered as a time of optimism, prosperity and glamour, films of the Kennedy era somewhat contradict this myth. Films representing electoral politics, particularly *Advise and Consent* (1962) and *The Best Man* (1964), address corruption within the system, and the underhanded manoeuvres employed by candidates in pursuit of victory. John Frankenheimer's *The Manchurian Candidate* (1962) and *Seven Days in May* address wider concerns regarding the overthrow of the American government by malevolent forces. *Fail-Safe* and *Dr Strangelove* both end with the dropping of atomic bombs, the president to varying degrees powerless to correct the systemic failures that lead to destruction. Given the influence of Kennedy on representations of the presidency, and the continued significance of the Kennedy era in American politics more generally, it is worth dwelling a little longer on some of the most notable examples from the period.

As J. Hoberman suggests, these films 'represented American politics as the province of demagogues, blackmailers and conspirators, placing one president after another in the terrifying light of some personal or public Armageddon.'[29] President Jordan Lyman (Frederic March) in *Seven Days in May* is a noble leader, trying desperately to ensure the safety of the United States by signing an anti-nuclear test ban treaty despite significant opposition from the public and within his own government. The film is possibly reflective of Kennedy's attempts to secure a similar agreement with the Soviet Union, which was ultimately achieved just months before his death. Although Kennedy's partial success in halting what seemed to be an inexorable march toward nuclear war has been celebrated, *Seven Days in May* offers a potent reminder of how delicate a grip the president had on nuclear affairs. Lyman's pursuit of the treaty has been an enormously stressful

29 J. Hoberman, 'When Dr No Met Dr Strangelove', *Sight and Sound* (December 1993), 16.

endeavour. As a result of this pressure, he is established at the beginning of the film as a frail and very sick man. The first scene shows the president having a routine physical examination, and his doctor urges him to take light exercise and rest to ease his dangerously high blood pressure. He goes swimming to unwind, and he reveals his aged body, with scrawny shoulders and a flabby chest. With the lowest popularity of any president in history because of his determination to sign a peace treaty with the Soviets, Lyman is portrayed as a beleaguered president, both physically and psychologically (he cannot tolerate the responsibility for launching a nuclear attack that would destroy mankind). Although his measured approach is valorised in comparison to the militaristic and aggressive General Scott (Burt Lancaster), the impression given is that, despite the best of intentions, the president remains a flawed and fragile human being when faced with the possibility of nuclear conflict. *Seven Days in May* articulates a profound doubt about the president's ability to exert full control over events – the film concerns the overthrow of the government in a military coup, a plot which Lyman, despite having the full resources of the national security apparatus at this disposal, has absolutely no knowledge or awareness of until it is revealed to him by Colonel Casey (Kirk Douglas). The psychological burden of the presidency, and its lack of control over the military, is established by *Seven Days in May*'s title sequence, which superimposes nuclear missiles to appear like prison bars over an image of the White House. This imagery suggests that the threat from, and potential use of, nuclear weapons incarcerates the presidency, and hinders its ability to preserve peace and security. The nation, symbolised by the feeble body of its president, is shown to be both imprisoned by its own horrifying creation (the bomb), as well as physically incapable of asserting control over this apparatus.

Both of the major films dealing with nuclear war, *Fail-Safe* and *Dr Strangelove*, explore the possibility of accidents in the chain of command. While tonally the two films could not be more different (*Strangelove* is a raucous comedy and *Fail-Safe* an earnest drama), they forge quite similar impressions of presidential impotence in the face of the nuclear threat. The President (Henry Fonda) in *Fail-Safe* is a slightly aged, calm, contemplative and rational individual, but his attempt to prevent a nuclear exchange between the United States and the Soviet Union is ultimately thwarted because of his inability to control all facets of his government and national security personnel. His isolation from his advisors for the duration of the film reinforces this lack of command, and he is eventually forced to sacrifice New York City to nuclear attack as a painful trade-off for the accidental bombing of Moscow. President Merkin Muffley in *Dr Strangelove* is an altogether more ludicrous creation, although the comedic tone of the film creates an intriguing conception of presidential power in the Kennedy era. Balding and bespectacled, President Muffley lacks the markers of heroic masculinity ordinarily associated with the presidency. The tone in which he converses with the belligerent Soviet premier verges on the obsequious, and forms a stark contrast with Kennedy's projections of a dynamic and aggressive attitude towards the Soviet Union. While *Strangelove* is primarily concerned with showing nuclear engagement as farce, like *Fail-Safe* it paints a horrifying picture of the inability of the president to manage the situation, with events spiralling out of control due to miscommunications, faulty technology, and rogue elements within the government and military establishment. The naïve belief in the benevolence of America's state institutions would not suffice in the nuclear age.

These issues become more pronounced in the 1970s. Hollywood's critique of the political system became more pointed, the burgeoning apprehension present in the films of the 1960s rendered more explicit in the following decade. Whereas the modern president was considered capable of confronting and overcoming problems of awesome magnitude, by the 1970s confidence in the power and agency of the individual had been gravely undermined by traumatic events: political assassinations, war, and institutional corruption. As Thomas Elsaesser suggests of a significant strain of Hollywood cinema produced in the 1970s,

> What the heroes bring to such films is an almost physical sense of inconsequential action, of pointlessness and uselessness: stances which are not only interpretable psychologically, but speak of a radical scepticism about American virtues of ambition, vision, drive.[30]

30 Thomas Elsaesser, 'The Pathos of Failure: American Films of the 1970s', in Thomas Elsaesser, Alexander Horwath and Noel King, eds, *The Last Great American Picture*

It is interesting that historians and political scientists describe the presidency in this period as 'imperilled'. Films released in the early- to mid-seventies such as *The Candidate*, *Executive Action*, *The Parallax View*, *Three Days of the Condor* (Sydney Pollack, 1975), *All the President's Men*, *Twilight's Last Gleaming* (Robert Aldrich, 1977) and *The Seduction of Joe Tynan* (Jerry Schatzberg, 1979) represent a political system paralysed by an atmosphere of suspicion and cynicism. By the 1970s, the Roosevelt-Capra era confidence that an individual with the requisite characteristics of nobility, integrity and honesty would inevitably triumph, had begun to be severely scrutinised. *The Candidate* chronicles systemic dysfunction in the American electoral process; *The Parallax View* and *Executive Action* concern the shadowy forces at work within the American government following the Kennedy assassination; *The Seduction of Joe Tynan* addresses the suffocating influence of corporate interests on the legislative process. *All the President's Men*, based on the account of *Washington Post* journalists Bob Woodward (Robert Redford) and Carl Bernstein (Dustin Hoffman) and their mission to uncover the truth about the Watergate scandal, is rather different. Like the Capra-era films, it celebrates the ability of sincere individuals to rescue the system from corrupting influences.

However, the overall impression created by Hollywood films of the 1970s is consonant with general concerns in the Nixon era surrounding the ability of elected politicians to overcome the overwhelming power of corporate interests, the mass media, and the military-industrial complex. By the end of the 1970s, Hollywood and Washington had begun to question the sanctity of the political system; as a result of his supposedly indecisive handling of the hostage crisis at the Iranian embassy, President Jimmy Carter had been largely dismissed as ineffectual. However, the institution itself was also under agitated inspection.

Show: New Hollywood Cinema in the 1970s (Amsterdam: Amsterdam University Press, 2004), 282.

The 1980s: Ronald Reagan and the Ultimate Convergence of Hollywood and Washington

The modern presidency, which had enjoyed enormous success in combating the Great Depression and winning World War II, wilted in the face of increased globalisation, and the overwhelming complexity of the post-war geopolitical environment. Where the system had been celebrated by Hollywood during the 1930s and 1940s, this confidence had largely vanished by the late 1970s. Ronald Reagan, a former Hollywood actor, was elected president in 1980. His presidency resulted in a new and even more complex relationship between the film industry and politics.

Although Ronald Reagan (1981–9) was celebrated for restoring American confidence after the debacles of the previous two decades, his successes were presentational rather than physical. As John Orman argues, 'while Reagan has been portrayed as a get-tough, no-nonsense, macho president by the media, Reagan has been just as unable to handle events in an uncertain world as Jimmy Carter.'[31] Despite his bullish approach to international affairs, Reagan had to contend with an environment in which America was 'no longer the dominant power that it once was.'[32] As the prosperity and power of other nations grew, the United States became 'more like other nations.'[33] However, Reagan injected something altogether different into presidential politics: where Roosevelt and Kennedy were famed for their ability to project images of strength and reassurance through their manipulation of mass media, Reagan employed his status as an ex-Hollywood actor to 'perform' the presidency as the symbol of a revitalised, powerful nation. As Gary Wills suggested, 'Reagan does not argue for American values; he embodies them.'[34] Norton reaffirms this:

31 John Orman, *Comparing Presidential Behavior: Carter, Reagan and the Macho Presidential Style* (New York: Greenwood Press, 1987), 169.

32 Rose, *The Postmodern President*, 4.

33 Ibid.

34 Garry Wills, *Reagan's America: Innocents at Home* (London: Heinemann, 1988), 4.

'What Reagan revealed, and the American people recognized, was not his possession but his representation of the qualities of leadership. *He was elected as signifier.*'[35] Reagan reinvested the presidency with its symbolic power, while simultaneously reaffirming the authority of the individual (even if this authority was illusory). Reagan's values were reliant upon two concepts that were hugely dependent on the construction of images: nostalgia for a stable and prosperous past that had supposedly slipped from America's grasp, and the valorisation of conventional, vigorous and uncompromising masculinity.

Reagan's approach to America's problems was unashamedly nostalgic. His invocation of the past was highly imagistic, often reliant upon the recollection of scenes from films rather than real events. Writing during Reagan's presidency, Michael Rogin argued that 'Reagan's easy slippage between movies and reality is synechdochic for a political culture increasingly impervious to distinctions between fiction and history.'[36] He erased the uncomfortable truths revealed in the previous two decades regarding the limitations of American power through the invocation of 'the post-World War II period of American international ascendancy, domestic social stability, and militant anticommunism.'[37] Instead of confirming the narrative that America must now be a nation among many other nations jockeying for global influence, 'Reagan's stories shared the individualist tilt of classical Hollywood narratives, effacing the importance of organized political action, economic social forces, and social movements throughout the nation's history.'[38]

Related to his individualist stance, Reagan placed a great deal of emphasis on notions of traditional masculinity. Although he was the oldest ever president, Reagan cloaked himself in the trappings of conventional manhood: tending to his ranch by chopping wood and riding horses at

35 Norton, *Republic of Signs*, 100. My emphasis.

36 Michael Rogin, *Ronald Reagan: The Movie, and Other Episodes in Political Demonology* (Berkeley: University of California Press, 1987), 9.

37 Daniel Marcus, *Happy Days and Wonder Years: The Fifties and Sixties in Contemporary Cultural Politics* (New Brunswick, NJ: Rutgers University Press, 2004), 60.

38 Ibid., 64.

home, he was tough and uncompromising with the Soviet Union abroad.[39] Again, the imagistic nature of Reagan's presidency comes to the fore: where the Carter presidency became synonymous with a nation as a 'softened, pampered, and ill-trained male body', Reagan used his tough-guy persona to return the United States to the forefront of the fight against communism through a reversion to the American figure of the cowboy.[40] As Norton suggests, 'Reagan exploited Western mythology for political advantage, presenting himself as the incarnation of this still popular archetype.'[41] In essence, Reagan's construction of himself as a cowboy sorting out America's problems suggests that the nation had been previously unable to meet its challenges simply because it had not been 'man' enough.

This masculinist, individualist bent is particularly manifest in the Hollywood films of the decade. Like the similarly conservative 1950s, the overtly political film is conspicuous by its absence. However, significant strains of Hollywood product in the 1980s conformed to Reagan's twin projects of reasserting America's military strength, and erasing the complexities of the previous two decades by celebrating traditional values of nuclear families and small towns. The films with a militaristic attitude towards global affairs, such as *Rambo: First Blood – Part II* (George P. Costmatos, 1985) and *Missing in Action* (Joseph Zito, 1984), were in keeping with Reagan's project of rehabilitating the Vietnam veteran and, by extension, the intention of the war itself. As Susan Jeffords contends, the revival of this maligned figure, and the repositioning of a traditional, muscular masculinity as the dominant force in society, was intended to regenerate the nation as a whole.[42] As Orman argues, 'In the mid-1980s, the veteran is transformed into the isolated but avenging angel of a reborn American patriotism, assertiveness, and toughness, in keeping with Republican calls

39 Susan Jeffords, *Hard Bodies: Hollywood Masculinity in the Reagan Era* (New Brunswick, NJ: Rutgers University Press, 1994), 12.

40 Ibid., 32.

41 Norton, *Republic of Signs*, 95.

42 Susan Jeffords, *The Remasculinisation of America: Gender and the Vietnam War* (Bloomington: Indiana University Press, 1989), 116.

for national greatness, militarism, and individualism.'[43] However, the recalibration of the Vietnam War in the American imaginary could not happen without assistance; it was largely dependent on the Hollywood dream factory. Reagan celebrated the return of the strongman in American culture, even if he was entirely fictional: after the release of hostages held aboard flight TWA 847 after it was hijacked by members of Hezbollah and Islamic Jihad in June 1985, Reagan stated, 'Boy, after seeing *Rambo* last night, I know what to do the next time this happens.'[44] The president's recourse to models of masculinity reconstructed in the realms of Hollywood cinema as a means of dealing with real political problems suggested that the distinctions between the political and cultural worlds had been further complicated in this period.

I think one can read the restoration of the Vietnam veteran as a beacon of American masculine and militaristic strength as part of a process that proved vital to Reagan's success as president. Although Reagan was no more in control of a delicate geopolitical environment than Carter, he *was* more successful at the management of his own image. Reagan's amnesiac approach to America's problems suggests he had constructed for the nation a highly selective, imagistic and seductive narrative of American supremacy. In the absence of *real* solutions, ideological ones were sought: the United States would recapture its greatness by reinvigorating its core values of individualism and self-reliance. While the rollback of the welfare state was divisive and controversial, Reagan's ability to perform the role of a reassuring father figure arguably rendered these policies more palatable. In essence, Reagan's presidency represents a further extension of a process which had begun during the Roosevelt administration, achieved maturation during Kennedy's era, and reached levels of *saturation* during the Reagan presidency: while it is arguable the president was ever 'real' in the sense that he was inevitably a mediated, constructed entity for the vast majority

43 Orman, *Comparing Presidential Behavior*, 97.

44 'Reagan Gets Idea from *Rambo* For Next Time', *The Los Angeles Times*, July 1st, 1985, <http://articles.latimes.com/1985-07-01/news/mn-10009_1_hostage-crisis>, accessed August 2012.

of people, I contend that it was Reagan who embraced the full potential of this process. As his speechwriter Peggy Noonan suggested,

> '"[T]he president's top aides who planned the day were no longer just part of the story – it was as if they were producers of the story. They were the line producers of a show called *White House*, with Ronald Reagan as the President." ... This particular mode of political representation "wasn't particular to that White House, *it was simply a trend that achieved its fullness in the Reagan era.*"'[45]

Timothy Raphael's work is illuminating in this regard. He argues that Reagan's former status as a Hollywood actor was ideal training for the presidency given its overwhelming reliance on performance, spectacle and stage-management. The comprehensive dominance of communications technologies over political life rendered such a process inevitable. By watching television, we consume acting performances regularly where once it was done only occasionally, and demand of our politics a similar visual language to our leisure pastimes: watching films and television. Invoking Frederic Jameson's diagnosis of our fascination with surfaces, images and representations in the postmodern moment, Raphael suggests, 'the cultural and the political, historically perceived to be semiautonomous spheres, have become virtually indistinguishable. Our engagement with politics is now thoroughly mediated by culture.'[46]

In essence, Reagan recast the presidency as a movie, starring himself in the lead role.[47] Although he could not retrieve the strength of the modern presidency because the world had fundamentally changed, he could assert at least an *image* of its former power. The success of Reagan's presidency is entirely in keeping with Guy Debord's suggestion that 'All that once was directly lived has become mere representation.'[48] Reagan's conflation of the worlds of politics and Hollywood entertainment renders the determined attempt by scholars in this field to maintain the distinction between the

45 Peggy Noonan, quoted by Timothy Raphael, *The President Electric*, 22.

46 Raphael, *The President Electric*, 12.

47 Wills, *Reagan's America*, 4.

48 Guy Debord, *The Society of the Spectacle* (translated by Donald Nicholson-Smith; New York: Zone Books, 1994), 12.

real and the fictional more difficult. It is my contention that the expansion, proliferation and diversification of the fictional presidency in mainstream film and television can be, at least in part, explained by Reagan's presidency.

What this brief exploration of the contours of Hollywood's relationship with American politics has revealed is a complex picture. While the film and television industries provide critiques of the presidents in power at the times they were produced, the consistent use of nostalgic imagery tends ultimately to celebrate the presidency overall as a *symbol* of the brilliance of the American system. The ultimate conflation of the industries of film, television and politics during the Reagan administration, with a concomitant reassertion of the power of the individual, adds further layers to this discussion. With the distinction between the 'real' and the 'fictional' further muddied, to what extent would future representations in Hollywood merely replicate dominant conceptions of the presidency's identity – racially, sexually, historically, mythologically? Or would this realisation of the presidency's artificiality provide the necessary cultural room to represent fictional leaders outside of these governing constructs? The intersection of these issues with questions of Hollywood genre, narrative, and iconography will form the basis of the forthcoming analysis and discussion. In essence, this book looks to examine the ways in which mainstream film and television have provided fortification to dominant mythological conceptions of America's presidency, its national identity and purpose. In so doing, I hope to provide an answer to Warren G. Rochelle's question of the fictional presidency:

> This Mr President, this colossus, is a far cry from most of the occupants of 1600 Pennsylvania Avenue, and why do we keep telling ourselves a story that can never be true, with a hero that can never be real?[49]

49 Rochelle, 'The Literary Presidency', 417.

CHAPTER 3

The Post-Cold War Presidency in Hollywood Cinema

> If Ronald Reagan was the fantasy elder come to lead the sons in triumphal battle against the Evil Empire, when the credits rolled and the sons awoke from that stardusted dream, most felt farther away from the promised land of adult manhood – less triumphal, less powerful, less confident of making a living or providing for a family or contributing productively to society. *And no new elder statesman, celluloid or otherwise, loomed on the horizon.*[1]

> Because we could never really know who the 'real' Bill Clinton was, and because there was no 'real' Bill Clinton to understand for the vast majority of Americans, the culture continued producing explanations for this president.[2]

> The end of the Cold War may be the ultimate stage in the demythologizing of the contemporary American presidency.[3]

The above quotations outline the intellectual ground upon which this chapter will be based. I will argue that the 1990s represent a fundamental sea change in Hollywood's representation of the presidency for three primary

1 Susan Faludi, *Stiffed: The Betrayal of Modern Man* (London: Vintage, 2000), 407. My emphasis.

2 Shawn J. Parry-Giles and Trevor Parry-Giles, *Constructing Clinton: Hyperreality and Presidential Image-Making in Postmodern Politics* (New York: Peter Lang, 2002), 1.

3 Harold M. Barger, 'The Incredible Shrinking Image: From Cold War to Globalist Presidency', in Anthony J. Eksterowicz and Glenn P. Hastedt, eds, *The Post-Cold War Presidency* (Oxford: Rowman and Littlefield Publishers, 1999), 57.

reasons: shifting conceptions of masculinity and what it meant to 'be a man' in a post-Civil Rights, postfeminist environment; the popularity of Bill Clinton who, despite being beset by scandal, and lacking many of the traits that had ensured electoral success for presidents that preceded him, won two presidential elections; and the relatively peaceful conclusion to the Cold War, the ideological conflict with the Soviet Union that had functioned as the organising narrative of American foreign and domestic policy for forty-five years.[4] How the United States should use its newly acquired status as the world's only remaining superpower was a product of heated debate: while many felt that an inward focus was essential after so many years of fighting battles abroad, others saw a unique opportunity for America to refashion the world in its own image. Furthermore, the cessation of what seemed a permanent conflict had enormous ramifications for traditional conceptions of masculinity, as Susan Faludi's analysis demonstrates.

From the vantage point of our contemporary political, social and economic crises, the 1990s now looks a benign period in Western history. The triumph of democracy over totalitarianism, of capitalism over communism, and the hope that the threat of nuclear annihilation had largely dissipated with the collapse of the Soviet Union, were greeted with overwhelming optimism in some circles. However, despite the outward appearance of calm, many aspects of society that had been held to be certainties underwent radical redefinition. As Shawn and Trevor Parry-Giles have suggested, the 1990s was 'a time of considerable political angst in the United States – a time when politics, both nationally and internationally, was in a constant state of flux and transformation.'[5] With America's global pre-eminence achieved, and seismic shifts in the global economy demonstrated by the booming information technology industries and the decline of traditional labour-intensive work, new paradigms had to be found to understand this rapidly changing global environment. Amidst all of this, who the president

4 I am aware that attaching the prefix 'post-' to the Civil Rights and feminist movements implies that they are at an end. I do not wish to suggest this (primarily because I am of the opinion that they certainly are not), but merely use the terms as culturally inscribed shorthand.

5 Parry-Giles and Parry-Giles, *Constructing Clinton*, 1.

should be and who he *was* were suddenly unanswered questions. The traditional, problematic association of the presidency with conventional masculine strength began to be undermined following the collapse of the Soviet Union. It is my contention that, once America had awoken from the Reagan dream and found there was no replacement, they sought to redraw, in various different guises and from wildly divergent points of inspiration, the traditional presidential-father in the Hollywood dream factory.

Films featuring the president in the 1990s were plentiful and diverse. Where the office had previously been treated largely with seriousness and respect in Hollywood cinema (its representation mainly the preserve of serious drama and biographical films), the 1990s saw the presidency represented in a wide variety of genres. In order to provide a broad impression of why this occurred, I will place particular emphasis on two opposing ends of the generic spectrum: this chapter will examine the presidency in the comedy (*Dave* and *The American President*) and action (*Independence Day* and *Air Force One*) genres. My discussion will provide some answers to the following questions: why did the fictional presidency proliferate in the 1990s? Do the representations of the president reflect contemporary anxieties surrounding the office, or are they more concerned with recycling older Hollywood genres and archetypes? If the texts are indeed nostalgic rearticulations of traditional forms, how does this impact upon our understanding of the fictional presidency, and its relationship with the real-world presidency? I will discuss all four films in relation to visual style, narrative, and iconography, and the ways in which generic conventions impact upon their representations of presidential power. First, I will flesh out the concerns with which I began this chapter: the changes occurring within the office as a result of America's Cold War victory, concomitant redefinitions of masculinity in the period, and the centrality of Bill Clinton in relation to these issues.

***

As Stephen Schier argues, 'the end of the Cold War … importantly altered the president's job description.'[6] George Bush Sr. was a victim of this shift:

6 Stephen E. Schier, 'A Unique Presidency', in Stephen E. Schier, ed., *The Postmodern Presidency* (Pittsburgh: University of Pittsburgh Press, 2000), 5.

although the demonstration of his masculine warrior credentials in the swift and successful execution of the Gulf War proved popular, he had no grand vision for where this New World Order would take the United States.[7] Moreover, he had considerable trouble in relating to ordinary Americans, as evidenced by the infamous news footage of him astonished by a supermarket barcode scanner. While he tried to reconfigure himself as a gentler, more conciliatory version of his predecessor, Bush failed to embody the presidential dichotomy of man and superman that Reagan had managed so adroitly.[8] He came across as a technocratic rather than emotional leader, and he was a step behind the times in which 'the hard-bodied male action heroes of the eighties [had] given way to a "kinder, gentler" US manhood, one that is sensitive, generous, caring, and perhaps most importantly, capable of change.'[9] To be kind to Bush, foreign policy now 'mattered little to a society persuaded that the great danger to its security had passed, that the time had come once again to enjoy a well-earned prosperity, too long deferred.'[10] To be cutting, and to quote Clinton's 1992 campaign slogan, 'It's the economy, stupid.'

As the Clinton campaign's now clichéd mantra suggests, the 1992 election was decided on domestic issues. A good record in the military and foreign affairs was deemed unnecessary: despite Bush's best efforts to position him as a draft-dodger, Clinton won the 1992 election comfortably. He was therefore the first president to not have served in the military since Franklin D. Roosevelt.[11] Clinton was able to win on a pluralistic platform that made a virtue of his lack of ideology: without the threat of communism and the absence of any other compelling 'ism' to fulfil the

7 Derek Chollet and James Goldgeier, *America Between the Wars: From 11/9 to 9/11: The Misunderstood Years Between the Fall of the Berlin Wall and the Start of the War on Terror* (New York: Public Affairs, 2008), 8.

8 Jeffords, *Hard Bodies*, 95–9.

9 Susan Jeffords, 'The Big Switch: Hollywood Masculinity in the Nineties', in Jim Collins, Hilary Radner and Ava Preacher Collins, eds, *Film Theory Goes to the Movies* (London: Routledge, 1993), 197.

10 Stephen Graubard, *The Presidents: The Transformation of the American Presidency from Theodore Roosevelt to George W. Bush* (London: Penguin, 2006), 648.

11 Schier, 'A Unique Presidency', 5.

role of villain in the American narrative, there was suddenly no need for 'isms' at all.[12] A public saturated with media that emphasised discontinuity and irony over consistency and conviction allowed Clinton to evade the numerous attacks on his character and personal behaviour, and avoid pursuing a consistent ideological project which may have backfired.[13] As Bruce Miroff argues, 'Who Clinton "really was" ... did not rest on a stable character structure or set of convictions'.[14] Indeed, 'who the president "really" was had become largely insignificant'.[15] Clinton revelled in his ambiguous status. He positioned himself as traditionally masculine, conforming to the dominant conception of the presidency, and sensitive, attuned to the less aggressive environment of the 1990s. Like the Hollywood heroes who had begun to explore their 'feminine sides' in the early 1990s, so too was the presidency subtly altering itself to remain attuned to the politics of the moment. Clinton was canny enough to realise that expectations of the presidency had altered, and by offering a 'newly sensitive, empathetic presidency', and distancing himself from the aggressive masculinity associated with the 1980s, he won power.[16]

However, there remained audible voices demanding that America not lay down its weapons after the Soviet Union's collapse. Charles Krauthammer and Richard Nixon implored the current political leadership to seize the opportunity to impose Americanism upon the world, ensuring that free market capitalism and democracy could flourish everywhere.[17] Francis Fukuyama controversially, and prematurely, argued that,

12 Bruce Miroff, 'Courting the Public: Bill Clinton's Postmodern Education', in Schier, ed., *The Postmodern Presidency*, 106–7.

13 With the end of the Cold War came the death of grand ideas about how to remake society: Clinton's only meaningful pursuit of a grand platform – the disastrous attempt at healthcare reform early in his first term – prompted him to declare in his 1996 State of the Union address that 'the era of big government is over'.

14 Miroff, 'Courting the Public', 112.

15 Ibid., 118.

16 Brenton J. Malin, *American Masculinity Under Clinton: Popular Media and the Nineties 'Crisis of Masculinity'* (New York: Peter Lang, 2005), 58.

17 Charles Krauthammer, 'The Unipolar Moment', *Foreign Affairs* 70/1 (1990/1), 23–33; Richard Nixon, *Seize the Moment: America's Challenge in a One-Superpower World* (New York: Simon and Schuster, 1994).

with the collapse of communism, 'history' had ended – the world had now realised that liberal democracy was the *ideal* form of government.[18] Girded by the collapse of the Soviet Union, Fukuyama suggested the move towards capitalism and democracy was an *inevitable, natural evolutionary process* for all nations.[19] However, the associated changes in dominant conceptions of masculinity, the presidency, and American national identity were not viewed entirely positively: Fukuyama worried that victory may cause men to become inert and complacent; 'the end of history would mean the end of wars and bloody revolutions. Agreeing on ends, men would have no large causes for which to fight.'[20] While shifting conceptions of masculinity and the presidency had demonstrated the Reagan-era 'hard body' to be untenable, there remained palpable apprehension regarding the 'soft body' that might replace it.[21]

This uncertain era was embodied by Bill Clinton, and ambiguity shrouded the presidency as an institution: was the president a hero or a villain? Who was he fighting, and what was he fighting for? From a position of global supremacy, with no more coherent, totemic enemies with which to grapple, and with a president who epitomised a contradictory age, these concerns manifested themselves in a cycle of Hollywood cinema diverse in style, genre, and tone. As Parry-Giles and Parry-Giles suggest, the ambivalence surrounding Clinton was explored by '[a] culture [that] continued producing explanations for this president.'[22]

***

The uncertainty that descended upon the presidency following Reagan's consummate performance of its competing demands left the office ripe for investigation, excavation and parody. Oliver Stone's *Nixon* psychoanalysed

18 Francis Fukuyama, *The End of History and the Last Man* (London: Penguin Books, 1992), ix.

19 Ibid., 48.

20 Ibid., 311. See also Tom Engelhardt, *The End of Victory Culture: Cold War America and The Disillusioning of a Generation* (New York: Basic Books, 1995).

21 Jeffords, *Hard Bodies*, 178–93.

22 Parry-Giles and Parry-Giles, *Constructing Clinton*, 13.

the disgraced former president, locating the reasons for Watergate in the traumas he suffered during childhood. Comedies such as alien invasion parody *Mars Attacks!* and *My Fellow Americans* (Peter Segal, 1996) caricature the president as bumbling and feckless, while *Dick* (Andrew Fleming, 1999) suggests it was Nixon's incompetence, rather than anything malevolent, that led to the Watergate scandal. Concerns regarding the influence of the media upon the political and electoral processes emerge in mockumentary *Bob Roberts* (Tim Robbins, 1992), and satirical comedies *Primary Colors* (Mike Nichols, 1998) and *Wag the Dog* (Barry Levinson, 1997). The cult of individualism that had enjoyed a considerable resurgence during the Reagan era persisted in the 1990s. While political thrillers of the 1970s, like *All the President's Men* and *The Parallax View*, constructed the presidency as *symbolic* of systemic malignancy within federal government, films of similar generic disposition in the 1990s render the president a physical presence, individually culpable for, or associated with, altogether more violent crimes, like the murder of a young woman in *Absolute Power* or *Murder at 1600*.

Absolute Power demonstrates the extent to which Hollywood demystified and denigrated the presidency in the 1990s. President Alan Richmond (Gene Hackman) is a ghastly creation; a drunken and lecherous man with a deadly penchant for sado-masochistic sex. In a more metaphorical fashion than the Lewinsky scandal, films like *Absolute Power* demonstrated how Hollywood deconstructed the presidential phallus by revealing the 'paltry' penis that exists beneath it. As Loren Glass suggested of the demythologisation of the presidency following the Lewinsky scandal, 'The penis – in the end a paltry thing – must be concealed if its fictional equation to the omnipotent phallus is to be sustained.'[23] I am primarily concerned with the breakdown of this equation: how Hollywood deconstructed the president *as a symbol*, revealing him to be ordinary, human, fallible, frail, and capable of heroism but also of weakness.

The first half of the chapter will investigate two comedies: *Dave* (Ivan Reitman, 1993) and *The American President* (Rob Reiner, 1995). I will argue

23 Loren Glass, 'Publicizing the President's Privates', *Postmodern Culture* 9/3 (1999), 3.

that *Dave* represents the presidency on the cusp of change at the start of Clinton's administration, a nostalgic yearning for a Capraesque 'common man' as president, and a rejection of the mean-spiritedness of the Reagan/Bush years. *The American President* is more firmly of the Clinton period, raising issues surrounding presidential identity, privacy, and the distinction between the man and the office (with particular emphasis on changing gender politics in relation to the presidency).

The second half will turn to the invention of the action hero president in science-fiction/disaster film *Independence Day* (Roland Emmerich, 1996) and action thriller *Air Force One* (Wolfgang Petersen, 1997). Through discussion of genre, narrative and *mise-en-scène*, I will argue that both films look to reinstate the heroic presidency which had become obsolete following the end of the Cold War. Because the complex international terrain in which the United States found itself after the collapse of the Soviet Union was unlikely to realise the utopian future envisioned by some, this dream would have to be enacted in the realm of fantasy: the motion picture.

The 1990s Presidency I: Comedy

Dave: The Return of the Capra Hero

Of the two comedies discussed, *Dave* is more straightforwardly Capraesque. Its narrative has notable similarities to *Mr Smith Goes to Washington*, where an ordinary, naïve and idealistic man from outside the political machine is whisked into government to serve the interests of a corrupt, powerful elite, but turns the tables on them to revitalise the principles on which the United States was founded. *Dave* is the story of Dave Kovic (Kevin Kline), an amiable 'Ordinary Joe' who runs a temporary employment agency in Washington, DC, but also happens to be the spitting image of the current president, Bill Mitchell (also Kevin Kline). Dave looks so much like the president he does part-time impersonation work to supplement his income. When Mitchell is incapacitated by a massive stroke while indulging in extra-marital sex with his secretary (Laura Linney), Dave is asked by Mitchell's nefarious Chief of Staff Bob Alexander (Frank Langella) to pose as the president. Alexander has designs on the presidency himself, and hopes to manipulate the guileless Dave into nominating him as vice president after pinning a scandal on the current incumbent, the decent and honest Vice President Nance (Ben Kingsley). Dave soon realises the Machiavellian machinations going on around him, and devotes his time as the 'acting' president to push a few solidly liberal reforms through Congress, while preventing Alexander from getting his clutches on the presidency.

Dave largely conforms to the formula of Capra's political films which, in concordance with Roosevelt's New Deal, were 'not concerned with the politics of social restructuring or revolution but with the politics of conversion and moral regeneration.'[24] Screenwriter Gary Ross confirmed the influence of this template when he said, 'A political film works if it's also an idealistic film ... People want to feel renewed about their politics ... Those films in the 30s worked because they understood what the right hero was, they weren't afraid of populism.'[25] The extent to which *Dave* is indebted to the political films of the 1930s is indicated by its similarities to Depression-era comedy *The Phantom President*, in which the colourless and lacklustre president is replaced by a charismatic lookalike. While the United States of the early 1990s was not experiencing anything like the convulsions of insecurity, fear and economic turbulence of the 1930s, *Dave*'s invocation of the cinema of the period raises an intriguing comparison: after long years of Republican rule which had brought the country to the edge of a precipice after the Wall Street Crash of 1929,

24 Leonard Quart, quoted in Lawrence W. Levine, *The Unpredictable Past* (New York: Oxford University Press, 1993), 251.

25 Gary Ross, screenwriter of *Dave*, quoted in J. Hoberman, 'Under the Rainbow', *Sight and Sound* 9/1 (January 1999), 14–15.
Aside from writing Hollywood hits like *Big* (Penny Marshall, 1988) and directing *Pleasantville* (1998), an allegory for the turmoil in American society during the McCarthy and Civil Rights eras, Gary Ross also worked as a speechwriter for Bill Clinton.

the United States began to question its democratic, capitalist identity.[26] Faith needed to be restored. Like Roosevelt's essentially conservative New Deal project, which sought not to revise but renew American democratic capitalism, Capra's populist political films called for 'a "kinder and gentler America" ... while endorsing both the economic system and political tradition.'[27]

In this regard, *Dave* appears to be reflective of similar impulses at work in the early 1990s. When Bush Sr. took office in 1989, he sought 'to make kinder the face of the Nation and gentler the face of the world.'[28] After Reagan's divisive social and economic policies, there was an appetite for at least partial rejuvenation of the American ideals of good neighbourliness and charity. For some, the end of the Cold War prompted an inward focus: after forty-five years of conflict, America's soul needed attention. Stella Bruzzi suggests that Hollywood's shift towards representations of sensitive and caring men and fathers in the 1990s demonstrated 'that men's greatest battles were now the internal rather than the external ones.'[29] I contend that this inward shift can be detected in *Dave*'s nostalgic recreation of a Capraesque representation of the presidency: now we have taken care of the world, we must take care of each other. In reality, while Bush failed to play the role of the gentle father figure because of his status as a corporate elitist, it fell to Clinton to recognise the mood of the times and play the role of the nice guy trying to help people. As Ben Dickenson notes, 'Hollywood liberals in the early 1990s greeted Bill Clinton's presidency with hopeful excitement.'[30] In relation to this, Martin Walker argues *Dave* is symptomatic

26 Bergman, *We're in the Money*, 92–109.

27 Brian Neve, *Film and Politics in America: A Social Tradition* (London: Routledge, 1992), 46.

28 George H.W. Bush, inaugural address, January 20th, 1989, quoted in Jeffords, *Hard Bodies*, 95.

29 Stella Bruzzi, *Bringing Up Daddy: Fatherhood and Masculinity in Post-War Hollywood* (London: British Film Institute, 2005), 156.

30 Ben Dickenson, *Hollywood's New Radicalism: War, Globalisation and the Movies from Reagan to George W. Bush* (London: I.B. Tauris, 2006), 33.

of a 'nice and nurturing' decade, 'characterised by innocence, readiness to believe and playing to the family audience.'[31]

However, Walker is correct to note that *Dave* was produced and released very early in Clinton's first term, before his presidency had taken shape (it was released in the US in May 1993, and Clinton had only taken office in January).[32] In concordance with this hesitation, I position *Dave* on the cusp of change within the presidency: the film articulates the changing attitudes towards (and demands of) the office in a post-Cold War, post-Reagan world, while also engaging with the modifications of traditional masculinity that emerged in wider culture in the late 1980s and early 1990s. Essentially, *Dave* appears to ask two questions: now that the Cold War is over, what role should the government play? How should the presidency evolve in accordance with this modified position? As Capra represented the American public as child-like and desperate for leadership, so *Dave* seizes upon this supposed 'new beginning' in American politics and society after the Reagan-Bush years to represent the president as a sensitive father figure who just wants to find his people jobs.

Dave's restorative strategy is apparent from the beginning, and demonstrates its symbolic indebtedness to Capra. Much as naïve country boy Jefferson Smith did upon arriving in Washington, DC in *Mr Smith Goes to Washington*, *Dave*'s camera takes a tour of much of the iconography that makes the city instantly recognisable. Here, however, the *viewer* is constructed as the innocent, and Washington, DC's monuments are uncomplicatedly established as icons of democratic virtue. The camera first soars across the Potomac River, tilting upwards to reveal the elegant line of symmetry between the Lincoln Memorial (seen here only from the back), the Reflecting Pool, the Washington Monument, and the Capitol Dome. The camera then glides effortlessly over the city, cutting to moving aerial shots of the Capitol Dome and boats rowing on the Potomac River, swooping towards and past the Jefferson Memorial (which is accompanied by an orchestral swell concomitant with the perceived import of this

31 Martin Walker, 'Clinton's Hollywood', *Sight and Sound* (September 1993), 13.

32 Ibid.

Founding Father), around the Washington Monument, before revealing the expanse of lawn at the back of the White House. The warm, gentle music, replete with soothing violins and trumpets, reinforces the notion that this is an adoring, wide-eyed, Capraesque treatment of the ideals of American democracy, symbolised by monuments to the nation's greatest leaders.

Giuliana Muscio suggests that Capra's heroes would visit historical monuments 'in moments of crisis', arguing that 'this didactic form and hagiography reduced American history to simplistic lessons aimed at … Americans searching for a return to a mythicized past innocence.'[33] The most famous examples in Capra's work are Jefferson Smith's pilgrimages to the Lincoln Memorial in *Mr Smith*: faced with the corruption of the present administration, Smith visits Lincoln to restore his faith in the system, to replenish American democratic ideals, to reaffirm his (and the nation's) virtuousness. *Dave* also finds this innocence in the elegant white marble of Washington, DC's monuments; the sequence is clean and smooth, the music affectionate and reverent. The camera's movement across Washington, DC implies a simultaneous mastery of, and comfort with, the city as the seat of benign American power. To deal with the uncertainty within the *contemporary* presidency, then, *Dave* employs old symbols of America's ideals to restore its confidence in the nation. In so doing, it correlates with Capra's frequent invocation of 'the notion or myth of some lost "golden age" in which life was purer and simpler'; a more innocent time when great men such as Lincoln, Washington and Jefferson held power, and we were not subjected to the fallible and insecure creatures of the recent past and present.[34]

In order to salvage these lost ideals, *Dave* must purge the presidency of the dishonesty, corruption and sleaze that blights its contemporary incarnation. President Mitchell is promptly established as indicative of this institutional malady, his characterisation functioning as a possible indictment of Reaganism: although Reagan himself managed to negotiate

33 Giuliana Muscio, *Hollywood's New Deal* (Philadelphia: Temple University Press, 1996), 75.

34 Neve, *Film and Politics in America*, 33.

the contradiction between his rhetoric and his actions to remain popular, his policies fostered a long period of selfish individualism and greed from which Western society has not yet recovered. Mitchell can be understood as simultaneously a Hollywood caricature of a Reaganite, and a Capraesque evil capitalist in the vein of *It's a Wonderful Life*'s (1946) Henry Potter. This is evidenced by Mitchell's desire to continue Reagan's work of rolling back the welfare state by closing homeless shelters and Head Start centres, and his Potteresque involvement in a 'Savings and Loans' scandal, whereby he and his chief of staff bribed federal regulators to allow larger than usual donations to be made by campaign contributors.[35] His marriage to First Lady Ellen Mitchell (Sigourney Weaver) has irretrievably broken down, and he sleeps wantonly with other women. Mitchell is portrayed as an insensitive, uncaring megalomaniac who committed all manner of crimes to win power, and will do anything to expand it. He is perfectly willing, for example, to implicate the innocent vice president in the fraud that he perpetrated in order to deflect attention and maintain supremacy. In Hollywood terms, Mitchell's presidency conforms to 'Capra's depiction of the depraving influences of governmental power', and Hollywood's general representation of Washington in the 1930s, where it 'became a symbol of the forces and developments that had derailed America from its destiny and led it astray.'[36]

Dave is, however, attuned to the imagistic nature of politics in the 1990s. As Hoberman suggests, '*Dave* defined the president in terms of

35 Not only does this remind one of Henry Potter in *It's a Wonderful Life*, it also recalls the Savings and Loan crisis of the Reagan era, whereby federal deregulation of the financial industry made fraud more likely, and more difficult to detect. It resulted in the failure of 747 savings and loan associations in the United States, requiring a federal bailout which partly caused the enormous budget deficits of the 1980s. Head Start centres are funded by government subsidy to provide children's educational, medical, nutritional and social services, and were established as part of Johnson's Great Society reforms in the mid-1960s to address systemic poverty. Reagan's presidency was largely defined as a repudiation of initiatives like this.

36 Lindholm and Hall, 'Frank Capra Meets John Doe', 34; Levine, *The Unpredictable Past*, 249.

his image.'[37] Mitchell is keenly aware of the need to present the *appearance* of caring about people and being a good husband and, like the villains of Capra's political films, uses the power of the press to deceive the public into believing this is his true identity. This public/private dichotomy is shown when he arrives back at the White House at the beginning of the film. While he is keen to offer the impression that he is a genial man in front of the journalists by holding his wife's hand and walking his dogs, as soon as he escapes the scrutiny of the cameras, he hurls the dog's leashes into the arms of an aide, and ignores his wife as they go their separate ways. Politically, he demonstrates his awareness of the public/private distinction, saying he could easily veto the bill which contains funding for the welfare programmes already mentioned, but he does not want to 'look like a prick'. However, he seems perfectly comfortable with actually *being* a prick; his only concern is *looking* like one. He hides behind rhetorical platitudes regarding America's glorious past, 'nostalgic for those days back then', while perpetrating crimes of fraud and adultery in the present. *Dave* appears to paint Reagan's nostalgic rhetoric as disturbingly hollow; a means of distracting the public from society's problems, and allowing the politicians to profit from them along the way. In presenting President Mitchell in this fashion, *Dave* gently satirises contemporary politics, which Bruzzi argues is 'so image-dependent that who the candidates are (in terms of character, the man behind the mask, etc.) has become an irrelevance'.[38]

Despite the overwhelming cynicism that characterised attitudes to politicians in the 1990s, *Dave* laments the turn towards an imagistic presidency, and articulates a profound longing for a resurgence of honesty, idealism and innocence in politics. It also recognises that, with the Cold War over, the ground upon which the presidency is based has shifted. Mitchell acknowledges as much: as he disappears for his clandestine tryst, he jokingly tells his staff, 'Call me if there's a war'. This throwaway line draws to the surface something rather intriguing about *Dave*'s conception of the presidency: although the Cold War is over and the threat of conflict has

37 Hoberman, 'Under the Rainbow', 14.

38 Stella Bruzzi, *New Documentary* [2nd edn] (London: Routledge, 2006), 147.

receded, the president as an office and a man has not evolved in a parallel fashion. Without the unifying force of global conflict, the old model of president is free to pillage the nation's wealth and exploit his powerful position for sexual gratification. Where a steely resolve and determination might have been necessary during the Cold War, Mitchell now simply appears cold and emotionless. As wife Ellen says to one of his (Dave's) typically terse responses, 'You don't change do you, Bill?' John MacInnes argues this is indicative of a shift in what constitutes the masculine ideal: what were once considered 'manly virtues', such as heroism, independence, courage, strength, backbone and virility, have been reconstituted as 'masculine vices' (abuse, aggression, coldness, detachment, an inability to empathise or be supportive).[39] In effect, President Mitchell's insensitivity and infidelity are not in keeping with the new era: he is an Old Man in a New Man's world. His behaviour demonstrates that, unlike the hard-bodied heroes for whom the 1990s represented a sensitive turn, he has not proven to be 'capable of change.'[40]

In accordance with this, *Dave* reveals the intransigent, unyielding Reaganite model of president (and man) to be ideologically and physically untenable: not only is the government budget in disarray because of excessive (and now unnecessary) military spending, Mitchell's stroke during adulterous sex undermines the construction of the virile, dominant and conventionally masculine presidency. As Richard Dyer argues, 'the penis ... is the symbol of male potency, the magic and mystery of the phallus, the endowment that appears to legitimate male power.'[41] By focusing on Mitchell's inability to withstand the physical exertions of the sexual act, *Dave* appears to question the functionality of this construction. *Dave* shows the Reaganite, 'hard bodied' presidency to be fragile and obsolete. As Glass suggests, the model of masculinity espoused by Reagan is 'increasingly embattled and lampooned in American popular culture', and is 'losing

39 John MacInnes, *The End of Masculinity* (Buckingham: Open University Press, 1998), 84.

40 Jeffords, 'The Big Switch', 197.

41 Richard Dyer, *The Matter of Images: Essays on Representations* (London: Routledge, 1993), 113.

[its] viability as ideological support for an American sex/gender system.'[42] Employed for comedic value, Mitchell's stroke demonstrates this construct to be decrepit, and presents *Dave* with the narrative coincidence it needs to reject the Reaganite model of presidency and masculinity, and renew the office for the softer and gentler 1990s.

To do so, *Dave* constructs its substitute president as a Capraesque hero for the post-Cold War period. Dave Kovic bears the essential characteristics of many of Capra's heroes: like Jefferson Smith, he is innocent and disbelieving of the government's mendacity, refusing to believe that the president would engage in fraud; like Smith and Deeds, he is naïvely patriotic, and his impersonations of President Mitchell come from a place of deep respect and adoration for the values his rhetoric espouses, rather than parody or mocking; he is exuberant and child-like in his behaviour.[43] Jeffrey Richards argues that all of Capra's heroes have 'an element of uninhibited boyishness about them, reflecting their innocence'.[44] Dave has similar characteristics: riding a bicycle to and from work figures him as a child, the absence of a motor vehicle further disassociating him from adult masculinity and its common associations of rapid movement, dynamism, and mechanised power.[45] He sings frequently and spontaneously ('Oklahoma!' and 'Hail to the Chief'). His photo opportunities as president construct him as youthful, energetic and playful: where Mitchell used his dogs for purely presentational purposes, Dave wrestles with them on the White House lawn; he does magic tricks for children at a homeless shelter (showing his caring, sensitive side, as well as his childish sense of wonder); he dances and plays the fool using a pair of robotic arms at a factory; he throws out the

42 Loren Glass, 'After the Phallus', *American Imago* 58/2 (Summer 2001), 554.

43 *Dave* conforms not only to a Capraesque model of hero, but is also in keeping with a contemporaneous trend in Hollywood cinema that idealised adult innocence: films like *Rain Man* (Barry Levinson, 1988), *Big* and *Regarding Henry* (Mike Nichols, 1991) feature child-like adult men who reveal the hypocrisy and selfishness of adult society through their innocent purity.

44 Jeffrey Richards, 'Frank Capra and the Cinema of Populism', in Bill Nichols, ed., *Movies and Methods*, 70.

45 While Dave does drive a car later, he does not own it and it is decidedly ordinary, and he is even pulled over by the police for a minor traffic violation.

first pitch at a baseball game with aplomb, celebrating his achievement by thrusting his arms into the air with boyish enthusiasm. This is welcomed by the news media in typically Capraesque terms, who celebrate Mitchell's (Dave's) transformation, saying that the president does not have to be 'a zombie. He could show some zip, some life, *even act like a child*.' Much as *Dave* appears to yearn for a return to a simpler, more innocent time, it appears to also desire a simpler, more innocent president to accompany this shift.

The scene in which Dave plays the fool alongside Arnold Schwarzenegger (playing himself) is crucial: Schwarzenegger, one of the poster boys of the militaristic and antagonistic Reagan era, is recast here as a children's nutritional expert, his musclebound physique employed as indicative of internal well-being and health, rather than outward strength. Although only a brief cameo, Schwarzenegger's presence shows the extent to which *Dave* is engaged in the renegotiation of Reaganite models of masculinity and the presidency.[46] Where he was celebrated by Reagan and Bush as 'Conan the Republican', emblematic of their tough stance in global affairs, *Dave* employs Schwarzenegger's evolution into a New Man to negotiate its reevaluation of the presidency. When Schwarzenegger wrestles Dave to the ground, it is done for laughs, not as a demonstration of masculine one-upmanship, and is greeted with fits of laughter from the audience of children. Schwarzenegger's performance here could not be further from the muscle-bound aggression of his action roles, and is in keeping the playful, friendly New Man (and New President) of the early 1990s.

This is not to say that the reformation of the presidency ends with a remodelling of the man himself. *Dave* also looks to rejuvenate the presidency's purpose, and does so again by recalling the politics of the 1930s, and

46 Jeffords notes the change in Schwarzenegger's star image in the early 1990s. Where in the 80s he played hypermasculine, violent and aggressive types in *The Terminator* (James Cameron, 1984), *Commando* (Mark L. Lester, 1985) and *Predator* (John McTiernan, 1987), the early 1990s saw a shift in his persona. He played an undercover cop who becomes a pre-school teacher in *Kindergarten Cop* (Ivan Reitman, 1990), and reworked his role as the 'relentlessly lethal' Terminator for the sequel, becoming a protective, nurturing surrogate father for John Connor. – 'The Big Switch', 199.

the films of Capra. Like Jefferson Smith, Dave is undeterred by the bullying tactics of the powerful elite (here embodied by his chief of staff) and 'insists on retaining his idealism, naïveté, youthful innocence.'[47] He cuts bloated, wasteful defence spending to save homeless shelters and, as his confidence in the position grows, introduces a government programme to guarantee jobs for everyone. This is *Dave*'s ultimate repudiation of Reaganism and its clearest return to the politics of populism, Capra and Roosevelt. This challenge is reinforced by one of the real-life congressmen who cameo in the film: in order to pay for the jobs programme, the government should 'cut Star Wars', an obsolete piece of technology following the Cold War, and the centrepiece of Reagan's militaristic agenda.

Dave acknowledges the origins of this policy on jobs: it is reported in the press as 'government activism unparalleled since the days of FDR.' In Hollywood cinema, Franklin Roosevelt was the man who saved the American system from the Great Depression. As Andrew Bergman suggests of Hollywood in this period, 'Roosevelt became an invaluable plot device ... an unseen sheriff cleaning up the town. The federal government remained the hero.'[48] After the crisis of faith which preceded Roosevelt's election, Roffmann and Purdy argue that Hollywood welcomed him as a messianic figure, and produced films in which 'a hero-redeemer, whether a populist country crusader bearing the strength of the pioneers or the liberal New Dealer representing a strong federal government, was ready to protect the "little people", the masses of innocent victims, from all manner of social parasites and selfish profiteers.'[49] Dave is clearly cut from similar cloth; a patriot who believes in the virtue of government activism, a non-politician with no vested interests, and an ordinary guy who helps the poor and disenfranchised find work.

47 Sam B. Girgus, *Hollywood Renaissance: The Cinema of Democracy in the Era of Ford, Capra, and Kazan* (Cambridge: University of Cambridge Press, 1998), 83.

48 Bergman, *We're in the Money*, 93.

49 Peter Roffmann and Jim Purdy, *The Hollywood Social Problem Film: Madness, Despair and Politics from the Depression to the Fifties* (Bloomington: Indiana University Press, 1981), 88.

It is clear against what Dave's rhetoric is positioned. When he says, '*Things aren't fine*. We've got so many problems we don't even want to look at them any more. The worst thing is, *we feel like we can't do anything about it*', this might be interpreted as a challenge to Reagan's small government agenda, as well as his amnesiac rhetoric which invoked a sentimental nostalgia to distract from America's post-industrial decline (a rhetorical strategy which President Mitchell also employs at the beginning of the film). If Reaganism was a repudiation of the New Deal, then *Dave* is Hollywood's attempt at its reinstatement. When Dave pledges that it will be the 'responsibility of this government to find a job for every American who wants one', he not only recalls Rooseveltian activism, but the Capraesque renewal of the system; a vote for a '"kinder and gentler America" – at least for those who are deserving – while endorsing both the economic system and political tradition.'[50] Like Capra, *Dave* does not challenge America's capitalist system, but argues that society will be improved through a reversion to traditionalism: the government can fulfil the role of Capra's 'good neighbour', reinstating faith in politics through 'moral regeneration rather than structural change'.[51] In Capraesque terms, Bush argued, 'We don't need to remake society, we just need to remember who we are.'[52] *Dave* fulfils this desire through a return to an America which had faith in the virtue of big government, believed in the honesty and integrity of its leaders, and was comfortable with the nation's purpose.

Dave completes its Capraesque project of renewal in its conclusion. Having violated the constitution in order to rescue it from the forces of corruption, Dave engineers a situation whereby he can relinquish power, imprison the despicable Alexander, and secure the presidency for the wholesome, honest ex-shoe-salesman vice president. The culmination of the corruption scandal is set, like *Mr Smith*, in the United States Senate,

50 Neve, *Film and Politics in America*, 46.

51 Ibid., 40.

52 George H.W. Bush, campaign announcement speech (Houston, Texas, October 12th, 1987), quoted by Michael Duffy and Dan Goodgame, *Marching in Place: The Status Quo Presidency of George Bush* (New York: Simon & Schuster, 1992), quoted in Jeffords, *Hard Bodies*, 102.

where 'Mitchell' (Dave) confesses his sins, fakes a stroke, and is therefore symbolically 'martyred'. When Dave says 'every one of these charges is completely and absolutely true', he completes the film's project of restoring honesty and integrity to American politics: rather than confuse, inveigle and obfuscate as Nixon did over Watergate, Reagan did over Iran/Contra, or Clinton would do over Lewinsky, Dave sticks to the 'common sense' idea that 'honesty is the best policy'. Where *Dave*'s beginning suggests that truth is a commodity in short supply in the era of image-based politics, by its conclusion it has restored this pillar of American values. In so doing, the film satisfies the demand, seemingly as real in the 1990s as it was in Capra's 1930s, 'for leaders who would rise above politics, who would be greater than the system, above petty argumentation, ordinary concerns, sordid selfish interests.'[53]

While obviously indebted to the title character's own martyrdom in Capra's *Mr Smith*, it is possible to read the ending as similar to *Gabriel Over the White House*. While Dave's political manoeuvres are nothing in comparison to President Hammond's flouting of the constitution in order to rescue America from the Great Depression, there is a similar *deus ex machina* employed in order to return American politics to normality. Hammond dies having saved America from economic cataclysm; Dave 'dies' having saved America from the forces of corruption and shysterism. While Capra is clearly the dominant reference point in *Dave*, there appears to be a more general appeal to the tone, style, and narrative structure of all the political films of the 1930s. As a cycle, the political films of the 1930s were primarily concerned with the rejuvenation of the American system in the wake of the Wall Street crash: the overarching sentiment of *Dave*, it appears, is a similar renewal of American ideals after the divisiveness and corruption of the Reagan years (and earlier). In so doing, *Dave* appears to take advantage of a new uncertainty regarding America's purpose in the world and the conception of its leader to revive liberal politics for a gentler, less aggressive era.

53 Levine, *The Unpredictable Past*, 243.

The American President: The President as Man and Office in the Clinton Era

Although it refers directly to Capra, *The American President* is more contemporary in its focus, addressing debates surrounding the presidency in the 1990s, and the Clinton administration in particular. It concerns President Andrew Shepherd (Michael Douglas) who, coming to the end of his first term, enjoys enormous popularity.[54] He is cautious with his power, saying his administration should 'only fight the fights [it] can win', which causes him to equivocate on his (broadly liberal) beliefs. He is also a widower with a young daughter. When he meets feisty and independent environmental lobbyist Sydney Ellen Wade (Annette Bening), Shepherd falls in love. However, the relationship prompts questions regarding the president's morality, patriotism and family values. Eventually, Shepherd's personal life and his presidency become so intertwined that he has to confront a difficult choice: forego his romantic interests to ensure the success of his legislative programme and safe passage to a second term, or convince the American people that it is possible to be in a relationship and be Commander in Chief at the same time.

Primarily, *The American President* addresses the distinction between Shepherd's status as a man and an office, and the tensions created in negotiating the transition between the two. Shepherd's experiences pre-empt many of those that Clinton would endure at the height of the Lewinsky

54 The casting of Michael Douglas as the president is an intriguing choice, given his association with many of the films that defined the backlash against not only feminism, but all 'special interest groups', such as ethnic minorities and homosexuals. His performances in *Fatal Attraction* (Adrian Lyne, 1987), *Basic Instinct* (Paul Verhoeven, 1992), *Falling Down* (Joel Schumacher, 1993), and *Disclosure* (Barry Levinson, 1994) confirmed him as 'the quintessential 1990s man-in-crisis'. – Donna Peberdy, *Masculinity and Film Performance: Male Angst in Contemporary American Cinema* (New York: Palgrave MacMillan, 2011), 46. ; For further discussion of Michael Douglas's position within the 'Backlash'/Masculinity-in-Crisis cycle of 1980s and 1990s Hollywood cinema, see Susan Faludi's work on *Fatal Attraction* in *Backlash: The Undeclared War Against Women* (London: Vintage, 1992), 147–52; and Bruzzi's discussion of *Falling Down* and the 'crisis' in masculinity, *Bringing Up Daddy*, 153–8.

scandal. I will examine the film as indicative of the issues circulating in culture during the Clinton era. This will involve an examination of the perceived anxiety surrounding the proximity of women (and femininity more generally) to the presidency, and the expanded role of the First Lady in the arena of public policy. I will examine these issues in some detail, with particular emphasis on dialogue and visual style. I will also discuss elements of the film that can be understood as nostalgic for an older, more traditional conception of the presidency.

The film's opening sequence is very similar to *Dave*'s nostalgic construction of American politics and the presidency. If anything, this montage is more achingly patriotic than *Dave*'s aerial tour of Washington, DC, employing potent images associated with American democracy in a reverent and adoring collage of the presidency. The orchestral score, whose deep violins ebb and flow throughout is, like *Dave*'s, stirring and emotional, emphasising this tone of admiration. The visual style is nostalgic: the colouring of the sequence is almost sepia-toned, the Oval Office bathed in a warm, comforting sunlight. The camera, largely employing close-ups, glides lovingly over various artefacts and portraits it showcases. The sequence opens with a bust of George Washington in profile, cross-dissolving to a close-up of the Star-Spangled Banner, an ornamental bald eagle, and various artefacts associated with American history (and are clearly designed to appear 'old'): book volumes entitled 'Messages and Papers of the Presidents', biographies of Thomas Paine, John Adams and Harry Truman, a visual rendering of the signing of the Declaration of Independence, before moving into various portraits of past presidents. The construction of the sequence conforms to Anne Norton's suggestion that

> As signifier the President calls up not only the American nation, the government, the executive branch, and the triumphant party (already a rich – and variable – assemblage of images) *but the mythic and historical associations that attach to the office and to its past and present occupants.*[55]

55 Norton, *Republic of Signs*, 91. My emphasis.

This sequence functions in a similar fashion, the wistful, pictorial style affirming *The American President*'s attitude towards the office as one of simultaneous proximity and respect.

As is always the case with the mythologisation of the past, however, certain elements are foregrounded and celebrated, while others marginalised and disavowed. In order to understand *The American President*'s construction of presidential power, it is important to note which presidents are remembered, and which are ignored or conveniently forgotten: George Washington (bust and portrait), John F. Kennedy, Harry S. Truman, Abraham Lincoln (bust), William Howard Taft, Lyndon Johnson, Woodrow Wilson, Andrew Jackson, Dwight Eisenhower, Theodore Roosevelt (in profile on a medallion), Ulysses S. Grant and Franklin D. Roosevelt are the presidents featured in the sequence. So while *The American President* is keen to present a reverent image of the office, it is a *selective* reverence. The absence of any president since Johnson suggests a possible denial of the events since Vietnam (particularly Nixon's Watergate crimes, the weakness and drift of the Ford/Carter years, and the divisiveness and military posturing of the Reagan/Bush era). Throughout the film, there are visual and aural references to past presidents, with particular emphasis on Lyndon Johnson's Great Society reforms (which might explain his presence in the portrait gallery rather than any associations with Vietnam), Woodrow Wilson's ability to negotiate his romantic pursuits and the formation of the League of Nations (the failure of this organisation is, however, not mentioned), and the portrait of a pensive Kennedy is shown twice more. Indeed, the strong association with Kennedy was a conscious decision by the filmmakers: production designer Lilly Kilvert suggested that they modelled the style of the White House on the Kennedy era, which itself was a reassertion of Thomas Jefferson's original conception of the building.[56] Like *Dave*, therefore, *The American President* takes the uncertainty surrounding the conception of the presidency in the 1990s and

56 Lilly Kilvert, production designer on *The American President*, quoted in Alex McGregor, 'This Old House', *American Cinematographer* 76/11 (November 1995), 84.

reverts to an older model of leadership, one perceived to have disappeared in the contemporary period. As demonstrated by the film's representation of the Republican opposition as mendacious, vindictive and self-serving, this absence is lamented.

The opening sequence is, however, rather different to the rest of the film, which revolves largely around the president's difficulties in managing his twin identities as a man and an office. It conforms to an old dichotomy around since the days of supreme monarchs: the notion of 'The King's Two Bodies', or the separation between the timeless office, and its present incumbent.[57] The scene which immediately follows the montage, for example, demonstrates the frenetic but micro-managed nature of the presidency: we see Shepherd arriving at work from the residence on a Monday morning, briefed on the events of the day by his secretary. He greets people along the way: he has to be reminded of the gardener's name, and is informed that it is one of his staff's birthdays, allowing him to appear as the caring, benevolent leader in tune with the day-to-day lives of the people who work for him. Bruzzi describes Shepherd's progress as 'tank-like', and this is an apt simile: nothing prevents the president from pursuing his pre-determined path to the Oval Office.[58] I would also suggest that the sequence demonstrates the stage-managing of the presidency rather astutely; like *Dave*'s almost instantaneous dissolving of the image of the president to reveal the reality that exists behind it, *The American President* illustrates how the intensity of activity render the minute details of everyday life which ordinary people take for granted (remembering someone's birthday or name, for example) to be an impossibility for someone as busy as the President of the United States. Were it not for his helpers, the man would be overwhelmed by the job. The sequence affirms the masculine,

57 For further exploration of this idea see Ernst Kantorowicz (1957), *The King's Two Bodies: A Study in Medieval Political Theology* (Princeton , NJ: Princeton University Press, 1997); Thomas Cronin, *The State of the Presidency* [2nd edn] (Boston: Little, Brown, 1980); Jeffrey Tulis, *The Rhetorical Presidency* (Princeton, NJ: Princeton University Press, 1987); Rossiter, *The American Presidency*.

58 Stella Bruzzi, 'Men's Cinema', in John Gibbs and Douglas Pye, eds, *Close-Up 03* (London: Wallflower Press, 2009), 200.

strident conception of the presidency as demonstrated by the rapid walk from elevator to Oval Office, reveals the Clintonesque cultivation of a vulnerable, accessible, human persona to be artificial (the president cannot remember names or birthdays on his own), while simultaneously offering sympathy for this inadequacy because, as Clinton himself suggested, 'You feel always never quite adequate to do the work; no one is smart enough, or wise enough, or strong enough.'[59]

The American President is engaged in the demystification of the presidency which occurred in this period. Clinton's admission of his own doubts and weakness reveal him to be part of this process. As Parry-Giles and Parry-Giles suggest, 'the tension between public and private typif[ies] contemporary constructions of presidentiality.'[60] This unease is in turn indicative of a process which Glass describes as the weakening of the presidential phallus; the death of the heroic, militaristic presidency at the end of the Cold War, coupled with the image-based means by which it was represented, led to an erosion of the awe with which the iconographic trappings of the presidency were ordinarily greeted. In this sense, the 'presidential phallus' is not focused solely upon the president's sexuality, but all the images of his power, including the Oval Office, Air Force One, Marine One, the US military, and the White House itself. To explore these icons is to divest them of at least some of their potency; their power resides largely in their invisibility, and their instinctive cultural association with American democracy and virtue.

The American President is engaged in a similar dismantling of the presidency's mystique, with a particular challenge made to the notion of the omnipotent, hypermasculine figure projected by previous Commanders in Chief. The film does so, however, in a largely playful way. Despite being commander of the world's largest army, for example, Shepherd has significant problems in asking Sydney out on a date. When he telephones Sydney,

59 Bill Clinton, interview for *The American President* (Philip B. Kunhardt Jr., Philip B. Kunhardt III, and Peter W. Kunhardt, PBS, 1999), quoted in Parry-Giles and Parry-Giles, *Constructing Clinton*, 170.

60 Parry-Giles and Parry-Giles, *Constructing Clinton*, 120.

she initially refuses to believe she is speaking to the president. She thinks it is her friend, Richard, doing his apparently uncanny impersonation of Shepherd. Having already appeared foolish by reacting badly to the president's earlier request she join him for a doughnut and a cup of coffee in the White House, Sydney continues to embarrass herself: in this instance, she compliments the president's buttocks, and hangs up. Shepherd calls her back, convinces her it is not the ruse she thinks it is, and eventually manages to ask her to accompany him to a state dinner with the President of France. Shepherd appears slightly bewildered by the exchange, uttering exasperatedly, 'This used to be easier.' Bruzzi argues that this line of dialogue is indicative of men's new anxiety regarding matters of dating and courtship in a postfeminist environment, but I would expand this to encompass the difficulty inherent in being simultaneously a fallible, human man and a supposedly omnipotent leader.[61] This is reinforced later in the film when Shepherd has similar difficulties in ordering Sydney flowers, because his status as president has dispossessed him of everyday modern conveniences such as a credit card: things used to be easier because he used to be just a regular guy. The 1990s brought the tension between being ordinary and extraordinary to the surface, and raised doubts about whether it was possible to be both. For Shepherd, everyday activities like ordering flowers or asking a woman out require the divorce of the man from the office, a separation shown to be almost impossible. Similarly, Sydney finds it very difficult to view Shepherd as merely a man. As she says when he asks if there might be a time when she can see him as an ordinary guy and not the president, 'This isn't a state of mind. You are the president.' As Heather Richardson Hayton argues of *The West Wing*, 'Sorkin regularly includes moments in the episodes that highlight the *impossibility* of separating the king's two bodies for either political or personal gain.'[62] I contend that it

61 Bruzzi, *Bringing Up Daddy*, 171.

62 Heather Richardson Hayton, 'The King's Two Bodies: Identity and Office in Sorkin's *West Wing*', in Rollins and O'Connor, eds, *The West Wing: The American Presidency as Television Drama* (Syracuse: Syracuse University Press, 2003), 67.

is the impossibility of achieving this distinction which forms the central focus of *The American President*.

Throughout, Shepherd is desperate to convince Sydney he is just an average guy, but his claims are persistently undermined by his 'presidential phallus'. When Shepherd attempts to see her outside an official state function by inviting her to the residence for meatloaf ('How presidential can that be?'), his assertion of ordinariness is undercut by the arrival of the presidential helicopter, Marine One, which Shepherd flippantly describes as his 'ride'. When Shepherd is then late for dinner, he asks his daughter to tell Sydney that he is simply talking to his dentist, when in reality he is discussing the final preparations for C-STAD, a missile defence system outside Tel Aviv, Israel. Lucy blows his cover almost immediately, but not before she tells Sydney that her father 'just wants you to think he's a regular guy.' The difficulty in achieving this separation reaches its apex when Sydney kisses the president in The China Room (a room Shepherd describes in distinctly folksy fashion as 'The Dish Room'), only for their romantic interlude to be interrupted by a secret service agent, who informs the president that Libya has just bombed C-STAD. Shepherd's inability to be an average man on a date without the responsibilities of his office providing obstacles is suggestive of debates occurring in popular culture in the period: while this date is decidedly more romantic than what we know of Clinton's relationship with Monica Lewinsky, it does appear to relate to Glass's characterisation of the Lewinsky affair 'as a series of desperate encounters squeezed into a schedule so busy and a space so small ... tragically underscor[ing] the scarce opportunities for pleasure in a regime so tightly and obsessively organized around work.'[63] Successfully reconciling and separating the two identities of being a man and a president is, it seems, impossible.

Shepherd, a widower of three years, also has significant anxiety regarding the sexual act because he 'has not done this in a pretty long time.' He is keen to impress upon Sydney that 'any expectations' she may have regarding his sexual performance because he is 'the most powerful man in the world' should be modified; she must remember that it is a 'political distinction

63 Glass, 'Publicizing the President's Privates', 15.

that comes with the office'. Shepherd is seemingly desperate to reinforce the distinction between his still potent 'phallus', by which Sydney has been hitherto intimidated, and his 'soft [and] vulnerable' penis.[64] This sequence is in keeping with an area of comedy described by Dyer, which 'plays on the anxiety caused by the gap between what male genitals are actually like and what they are supposed to be like.'[65] I argue this discrepancy is even more hyperbolically inscribed in *The American President*: the gap between the all-powerful presidency, and the ordinary man who occupies it, makes the distinction between the 'phallus' and the 'penis' that much more apparent. The assumed power of the presidency is further undermined by the fact that Sydney initiates sex, undressing while Shepherd pontificates over a strategy for the future of their relationship. Shepherd's hesitation and Sydney's assertiveness are perhaps indicative of the modification of gender roles in wider culture, and a more relaxed attitude towards female pursuit of sexual gratification. The sequence conforms to shifts in wider cultural conceptions of masculinity: Shepherd's uncertainty that he can fulfil expectations of inherent, assumed male sexual prowess confirms Anthony Clare's assertion that, in the 1990s, 'phallic man, authoritative, dominant, assertive – man in control not merely of himself but of woman – is starting to die.'[66] Here, *The American President* participates in the erosion of the hypermasculine president in the post-Cold War environment, within its overall project of separating the office and the man. In essence, the office remains powerful, even if the man does not.

In correlation with *The American President*'s investigation of the fragility and artificiality of the traditionally masculine presidency, the character of Sydney prompts an exploration of the contemporaneous anxiety regarding the role of women in relation to the president. Hillary Rodham Clinton's legislative agenda expanded the role of First Lady to include matters of

64 Richard Dyer, *The Matter of Images: Essays on Representation* [2nd edn] (London: Routledge, 2002), 113.

65 Ibid., 115.

66 Anthony Clare, *On Men: Masculinity in Crisis* (London: Chatto and Windus, 2000), 9.

public policy and debate.[67] As Schier suggests, 'Gone was the decorative and subordinate homebody; in her place was an assertive and independent political force working alongside her spouse.'[68] Rodham Clinton's treatment by the press was in keeping with a wider 'backlash' against the feminist movement which took place through the 1980s and into the 1990s.[69] Because Rodham Clinton was unashamed of the fact that 'she chose to practice law rather than stay home and bake cookies', she was constructed by the press as 'symbol of hard-edged feminism', and an 'embodiment of all that was wrong with the sixties'.[70] Rodham Clinton's construction of herself as career woman, lawyer and politician was treated with fear and suspicion.[71] Faludi suggests that figures such as Rodham Clinton, Sarah Brady and Janet Reno (Clinton's Attorney General) were singled out for particular vitriol because they 'were women who were most prominently showcased by the culture as independent, self-sufficient, and unintimidated by men.'[72] She argues that with the end of the Cold War, the dominant American male myth of serving as provider for, and protector of, women, had been eroded.[73] In this formulation, it appears the conservative establishment demanded

67 Such was Hillary Rodham Clinton's influence upon her husband's political career, they were often referred to in the media as 'Billary', the kind of conjunction commonly given to celebrities. More recent examples include 'Bennifer' (Ben Affleck and Jennifer Lopez), and 'Brangelina' (Brad Pitt and Angelina Jolie).

68 Schier, 'A Unique Presidency', in Schier, ed., *The Postmodern Presidency*, p. 3.

69 Susan Faludi argues this was a conservative reaction by the culture machine to the emancipation of women; an attempt 'to push women back into their "acceptable" roles – whether as Daddy's girl or fluttery romantic, active nester or passive love object.' – Faludi, *Backlash*, 16.

70 Shawn J. Parry-Giles, 'Mediating Hillary Rodham Clinton: Television News Practices and Image-Making in the Postmodern Age', *Critical Studies in Communication* 17/2 (June 2000), 207.

71 While First Lady, Hillary Rodham Clinton was a divisive figure. She was 'a leader in advocating and promoting gender equality and women's rights policies during her husband's administration', but was simultaneously 'a "lightning rod" for critics of the administration.' – Barbara Burrell, 'The Clintons and Gender Politics', in Schier, ed., *The Postmodern Presidency*, 40.

72 Faludi, *Stiffed*, 414.

73 Ibid., 417.

that the First Lady conform to traditional gender roles, functioning not as a political entity in her own right, but as the most visible evidence of the president's ability to protect and defend his citizens.[74]

Like Rodham Clinton, Sydney proves to be a political problem for the president because she is an individual with an agenda (in this case an environmental lobbyist looking to pass a bill that will commit the United States to cutting greenhouse emissions). This speaks to a wider concern regarding women's involvement in, and proximity to, the presidency. As shown by the media treatment of Rodham Clinton, it was deemed problematic for a woman to be close to the presidency and simultaneously hold political power. As would prove to be the case with the public fascination with, and investigation of, Clinton's affair with Lewinsky, 'the feminist tenet that the "personal is political" confirmed sexuality, gender relations and pornography as crucial areas of public debate.'[75] *The American President* explores the anxiety and uncertainty regarding the president having a sexual relationship with a single woman: Shepherd's poll ratings plummet as a result, and his patriotism and family values are questioned. Sydney is constructed in similar ways to Rodham Clinton: just as the First Lady was caricatured as a radical feminist, so Sydney is figured as similarly threatening. A photograph of her at an anti-apartheid rally in which an American flag was burned emerges, causing a headache for the Shepherd administration.

The context of the photograph is considered unimportant: Sydney participating in a protest in which an American flag was burned simply feeds into suspicions that she is dangerously politicised, and Shepherd's association with her is unpatriotic. In a similar fashion to the press's treatment of Rodham Clinton, 'visuals are decontextualized from their original stories and then recontextualized within alternative narratives to substantiate the contentions of journalists' (and, in this case, the opposition party).[76] *The American President* is critical of this process, arguing that this divisiveness

74 Rodham Clinton's treatment by the press when she ran for president in 2008 will be explored in relation to the fictional female presidency in Chapter Six.

75 Glass, 'Publicizing the President's Privates', 9.

76 Parry-Giles, 'Mediating Hillary Rodham Clinton', 211.

and partisanship is corrupting American politics, but that leadership is required to nullify this turn. Shepherd's silence on the issue simply allows the image to speak for itself.

Shepherd's romantic pursuit of Sydney while simultaneously pursuing legislative success reaches breaking point when the controversy surrounding his private life causes him to lose popularity. He can only regain support by shelving the carbon emissions bill on which Sydney is working, thereby breaking a promise to her. Shepherd is beleaguered by the attempt to negotiate his twin identities, and this is rendered visually as he walks to the Oval Office at the end of another bruising day at work, having faced up to the choice between his job and his relationship. Where the opening march to the Oval Office was characterised by authoritative movement, and Shepherd was surrounded by an entourage of staff, here he is alone. In correlation with his shuffling pace, the camera movement is slow. His appearance is unkempt: his shirt undone and tie hanging loosely around his neck, and the music is sombre. In a shot which forms a contradictory echo to the confident stride at the film's beginning, Shepherd is shown walking alone in the dark, ambling towards his office, weighed down by his responsibilities. This is reaffirmed by the subsequent shot which frames him at a distance, from outside the Oval Office door. This conforms to production designer Lilly Kilvert's suggestion the film might have been retitled 'The American Prisoner'; Shepherd is small and isolated, incarcerated in the building in which he works, held captive by responsibilities which he carries, the large pillars almost functioning as prison bars.[77] Through these shots, *The American President* suggests the irreconcilability of the president's identity as a man and an office: the individual is literally dwarfed by the size of the job.

The American President resolves the negotiation between the president as man and as office through a visually and rhetorically striking sequence: Shepherd's intervention at a press conference where he faces down Rumson's accusations, rediscovers his liberal values, and positions himself simultaneously as the sensitive, caring, articulate New Man, and the tough, aggressive

77 Lily Kilvert, quoted in Alex McGregor, 'This Old House', 83.

president determined to fight for his beliefs. Throughout, Shepherd has attempted to conform to a traditional, 'strong, silent' model of masculinity in relation to the character debate. However, such an approach will not suffice in a rapidly altering media environment dominated by images that are decontextualised and recontextualised. Here, his refusal to retaliate is viewed as weakness. In this scene, articulacy becomes a means of restoring the president's strength, and this rediscovered power is illustrated through visual style and music. Indeed, the sequence renders *cinematic* the presidential press conference, which are formally rather staid, unflashy and statically framed.

Throughout the press conference, Shepherd remains still. Potency is captured here through stasis: a refusal to budge. At the film's beginning, and in wider visual culture, the president's strength is ordinarily captured through dynamic movement. Here, Shepherd's stillness is indicative of his authority and command: he is in complete control of the situation. The emphasis on the president's sturdiness is affirmed through cutaways to the press and Shepherd's staff as they watch and listen, awestruck by his articulacy, determination and forthrightness. Shepherd employs the pithy phrases associated with good presidential rhetoric, such as his challenge to Rumson's opposition to his membership of the American Civil Liberties Union ('Why aren't you Bob?'). These are combined with erudite critiques of the state of contemporary American politics, particularly the use of nostalgia in political campaigning (which might be interpreted as a challenge to Reagan's simplistic celebration of America's past), and articulate defences of more complex aspects of American citizenship, such as the right to burn the flag. The camera movement renders visual this new confidence and determination: interspersed between the commanding medium shots of Shepherd at the podium are moving shots through the press corps, as well as a downwards-tilting point-of-view shot from the podium, and upwards-tilts from the press's perspective. These reinforce Shepherd's dominance over the room, and reassert his status as leader. This speech becomes a reassertion of the initial conception of the president as a dynamic, forceful and traditional masculine figure.

As Shepherd's speech gathers pace and momentum, the camera moves around him and, as he reaches a crescendo in his savage criticism of

Rumson's juvenile strategy, it moves slowly in from a distance, settling into a medium close-up of him. This movement is suggestive of both mastery and intimacy; the wider angle confirms his command of the room, but the shift into close-up brings us closer to the president (looking directly into the camera assists this impression), combining the two personae which Shepherd has hitherto found impossible to reconcile: Shepherd is now simultaneously a man *and* the president. Shepherd appears to have realised that in this image-dominated age it is dangerous and politically naïve to let images simply speak for themselves. The camera conducts a similar movement toward Shepherd when he talks about his legislative programme, the repetition further illustrating the reconciliation of these two identities: in recognising the crime bill he has drafted as a worthless piece of centrist equivocation, and the environmental bill as fundamental to America's future, he simultaneously rescues his presidency and his relationship with Sydney. Having rhetorically eviscerated Rumson's superficial campaign, Shepherd stridently asserts, in simple, direct terms: 'My name is Andrew Shepherd, and I am the president', a line which ultimately fuses his personal and political identities. The orchestral swell and cathartic release which accompanies this assertion affirms this reconciliation. The essence of this sequence is control through stability, Shepherd realising that he is able to be both man and president if he stays true to his beliefs. Indeed, as Shepherd suggests, 'Being president of this country is entirely about character'; being president is inextricably linked to your identity as a man, and you cannot separate the two. As in *Dave* and the Capra tradition, the presidency is shown to be a wholly benign institution as long as it is occupied by men of good character – Shepherd has character, Rumson certainly does not.

The dialogue exchange between Shepherd and Sydney immediately before the president delivers the State of the Union underlines the merging of his two identities. When Sydney asks how he managed 'to give a woman flowers and be president at the same time', Shepherd replies, 'It turns out I've got a rose garden.' Shepherd's final line demonstrates the eventual understanding that he is able to be both man and president. It conforms to the conception of the White House as 'both a residence and an office ... architecturally constructed and symbolically understood to contain both domestic and professional activities under one roof.'[78] The anxiety surrounding sexual activity in the White House, and the problematic status of the unmarried couple within such a setting, is ultimately resolved. The White House is both a private and public space and the president is both a private and public individual. In essence, *The American President* tackles a contemporaneous anxiety within the office, and employs an old dichotomy (The King's Two Bodies) as a means of resolving it.

The 1990s Presidency II: Action

As suggested at the start of this chapter, the Cold War generated two competing impulses in American politics and society: turn inward, and tend to domestic problems, or seize the opportunity afforded by the collapse of communism to remake the world as a democratic, capitalist utopia. The next half of this chapter will address the ways in which Cold War archetypes were employed to negotiate the terrain of this New World Order, a turn embodied by the construction of the 'action hero' president in *Independence Day* and *Air Force One*. Unlike *Dave* and *The American President*, which viewed the Cold War victory as the opportunity to repudiate the worst excesses of Reaganism and revert to Capraesque and Rooseveltian political models, *Independence Day* and *Air Force One* demonstrate concern regarding the sudden absence of an uncomplicated enemy like the Soviet Union, and an associated softening of the presidency. To combat this, they reconstruct the tough, aggressive, militaristic presidency which dominated the Cold War landscape, and re-establish old enemies for him to fight.[79]

78 Glass, 'Publicising the President's Privates', 15.

79 As Malin argues, the 1990s did not see old models of masculinity simply cast aside, but the 'new '90s masculinity [was] accompanied by a concomitant anxiety associated with traditional male values.' – Malin, *American Masculinity Under Clinton*, 10.

How this reassertion of traditionalism was negotiated within the Clinton era will form the basis of the rest of this chapter.

Neither *Independence Day* nor *Air Force One* has been afforded much serious critical attention, and the scholarship that does exist is dismissive of the films' political implications. Christensen and Haas regard *Independence Day* as an apolitical recycling of the president as archetype, and that any intentional political agenda seems 'marginal at best.'[80] Geoffrey Macnab suggests *Air Force One* is 'implausible' and 'deeply muddled' in its geopolitical viewpoints.[81] Novelist and critic Adam Mars-Jones describes the film as 'preposterous' in its vision of America as an uncomplicated vision of moral rightness, the character of the president 'a composite of every dreary virtue that America imagines it would elect if given the chance'.[82] What these critics fail to recognise is the importance of context: why did the 'action hero' president emerge in the 1990s? In this section I will look to assert the cultural significance of both films as reactions to the political landscape of the period, and the ways in which they resurrect old forms in order to achieve this.

Reborn on the Fourth of July: The American President, Cold War Nostalgia and Independence Day

Independence Day concerns mankind's war with an invading race of intergalactic space aliens. The film takes place over seventy-two hours: the bloodthirsty monsters arrive on 2 July to wreak global destruction, laying waste to the major American cities of Los Angeles, Washington, DC, and New York (other nations are subjected to a similar onslaught, although they are barely glimpsed). The surviving humans regroup on 3 July, assemble a

80 Christensen and Haas, *Projecting Politics*, 9.

81 Geoffrey Macnab, '*Air Force One*', in José Arroyo, ed., *Action/Spectacle Cinema: A Sight and Sound Reader* (London: British Film Institute, 2000), 250–2.

82 Adam Mars-Jones, 'Get Me out of Here', *The Independent*, Thursday, September 11th, 1997, <http://www.independent.co.uk/arts-entertainment/get-me-out-of-here-1238525.html> accessed April 2010.

scrappy counter-offensive, and secure ultimate victory on Independence Day itself (4 July). In keeping with the disaster genre, *Independence Day* features a large ensemble cast, with characters from a variety of ethnic and class backgrounds. Russell Casse (Randy Quaid) is an alcoholic, working-class Vietnam veteran (now an unsuccessful crop-duster) who has a complex relationship with his three mixed-race children, one of whom has a chronic illness. Captain Steven Hiller (Will Smith), an African American fighter pilot and aspiring astronaut, is in a relationship with stripper Jasmine (Vivica Fox), who has a young son, Dylan (Ross Bagley), from a previous relationship. David Levinson (Jeff Goldblum) is a Jewish technician working for a cable company, and is estranged from his ex-wife Constance (Margaret Colin). Constance left David to work as the Press Secretary to the President of the United States, Thomas Whitmore (Bill Pullman). Whitmore has his own difficulties: despite his heroics in the Gulf War, he is deemed a weak and ineffectual leader, hamstrung by the need for compromise in America's divided government. In keeping with the conventions of the disaster movie, the characters' problems are rendered insignificant when the malevolent aliens materialise, and the human race unites to confront the threat. Leading this response is President Whitmore, who recovers the strength and assertiveness required of a military leader to save his country and, by extension, the world. During a period in which the presidency was in flux, *Independence Day* elects to return to the 1950s and the alien invasion narrative as a means of cultural rebirth, eviscerating the problems that blighted the United States in the following decades, and supposedly weakened the presidency as an institution.[83]

Independence Day conforms to the disaster genre's narrative template outlined by Nick Roddick: although society prior to the catastrophe is

83 My analysis departs from other discussions of the film, particularly Michael Rogin's *Independence Day: Or, How I Learned to Stop Worrying and Love the Enola Gay* (London: British Film Institute, 1998), which argues the film participates in the nostalgia for World War II that occurred in American culture following the Cold War. I do not look to refute these arguments, as there is plenty of compelling evidence within the film to suggest this is the case, but my approach is different, and one specific to *Independence Day*'s representation of the *presidency*.

blighted by the breakdown of traditional models (in particular gender roles and 'family values'), the calamity affords the opportunity to expunge problematic aspects of society and remake the world along traditional lines.[84] This structure invites comparison with Mark Jancovich's suggestion that Cold War invasion narratives tend to be resurrected at times of turmoil and uncertainty, when traditional values require reassertion. The 1950s invasion cycle has been ordinarily discussed through the prisms of Cold War paranoia and fears of communism: films such as *The Day the Earth Stood Still*, *Invasion of the Body Snatchers* and *The Thing from Another World* 'presented America in the grip of an emergency, and ... these emergencies dramatised the need for consensus, of pulling together.'[85] However, Jancovich challenges the view that the 1950s invasion films were *only* allegorical of the communist threat: they were 'at least as concerned with internal changes within American life'.[86] Given the relatively tranquil geopolitical environment America faced in the 1990s, this suggestion is instructive.[87]

Independence Day reflects some of these changes in American society: the decline of 'family values' embodied by an unmarried mother who works as a stripper (who dares to take her young son to *work* with her), an alcoholic single father who cannot provide for his sick child, and a woman who leaves her unmotivated husband to pursue a career in politics. The arrival of the aliens re-establishes the 'consensus' demanded of the disaster narrative, albeit one that has its foundation in cultural politics more suited to the 1950s than the 1990s. *Independence Day*'s pre-disaster malaise conforms to Susan Sontag's conception of the 1950s invasion movie: 'Again and again,

84 Nick Roddick, 'Only the stars survive: disaster movies in the seventies', in David Bradby, Louis James and Bernard Sharratt, eds, *Performance and politics in popular drama* (Cambridge: University of Cambridge Press, 1980), 243–71.

85 Peter Biskind, *Seeing is Believing: How Hollywood Taught Us to Stop Worrying and Love the Fifties* (London: Pluto, 1983), 103.

86 Mark Jancovich, *Rational Fears: American Horror in the 1950s* (Manchester: Manchester University Press, 1996), 3.

87 For an explanation for the resurgence of the disaster genre in the 1990s, see Geoff King, *Spectacular Narratives: Hollywood in the Age of the Blockbuster* (London: I.B. Tauris, 2000), 154.

one detects the hunger for a "good war," which poses no moral problems, admits of no moral qualifications.'[88] Such a conflict will enable the nation to return to an imagined time that was more stable and less complex. The construction of the president is central to this process: how Whitmore is established initially as a compromised, emasculated 1990s president before being reborn as a militaristic, 1950s 'cold warrior' will form the basis of the rest of this discussion.

***

Michael Rogin argues *Independence Day* is 'the defining motion picture of Bill Clinton's America', and the films' opening scenes are illustrative of the era's modified models of masculinity and the presidency.[89] Whitmore's introduction reflects the new intimacy and familiarity with the president. While we are accustomed to being introduced to the chief executive when he is at *work*, dressed in a suit connotative of power and traditional masculinity (demonstrated by the opening to *The American President*), Whitmore is shown at the very beginning of his day. Relaxing on the bed in a grey T-shirt, watching television while his daughter sleeps beside him, it is crucial that the film does not introduce him immediately as the president. This reinforces his ordinariness: he could be anybody having arisen from sleep. Speaking to his wife on the telephone as she is away on business, Whitmore is constructed as a 'New Man', responsible for childcare. Lampooning Clinton-era anxieties surrounding sex and the presidency, Whitmore makes an off-colour joke about lying 'next to a beautiful brunette', which raises the spectre of Clinton's extra-marital affairs: from the Gennifer Flowers allegations during his 1992 campaign, to the Lewinsky scandal of two years after the film's release. *Independence Day* is quick to dissolve this tension by panning across to reveal the 'brunette' to be his young daughter, and the conversation turns to domestic matters regarding the child's bedtime.

Like Shepherd in *The American President*, *Independence Day* immediately establishes Whitmore as familiar and approachable (rather like

88 Susan Sontag, *Against Interpretation* (London: Vintage, 2001), 219.

89 Rogin, *Independence Day*, 13.

Clinton), yet somehow more wholesome. These characteristics are further demonstrated later when his wife says he is a terrible liar, and to 'stick to the truth, it's what you're good at.' It corroborates the suggestion that Clinton sought to cultivate a vulnerable and accessible image following the intrusion into his private life in 1992.[90] However, the ability to maintain this intimacy alongside the heroic imagery expected of presidential leadership generated some concern in the period. This apprehension is evident in the construction of Whitmore, although his character appears to be in a more visible crisis of masculinity: he is not a strong enough father figure to have ensured his child went to bed at a suitable time, and is gently chastised by his wife for this.[91]

However, unlike *The American President*, *Independence Day* expresses discomfort with this domesticated presidency. In the television programme that is on when Whitmore is introduced, he is derided as an indecisive, dithering chief executive whose 'salad days' are over. Despite his credentials as a Gulf War hero, these achievements in *military* leadership are dismissed as insufficient preparation for success in political office. As Amy Taubin suggests, 'President Whitmore finds himself incapable of making decisions when the circumstances are less black and white'.[92] As one of the TV pundits declares, 'They elected a warrior and they got a wimp.' Whitmore feels beleaguered by the overwhelming need for compromise in government. While this is indicative of the continuous battles Clinton endured with the Republican Congress in the mid-1990s, *Independence Day* suggests that dynamic, assertive, conventional masculinity is impeded by democratic government. Whitmore's weakness is suggestive of Fukuyama's argument that, in the post-Cold War environment, men would become inert and complacent.[93] Once a war hero, but now a struggling and unpopular president

90 Parry-Giles and Parry-Giles, *Constructing Clinton*, 31.

91 Whitmore's initial construction is entirely in keeping with Pullman's star persona. Not recognised as being a conventional 'leading man', Pullman often portrayed ineffectual husband/boyfriend figures in films such as *The Last Seduction* (John Dahl, 1994) and *Sleepless in Seattle* (Nora Ephron, 1993).

92 Amy Taubin, 'Playing it Straight', *Sight and Sound* (August 1996), 8.

93 Fukuyama, *The End of History*, 300–13.

left at home to look after his child, Whitmore is the embodiment of the suggestion that 'the warrior without war is bereft, drowning in an anomic sea of meaningless routine.'[94] Whitmore is cast as a victim of his circumstances. As Barger argues, the post-Cold War presidency has to deal with all manner of new challenges at home and abroad, but 'the absence of a clearly perceived external threat ... has reduced the strategic, psychological and symbolic underpinnings that served for nearly half a century to define the modern presidency.'[95] As a war hero, Whitmore is clearly unaccustomed to dealing with this level of complexity, and without an environment in which he can perform traditional heroism, he appears emasculated.

Even the arrival of the alien ships is not enough to prompt a decisive response from Whitmore. While the level of threat remains uncertain, Whitmore's lack of leadership is demonstrated through the film's use of camera movement and framing. He is consistently positioned either to the right or left of frame, never at the centre; he is not allowed to dominate the image.[96] His dialogue is similarly indecisive: 'We *may* need to upgrade to Defcon 3', indicating his hesitancy in the face of peril.[97] Following this line of dialogue, the camera tracks backwards sharply, distancing itself from the president, and further establishing this impression of indecisiveness and lack of control. His inability to impose his authority on the situation causes his advisors to argue amongst themselves, fostering further discord

94 Michael Kimmel, *Manhood in America: A Cultural History* (New York: Free Press, 1996), 321.

95 Barger, 'The Incredible Shrinking Image', 58.

96 This is in marked contrast to President Shepherd's press conference in *The American President* – centrality of framing indicates control and mastery over the situation, whereas Whitmore's decentred positioning is indicative of his weakness.

97 Indeed, Whitmore's indecisive dialogue is indicative of the uncertain terrain on which he finds himself. This is firmly allied to the film's post-Cold War context, in which the impression of the president as the 'omnipotent, omniscient, and trustworthy' leader has frayed substantially. Whitmore's lack of knowledge is indicated by his press secretary's suggestion that 'Our position is we have no official position', and Whitmore's own acknowledgement that 'We don't yet know enough about what we're dealing with to make any kind of intelligent judgements.' – Barger, 'The Incredible Shrinking Image', 57.

and lack of direction. Prior to a news broadcast showing the spaceships arriving over Moscow, Whitmore's press secretary runs towards him, the camera tracking her movement. This shot illustrates the chaos and turmoil surrounding the president, his weakness indicated by his stasis within the surrounding hubbub. Despite his status as the president, he is curiously undifferentiated from the others that surround him: when he is informed by the general that they have sent out a helicopter on a reconnaissance mission, the medium-long-shot of the president surrounded by his advisors, standing slightly to the left of frame and slightly behind his press secretary indicates that, although he is the most powerful person in the room, he is simply unable to exert that power, his indecisiveness rendering him incapacitated (see Figure 3.1).

3.1 President Whitmore (Bill Pullman) disappears into the background in *Independence Day* (dir. Roland Emmerich, Twentieth Century Fox, USA, 1996)

His attempt to display conventionally masculine, presidential leadership by remaining at the White House to preserve an image of calm is undermined by the *mise-en-scène*, which continues to frame him in two-shot with either his press secretary or secretary of defence. His lack of command over the situation is illustrated throughout this section of the film; despite his pleas for people to 'leave these cities in an orderly fashion' in his address to the nation, the sudden cut to scenes of panic and chaos undermines his calls for calm and his display of strength. Indeed, it renders his attempt to project bravery and unwavering determination as the punchline to a joke. At this point, people are acting *around* President Whitmore, his lack of individual agency and decisive leadership demonstrated by the *mise-en-scène*.

Following the destruction of the major cities, the president and his closest advisors sit aboard Air Force One, discussing their options in the face of a seemingly implacable alien threat. The president's impotence is further emphasised in this sequence: while arguments rage around him, he remains conspicuously silent. The secretary of defence insists the president launch a counter-offensive with full nuclear capability, while David, the scientist who deciphered the alien signal which saved their lives, demands that this option not be allowed. The camera positioning performs a vital function, placing the president in the middle of the argument, trapping him between opposing viewpoints with no way out: David is positioned to the president's left, the secretary of defence and general directly in front of him, before David's father emerges from the president's right-hand side to encircle him fully. While the others argue, Whitmore remains silent, at one point holding his head in his hands.[98]

Independence Day's deconstruction of the omnipotent, omniscient presidency reaches its apex in the sequence in which the secretary of defence reveals the existence of Area 51, a top secret military installation which has been holding the remnants of an alien spacecraft and its passengers since the Roswell Incident in 1947.[99] The president's powerlessness is exacerbated by this revelation: he has been entirely kept in the dark about this facility and he is made to look foolish when, attempting to speak from a position

98 Silence is not always necessarily indicative of weakness in the representation of presidents. Kennedy's silence in *Crisis* (Robert Drew, 1963) is indicative of his considered, measured approach to the Civil Rights demonstrations. However, the formal construction of this sequence in *Independence Day* reinforces the president's weakness: surrounded by chaos, Whitmore appears exasperated and isolated. Pullman's performance and body language reaffirm this reading.

99 The Roswell Incident has become something of an overdetermined point of reference for conspiracy theorists who believe the American government has hidden the existence of extra-terrestrials. Suggestions of a cover-up became more mainstream in the 1990s after the success of *The X-Files* (Chris Carter, 1993–2002).

of authority in denying its existence to David's father, he is told that such a denial is 'not entirely accurate'. Whitmore's look of helplessness here, articulated by Pullman's body language (shoulders dropped, his mouth agape), lack of dialogue and the film's camera positioning, is amplified, ultimately trapping him literally and figuratively, with no room for escape.

However, this sequence appears to be a turning point for Whitmore, who from then on becomes more dynamic and assertive. The conventional *tabula rasa* of the disaster film comes to the rescue of the individualistic, militaristic presidency: at a stroke, *Independence Day* erases all the barriers that had hitherto hindered the president's progress. It is revealed that the Vice President and the Joint Chiefs of Staff have been killed in an alien attack. Whitmore also fires Secretary of Defence Nimzicki (James Rebhorn), erasing the spectres of conventional militarism (Nimzicki had been agitating for a full nuclear attack against the alien craft) and governmental conspiracy and intrigue (his prior knowledge of the captured alien spacecraft). No longer will Whitmore have to battle with government bureaucracy to attain consensus: he is in sole command of his nation.

In keeping with the backlash against 'special interest groups' that Reagan instituted, reinforced by Hollywood's demonisation of the counterculture in films like *Forrest Gump* (Robert Zemeckis, 1994), *Independence Day* performs a cleansing of the social problems that are supposed to have blighted the United States since the 1960s.[100] The removal of this complexity enables further restitution of individualistic, masculine agency to the president. During the initial alien assault, the film's hyperbolically caricatured homosexual, Marty (Harvey Fierstein), is one of the many victims of a fire which rips through a highway tunnel. Social misfits and miscreants likened to those who participated in the counter-cultural movements

100 The film's desperation to return to this earlier period is indicated by the numerous references made to the 1950s: *The Day the Earth Stood Still* is on television in the Casse family trailer, Marty says the satellite interference caused by the alien spacecraft has made every station behave 'like it's the 1950s', and one of the misfits on top of the US Bank Tower hopes the aliens 'bring back Elvis'. Overall, it seems *Independence Day* hopes the alien invasion will bring back the 1950s in its entirety – socially, politically and culturally.

of the 1960s are obliterated atop the US Bank Tower in downtown Los Angeles. The only meaningfully differentiated character among them, stripper Tiffany, is portrayed as stupid and grossly naïve. According to Geoff King, 'The denizens of the rooftop are presented as a fake, metropolitan and decadent version of the kind of redemption that is only really available to those strong enough to engage more violently with the alien.'[101] The treatment of these characters is highly problematic: I contend they function as emblems of the difficulties created by the permissive, pre-disaster society. It is clear how *Independence Day* views the social progress of the previous three decades: in order to complete the narrative's project of restoring traditional values, these characters must be jettisoned. With Whitmore's wife presumed dead, and with her, the activist model of First Lady considered a 'symbol of hard-edged feminism' in the Clinton era, the forces that together constituted 'a frontal assault on the traditional way that men had defined their manhood' in the preceding decades have been almost instantaneously eliminated.[102] Like a family-friendly Rambo, the reclamation of his individualism confirmed, Whitmore is now free to reassert a traditional model of masculinity and the presidency. He is reborn as the individual 'pitted against the horde of pretenders to the masculine crown'; in this case, an implacable race of aliens.[103]

This rediscovered confidence is articulated quite clearly by the film's *mise-en-scène*: the arrival of Air Force One at the Nevada facility is greeted with a rousing, jingoistic orchestral score on the non-diegetic soundtrack, replete with a series of military drum rolls. A long shot of the aircraft landing

101 King, *Spectacular Narratives*, 26.

102 Kimmel, *Manhood in America*, 280.
Indeed, it might be argued that the First Lady's death is indicative of the conservatism of the disaster narrative: having not fulfilled the expectations of her gender, and defied her husband's pleas for her to return home sooner, she has paid the ultimate price for her independence and assertiveness. Such narrative processes are indicative of what Faludi discusses in *Backlash*; pushing women back into their 'acceptable' roles. These issues will be further addressed in the discussion of *Air Force One*. It is vital to note that the women who accept their subordination to men in *Independence Day* survive the war. – Faludi, *Backlash*, 16.

103 Kimmel, *Manhood in America*, 307.

creates the impression of a dominating presence on the landscape, with the words 'United States of America' emblazoned conspicuously across its side. The president emerges, striding purposefully from the front, greeted with the requisite military salute from the soldiers stationed at the base. This is followed by a low-angle long shot from inside the base, where the doors open to greet the president, the aeroplane dominating the image from the background, dwarfing the facility. The framing of Air Force One, which magnifies its size, is clearly intended to create a powerful impression of the presidency, with a force similar to that possessed by the invading aliens.

It is here that the president regains his agency, demanding that he be allowed to see the facility despite the protestations of his advisors and subordinates. 'Open the door!' he exclaims, and he strides into the room with purpose, positioned in the centre of the frame. The tracking shot into the facility could be interpreted as the president's point of view, as his exclamation 'My God!' directly precedes the cut, which then positions him centrally, flanked by his most senior advisors who are standing behind him. The simplicity of his language here is in marked contrast to his earlier indecisive words: he is assertive, strident and dominant. The camera tracks backwards, following his movement as he marches into the building. This is in striking distinction to the scenes immediately following the alien arrival, where Whitmore blended into the background. Although the president continues to be framed in two-shot with other, more marginal, characters, the film's *mise-en-scène* is gradually manoeuvring agency to him. This process culminates in the scene in which he communicates telepathically with the captured alien, allowing him to see the horrifying invasion they are planning. This positions the president as the dynamic centre of the American response, allowing him to delegate responsibilities to soon-to-be astronauts Hiller and Levinson from a position of ultimate authority.

The final confirmation of Whitmore's transformation is demonstrated by his stirring, patriotic address to the improvised military force hastily assembled to launch the counter-offensive. Like Shepherd at the conclusion of *The American President*, Whitmore's speech affirms his position as the individual in command: the camera positioning, framing and movement function to unite the nation (and the world) in a common, primal desire to survive. Crane shots emphasise the collective national unity the president's speech inspires; the cutaways to various peripheral characters emphasise the multicultural nature of the United States; the tracking shot which starts from a distance to end in tight close-up of Whitmore issuing his final rallying cry creates an impression of a president who has recognised the significance of his role, broken the shackles imposed upon him by governmental bureaucracy, and seized the opportunity to reinstate the president as the nation's reassuring, commanding father.

This is emphasised by the conclusion of his speech, which is met with a rapturous round of applause, an orchestral crescendo on the non-diegetic soundtrack, close-ups of pilots cheering and saluting him, and book-ended by two crane shots once again emphasising collective unity. Whitmore's strength is finally confirmed as he too takes up arms, flying a plane into battle. When Whitmore asserts, 'I'm a combat pilot, I belong in the air', he abandons the words on which he has hitherto been dependent, and demonstrates his masculine prowess through heroic actions. Through this, *Independence Day* has completed its project of restoring individual masculine agency to the presidency.

The metaphorical cleansing which the alien invasion has enacted, and which Whitmore has seized upon, reaches its conclusion in *Independence Day*'s final scene where Hiller and Levinson return from space, having destroyed the alien mothership and rescued mankind from extinction. They are greeted by President Whitmore and his daughter, Levinson's father, Constance, Jasmine and Dylan. Following the crisis, traditional gender roles are reinstated: Jasmine and Steven married before the latter rode into battle, with the chapel scene also confirming the reconciliation between Constance and David. Both women bound up to the heroic pilots, fulfilling the expectation of dutiful wives welcoming their brave men home from battle (David, decidedly uncomfortable with conventional markers of masculinity previously, has taken up cigar-smoking in celebration). The barren desert landscape seems indicative of *Independence Day*'s rejuvenated United States, returning the nation to its foundational, frontier myth.[104]

104 As Geoff King suggests, 'This version of the renewed frontier experience produces the appearance of enemies that are unambiguously defined and against which a clear definition of a virtuous self can be articulated.' – King, *Spectacular Narratives*, 19.

This final scene marks *Independence Day* out from Reaganite visions of American society, and can certainly be viewed as a Clintonesque image (if not a Clintonesque presidency). It is the perfect picture of multicultural, pluralistic, tolerant harmony: the Jewish scientist and the African American fighter pilot/astronaut, their wives and children, with the WASP president (now a single father) in powerful and assertive command, can now realise the post-Cold War dream of a united, uncomplicated and victorious America (as long as everyone remains heterosexual). The conclusion is entirely in keeping with the generic conventions of the disaster film, in which the social and cultural problems that preceded the catastrophe are resolved 'through the ritualized legitimation of strong male leadership, the renewal of traditional moral values, and the regeneration of institutions like the patriarchal family.'[105] Far from being symbolic of millennial tension, as it is so often understood, the triumphalist tone of the film's conclusion indicates that *Independence Day* is ecstatic about the coming millennium; as Taubin suggests, '*Independence Day* is a feel-good picture about the end of the world'.[106] However, its optimism is distinctly reactionary and nostalgic. The reworking of the president into a traditionally masculine, Cold War warrior is indicative of this process.

'Get Off My Plane!': Air Force One

While *Independence Day* works hard to restore individual agency and traditional masculinity to its president through visual strategies and narrative structure, *Air Force One* is more straightforward in its expectations of the office in the post-Cold War environment. The film concerns the hijacking of the eponymous presidential aircraft by a group of radical Kazakh nationalists who feel aggrieved at the disintegration of the Soviet Union, and the responsibility of President James Marshall (Harrison Ford) for

105 Michael Ryan and Douglas Kellner, *Camera Politica: The Politics and Ideology of Contemporary Hollywood Film* (Bloomington: Indiana University Press, 1990), 52.

106 Taubin, 'Playing it Straight', 6.

the capture and imprisonment of their beloved leader General Ivan Radek (Jurgen Prochnow). Marshall's determination to thwart tyranny and oppression, and his refusal to negotiate with those who employ these tactics, is severely tested by the terrorists. They threaten to murder the president's wife Grace (Wendy Crewson) and daughter Alice (Liesel Matthews), and everyone on board, should their demands not be met. Terrorist leader Ivan Korshunov (Gary Oldman) forces Marshall to choose between his love for his wife and daughter, and loyalty to his country. While Vice President Kathryn Bennett (Glenn Close) and Defence Secretary Walter Dean (Dean Stockwell) attempt to come to an agreement with the terrorists from the ground, it becomes apparent that a diplomatic solution is likely to end in failure, and the efficacy of United States' foreign policy, her standing in the world, and the safety of everyone on board Air Force One lie squarely in the hands of President Marshall. As one of various promotional taglines used for the film suggests, 'The fate of a nation rests on the courage of one man.' Using his combat experience in Vietnam, his considerable strength of physique and of character, Marshall successfully outfights and outwits the terrorists to win the day.

I will examine *Air Force One* as a regressive text, resurrecting a Reaganite conception of the presidency and its simplistic, Manichean attitude towards international affairs. How the film reconciles the shifts in conceptions of masculinity that occurred in the 1990s with an uncomplicated, Cold War vision of the presidency is essential to my discussion. While Bill Clinton's message, eagerly lapped up by the electorate, was the promise of physical security and material plenty, the fictional Marshall is more concerned with seizing the opportunity afforded by the end of the Cold War to recreate the world in America's image, making it safe for freedom and democracy. I will examine the film's adoption of the narrative structure of the 1980s action film (particularly *Die Hard* [John McTiernan, 1988]), the star persona of Harrison Ford and its similarities with Reagan's bifurcated father/warrior image, and the means by which *Air Force One* reasserts traditional models of gender, masculinity and the presidency through *mise-en-scène*, character and performance.

The influence of *Die Hard* on *Air Force One*, and the action genre in general, cannot be underestimated. Rick Altman argues that '*Die Hard* has almost become a generic label in [its] own right', the film's iconographies, narrative structure and action set-pieces reworked in a variety of settings: on a boat (*Under Siege* [Andrew Davis, 1992]), on a bus (*Speed* [Jan de Bont, 1994]), at a Pittsburgh Penguins ice-hockey match (*Sudden Death* [Peter Hyams, 1995]).[107] As Larry Gross suggests of the narrative structures in the *Die Hard* series and its clones, 'An implacable killing force/situation is unleashed in an isolated space and on a small group of people, resulting in one spectacular disaster after another, until the force/situation is either subdued or escaped.'[108] The similarities between this formula and *Air Force One* are obvious, but *Die Hard*'s Cold War context is also vital: the villains in *Air Force One* have a similarly uncomplicated malevolence (albeit for nationalistic rather than financial objectives). The main scoundrel of the piece, Ivan Korshunov, may not possess the suave sophistication of Hans Gruber (Alan Rickman), and is significantly more extravagant in both his mannerisms and demands, but he does continue a strong tradition within Hollywood action thrillers that cast British actors in the roles of European villains. 'Double-othering' villains in such a fashion allows films like *Die Hard* and *Air Force One* to establish the enemy with definitive certainty, effectively establishing the battleground as a Manichean division between good and evil, and rendering the American hero as an uncomplicated bastion of righteous strength.

Although *Die Hard* has a somewhat parodic attitude towards its hero, John McClane (Bruce Willis), and makes numerous references to John Wayne, Rambo, and Roy Rogers, he is a nostalgic figure, and indicative of a process within Hollywood action cinema of the 1980s that sought to restore a conventional, individualistic brand of heroism to its male protagonist. According to Stephen Keane, McClane 'is the epitome of the self-reliant, self-effacing modern hero, squaring up to the technological terrorists with ingenuity and true grit.'[109] A similar process is apparent in *Air Force One*,

107 Rick Altman, *Film/Genre* (London: British Film Institute, 1999), 47, quoted in Stephen Keane, *Disaster Movies: The Cinema of Catastrophe* (London: Wallflower Press, 2001), 70.

108 Larry Gross, 'Big and Loud', in Arroyo, ed., *Action/Spectacle Cinema*, 5–6.

109 Keane, *Disaster Movies*, 64.

although how these masculine traits are restored to the *presidency* raises a number of intriguing questions regarding the expectations of the office in this period. I will now discuss the manner in which these elements intersect with *Air Force One*'s determination to reconstruct the heroic, Reaganite, Cold War-era presidency.

Marshall conforms closely to what Orman describes as the 'macho presidential style', the quintessential example of which was Ronald Reagan: looking to restore traditional masculinity to the presidency after the perceived 'feminine' weakness of the Carter years, Reagan portrayed himself as competitive, athletic, decisive, unemotional, strong, aggressive and powerful, all considered the characteristics of a 'real man'.[110] President Marshall is similar in construction. His athleticism and strength are demonstrated at various stages throughout: he is able to overcome physical challenges from other men and escape strictures placed upon him using improvisation and brute strength. He manages to cling on to the plane when the baggage deck is suddenly opened while in mid-air, and while many other men fall to their deaths, Marshall's upper body strength allows him to be pulled to safety. Like McClane in *Die Hard*, he is wounded, but improvises a bandage, replaces his jacket (much like a suit of armour or uniform), and carries on. His decision to allow his press secretary to be killed rather than reveal himself, his refusal to negotiate with the terrorists, and his steely resolve in flying the plane despite his inexperience with such large aircraft, are all illustrative of his tough, strident and forceful masculinity. Indeed, Marshall's feats of derring-do conform to the 1980s 'depiction of the indefatigable, muscular, and inviolable masculine hard body [which] became the linchpin of the Reagan imaginary'.[111]

The president's tough, Cold War posture is apparent from the film's beginning as he outlines a radical shift in foreign policy in a speech in Moscow. Having worked with the Russian authorities to apprehend the dastardly General Radek, Marshall states aggressively that America will no longer allow such tyranny to proceed unchecked. His forthright assertion

110 Orman, *Comparing Presidential Behavior*, 8.
111 Jeffords, *Hard Bodies*, 25.

that America 'will never negotiate' with terrorists can be understood as a reversion to a Reaganite foreign policy founded upon 'a hawkish [and] muscular lack of diplomacy'.[112] Why *Air Force One* feels the need to adopt this aggressive stance given the relative geopolitical tranquillity of the mid-1990s is perhaps more difficult to explain. I concur with Faludi's suggestion that Reagan's departure left a gaping chasm in the masculine conception of the presidency, but the desire to believe in the strength of the nation and its president did not simply disappear. Where Clinton was content to pursue a tentative foreign policy, avoid direct conflict, and look after the nation's bank balance, the traditional conception of the president as a Reaganite strongman migrated into the fictional realm of Hollywood cinema. President Marshall is indicative of an implicit desire to return to the conventional masculine bombast of the Reagan era, with 'America ... once again sitting tall in the saddle, willing to take on all comers, asserting its dominance in world affairs'.[113]

This bullishness is reflected in the visual construction of Marshall both during and immediately following the delivery of the address. In marked contrast to President Whitmore's hesitancy at the beginning of *Independence Day*, *Air Force One* is swift and straightforward in its construction of Marshall as a powerful and authoritative presence. When he is introduced by the Russian President Petrov (Alan Woolf) as a 'brave man' and 'one of the world's greatest leaders', the slow track into his face from distance individuates him from the other dignitaries. The camera positioning clearly reflects Marshall's individual agency and strength: whereas the speech begins by positioning him slightly to the right of centre, once his chief of staff and national security advisor realise he is deviating from the original script, Marshall is positioned centrally, in medium close-up, as he outlines the radical departure in American foreign policy. He is entirely in command.

Unlike Clinton (or Shepherd, in the early stages of *The American President*), Marshall will not poll-test or triangulate a policy he 'knows to

112 Tasker, *Spectacular Bodies*, 92.

113 Kimmel, *Manhood in America*, 291.

be morally right', and this confident belligerence is, as at the conclusion of *The American President*, rendered visual by his stasis and central framing. Cutaways to his chief of staff looking flummoxed by this shift, and downwards tilting point-of-view shots from the president's podium looking at the audience, further reinforce this image of Marshall's individualism and independence. He receives a standing ovation, which is immediately followed by a shot of Air Force One, framed from distance, the camera tilting upwards to reveal its magnificent size. The orchestral score, introduced in the credits sequence which preceded Radek's capture, is employed here. Its bombastic trumpets and militaristic drumrolls lend a patriotic tenor to proceedings, creating a motif which is utilised throughout to reinforce the president's authority and strength. It is possible to interpret the introduction of the plane as illustrative of the presidential phallus: following Marshall's assertion of presidential power, the film employs a symbol of the office's potency, virility and manliness.[114] Unlike *The American President*'s employment of the phallus in order to generate humour regarding the separation between man and office, here the plane is revealed as a symbol of overwhelming power, the heft of which is appropriate to the president's command. The plane's introduction is followed by a backwards tracking shot following the movement of the president and his advisors as they leave the event, Marshall's brisk movement almost forcing the camera backwards. When his advisors question his new policy, Marshall states, 'I know exactly what I committed us to', indicating that his control and authority should not be in question, a confidence reflected by his control of the positioning and movement of the camera.

Marshall clearly conforms more closely to a Reaganite presidential ideal than a Clintonian one: as Jeffords suggests, 'in order to be the embodiment of Reagan democratic ideals, he must be both muscular and independent of mind.'[115] Marshall is unconcerned with consensus, being wholly devoted to doing what he believes to be right, whatever the consequences. His closest advisors chastise his decision to improvise a new speech, and are concerned at the ire such a radical departure in foreign policy will provoke

114 Clare, *On Men*, 8.
115 Jeffords, *Hard Bodies*, 41.

from a hostile Congress. Marshall refuses to be bullied, simply stating, 'It's the right thing to do, and you know it.' The economical introduction of Marshall, which establishes his strident, authoritative masculine presence through dialogue, framing and camera movement, suggests that he is a sturdy presence that will prove reassuring when the later chaos occurs.[116] *Air Force One* looks to reclaim a space for traditional masculinity and a militaristic presidency in a post-Cold War context, and it appears to do so by invoking the attitudes and discourses that dominated the Reagan era.

As Marcus suggests, 'Reagan's persona evoked the post-World War II period of American international ascendancy, domestic social stability, and militant anticommunism.'[117] *Air Force One* articulates a similar desire: while the post-Cold War context renders it unnecessary for the president to appear militantly anticommunist, its choice of villain, a Kazakh nationalist with a maniacal desire to reform the Soviet empire, raises this spectre. As Macnab suggests of *Air Force One*, 'it becomes apparent that the evil empire is still evil as far as Hollywood is concerned.'[118] Once the hijackers have been defeated, Marshall still has to contend with a fleet of MiGs sent from Radek loyalists in Kazakhstan to take down Air Force One. The fighter aircraft are a potent symbol of Cold War Soviet expansionism, having been deployed by the communist regimes in the Korean and Vietnam wars. So desperate is *Air Force One* to reconstitute the allegedly Manichean dichotomy between the wholesome and benevolent United States and the straightforwardly evil Soviet Union, when American fighter jets arrive to thwart the MiGs, Marshall exclaims excitedly, 'Good guys are here!'

Korshinov reacts with emotional, patriotic awe when Radek is released and the strains of socialist anthem 'The Internationale' are heard over the radio. The song's lyrics, particularly

> This is the final struggle
> Let us group together, and tomorrow

116 See Bruzzi, 'Men's Cinema', for analysis of *Dirty Harry*'s 'slick, functional' visual style and the associated construction of traditional, authoritative masculinity – 192–3.

117 Marcus, *Happy Days and Wonder Years*, 60.

118 Macnab, '*Air Force One*', 251.

The Internationale
Will be the human race

appear to position *Air Force One*, like *Independence Day*, as the final redemptive battle which the peaceful conclusion to the Cold War had failed to deliver. While all the rhetoric employed by Marshall points to a tough, militaristic approach to tyranny in the Cold War mould, so does this direct confrontation with 'Soviet communists' allow him to fight, and win, the final battle of the protracted war which defined American ideals and policies for half a century. These iconographic references demonstrate that the Soviet Union and communism remain the definitive enemy, despite *Air Force One*'s post-Cold War context.

Marshall's status as a combat veteran of the Vietnam War is essential to *Air Force One*'s reconstruction of the heroic Cold War presidency, and another way in which the film defines its president as distinct from Clinton. Marshall's strength and clarity of purpose are vigorously reinforced by the knowledge that he was a Medal of Honour winner, and that 'he knows how to fight.'[119] In a similar fashion to *Independence Day*'s Russell Casse, *Air Force One* recasts the Vietnam veteran as saviour. Whilst *Independence Day* attempts to expunge the war from the American record by killing its soldier in a noble sacrifice, *Air Force One* does not disavow the conflict entirely; Marshall's status as a successful soldier is indicative merely of his battle-hardened, hypermasculine character, and he fought in the Vietnam War for all the right reasons: defending freedom and defeating tyranny, ideals which he has carried over into his presidency. While it might be true that the Vietnam War 'is invariably referred to by Americans as a tragedy or a national trauma', *Air Force One* attempts to reclaim the alleged purity of its initial purpose by demonstrating that the skills Marshall learned in

119 Marshall becomes evocative of Reagan's desire to transform the Vietnam veteran from an 'emotionally fragile and socially disoriented' figure into 'the isolated but avenging angel of a reborn American patriotism, assertiveness, and toughness'. – Marcus, *Happy Days and Wonder Years*, 97.

Vietnam would subsequently be put to righteous use.[120] Indeed, the casting of a Vietnam veteran as the American president completes the process begun in the Reagan era to rehabilitate the veteran as an icon of American manhood.[121] President Marshall's construction represents the concluding point of the Vietnam veteran's journey 'from child to adolescent to father, from outsider to leader, from destructive rebel to wise patriarch, from feminine to masculine.'[122]

However, *Air Force One*'s rejuvenation of the Reagan-era Cold Warrior president is not entirely unaffected by shifts within Hollywood's representations of masculinity in the 1990s, nor by Harrison Ford's own evolving star image. As one of the prominent action heroes of the Reagan era, Ford could be said to embody many of that period's neo-imperial ideologies. Where Reagan expounded the virtue of a return to the rugged individualism upon which the country was founded, so too did Ford embody these ideals in his portrayals of Han Solo in the *Star Wars* trilogy (1977–83) and the eponymous fortune hunter of the *Indiana Jones* films (Steven Spielberg, 1981–9).[123] However, prior to *Air Force One*, Ford would also perform Jeffords' 'Big Switch', whereby the Reagan era 'hard bodies' gave way to kinder, gentler husband/father images.[124] This is most apparent in *Regarding Henry* (Mike Nichols, 1991), in which Ford's cruel and unpleasant lawyer, the very embodiment of corporate excess of the Reagan years, is reincarnated as a caring, attentive father and husband following a bullet

120 Trevor McCrisken, *American Exceptionalism and the Legacy of Vietnam: American Foreign Policy since 1974* (Basingstoke: Palgrave Macmillan, 2003), 26.

121 Jeffords, *The Remasculinization of America*, p. 116.

122 Ibid., 143.

123 As Adam Knee suggests, these roles 'aligned Ford with a certain old-guard – indeed nostalgic – and also distinctively American masculinity ... the particular neo-imperialist ethos implied therein clearly aligned with Reagan-era conceptions of America as an ascendant economic power'. – Adam Knee, 'Harrison Ford: A Well-Tempered Machismo', in Robert Eberwein, ed., *Acting For America: Movie Stars of the 1980s* (London: Rutgers University Press, 2010), 161.

124 Jeffords, 'The Big Switch', 196–208.

wound to the head.[125] It can be argued that Ford began this transformation earlier than the more obviously musclebound action heroes of the period. He performed humane, thoughtful roles in films such as *Witness* (Peter Weir, 1985) and *Frantic* (Roman Polanski, 1988), both of which were predicated on the rescue and/or protection of women. As Adam Knee argues of Ford, 'the macho dimensions of his star image [are tempered] as it evolves', combining 'rugged, virile masculine sexual attractiveness' with 'husbandly and fatherly concern for his loved ones.'[126] Prior to *Air Force One*, Ford would hold these two competing notions in unison in his role as CIA operative Jack Ryan in *Patriot Games* (Phillip Noyce, 1992) and *Clear and Present Danger* (Phillip Noyce, 1994), in which the safety of his wife and daughter are predicated on his physical strength and tactical nous.

While Schwarzenegger and Stallone may have reflected Reagan's uncompromising rhetorical stance in foreign affairs, Ford's combination of action heroics and familial role as a protective father is perhaps a closer reflection of the bifurcation of Reagan's image as president. As Marcus suggests, 'Reagan's paternal rhetoric fit his stance as a father figure', constructing himself as simultaneously tough and aggressive, but also reassuring and nurturing.[127] *Air Force One* represents the final conjunction of the divided Reagan persona, and is in keeping with Hollywood's desire in the 1990s to hold in unison images of men as 'both warrior and father, both defender and provider, both killer and nurturer.'[128] In so doing, it conforms to Jeffords' suggestion that Hollywood's representation of masculinity in this decade was not a straightforward rejection of the 'hard body' heroics of the Reagan era, but an adjustment of this image in order to 'incorporate

125 Bruzzi describes *Regarding Henry* as 'a saccharine indictment of 1980s hyper-masculinity' in which 'the ambitious, detached father … return[s] to his home and family and learn[s] to be a dad again.' – *Bringing Up Daddy*, xii.

126 Knee, 'Harrison Ford', 161.

127 Marcus, *Happy Days and Wonder Years*, 83.

128 Jeffords discusses this shift in relation to Clint Eastwood's star image and his performance in *Unforgiven* – *Hard Bodies*, 178–93.

a domestic component, one that acknowledges the family as the final justification for any foreign interventions.'[129]

***

Although the protection of Marshall's family is the ground on which the Cold War's final battle is fought in *Air Force One*, the incorporation of this 'domestic component' is not without its casualties: in order for Marshall to embody the warrior/father masculine archetype outlined above, obvious counterpoints need to be constructed. As Faludi suggests, 'As much as the male paradigm demanded a clear mission, an enemy, and a frontier, it also required dependents – women and children to fight the mission *for*, to rescue from the enemy, and to homestead with on a conquered (but still insecure) frontier.'[130]

These 'dependents' are provided by the characters of Vice President Kathryn Bennett and The First Lady, Grace Marshall. Bennett is, while not an unsympathetic character, indicative of the chaos and indecision which exists in the absence of Marshall's authority. Close's performance reinforces this sense of powerlessness. Her initial negotiations with the terrorists are wholly unsuccessful, perhaps because her monotone, over-rehearsed approach to hostage negotiation is painfully inadequate in the face of such a ruthless, uncompromising enemy. She is unable to depart from the rehearsed script, uttering meaningless platitudes such as, 'We're doing everything we can'. Close's purposely robotic delivery is in marked contrast to Marshall's ability to think on his feet and act decisively; his masculine autonomy thrown into stark relief by Bennett's conformity

129 Ibid., 191.
Although relegated to secondary importance, the hostage situation aboard Air Force One recalls the Iranian hostage crisis that beleaguered Carter's presidency. Here, however, the president is tough, dynamic and forceful in his approach to the crisis, where Carter had been supposedly weak and impotent. Indeed, Jeffords argues the hostages held in the embassy became symbolic for the national body – weak and imprisoned. In *Air Force One*, they are physically rescued by the president himself and, therefore, the national body remains strong. – Jeffords, *Hard Bodies*, 36–7.

130 Faludi, *Backlash*, 417.

and indecision. She consistently struggles to keep her emotions in check, tears welling up in her eyes when Doherty is executed, and she is hesitant when confronted with the choice to sign a document that would put her in charge due to the incapacity of the president. *Air Force One* is at pains to construct her as everything Marshall is not: weak-willed, passive, indecisive, uncertain and, perhaps most problematically of all, soft. She even raises the possibility of a negotiated settlement with the terrorists, which is quashed immediately by Marshall, using a childishly patronising maxim to convince her: 'If you give a mouse a cookie, he's going to want a glass of milk.' Her ability to function effectively is only attained once contact with Marshall has been established, and she becomes the president by proxy, merely reasserting orders she has received from him: 'Your Commander in Chief has issued you with a direct order. DO IT!'

The other figure through which *Air Force One* constructs Marshall as the heroic president is the First Lady, Grace. Her narrative arc conforms to that of Holly Gennero in *Die Hard*: although initially figured as a strong, independent career woman, when faced with the grave threat of terrorism, she retreats into a more conventional, passive state of femininity, cowering before the ruthless evil of Korshinov. Bruzzi argues that 'passivity in *Die Hard* resides quite explicitly with Holly', and Grace's characterisation follows a comparable pattern.[131]

Grace's initial representation recalls the pivot away from the First Lady as ceremonial housewife that occurred during the Clinton administration.[132] Visually, she is constructed in a similarly professional manner: hair tied back, dressed in elegant, but demure, evening wear. Her equality with Marshall, and her active role within his presidency, is rendered visually: when discussing their earlier campaign to get Marshall elected to the House of Representatives, they perch on the front of the desk, rendering them of almost identical height. The camera tracks almost imperceptibly forward and left, framing the two characters alongside each other, positioning the

131 Bruzzi, 'Men's Cinema', 213.
132 Schier, 'A Unique Presidency', 3.

presidential seal hanging on the wall behind perfectly between them (see Figure 3.2).

3.2 President Marshall (Harrison Ford) and The First Lady (Wendy Crewson) discuss their partnership in *Air Force One* (dir. Wolfgang Petersen, Columbia Pictures, USA, 1997)

Their subsequent embrace completes this impression of an equal partnership, the dialogue, camera movement and framing all working to suggest that the success of Marshall's presidency is to a large extent contingent on Grace's love, support and political acumen.

The conventions of the action genre, however, do not allow *Air Force One* to persist with this construction of equal power relations. Grace does initially demonstrate courage in her confrontations with Korshinov, but fear is etched across her face, with tears rolling down her cheeks. The contrast with her initial appearance before they board the plane, in which her appearance is indicative of her powerful position, is stark. Often framed in close-up, the film seems to revel in her repositioning as the 'damsel in distress', and she is relegated to issuing cries for help, howls of anguish, and whimpers in the face of the monstrous villain. Held at gunpoint, dragged from the room in which the hostages are held, and forced to witness Korshinov issue Marshall with a horrible beating, Grace can only sit powerlessly and wait for her husband's courage, ingenuity and brute strength to overcome the terrorists and rescue herself and Alice. *Air Force One* dismantles the initial construction of the equal relationship between the president and the first lady, proving to be more concerned with the reconstruction of the heroic presidency through the implementation of a narrative structure predicated on the protection of women and children. Unlike *The American President*, which explores the changing gender dynamics within the presidency, *Air Force One* simply polices its female characters back into traditional gender roles, recast as passive figures entirely dependent on the president's great courage for guidance and rescue.[133]

The rendering of Grace as simply Marshall's 'goal' neatly encapsulates the evolution of the First Lady's representation over the four films discussed in this chapter, and the position's significance in wider culture during the period. The comedies are ultimately celebratory of the more activist First Lady model embodied by Hillary Rodham Clinton: Ellen Mitchell uses her marriage to the president to pursue her own platform and agenda, with particular emphasis on the plight of the homeless. Sydney Wade is career woman first, and the president's partner only later. Having explored the controversial implications of her involvement with the president, the film ultimately comes down on Sydney's side (indeed, in much the same way as Shepherd, she has 'character', and is therefore an appropriate romantic interest for the president). The disaster movies, perhaps unsurprisingly given the genre's conservatism, re-establish the traditional First Lady model as the ideal. In *Independence Day*, Marilyn Whitmore is punished for her independence from her presidential husband, as she dies from internal bleeding after her helicopter crashes when the aliens attack. In *Air Force One*, Grace Marshall's equal footing with her husband is erased once the terrorists take over the plane: she becomes a figure to be protected and rescued. This development of more conservative images of the First Lady in Hollywood cinema is in some ways reflective of the news media's treatment of Hillary Rodham Clinton: where she began as a symbol of feminism during Clinton's first term, she was eventually recast in the more dutiful role as supportive wife once the Lewinsky scandal broke, and she became more popular.[134]

133 Faludi, *Backlash*, 16.

134 Parry-Giles and Parry-Giles, 'Mediating Hillary Rodham Clinton', 205–26.

Indeed, the desperation to reposition Grace as the president's 'goal' is somewhat hysterically rendered in the climax of *Air Force One*. Their embrace aboard the rescue aircraft, and the eventual sinking of Air Force One beneath the waves, occur almost simultaneously. Although the computer generated fakery of the plane's crash is obvious, *Air Force One* is keen to represent this spectacle. This might seem curious given the manifest inadequacy of the special effect, but it demonstrates the extent to which *Air Force One* is anxious to reconstruct the traditional, heroic presidency, and to re-establish traditional gender roles. It may also speak to the tenuousness of the heroic presidential archetype: both *Independence Day* and *Air Force One* are dependent upon some fairly blunt narrative tools in order to achieve the restoration of the heroic presidency, either expunging those figures that have obstructed its realisation, or enforcing a traditional framework through which they are represented. In *Air Force One*, the restoration of traditional masculinity to the presidency proves of paramount concern. As Dyer suggests of the Western narrative tradition, 'the drive to a climax is so bound up with the promise of a woman at the end that all stories seem to be modelled on male sexuality.'[135] It is therefore possible to interpret the plane's plunge into the ocean immediately prior to Marshall's safe reunion with Grace and his daughter aboard the newly christened 'Air Force One' as the symbolic representation of the point of orgasm.[136]

If narrative and male sexuality are both goal-orientated, then the pleasures of watching the plane falling apart beneath the waves, the water cascading into the air, perhaps demonstrates the conflation of the two processes. Despite her initial construction as a First Lady in the Clinton mould, Grace's subsequent relegation to Marshall's 'goal' renders her inactive, allowing *Air Force One* to reconstruct the heroic presidency through recourse to a conventional narrative template. Much as 'social order' is restored at the conclusion of *Die Hard* 'through the restitution of masculinity to the

135 Dyer, *The Matter of Images*, 120.

136 Given that Marshall and Grace were interrupted in the middle of their embrace immediately prior to the hijacking would corroborate Bruzzi's notion that 'masculinity in cinema is so often predicated upon sexual frustration' that 'action supplants the sexual act'. – Bruzzi, 'Men's Cinema', 210.

father', *Air Force One* restores the image of the heroic presidency through a similar reassertion of traditional masculine power.[137] This renewal is triumphant: as the heroic Marshall embraces his family, the sun rises over the clouds, and the new Air Force One and accompanying fighter jets zoom out of sight, it is, as Ronald Reagan suggested during his re-election campaign in 1984, 'Morning in America' once again.

***

It is apparent from the films discussed that Hollywood reacted to, and participated in, the redefinition of the presidency in the 1990s. The fictional presidency in this period can be characterised by both uncertainty and ambivalence. One can also discern an encroaching conservatism over the course of the decade: if *Dave* (1993) is a repudiation of the Reaganite model of president, then *Air Force One* (1997) is its qualified reinstatement. The treatment of women in both sets of films confirms this conservative turn. Indicative of the treatment of Hillary Rodham Clinton in the media, these four films demonstrate growing hesitation surrounding the proximity of women to the presidency, and the continued backlash against the feminist movement.

While all four films are concerned with the contemporaneous redefinition of the presidency in the post-Cold War environment, they are manifestly nostalgic. Although Clinton's chameleonic ability to change positions and identities may have been popular with a nation prosperous and at peace, the desire for a more traditional, stable model of president (and man) appears to have migrated into Hollywood cinema. This longing is evidenced by the montages of former presidents that begin *Dave* and *The American President*, enacted by the Rooseveltian activism of Dave Kovic, and the eventual determination of President Shepherd to pass environmental and gun legislation. The action films are similarly nostalgic in approach, although they are more aggressive: problems that have hindered the heroic presidency are violently dispatched, the restitution of individual masculine power to the president being of core concern. The fact that

137 Bruzzi, *Bringing Up Daddy*, 139.

both Whitmore and Marshall are war veterans is no coincidence: where military experience was absent in Clinton, so it was explicitly present in his fictional counterparts.

All four films, however, valorise the agency of the individual, and celebrate the presidency, in an era of ambiguity. *What* the president's role should be in the 1990s appears to be the films' primary worry: the comedies urge the revitalisation of the dynamic, activist presidency tending to domestic problems, harking back to the era of Capra and Roosevelt. In essence, America should use its Cold War victory to fix the problems it has neglected for so long. The action films yearn for a similar vigour, albeit much more militaristic, and dependent upon the reconstitution of a coherent and unproblematic enemy for its realisation. To combat invading aliens or terrorists bent on re-establishing the Soviet Union, traditional models of masculinity are required: an ascendant United States grounded in the social politics of the 1950s, with Ronnie Rambo at the helm.

CHAPTER 4

The West Wing: Continuity and Change from Clinton to Bush

The West Wing premiered on NBC in the United States in September 1999. Despite protestations from the network that public cynicism about politicians in the aftermath of the Lewinsky scandal would deter viewers from watching a programme so staunchly optimistic about the political process, *The West Wing* defied initial expectations to become a critical and commercial hit. The programme capitalised on general disenchantment with politics to present a buoyant, inspiring vision of the American presidency, conforming largely to the template established in classical Hollywood cinema by Frank Capra. As Chris Lehmann argued rather disparagingly, *The West Wing* 'offers a pointedly sunny weekly fable about the unassailable motives and all-too-human foibles of the nation's governing class which verges on the Capra-esque.'[1] Although *The West Wing* is certainly not beholden to the same brand of populist ideology that saturates Capra's political films, the influence is clearly a crucial one. *The West Wing* is heavily indebted to the Capraesque notion that the American system is inherently good, and it can achieve great things if it is maintained by honest, hard-working individuals with noble intentions. In comparison with the period of uncertainty and malaise in which Capra enjoyed his greatest success, the social and political context from which *The West Wing* derives is more benign. However, both perpetuate the fundamental belief in the United States' ability to achieve good things if it is governed by good people. This

1 Chris Lehmann, 'The Feel-Good Presidency: The Psuedo-Politics of *The West Wing*', in Rollins and O'Connor, eds, *The West Wing*, 215.

idea was as influential when the *The West Wing* premiered in 1999 as it had been when it was explored by Capra's Depression-era films.[2]

A long-form serial drama about American politics and the presidency was perhaps the inevitable concluding point to a decade in which representations of the president in mainstream cinema had become frequent and pervasive. As demonstrated by the previous chapter, the Capraesque political film had enjoyed a brief resurgence in the 1990s. *The West Wing*'s most obvious antecedent is the Aaron Sorkin-scripted *The American President*. As Bruzzi argues, *The American President* has increasingly been viewed as Sorkin's rehearsal for the expanded investigation of the presidency in *The West Wing*.[3] However, *The West Wing* 'becomes more openly political, institutional and complex' in comparison to its cinematic predecessor, balancing the obvious fascination with the presidency as an institution and a man with a thirst to investigate the policy and legislative processes which dominate the daily activity of White House staff.[4] I am more concerned here with the characterisation of President Bartlet and the programme's representation of presidential power.

The West Wing's breadth and depth presents a daunting task for a scholar: running at seven seasons and over one hundred hours, how does one decide on which aspects to focus, and which to neglect? My decisions have been largely contingent upon what the existing literature has addressed: much of the research focuses upon the relationship between President Josiah Bartlet (Martin Sheen) and Bill Clinton, and where there are broader discussions of the presidency in relation to American national

2 I began with this discussion primarily because so much of the literature on *The West Wing* neglects to mention that it is a television drama that emerges from a particular tradition of American cinema and television.

3 Bruzzi, 'Men's Cinema', 199.

4 Jason P. Vest, 'From *The American President* to *The West Wing*: A Scriptwriter's Perspective', in Rollins and O'Connor, eds, *The West Wing*, 137.
Indeed, the programme's complexity and detail, in conjunction with its superior writing and performances, has resulted in *The West Wing* being discussed primarily in relation to the notion of 'quality' American television drama, earlier examples of which include *Hill Street Blues* (1981–7), *L.A. Law* (1986–94) and *ER* (1994–2009).

identity, little attention has been paid to the ways in which these issues are explored in relation to the programme's visual dynamics. Furthermore, there has not been much focused analysis of the characterisation of Bartlet himself. With this in mind, I have split this chapter into two sections: the first will address the ways in *The West Wing*'s visual style evolved over its duration, with particular emphasis on the president's use of military action in the pre- and post-9/11 periods. For all the work that has been done regarding the impact of 9/11 on popular culture, scant attention has been paid to *The West Wing*'s complex relationship with this traumatic event. With this in mind, the second section will address Bartlet's brief course of psychotherapy, in which he comes to terms with his difficult relationship with his deceased father, and the awesome challenges faced by the president during the 'war on terror'. I look to expand upon and re-evaluate the existing scholarship on *The West Wing*: now that the programme has been absent from our screens for more than a decade, it is possible to obtain critical distance from old debates surrounding the programme's verisimilitude, historical and political accuracy, and its relationship to the 'real' Clinton administration. It is time to consider *The West Wing* as a fictional drama which commented upon the world around it, rather than a programme in thrall to its (admittedly cultivated) relationship with the political reality.

***

As *The West Wing* has already attracted a substantial amount of critical attention, I must first survey the field and carve out the intellectual ground on which my analysis will be based. To many, the body of work that already exists might suggest *The West Wing* has been sufficiently covered in scholarship. However, the selective attention paid to the programme, focused primarily on its first four seasons, has resulted in a hardening of the critical consensus around a few, very limited, aspects of the programme's composition. The critical focus tended towards the programme's relative pedagogic merits, the historical and political accuracy of Sorkin's vision, and its relationship to the real world.[5] It was the political persuasion of the

5 Staci Beavers, '*The West Wing* as a Pedagogical Tool: Using Drama to Examine American Politics and Media Perceptions of Our Political System', in Rollins and

programme which enraptured critics in *The West Wing*'s early days, as it was simultaneously celebrated and derided for its determinedly liberal vision. Many critics suggested that *The West Wing*'s enslavement to a rigid liberal ethos resulted in a wildly inaccurate impression of American politics: the administration suffered no inner conflict, no power struggles, none of the senior staff were hungry for perks, privilege or position, all were devoted to their great and glorious leader President Bartlet, and they worked tirelessly to serve him and his vision of a liberal, tolerant and fair America. As John Podhoretz suggests in his vitriolic attack on the political leanings of the show, '*The West Wing* ... is nothing more or less than political pornography for liberals'.[6]

The West Wing's similarities with the Clinton administration were the predominant feature of much academic criticism of the programme in its early days. As Lehmann suggests, *The West Wing* offers 'a version of Clintonism with both moral gravitas and political backbone'.[7] Peter Rollins and John O'Connor's edited collection sought in various ways to establish the similarities and discrepancies with the Clinton White House. Despite Sorkin's protestations to the contrary, journalists and academics were quick to identify the potential real-life inspirations for many of the *The West Wing*'s central characters. Sharon Waxman suggests that although Sorkin might have balked at the inclination to compare *The West Wing* to political reality, it is difficult to ignore the resemblances to Clinton's senior staff.[8] Almost all the main cast met Clinton himself at one point or

---

O'Connor, eds, *The West Wing*, 175–86; Myron A. Levine, '*The West Wing* (NBC) and The West Wing (DC): Myth and Reality in Television's Portrayal of the White House', in Rollins and O'Connor, eds, *The West Wing*, pp. 42–62.

6 John Podhoretz, 'The Liberal Imagination', in Rollins and O'Connor, eds, *The West Wing*, p. 223.

7 Lehmann, 'The Feel-Good Presidency', 215.

8 As Waxman argues, 'fictional deputy chief of staff Josh Lyman (Bradley Whitford) is derivative of former White House aide Paul Begala; that hunky, single speechwriter Sam Seaborn (Rob Lowe) is inspired by single former Clinton aide George Stephanopoulos; or that neurotic press secretary C.J. Cregg (Alison Janney) is somehow related to former Clinton press secretary Dee Dee Myers, one of Sorkin's script

another.[9] Sheen said that Bartlet was in part modelled on the best aspects of Clinton, Jimmy Carter and John F. Kennedy, and by adopting the positive characteristics of three real presidents one might be able to constitute a great fictional one, devoid of the moral or intellectual weaknesses which inevitably plague real men.[10] Although Sorkin seemed preoccupied with establishing his vision as fictitious, it is difficult to dispute that *The West Wing* attempted to cultivate, and benefit from, its perceived close relationship with the Clinton White House, and the real world of American politics in general. As Donnalyn Pompper suggests, '*The West Wing* ... uses actual former and current political figures as consultants for authenticity in telling the stories.'[11] However, although the suggestion that Bartlet's White House is merely a 'conscience-haunted upgrade' of Clinton's is a compelling one given the myriad ways in which the programme's early promotional strategies stressed its close relationship with its real-life counterpart, such an assertion paints only part of what becomes an increasingly complex picture.[12]

Two books on *The West Wing* attempted to shift the debate towards a more nuanced understanding of the programme's representation of politics. Trevor and Shawn Parry-Giles's intervention is particularly useful in relation to this chapter: their work represents the first concerted attempt to move away from discussions of the programme's realism towards

---

consultants.' – Sharon Waxman, 'Inside *The West Wing*'s New World', in Rollins and O'Connor, eds, *The West Wing*, 204.

9 *West Wing* actors were also given tours of the Clinton White House during the show's first season, and there were high-profile meetings between real White House staffers and their fictional counterparts – John Spencer, who played Bartlet's Chief of Staff Leo McGarry, met with Clinton Chief of Staff John Podesta, and Alison Janney, who played Bartlet's Press Secretary C.J. Cregg, opened a midday briefing for White House spokesman Joe Lockhart. – Peter Rollins and John O'Connor, 'Introduction', in *The West Wing*, 6.

10 Martin Sheen, 'Martin Sheen shares worldview on *Charlie Rose*', October 14th, 2002, <http://martinsheen.net/id110.html>, accessed August 2012.

11 Donnalyn Pompper, '*The West Wing*: White House Narratives That Journalism Can't Tell', in Rollins and O'Connor, eds, *The West Wing*, 25.

12 Lehmann, 'The Feel-Good Presidency', 214.

a greater appreciation of its status as fictional drama.[13] They are concerned with the series' nationalism, and the president's role within this construction: 'the center of all national action, the source of all national identity in *TWW*, comes from a heroic, white, male president who is strongest when exerting military force.'[14] My work will build upon this discussion, examining more closely the aesthetic strategies *The West Wing* employs in its representation of the president, and the ways in which these techniques reaffirm or complicate understanding of presidential power.

Melissa Crawley adopts an auteurist approach to *The West Wing*, arguing that Sorkin's influence on the programme results in the construction of the presidency as a primarily emotional institution; 'the president is a structure of feeling.'[15] Crawley makes the intriguing suggestion that *The West Wing*'s idealised portrayal of the president is similar to the ways in which reverence for the office is inculcated in American citizens during childhood. Crawley argues *The West Wing* is a fairly conservative celebration of the American presidency, nostalgically reconstructing the president as a pseudo-religious figure of national conscience in a period in which such conceptions were thought to have been lost; 'rather than contributing something new to this [presidential meaning] system, Sorkin's drama merely asked the audience to remember it.'[16] This argument raises significant issues in relation to Bartlet's course of psychotherapy, and the programme's critique of the Bush administration to which I will return later.

Janet McCabe's intervention, as part of the 'TV Milestones' series, represents the most significant investigation of the political implications of *The West Wing*'s visual style to date. Born of her extensive work into the aesthetics and industrial facets of 'quality' television drama, this volume offers a broad account of the programme's origins, its position as a network show pursuing an upmarket audience demographic, the authorial influence

13 Trevor Parry-Giles and Shawn J. Parry-Giles, *The Prime-Time Presidency: The West Wing and US Nationalism* (Chicago: University of Illinois Press, 2006), 13.

14 Ibid., 158.

15 Melissa Crawley, *Mr Sorkin Goes to Washington: Shaping the President on Television's The West Wing* (London: McFarland and Company, Inc., 2006), 10.

16 Ibid., 194.

of Sorkin on its idealistic tone, and the shifts in narrative focus and structure that accompanied the arrival of producer John Wells in season five. Where McCabe's work differs from the other literature on *The West Wing* is in its willingness to discuss the programme's stylistic and tonal changes brought about by the presidency of George W. Bush, 9/11 and the 'war on terror'. She acknowledges the aesthetic changes that occurred across the programme's run, arguing that the romanticism of the Steadicam gave way to a darker, sepia-toned vision of 'what presidential power looked and "felt" like.'[17] In addition, she explores the impact this vision had on the programme's representation of race and gender. Drawing upon Faludi's work on the 'war on terror' and representations of gender, McCabe focuses particularly on the kidnap, and subsequent rescue, of Bartlet's youngest daughter Zoey (Elisabeth Moss) at the end of season four as indicative of a tendency within post-9/11 visual culture to restage the 'captivity narrative' most readily associated with the American frontier.[18] She argues that *The West Wing* 'made sense' of the United States' position in the post-Cold War and post-9/11 worlds, at first 'dialoguing with the troubled Clinton administration' before turning its attention to acting as the 'liberal imagination to a conservative reality' during the Bush presidency.[19]

This chapter will build upon McCabe's initial intervention, wrest the critical initiative away from discussions of political and historical accuracy, and maintain steadier focus on the presidency itself. It will examine in close textual detail the evolution of the programme's visual style, provide political explanations for these shifts, and explore the resultant impact upon our understanding of the fictional presidency in the post-9/11 period. What does the aesthetic style of *The West Wing* reveal about its attitude towards presidential power? What picture does it offer of presidential control, authority and mastery? I will examine how *The West Wing* evolved in response to the seismic, almost simultaneous shocks to its liberal ethos: the installation of George W. Bush as president in 2001, and the 9/11 terrorist

17 Janet McCabe, *The West Wing* (Detroit: Wayne State University Press, 2013), 60.

18 Ibid., 101–4.

19 Ibid., 85.

attacks on New York and Washington, DC later that year. There was a certain level of critical interest in how *The West Wing* might be compelled to dilute its unashamed liberalism in the wake of these events. Rollins and O'Connor argued that 'the parallels that had been established between [Clinton's] real life and Bartlet's scripted situations ... would likely have to be changed to accommodate a new chief executive.'[20] However, there has been little attempt to formulate a coherent, critical understanding of how the programme changed stylistically to address these issues.

I will examine *The West Wing* as a fictional drama, with a *specific vision* of the presidency and American politics. Despite evidence to the contrary, *The West Wing* has never intended to be a strictly accurate picture of the modern (or postmodern) presidency, but set out with a clear agenda to revitalise interest and passion in politics and public service.[21] As Pamela Ezell suggests, *The West Wing* was not designed to replicate politics-as-usual, but rather to present a fantasy vision of American politics.[22] As Rose Marie Berger observed, 'If this is not how the White House actually is, it's how it should be'.[23] After the moral and political equivocations of the Clinton period, Sorkin's creation 'seemed the perfect antidote for a nation weary of human frailty in its ultimate leader.'[24] As Sorkin asserted, 'The appearance of reality is more important than reality', suggesting that *The West Wing* was perfectly willing to take advantage of its carefully constructed façade of authenticity to offer a critique of the turbulent period of which it was part.[25]

20 Rollins and O'Connor, 'Introduction', 3.

21 Indeed, as Sorkin suggested, *The West Wing* is his 'valentine to public service' (September 27th, 2000), quoted in Crawley, *Mr Sorkin Goes to Washington*, 77.

22 Pamela Ezell, 'The Sincere Sorkin White House, or, the Importance of Seeming Earnest', in Rollins and O'Connor, eds, *The West Wing*, 164.

23 Rose Marie Berger, 'Scripted Hope in *The West Wing*', *Sojourners* (May 29th, 2000), 61, quoted in Pompper, 'Narratives Journalism Can't Tell', 29.

24 Ezell, 'The Sincere Sorkin White House', 160.

25 Ibid.

The West Wing, Visual Style and the War on Terror

While the Bush administration's execution of the 'war on terror' is not explicitly identified in *The West Wing*, through the acknowledgment and exploration of the terrorist threat on the United States, the programme is engaged in a complex critique of the events which followed 9/11. Much has been written regarding the representation of 9/11 and the 'war on terror' in popular culture, with a general impression that mainstream cinema and television has failed to engage fully with the trauma caused by the event and its aftermath. The two most high-profile Hollywood films representing 9/11 – *World Trade Center* (Oliver Stone, 2006) and *United 93* (Paul Greengrass, 2006) – were criticised for failing to interrogate what the terrorist attacks meant in relation to America's national identity and purpose. Faludi argues both films are symptomatic of a tendency in American culture to 'replicate' 9/11, but 'not delve' into its implications.[26] Slavoj Žižek suggested that, by attempting only a realistic recreation of the catastrophe itself, 'both films are restrained from taking a political stance and depicting the wider context of the events.'[27] Karen Randell argues that *World Trade Center*'s filtering of 9/11 through the generic conventions of the Hollywood disaster movie is indicative of a culture unable to accept that the event occurred at all.[28]

The response of the Bush administration might explain the inability to comprehend 9/11. Bush's rhetoric in the aftermath of the attacks manufactured an undemanding narrative: the attacks were an act of war and, in Manichean fashion, the president divided the world into those

26 Susan Faludi, *The Terror Dream: Myth and Misogyny in an Insecure America* (New York: Picador, 2007), 3.

27 Slavoj Žižek, 'On 9/11, New Yorkers faced fire in the minds of men', *The Guardian*, September 11th, 2006, <http://www.guardian.co.uk/commentisfree/2006/sep/11/comment.september11>, accessed August 2012.

28 Karen Randell, '"It was Like a Movie": The Impossibility of Representation in Oliver Stone's *World Trade Center*', in Jeff Birkenstein, Anna Froula and Karen Randell, eds, *Reframing 9/11: Film, Popular Culture, and the 'War on Terror'* (New York: Continuum, 2010), 141–52.

that are 'good' (America and her allies), and those who are 'evil' (Osama Bin Laden, al-Qaeda and its supporters and defenders, and 'The Axis of Evil' – Iraq, Iran, and North Korea); those who support terror and those who oppose it ('You are either with us, or you are with the terrorists').[29] As Reza Aslan suggests,

> it was cinema, and popular culture in general, that, more than anything else, helped cast the disturbing events of 9/11, and the even more disturbing events that followed, into an easily accessible, easily digestible *story*, one in which everyone had a role to play, as either hero or villain, good or evil, 'with us' or 'against us'.[30]

Jeff Birkenstein, Anna Froula, and Karen Randell concur with this suggestion, arguing that 'the official 9/11 response impeded the creation and use of a constructive post-traumatic language, one that is still needed both to historicize and to cope with the traumas of this national and international event.'[31] Susan Sontag attracted vehement criticism for suggesting that the official response to 9/11 infantilised the public, arguing that the refusal to challenge the policies pursued by the Bush administration was deeply troubling for the future of American democracy.[32]

In essence, Bush's crude response, founded on the straightforward divisions between 'good' and 'evil' most common in Hollywood narratives, prevented any therapeutic treatment being administered to the nation. The event could be relived repeatedly (the footage of the planes crashing into the World Trade Centre shown so frequently on news networks that one became desensitised to the violence), but it could not be problematised,

29 George W. Bush, State of the Union address, January 29th, 2002, <http://edition.cnn.com/2002/ALLPOLITICS/01/29/bush.speech.txt/>, accessed August 2012; George W. Bush, address to joint session of Congress, September 20th, 2001, <http://edition.cnn.com/2001/US/09/20/gen.bush.transcript/>, accessed August 2012.

30 Reza Aslan, 'Foreword', in Birkenstein, Froula, and Randell, eds, *Reframing 9/11*, xii.

31 Jeff Birkenstein, Anna Froula and Karen Randell, 'Introduction', in Birkenstein, Froula and Randell, eds, *Reframing 9/11*, 3.

32 Susan Sontag, 'The Talk of the Town', *The New Yorker*, September 24th, 2001, <http://www.newyorker.com/archive/2001/09/24/010924ta_talk_wtc>, accessed August 2012.

and the official version could not be doubted. Any serious attempts to understand the event would have disturbed the fragile narrative construct on which much of the response was based. As Henry Giroux argued of 9/11 and the rhetoric surrounding it, 'Dialogue, reason, and thoughtfulness slowly disappeared from the public realm as every encounter was framed within circles of certainty, staged as a fight to the death.'[33]

The representation of George W. Bush is crucial in this regard. He looked to restore the heroic presidency through recourse to old Western tropes: as Faludi suggests, 'The attack on home soil triggered a search for a guardian of the homestead, a manly man, to be sure, but one particularly suited to protecting and providing for the isolated American family in perilous situations.'[34] While Bush had run for president in 2000 on a platform of 'caring conservatism', after 9/11 he recast himself as a cowboy in the Old West to fulfil the role Faludi claims the American people craved. To do so, Bush employed the language of the movies: Osama Bin Laden was 'Wanted: Dead or Alive', the president channelling John Wayne in *True Grit* (Henry Hathaway, 1969) by promising to 'smoke him out of his cave' (rhetoric which was parodied in Michael Moore's *Fahrenheit 9/11* [2003]). The popular conceptions of Bush and his post-9/11 policies are summarised by television film *DC 9/11: Time of Crisis* (Brian Trenchard-Smith, 2003), which represents the president (Timothy Bottoms) as 'a Kryptonite-proof commander in chief ... part Hulk Hogan, part Rambo, and part Dirty Harry'.[35] In essence, Bush portrayed himself, and was portrayed, as the tough, strident, conventionally masculine warrior, who distilled an enormously complex international situation into a series of binary oppositions: America was wholesome and good, and terrorists were 'cowards' and 'evil-doers'. Where the situation was complex and uncertain, Bush's rhetoric provided clarity.

33 Henry Giroux, *Hearts of Darkness: Torturing Children in the War on Terror Paradigm 2010*, excerpted in 'Torturing Democracy', *Truthout*, <http://www.truth-out.org/torturingdemocracy67570>, quoted in Sara Brady, *Performance, Politics and The War on Terror* (London: Palgrave Macmillan, 2011), 20.

34 Faludi, *The Terror Dream*, 191–2.

35 Ibid., 63.

It was a basic narrative that justified an exercise of power that proved enormously damaging to the United States' reputation. On September 16th 2001, Vice President Dick Cheney stated that in order for the nation to triumph over the terrorists, it would have to explore 'The Dark Side'.[36] Although the 'war on terror' involved initial, fairly conventional military interventions in Afghanistan and Iraq, Arthur Schlesinger Jr. argued 'the Bush administration's extra-legal counterterrorism program presented the most dramatic, sustained and radical challenge to the rule of law in American history.'[37] Passed in October 2001, the Patriot Act significantly undermined the civil liberties of Americans. The legislation dramatically reduced restrictions on law enforcement agencies' abilities to search telephone, e-mail communications, medical, financial, and other records. It also broadened the discretion of law enforcement and immigration authorities in detaining and deporting immigrants suspected of terrorism. Outside the legislative arena, further extraordinary measures adopted were the illegal arrest, detention and (in some cases) torture of 'enemy combatants' suspected of involvement with terrorism at Guantanamo Bay, some of whom were incarcerated for several years without being formally charged or tried. Another measure adopted, known as 'extraordinary rendition', involved the arrest and secret deportation of foreign nationals, suspected of terrorist offences despite an absence of hard evidence, to a location more amenable to illegal practices of torture. These crimes have severely undermined America's reputation as a paragon of freedom and virtue. As Aslan suggests of the psychological impact of these illegalities, 'The narrative that Americans constructed to help make sense of 9/11 no longer seems so straightforward and uncomplicated as it so often does in the movies.'[38] The basic story of a battle between 'good' and 'evil' would not suffice given the obvious moral ambiguity of the 'war on terror'.

36 Dick Cheney, 'Interview on *Meet the Press*', September 16th, 2001, <http://www.freerepublic.com/focus/f-news/525111/posts>, accessed August 2012.

37 Arthur Schlesinger Jr., quoted in Jane Mayer, *The Dark Side: The Inside Story of How the War on Terror Turned into a War on American Ideals* (New York: Random House, 2008), 8.

38 Aslan, 'Foreword', xii.

It is my contention that *The West Wing* represents the most sustained popular cultural critique of the policies pursued by the Bush administration following 9/11. As McCabe suggests, *The West Wing* attempted, 'for better or worse, to give voice to America desires and beliefs at a time when public opinion lurched rightward and sought comfort in traditional core values.'[39] The programme reacted quickly to the terrorist attacks: 'Isaac and Ishmael', which premiered on October 3rd, 2001, was one of the earliest fictional explorations of the terrorist threat and post-9/11 American foreign policy. The episode existed outside the narrative arc of the programme, featuring the president's senior staff debating American foreign policy and the terrorist threat with young visitors to the White House during a security alert. The episode was widely derided as a pious and pretentious response to the atrocity but, as Parry-Giles and Parry-Giles note, it offered 'a different discourse than those [of] President Bush and other public officials. It presented a dialogic rhetoric that symbolically invited participation and disputation about the terrorism confronting the United States.'[40] 'Isaac and Ishmael' can be distinguished from many of the other immediate responses to the attacks in popular culture, as it sought to comprehend 9/11 in a period in which 'even many of the most astute critics refused to place the events in a political or social context from which they might be understood'.[41]

I will demonstrate, through a discussion of visual style, how *The West Wing* continued this critique through its third, fourth, and fifth seasons, evolving from post-Cold War confidence in America's unchallenged global position, to a post-9/11 sense of unease regarding the exercise of force. To illustrate this, I will examine four episodes in detail: 'A Proportional

39 McCabe, *The West Wing*, 99.

40 Parry-Giles and Parry-Giles, *The Prime-Time Presidency*, 160. Indeed, *The West Wing* lost its critics' choice award to *24* in the year following 9/11, a programme which espouses many of the same attitudes promoted by the Bush administration in its response to the 9/11 attacks. I will explore *24*'s representation of the 'war on terror' in relation to its fictional presidency in Chapter Five. – Ezell, 'The Sincere Sorkin White House', 172–3.

41 Lynn Spigel, 'Entertainment Wars: Television Culture After 9/11', *American Quarterly* 56/2 (2004), 239.

Response', from the programme's first season, chronicles Bartlet's first use of military force after an American aircraft is blown up by Syria, and is indicative of the optimistic and relaxed attitude towards American military power in the immediate post-Cold War period; 'Posse Comitatus', from the third season, shows Bartlet wrestling with a post-9/11 conundrum: whether or not to assassinate a foreign leader who has orchestrated terrorist attacks on the United States; 'Gaza' and 'Memorial Day', from the fifth season, feature Bartlet resisting calls for a full-scale military assault on the Gaza Strip following a terrorist attack against American personnel in Israel. I will examine the ways in which *The West Wing*, through camera movement, framing and *mise-en-scène*, distinguishes President Bartlet from President Bush, and places him in various poses that invite comparison with more measured and appropriate real-life models of presidential power. Through the exploration of the ill-defined 'terrorist threat' on the United States, *The West Wing* raises significant issues regarding the appropriate exercise of executive power and its limitations in an interdependent and globalised world, significantly countering the stark divisions peddled by the Bush administration. The representation of President Bartlet works to complicate Bush's notion that, in the war against terror, 'you are either with us, or you are with the terrorists.'

'A Proportional Response'

Although 'A Proportional Response' also features developing narrative arcs such as Sam's relationship with a sex worker and the appointment of Charlie as the president's personal aide, its central concern is with Bartlet's decision to take military action against Syria. The president dismisses the military's calls for a measured response to the attack in favour of something more aggressive, but he is ultimately reined in by his closest advisors. The episode is optimistic about America's use of military power, showing that although Bartlet looks to avenge the death of his physician through the violent annihilation of civilians, the system of checks and balances is robust, and the president is placed back upon an appropriate path. This first season episode is indicative of America's confident post-Cold War attitude towards incursions in foreign lands, secure in its status as the last remaining superpower, and responsible in the ways in which it wields this unchallenged authority.

This episode participates in the re-evaluation of the president's role in the post-Cold War geopolitical environment. While *Air Force One* and *Independence Day* attempted to reinstate the heroic presidency through a return to old forms and certainties, *The West Wing* is more complex. While acknowledging America's unrivalled position at the head of the global community, 'A Proportional Response' also articulates the more diffuse threat environment following the collapse of the Soviet Union. Simultaneously, it addresses issues surrounding presidential power within this new context – although Bartlet has the *means* to conduct the nation's affairs in a bullish, confrontational and militaristic manner, *The West Wing* suggests that America did not achieve its enormous power by engaging in such behaviour (a matter open to considerable debate), and its reputation would be significantly undermined should it resort to such action. In this way, *The West Wing* 'remains within a long tradition that represents the US in discourses of innocence and pureness of will', the programme's early seasons capturing a moment in which America was more at ease with itself and less restless in international affairs.[42]

'A Proportional Response' begins with Bartlet adopting a more familiar, Cold War-style military posture. The president is introduced as he marches to the Oval Office, the camera tracking leftwards along the walkway outside past the windows, glimpsing the portrait of George Washington which hangs on the wall, before moving rightward, following Bartlet and Leo (John Spencer) after they stride into shot. The camera is pushed backwards by Bartlet's march into his secretary's office, pivots, and then is propelled along behind him as he enters the Oval Office. As he reaches his desk, the president complains at not being able to locate his reading glasses, the camera circling around him as he remonstrates with his staff.[43] The vigorous

42 Simon Philpott and David Mutimer, 'Inscribing the American Body Politic: Martin Sheen and Two American Decades', *Geopolitics* 10/2 (2005), 335–6.

43 The similarities with President Shepherd's march to The Oval Office at the beginning of *The American President* are immediately apparent, albeit achieved in *The West Wing* through Steadicam rather than the traditional editing techniques of its predecessor. – Bruzzi, 'Men's Cinema', 199.

movement here appears to reflect Bartlet's impatience to exact retribution – it is driven by his strident march into the office, and then swirls around him as he laments the absence of his spectacles. Crucially, the smooth nature of the camera movement, enabled by the use of Steadicam, also lends an aura of presidential power to proceedings: it is Bartlet's agency which is motivating this whirlwind of activity, the balletic movement of the camera around him demonstrating his ultimate control over the situation. Bartlet's desire for control is reinforced by the glimpse of Washington's portrait: the president's complaint that failure to take swift and decisive action in response to the terrorist attack makes him look 'candy-ass' might be indicative of a desire to live up to Washington's astounding military accomplishments in commanding a victory in the American War of Independence.

As demonstrated by the opening sequences of *Dave* and *The American President*, comparison with the achievements of the Founding Fathers is a traditional means of assessing presidential performance and, as Barry Schwartz suggests, Washington is America's 'heroic prototype'.[44] Furthermore, as Mark Kann observes, Washington was considered by ministers, writers, and citizens to be 'the father of the country'.[45] Having never served in the military, Bartlet is anxious to prove his competence in matters of national defence, and demonstrate that he is capable of behaving heroically in the same ways as his predecessors, or 'fathers', are perceived to have. However, what Bartlet has not yet come to understand is that, following the collapse of the Soviet Union, 'the international environment … [did not] lend itself to the kinds of strong, dynamic leadership that were required during the Cold War.'[46]

The West Wing articulates the delicate balance the United States attempted to strike in the aftermath of the Cold War between interventionism and isolationism, and 'A Proportional Response' draws attention to the pitfalls faced by the president in making such decisions. As Barger

44 Barry Schwartz, 'The Character of Washington: A Study in Republican Culture', *American Quarterly* 38/2 (Summer 1986), 218.

45 Mark Kann, 'Manhood, Immortality and Politics During the American Founding', *The Journal of Men's Studies* 5 (November 1996), 79.

46 Barger, 'The Incredible Shrinking Image', 77.

suggests, the international environment was 'increasingly intractable and more complicated' following the collapse of the Soviet Union.[47] In accordance with this observation, *The West Wing* employs another presidential image, which both reinforces and undermines Bartlet's assertion that any kind of aggression against America must be met with 'total disaster': following the scene in the Situation Room, we cut to a portrait of President Theodore Roosevelt hanging in the eponymous Roosevelt Room. Roosevelt was renowned for his robust masculinity, having been an explorer, hunter and soldier, and was a firm advocate of interventionism where the interests of the United States were directly threatened. His corollary to the Monroe Doctrine, an 1899 speech entitled 'The Strenuous Life', argued that

> while a nation's first duty is within its own borders, it is not thereby absolved from facing its duties in the world as a whole; and if it refuses to do so, it merely forfeits the right to struggle for a place among the peoples that shape the destiny of mankind.[48]

Roosevelt's words appear to justify Bartlet's doctrine of intervention, the fictional president's policy further reinforced by Roosevelt's later suggestion that civilisations which enjoy sustained periods of tranquillity and prosperity are unlikely to achieve true greatness. Reflective of discourses surrounding America's national mission in the post-Cold War environment, the 'loss of the virile fighting qualities' would cause enormous problems for any nation, however 'cultured' and 'prosperous' they may be.[49] However, aside from the teddy bear, perhaps Roosevelt's most famous contribution to popular culture was his oft-quoted maxim for American foreign policy: 'Speak softly and carry a big stick'. This phrase is widely understood to suggest that negotiation and diplomacy are the foundation of any successful foreign policy, and overwhelming military force should only ever

47 Ibid., 59.

48 Theodore Roosevelt (1899), *The Strenuous Life: Essays and Addresses* (New York: Cosimo, 2006), 16.

49 Theodore Roosevelt, 'Address before the University of Berlin, May 12th, 1910', in Theodore Roosevelt, *Roosevelt, His Life, Meaning and Messages* (New York: Current Literature Publishing, 1919), 1066.

be deployed as a last resort. The adage appears to advise caution wherever possible, something Bartlet's initial strategy certainly does not.

The president's wish to inflict maximum possible damage in retribution for the crime is challenged by the Chairman of the Joint Chiefs of Staff, Admiral Fitzwallace (John Amos), who argues that such a response would be immensely damaging to America's standing on the international stage. The only acceptable option is to remove a transmitter and an intelligence headquarters, a more measured approach. Bartlet's acceptance of the limitations placed on his exercise of power is accompanied by a distinct shift in visual style and *mise-en-scène*. Where previously the camera was propelled along by Bartlet's desire to act aggressively, the withdrawal from this confrontational position has an inverse impact. When Bartlet gives the order for the drastically curtailed military response, the camera tracks in on his face to settle into a profile shot, and he is quiet, with his head slightly bowed. In contrast to his bullish attitude, here the president is contemplative and withdrawn.[50] He reinforces his uncertainty when he leaves the room, stating, 'I honestly don't know what the hell we're doing here.' Bartlet's insecurity is reiterated later in the episode as he prepares to address the nation regarding the intervention. As he discusses his televised address with speech writers Toby (Richard Schiff) and Sam (Rob Lowe), Bartlet is suddenly frozen in position, hemmed in between the two other men as they discuss the content of the speech. The *mise-en-scène* is chaotic and cluttered, as people bustle in the background, and where previously the camera had moved swiftly and elegantly through the Oval Office, now it is largely static and uses more traditional techniques of shot-reverse-shot to capture the conversation between Bartlet and his advisors. This sense of confusion is reinforced by the inability of the intelligence services to determine whether the military strike was actually successful in hitting its targets, Bartlet's impatience erupting when he bellows, 'Oh for crying out loud, will someone get on to CNN to find out if we hit anything?' This is

50 Bartlet's posture here recalls the representation of John F. Kennedy as contemplative and considered, as shown in *Crisis* (1963), and memorialised by Aaron Shikler's official White House portrait of him.

indicative of Barger's suggestion that the global communications revolution has effectively downsized the presidency, as the office no longer has a monopoly over information and knowledge.[51]

Therefore, *The West Wing* appears to be making a wider point regarding the reduction in presidential power following the Cold War. This critique is achieved through shifts in visual style: where Bartlet attempted to recreate the militaristic Cold War presidency, the use of Steadicam reflected his stridency and aggression. When the president's ability to act with this level of authority is challenged, the less mobile camera implies that the president is no longer the all-knowing being he was perceived to be during the Cold War, simultaneously acknowledging that the geopolitical environment in which Bartlet operates is decidedly more complex.

However, this is not to say that 'A Proportional Response' laments this supposed decline in the president's power. The tone and style of the episode is far more indicative of contemporaneous discourses surrounding the United States as the world's only 'indispensable nation', and is optimistic about the nature of American power and her position globally. While the president may feel the punishment does not reasonably atone for the crime, this option ensures that America behaves in a righteous and acceptable manner, always ensuring that the risk to civilians and American personnel is kept to an absolute minimum. Bartlet could, as Leo suggests, 'conquer the world like Charlemagne' if he so wished, because America sits unchallenged astride the globe, but this would not be in keeping with the values on which the nation was founded. Indeed, the measured response to the attack is indicative of the Clintonian notion that America will only maintain its global hegemony through the responsible exercise of its awesome power. As National Security Advisor Anthony Lake suggested of America in the post-Cold War moment,

> Our leadership is sought and respected in every corner of the world. ... Around the world, America's power, authority, and example provide unparalleled opportunities to lead.[52]

51 Barger, 'The Incredible Shrinking Image', 77.

52 Anthony Lake, 'From Containment to Enlargement' (September 21st, 1993), quoted in McCrisken, *American Exceptionalism and the Legacy of Vietnam*, 161.

This reinforces the neoconservative notion of the 'unipolar moment', whereby following the collapse of the Soviet Union, America is 'the only country with the military, diplomatic, political and economic assets to be a decisive player in any conflict in whatever part of the world it chooses to involve itself.'[53] Crucially, however, *The West Wing* is keen to align itself simultaneously with this 'unipolar moment', and to the optimistic discourses surrounding America's inherent 'innocence and pureness of will' which have proliferated in mainstream Hollywood films about American politics.[54] As Leo tells Bartlet,

> We're behaving as a superpower ought to. … It's how you behave if you're the most powerful nation in the world. It's proportional, it's reasonable, it's responsible, it's merciful.

Leo ultimately convinces Bartlet of this course of action when he says, 'It's what our fathers taught us.' Given the references to Washington and Roosevelt earlier in the episode, we can presume that Leo refers not to their biological fathers but the presidential forefathers, who argued for reasonable and appropriate measures in response to America's enemies.[55] Indeed, the *idea* of America is based on the desire to escape the kind of tyranny and aggression which characterised colonial rule, a lesson which Bartlet has just learned. Despite great military success, Washington was known for his restraint, his sense of duty and his pacifism.[56] Roosevelt had a similarly ambivalent relationship with military action because, despite being known for his 'cowboy' image, he won a Nobel Peace Prize in 1906 for successfully negotiating an end to the Russo-Japanese War. In taking heed of the lessons handed down to him from his presidential predecessors, Bartlet is learning to become a 'Patriot-King'; a towering leader who is resolute

53 Krauthammer, 'The Unipolar Moment', 24.

54 Philpott and Mutimer, 'Inscribing the American Body Politic', 335.

55 This notion will be developed in the next section of this chapter in which I examine Bartlet's attempts to negotiate his complex relationship with his own biological father and his presidential forefathers.

56 Schwartz, 'The Character of Washington', 206.

and determined, but also intelligent, pious, moderate and reasonable in ways that the monarchs which ruled America under colonialism were not.

This tone of optimism and confidence is most clearly demonstrated through the use of music, which recycles the triumphant orchestral title theme in various guises throughout. This becomes most apparent when Bartlet has relaxed his frustrated aggression, and introduces himself to his new aide, Charlie (Dulé Hill), discussing with him ways in which they might be able to outlaw the weapons which killed Charlie's mother. The exchange is handled in close-up, creating a feeling of spatial and emotional proximity to the president: he is a warm, comforting and reassuring presence. Charlie's awe and respect is clearly intended to be replicated by the audience: Bartlet is the embodiment of the benign use of American political and military power in the post-Cold War environment. The use of the music here underlines this impression, lending a warm, genteel feel to the exchange, and emphasising the overwhelming reverence the programme has for the president. This worshipful attitude is reinforced as Bartlet begins to deliver his speech: the camera, as it had done earlier in the episode, moves lithely around the room, capturing the awe-struck faces of his senior staff as they witness a presidential moment. Charlie is instantly integrated into the group when he says, 'I've never felt like this before', emphasising the notion that the president's staff are in the presence of true greatness.

'Posse Comitatus'

In marked contrast to the tone of optimism regarding America's foreign policy shown in 'A Proportional Response', the third season's finale, 'Posse Comitatus', throws many of these initial assumptions into doubt. Where in the earlier episode the course of action seemed obvious, the enemy limited and easily defined, this post-9/11 narrative challenges the notion of certainty.[57] Bartlet is faced with the difficult decision to assassinate an ally of

57 The 'Posse Comitatus' Act of 1878 was designed to limit the power of local governments and law enforcement agencies to use federal military personnel for law

the United States, Qumari defence minister Abdul Shareef (Al No'mani), who is thought to have orchestrated terrorist attacks against American interests.[58] Bartlet's decision is framed by his attendance in New York at a performance of *The Wars of the Roses*, an adaptation and abridgement of Shakespeare's tripartite *Henry VI*. Aside from the assassination, the episode also covers Bartlet's first meeting with his election opponent, Republican Robert Ritchie (James Brolin), and the murder of Simon Donovan (Mark Harmon), the Secret Service agent assigned to protect C.J. (Allison Janney) after she received death threats. I will now analyse this episode as indicative of *The West Wing*'s attitude towards American power in a post 9/11 environment, and how the stylistic shifts which accompany this change impact upon the representation of the president.

The representation of the Situation Room demonstrates the most apparent difference between the pre- and post-9/11 episodes. Where 'A Proportional Response' framed the majority of exchanges from table height, the establishing shot of the Situation Room here is taken from the floor, the camera lurking in the corner of the room before slowly shifting towards the table as the military officials begin discussion. In direct contrast to the more traditional framing devices of the earlier episode, which create a sense of control over proceedings, this unusual camera angle perhaps reflects the paranoia and uncertainty of the situation. Bartlet acknowledges the absurdity of the circumstances, but his attempts at humour are contradicted by the visual style which emphasises the moral ambiguity of the situation, and the burden placed upon him.

The psychological pressure on Bartlet is demonstrated when he meets Abdul Shareef at the White House, the president's interiority explored through close-up. As Shareef extends his hand to him, Bartlet whispers under his breath, 'Not in the Oval Office.' The look of guilt on Bartlet's

---

enforcement. In essence, its passage sought to prevent the possibility of a military dictatorship in the United States, and any action made by the military on American soil must exist within the Constitution or an Act of Congress.

58 Qumar is a fictional country, although it can be understood as akin to Saudi Arabia – an ally of the United States, but it is a bond forged by necessity rather than mutual affection.

face, in conjunction with the solemn and statuesque figures of Leo and Admiral Fitzwallace who stand behind the president framed in contemplative profile shot, reinforces the notion, perpetuated throughout the life of *The West Wing*, that the office is a sacred space (one may not swear or malign the president within its walls, for example). Bartlet cannot bring himself to perform such an act of betrayal in what he perceives to be a sanctified location. The refusal to shake Shareef's hand indicates Bartlet's unwillingness to demean the presidency: if he must act outside the bounds of American law to protect the nation, he will attempt to do so without blemishing the hallowed halls in which he works. This action must be taken *outside* the presidency, both physically (the action must not occur on American soil), and constitutionally.

Because 9/11 did not happen within the fictional world of the programme, *The West Wing* is able to sidestep the tendency within popular culture to constantly relive it, and is thus afforded the critical space to allude to its implications in various ways. *The Wars of the Roses* contains weighty themes regarding a once ordered nation thrown into chaos and barbarism as moral codes are subverted in the pursuit of revenge and power. This might be interpreted as roughly analogous of America's abuse of power in retaliation for the 9/11 attacks: the play laments the decline of chivalry in battle, with the assassination of Shareef employed to comment upon the extra-legal tactics adopted in the 'war on terror'.[59] The theatre visit also raises the spectre of Abraham Lincoln who, like Bartlet, had to adopt extra-legal strategies to save the nation, violating the rights of individual states by signing the Emancipation Proclamation in 1863. Bartlet's similarly difficult decision is lamented by *The West Wing* as a tragedy: the themes of the play, the plot to assassinate Shareef and the death of the Secret Service agent appear to function as a microcosm of the trauma America has experienced and was experiencing, and the loss of innocence which has accompanied her actions in the 'war on terror'.

59 For broader discussion of the themes of Shakespeare's *Henry VI* plays, see Stuart Hampton-Reeves and Carol Chillington Rutter, *The Henry VI Plays* (Manchester: Manchester University Press, 2006).

The montage sequence which best encapsulates this notion is one in which Simon's bullet-riddled body is examined by police as it lies on the floor of the convenience store, cross-cut with C.J. sitting on a bench outside the theatre weeping over his death, and Bartlet contemplating the best course of action regarding Shareef. The non-diegetic music which underpins the sequence is Jeff Buckley's cover of Leonard Cohen's 'Hallelujah', a painful and elegiac song which ties all the disparate narrative strands together to form a coherent depiction of America's loss of innocence.[60] As McCabe argues of 'Hallelujah' in *The West Wing*, 'Weaving biblical references into this melancholic hymn to love, gospel rhythms mixed with a waltz, the song sung by Buckley textually layers with intricacy and nuance the personal cost of political power.'[61] There is most certainly a personal dimension to this sequence, as it demonstrates Bartlet's acceptance of the incredible burdens of the office during the 'war on terror', but, given the common synonymy of the president and the country, it is fairly clear that this tragedy is also a national one. The roses which Simon bought for C.J. lie smashed and strewn across the convenience store floor, calling to mind both the name and subject matter of the play – a ruinous war which destroys a nation which was once perfect.

This process of mourning lost innocence through stylistic choices reaches its apogee in the sequence in which Bartlet orders the assassination of Shareef. Bartlet leaves his theatre seat to discuss the action with Leo. The president's fears regarding the assassination coalesce around the inevitable questions that will be raised regarding America's (ab)use of power. In contrast to 'A Proportional Response', Bartlet is hesitant not only because of the illegality of the action, but also because due process has not been allowed to take place. 'It's just wrong, absolutely wrong', he repeats to Leo. Leo's perspective is more akin to the Bush/Cheney attitude, arguing that Shareef is a bad person and that killing him is the only way to keep America

60 Despite being the newer version of the song, Buckley's 'Hallelujah' has become, in many ways, its definitive version. It is a painful, nostalgic elegy to lost love, and Buckley's mournful rendition of it makes it seem somehow older than Cohen's original.

61 McCabe, *The West Wing*, 81.

safe, despite the legal and ethical ramifications of the decision: as Vice President Dick Cheney suggested in the days following 9/11,

> We also have to work, though, sort of the dark side, if you will. ... A lot of what needs to be done here will have to be done quietly, without any discussion, using sources and methods that are available to our intelligence agencies, if we're going to be successful. That's the world these folks operate in, and so it's going to be vital for us to use any means at our disposal, basically, to achieve our objective.[62]

The theatrical setting is interesting too because Cheney's 'dark side' has been described by Jane Mayer as a sort of 'back stage' in which the war against terrorism could be conducted.[63] Furthermore, *The West Wing* uses lighting to render visual Bartlet's movement over to this 'dark side'. Reminiscent of the vivid contrast of *film noir*, Bartlet expresses his reservations as his face is bathed in brilliant light, where the more determined Leo is shrouded in ominous shadow. When Bartlet says the action will cause America to 'join the league of ordinary nations', this is in distinct contrast to 'A Proportional Response', where America's limited use of force is understood to be necessary to maintain her status as a world leader.

Bartlet's utterances regarding America's diminished international stature are obviously designed to raise the spectre of the 'war on terror' and, specifically, to draw attention to the damage which the extra-legal activities of the Bush administration have done to America's reputation. Have Bartlet's (and therefore Bush's) actions moved the United States away from being the world's righteous superpower to being merely another nation, similarly capable of the kinds of heinous acts of which her enemies are frequently guilty? As Bartlet begins to accept Leo's perspective as the only course of action available, he literally moves into the shadows. In essence, he crosses over to Cheney's 'dark side'. Bartlet eventually gives the order to kill Shareef with his head bowed, his face entirely obscured by darkness (see Figure 4.1), the movement away from the light into the darkness

62 Dick Cheney, interview on *Meet the Press*, September 16th, 2001, <http://emperors-clothes.com/9-11backups/nbcmp.htm>, accessed August 2012.

63 Mayer, *The Dark Side*, 9–10.

seemingly indicative of Bartlet's transformation from the righteous and confident president in 'A Proportional Response', to an altogether weaker, more frail Commander in Chief who, skulking in the shadows, must keep the crimes he has committed a secret from the American people; only *he* can carry the burden.

4.1 President Bartlet (Martin Sheen) orders the assassination of Abdul Shareef in 'Posse Comitatus', season three, *The West Wing* (dir. Alex Graves, Warner Brothers Television, USA, 2002)

In a marked shift, the confident and bullish tone of voice Bartlet had in 'A Proportional Response', in which he rhapsodised about the power of the Roman Empire and the similar strength which America possesses, gives way to a whimper – Bartlet forlornly whispers 'Take him' to Leo when he gives the order to kill Shareef. This process reaches its conclusion when Bartlet is informed of Shareef's death. Images of Shareef being gunned down on the remote airstrip in Bermuda are cross-cut with the conclusion of the play, which prophesises a turbulent future for England despite the impression that peace has been achieved. Bartlet now walks over to Leo. Leo is framed between the darkened balusters of the balcony, visually implying that the decision has imprisoned him. Bartlet receives the news and then moves behind the curtain, his profile shown in black silhouette. A careful combination of contrast lighting, and the employment of the theatrical display as a metaphor for the condition of the United States, draw one to the conclusion that Bartlet's decision means a troubled future for him and for the nation.

Many of the stylistic techniques employed in this episode – the close-up, the elegiac pop song, the ominous and sombre orchestral score, the sharp contrasts in lighting, and the theatrical references – all function to emphasise that Bartlet's decision was one of painful and enormous significance; dwelling upon it as he did showed him to be a man of conscience, moral fibre and awesome intelligence, and having to abandon his principles for the 'greater good' is, ultimately, tragic. The contrast with Bush, who was impatient, over-zealous and guided by a disturbing level of conviction given the complexity of the 'war on terror', could not be more apparent. As the theatre location suggests, Bartlet is more like Lincoln, forced out of necessity to act outside the parameters of the constitution to save the nation.[64] Despite taking the course of action he did, the formal techniques *The West Wing* employs show a man of Bartlet's temperament to be worthy of the office.

Having constructed Bartlet in the guises of Abraham Lincoln and, in the earlier episode, George Washington and Theodore Roosevelt, *The West Wing* provides further reiteration of his distinction from Bush by establishing his opponent for re-election as effectively an impersonation of the United States' then-current president. As Bartlet indulges in a cigarette after making the difficult decision, Governor Robert Ritchie arrives at the theatre having been stuck in traffic following his attendance at a baseball game (a leisure pursuit for 'ordinary Americans'). The episodes prior to this have hinted at the binary opposition between the two men, but this first meeting renders the contrast explicit – Bartlet is an Ivy League-educated intellectual and a Nobel Prize-winning economist with a profound understanding of international affairs, whereas Ritchie is populist, inarticulate and ignorant. Ritchie's grey hair, Southern accent and the fact that he is governor of Florida make it fairly obvious that he should be understood as symbolic of George W. Bush (whose brother Jeb was governor of Florida when Bush became president), infamous for his bumbling speeches, lack of

64 I will conduct a psychological analysis of this sequence later on in the chapter.

knowledge of international affairs and anti-intellectualism. The two men engage in a tête-à-tête as they sit across from each other. When Bartlet tells Ritchie that the Secret Service agent was murdered, Ritchie responds, 'Crime, boy, I don't know.' His folksy vocabulary and acknowledgement that he is ignorant regarding solutions to such problems immediately identify him as insufficiently serious to hold the position of president. Indeed, Bartlet says as much when he accuses Ritchie of turning 'being unengaged into a zen-like thing.' The moral ambiguity of the 'war on terror' demands a president of Bartlet's intellectual and moral stature.[65]

'Posse Comitatus' is illuminated via comparison with 'A Proportional Reponse' as it emphasises the uncertainty in America's global position after 9/11. While there is confusion and hesitancy regarding the bombing of the Syrian intelligence agency in the earlier episode, the tone and style is clearly one of optimism regarding America's exercise of military power. The conclusion of the episode – Bartlet addressing the American people via television broadcast – demonstrates the openness and transparency between the post-Cold War president and the public; the comforting notion that, although America still has enemies, they are insufficiently equipped and far too remote to pose any lasting threat and that, should the situation so demand, the president is able to 'blow them off the face of the earth with the fury of God's own thunder.' By marked contrast, the conclusion of 'Posse Comitatus' posits almost the opposite notion, and offers a powerful indictment of the position of the United States after 9/11 – Bartlet undertakes an illegal action to dispose of a foreign leader, he violates both US and international law, and there is no transparency regarding the action because of its incendiary nature. We are left in no doubt at the end of 'Posse Comitatus' that America is a more dangerous, more insecure and more troubled nation than the one in 'A Proportional Response', a grave situation that demands a contemplative and intellectual

65 As Parry-Giles and Parry-Giles suggest, 'The episode also resolves the ideological dissonance over the president's reelection, suggesting that his moralism and intellectualism prepare him for wartime necessities and that Ritchie lacks such intellectual prowess.' – *The Prime-Time Presidency*, 148.

leader to guide the United States through the morally murky waters of the 'war on terror'.

'Gaza' and 'Memorial Day'

The inability of Bartlet to control his nation's destiny is explored in great detail at the conclusion of season five, in which a US convoy on a fact-finding mission in Israel becomes the victim of a roadside bombing by a Palestinian terrorist group. The incident prompts vociferous calls for Bartlet to bomb parts of Gaza, which could mire the United States in an unwinnable war in the Middle East and invite reprisals at home. Bartlet resists calls for military action, ultimately inviting Israeli and Palestinian representatives to Camp David to resolve the crisis. In this section I will examine the ways in which the visual style reflects the chaos and complexity of the situation it represents. Where 'A Proportional Response' might be described as strident, bullish and confident, and 'Posse Comitatus' as dark, sombre and introspective, 'Gaza' and 'Memorial Day' illustrate the inability of the president to control unpredictable global events in the post-9/11 environment. It is clear from the dialogue, visual style and tone of this narrative that the reference point is the military incursion in Iraq, and the conciliatory and pragmatic Bartlet an antidote to the strident aggression of Bush.

In contrast to the elegant use of Steadicam in the opening scenes of 'A Proportional Response', which created a sense of certainty and stability despite the difficult situation, the breaking news of the bomb in Gaza is captured within the White House's communications bullpen through the use of handheld camera, lending not only a feeling of (manufactured) liveness to proceedings, but also an overwhelming sense of *un*certainty and fear. Handheld camerawork has its roots in direct cinema and observational documentary, but its use has proliferated in the post-9/11 period: some examples include the terror-themed action-thriller series *24*, the films of Paul Greengrass (*The Bourne Supremacy* [2004], *The Bourne Ultimatum* [2007] and *United 93* [2006]), *Children of Men* (Alfonso Cuarón, 2006), and *The Hurt Locker* (Kathryn Bigelow, 2008). Its employment is designed to create an aura of realism and a sense of events unfolding before our eyes, a stylistic inheritance from the pioneers of direct cinema in the 1960s. As McCabe suggests, the shaky mobile camera creates a sense of spontaneity and intimacy.[66] It has also become a kind of aesthetic shorthand for 'breaking news', especially given the preponderance of user-generated footage depicting the 9/11 attacks and the 7/7 London bombings broadcast on major news networks. Indeed, *The West Wing*'s adoption of techniques more readily associated with documentary and news footage demonstrates the extent to which 'representations of the [9/11] attacks are paradigmatic of the accelerating conflation of news and entertainment.'[67]

Having established what is going to happen in the pre-credits sequence, the first scene begins with the on-screen title '7:31am. Prior to the Explosion', with Toby and Josh (Bradley Whitford) being tracked by Steadicam through the halls of the West Wing into the communications bullpen, the conversation then shifting to C.J. and Toby discussing pharmaceutical imports from Canada. Flashback sequences of Donna (Janel Moloney) in Gaza are then followed by a conversation between National Security Advisor Kate (Mary McCormack) and Josh regarding poppy production in Afghanistan, again captured by Steadicam, before news of the attack breaks. These sequences can be characterised by a sense of stability, of natural order and flow, illustrative of a White House in control and command despite the challenges of the day. Following the onset of crisis precipitated by the attack, the visual style switches suddenly to handheld camera, cutting between Josh, Toby, Will (Joshua Malina), C.J. and C.J.'s assistant Carol (Melissa Fitzgerald) as they attempt to discern what has actually happened. The uncertainty is reflected in the camera movement, panning wildly across the room between Carol and C.J. as they struggle to contact their people on the ground in Gaza because of poor mobile reception. The sense of events unfolding before our eyes is reinforced when C.J. spots Toby's ex-wife Andy (Kathleen York) on a live news broadcast from Gaza as she speaks to Toby on the phone.

66 McCabe, *The West Wing*, 76.

67 Richard Schechner, '9/11 as Avant-Garde Art?', *PMLA* 124/5 (2009), 1822, quoted in Brady, *Performance, Politics, and the War on Terror*, 23.

This combination of handheld camera, lack of knowledge, technological difficulties and the news broadcast all function to create not only an overwhelming sense of immediacy, but also to capture a moment of uncertainty and lack of control: in this environment of chaos, the pretence that the president is in command of events can no longer be maintained. Indeed, he is entirely absent from these early scenes, in marked contrast to his consistent presence in 'A Proportional Response'. Furthermore, such a sequence directly challenges many critics of *The West Wing* who argue that the 'walk-and-talk' style dominates for the duration of the show's existence, creating a visual register of 'ceaseless forward motion.'[68] The characters within this sequence remain static, their *lack* of movement indicative of their *lack* of knowledge; the shaky, seemingly improvisatory camerawork illustrative of the pervasive feeling of insecurity.

President Bartlet is not immune from helplessness and uncertainty. When Leo tells the president of the terrorist attack in 'A Proportional Response', Bartlet responds with vaguely biblical language vowing to destroy the culprits. In 'Gaza', the president can only respond with a whimpering 'Oh God' when told of the deaths of the congressmen. His reaction to the death of Admiral Fitzwallace is met with stunned silence, in marked distinction from the vengeful, Old Testament-style rhetoric of the earlier episode. Although Bartlet might have been frustrated at the limited options available to him in 'A Proportional Response', at least there was comfort in knowing who the perpetrators were, and what the best course of action was in dealing with them. 'Gaza' contains no such reassurance. This level of doubt is reflected in Bartlet's angry summary of the events as he sees them:

> We don't know who did this or even if they meant to. Don't know how we'd hit them even if we did find out. Don't know who these guys were that the chairman arrested or why. Is there anything, anything at all, that we *are* certain of? Other than three US officials were brutally murdered?

Bartlet's candid expression of doubt is in marked contrast to the definitive nature of much of Bush's rhetoric on 9/11: unwavering in his confidence,

68 Guy Rundle, '*The West Wing*: BFI Television Classic', unpublished manuscript, 45.

Bush asserted, 'Make no mistake, the United States will hunt down and punish those responsible for these cowardly acts.'[69] Bartlet possesses no such self-assurance, as demonstrated by his visit to Admiral Fitzwallace's wife. Gazing downwards, Bartlet utters a similarly hackneyed maxim: 'The people responsible will be found and brought to justice.' However, the line is uttered robotically, with no conviction: he says what is expected of a president, but nobody really believes it. Mrs Fitzwallace acknowledges the capricious nature of world events when she says, 'Don't promise that. I know the world.' Where Bush painted the 'war on terror' as an uncomplicated battle that would result in the inevitable victory for the forces of good over the forces of evil, here Bartlet and Mrs Fitzwallace acknowledge the complexity of the international situation, and that the righteous do not always triumph.

This decline in confidence is rendered visually: Bartlet's exit from the Situation Room is not in the grand manner that is normally afforded the Commander in Chief in *The West Wing*. Having reacted angrily to the lack of information available, held a brief moment of silence in honour of those that have perished, and ordered contingency plans for a military response, he walks out of the room. Instead of a Steadicam being employed to follow his masculine strides, his movement is statically framed through a partially closed blind in medium-long shot, and the door closes behind him. The stasis of the camera, and its distance from Bartlet, appear indicative of a feeling of powerlessness, and an inability to undertake a course of action which does not mire the United States in an intractable conflict.

Bartlet's changing relationship with the use of rhetoric is also significant in relation to the post-9/11 environment and Bush's 'war on terror', as well as the shifting attitude of the programme towards military intervention and diplomacy. In 'A Proportional Response', Bartlet was comfortable with using biblical rhetoric in his response to the terrorist attack. In 'Memorial Day', when Bartlet has to address the American people via

69 George W. Bush, 'US "Will Hunt Down And Punish" Terrorists, Bush Says', September 11th, 2001, <http://www.defense.gov/news/newsarticle.aspx?id=44914>, accessed August 2012.

live television broadcast, he changes the speech written for him at the last minute, removing phrases such as 'tyranny of terror' and 'death mongers', dismissing the language as something out of the novels of J.R.R. Tolkien. In contrast to Bush, whose inflammatory 'Axis of Evil' speech in 2002 had an adverse effect on America's ability to negotiate with rogue states such as Iran and North Korea, Bartlet appears wary of using the wrong words for fear of making things worse. Bartlet refuses to construct a fantastical, pseudo-biblical narrative of good versus evil, which is both inaccurate and inflammatory. The muted tones with which he condemns the attack are greeted with howls of derision from a hostile Republican opposition, but Bartlet refuses to budge, appearing measured, careful and moderate where the opposition are hasty, reckless and disproportionate.

In addition to the visual style being reflective of a president hamstrung by the unpredictability of world events, *The West Wing* takes the opportunity to issue a damning critique of Bush-era foreign policy. In discussion with Toby as he practices his pitching before the traditional Memorial Day baseball game, Bartlet rages at the increasingly vociferous calls for him to bomb the Palestinian territories,

> Sure, hell, it's practically the American way. And who cares if it's exactly what those lunatics want? They push, we push back and they've got the holy war they've been praying for, with 1001 recruits to fight the big kid on the other side of the Atlantic. It's like bad Shakespeare. They're just waiting for me to play my role and chuck a big fat one down the middle.

Using language associated with the United States' national pastime as a potent metaphor, Bartlet here appears to be commenting simultaneously on the history of American foreign policy, the heavy-handed nature of the Bush administration, and the increasingly beleaguered nature of the presidency in the post-9/11 environment. Where Bush reacted to events impulsively and without hesitation, Bartlet is altogether more considered in what is a delicate atmosphere. The intervention in Iraq under the guise of protecting America from terrorism following 9/11 is clearly the reference point, with *The West Wing* attempting to draw subtle comparisons with earlier, real-life presidents and their management of major crises. When his military advisors suggest action should be taken now and evidence sought later, Bartlet rages,

> Are you suggesting we use the attack on our congressional delegation as a pretext for an attack on a country we don't know to be responsible? … I'm not going to bomb the Middle East because it will make everybody feel better!

The vitriol with which he expresses himself here appears similar to the criticisms levelled at the invasion of Iraq, based on vague intelligence (as it happens, completely false) that Saddam Hussein was somehow involved in the 9/11 terror attacks, and possessed weapons of mass destruction. Rather than adopt the reckless, incendiary diplomacy of the Bush administration, Bartlet's strategy appears more akin to representations of John F. Kennedy's handling of the Cuban Missile Crisis in October 1962.[70] His refusal simply to bomb Gaza into submission is reminiscent of Kennedy's attempt to control the conflict with the Soviet Union over Cuba, and dictate the course of events without resorting to violence. In another reminder of the way Kennedy handled the crisis, Kate suggests Bartlet could rescue the peace summit at Camp David by simply 'ignoring everything that has happened in the past twenty-four hours', reminding one of how Kennedy held Khrushchev to an earlier agreement which he had since rescinded. When Bartlet decides to pursue a peaceful, negotiated solution to the crisis and dismisses Leo's further calls for military intervention, he stands with his back to camera in front of the Oval Office window looking out, in a pose clearly evocative of the famous photograph of Kennedy at the window, itself referenced at the conclusion of the programme's title sequence. By invoking Kennedy in these ways, *The West Wing* appears to offer an alternative, pre-Vietnam model of presidential intervention to the heavy-handed response of the Bush administration. This impression is further underlined by a dialogue exchange between C.J. and Toby:

70 Given that Sheen played Kennedy in the eponymous 1983 television miniseries, it is conceivable that he will have channelled some of his portrayal of Bartlet through that performance.

> C.J.: Do you ever look around and think, 'If we're the ones in charge, this country's in a helluva lot of trouble'?
> Toby: Till I spend time with the other guys.

In effect, *The West Wing* offers an alternative version of reality: Bush-era Republicans are far too gung-ho for such a delicate international situation, and only Bartlet possesses the calm and intellect to achieve a peaceful end to the crisis.

Bartlet is often conspicuously silent when discussing the most appropriate course of action in Israel. He has been often described as a pseudo-religious figure, priest-like in his commitment to his duty, and unwavering in his faith.[71] In keeping with such an understanding, Bartlet is given two opposing points of view from which to decide, and *The West Wing* represents them in a binary fashion, seemingly using the conventional angel/devil metaphor so common in narrative storytelling (see Figure 4.2).

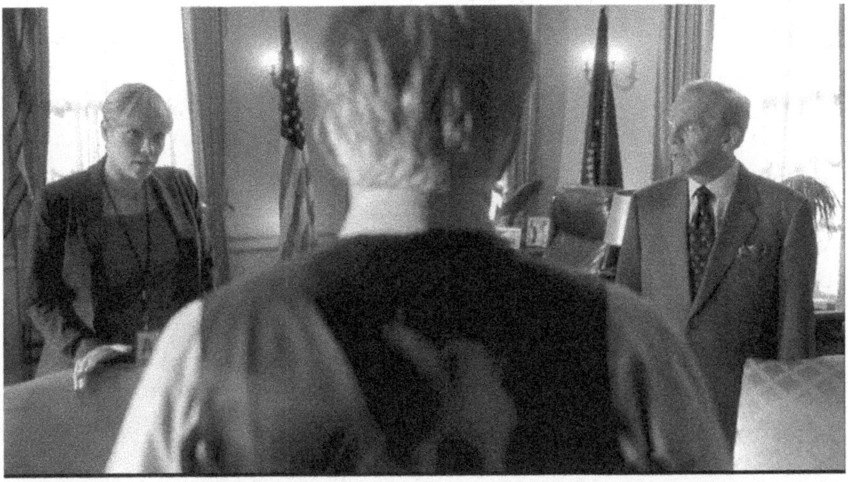

4.2 President Bartlet contemplates military action in Israel with his advisors in 'Memorial Day', season five, *The West Wing* (dir. Christopher Misiano, Warner Brothers Television, USA, 2004)

71 Crawley, *Mr Sorkin Goes to Washington*, 163.

Whereas Leo is committed to the military option, Kate feels that a diplomatic solution can be achieved. In deciding between war and peace, the camera is positioned behind Bartlet, with Kate framed on his left shoulder, Leo his right, creating the impression that Bartlet is caught between two opposing points of view, and two competing understandings of American foreign policy. That Bartlet ultimately chooses a peaceful, diplomatic negotiation over armed conflict by inviting the Israelis and the Palestinians to Camp David demonstrates the extent to which *The West Wing* offers an idealised vision of presidential power, and a clear alternative to Bush's handling of the 'war on terror'.[72]

Psychologising the President: Bartlet the Man/Bartlet the President

Josiah Bartlet represents the richest, most detailed and psychologically complex fictional president in film and television history. The fictional presidents discussed in the previous chapter are *textually* and *ideologically* intricate: the films graft older generic forms onto contemporary concerns surrounding the presidency in order to construct competing models of presidential leadership. However, *The West Wing* combines a similar complexity with a psychological exploration, investigating President Bartlet as man with a history; a fallible human being who had a troubled childhood and a difficult relationship with his father, and whose formative experiences are problematically, but inevitably, brought to bear on his presidency.

72 Bartlet's decision to invite the Israeli and Palestinian leadership to Camp David also invites comparison with President Jimmy Carter, who sought to resolve tensions between Israel and Egypt through careful, diplomatic negotiation. These processes culminated in thirteen days of secret discussions at Camp David, a direct result of which was the 1979 treaty between the two countries that ended thirty years of conflict. Again, this shows Bartlet's difference from Bush, and how the programme models him on earlier examples of presidential leadership.

Following the revelation of his multiple sclerosis at the end of the second season, *The West Wing* explores Bartlet's youth, and his relationship with his father, through flashback. This process is given fuller and clearer articulation halfway through the third season and beyond, as the president undergoes sporadic psychotherapy. This process becomes wedded to the programme's response to the 9/11 terrorist attacks, with Bartlet exorcising the ghost of his own father through an acceptance of the overwhelming burden of the presidency, culminating in his illegal assassination of Qumari Defence Minister Abdul Shareef. As Stanley Renshon, psychobiographer of Bill Clinton and George W. Bush, suggests, 'An absolutely critical question is this: Is the president's ambition primarily *personal* or *public*?'[73] Given the magnitude of events with which the presidency has to contend in the post-9/11 environment, *The West Wing* clearly feels it is necessary that Bartlet lay to rest the influence of his father in order to fulfil expectations of the office. As suggested previously, *The West Wing*'s tone and visual style changed substantially after 9/11. This section will address President Bartlet's character more specifically, and the ways it evolved in response to this traumatic event. This is the fundamental issue at the heart of *The West Wing*: Bartlet sits at the centre of a therapeutic narrative that looks to come to terms with the Bush administration's 9/11 policies and the 'war on terror'. Will Bartlet overcome the desire to please his now-deceased father and accept the awesome responsibilities of the presidency? I will demonstrate how *The West Wing* uses psychotherapy to establish Bartlet as a president worthy of leading the United States in this environment.

***

The exploration of the son's relationship with the deceased father prompts inevitable discussion of Sigmund Freud. Freud's theories surrounding the Oedipal complex and the primal father are now so familiar in popular psychology that they hardly require further reiteration but, for the sake of clarity, and to begin unpicking his theories and their relationship to *The West*

73 Stanley A. Renshon, *In his father's shadow: the transformations of George W. Bush* (Basingstoke: Palgrave Macmillan, 2004), 60.

Wing, I will sketch them briefly here. The Oedipal struggle emerges when the young boy realises the father to be a rival for his mother's love, resulting in an ambivalent relationship whereby the son resents and hates his father, but also strives to emulate him. In order to overcome this complex, Freud argues, the sexual rivalry between father and son must be dissolved, and replaced by the son's identification with the paternal figure. While Freud's case studies demonstrated that *real* fathers were often disappointing, weak and ineffectual, the construction by the son of the idealised *primal* father begins a complex process, whereby the son tries to emulate the characteristics of this partially invented figure, while simultaneously repressing the reality of his father's inadequacies. Freud suggests that the origin of religion lies in an infantile longing for the absent, idealised father figure because, while the son may have had an ambivalent attitude to his father in life, the guilt engendered by his death results in 'the dead father becoming stronger than the living one had been.'[74] This guilt is then internalised by the son in the form of his superego which, Freud argues, is the idealised version of the self in the guise of the dead father.[75]

Of particular importance to *The West Wing*, and the American presidency in general, is Freud's extrapolation of this process into a wider formulation of the cultural superego, which posits the notion that the 'impression left behind by the personalities of great leaders' fashions a collective superego for an entire epoch of civilisation.[76] While these leaders may have been ridiculed, derided and generally maltreated in life, they 'attain divinity' in death.[77] This raises significant issues with regard to the characterisation of President Bartlet, as his psyche appears to be engaged in a battle to appease his father, while simultaneously fulfilling the expectations handed down to him from his presidential forefathers. Indeed, in their examination of Richard Nixon's psychology, Vamik D. Volkan, Norman Itzkowitz and

74 Sigmund Freud, 'Totem and Taboo', *The Origins of Religion: Totem and Taboo, Moses and Monotheism and Other Works* (London: Penguin Books, 1990), 204.

75 Sigmund Freud, 'Civilisation and its Discontents', in *Civilization, Society and Religion* (London: Penguin Books, 1991), 325.

76 Ibid., 335.

77 Ibid.

Andrew W. Dod identify a facet of Freud's Oedipus complex which is fundamental to the characterisation of Bartlet. In order to deal with the 'continuing influence of the complex', the adult may 'maintain certain unconscious manoeuvres in his personality'.[78] This would happen if the individual lacked the requisite psychological preparedness to surpass the father's achievements. This appears to be a defining characteristic of Bartlet's fictional presidency: a hesitancy to do what is right for fear of incurring the wrath of his intellectually inferior father. Essentially, in Freudian terms, Bartlet does not appear to be engaged in the common battle between his ego and his id, but between his own superego (his biological father) and the collective, cultural superego (his presidential fathers).

I will explore these issues through a close analysis of a handful of episodes of *The West Wing*: from the second season finale, 'Two Cathedrals', which, through flashback, captures Bartlet's difficult relationship with his father; the three episodes from the third season which deal explicitly with Bartlet's psychology ('The Two Bartlets', 'Night Five', and 'Hartsfield's Landing'); and then the final two episodes in which Bartlet attends therapy sessions ('Posse Comitatus' and 'Holy Night'), which deal with the president's conscience before and after the assassination of Shareef. This is an attempt to craft a psychological portrait of Bartlet that is not immediately self-evident from the text, examining how his psyche is excavated visually and narratively, building an impression of the ways in which *The West Wing* articulates Bartlet's difficulties in reconciling his presidency with his personal life. My analysis will revisit Freud's theories surrounding the Oedipal complex and the primal father to determine the ways in which Bartlet's psychosis is established, understood, and ultimately contained, remedied by his acceptance of the enormity of the presidential role, and the appreciation of his position within a historical lineage. I challenge Jeff Smith's suggestion that the psychological exploration of Bartlet is undeveloped because *The West Wing* is primarily interested in the presidency, not the

78 Vamik D. Volkan, Norman Itzkowitz and Andrew W. Dod, *Richard Nixon: A Psychobiography* (Chichester: Columbia University Press, 1997), 15.

personality.[79] I contend that the two are not mutually exclusive: the man *makes* the president, and to a significant degree it is the personal foibles that ultimately determine presidential performance. Given the gravity of the international situation in which he finds himself, Bartlet's self-inspection is crucial as an illustration of his conscience and morality during the 'war on terror'. Although the president's therapy does not *dominate* the narrative structure of *The West Wing* in the way that Tony's (James Gandolfini) does in *The Sopranos* (David Chase, HBO, 1999–2007), it performs an important function in the characterisation of the president. Through my analysis, I will demonstrate how the programme is engaged in a reversal of the feminist maxim 'the personal is political': in *The West Wing*, the political is almost certainly personal.

There is a rich and varied body of scholarly work which applies psychoanalytic methodologies to biographical studies of former presidents, a phenomenon which is perhaps reflective of a compulsion in the postmodern era to understand the president as a human being rather than an aloof and distant figurehead. As George Reedy suggests, the presidency 'was a magnifying glass which would reveal any latent neuroses affecting its incumbent.'[80] Investigations such as Doris Kearns Goodwin's psychological portrait of Lyndon Johnson, Volkan, Itzkowitz and Dod's analysis of the psychology of Richard Nixon, Renshon's investigations of Clinton and Bush Jr., and Charles Strozier's excavation of Abraham Lincoln's psyche, all appear to identify their relationships with their parents as fundamental to an understanding of their presidencies. The sheer amount of scholarship that exists regarding the psychology of the president, and *The West Wing*'s participation in this tradition, affirms my suggestion that a psychological analysis of Bartlet's relationship with his father will generate greater understanding of the programme's representation of the president as a man and an institution.

There is a pattern established in these psychobiographies regarding the president's relationship with his parents: to a greater or lesser degree, the father is the parent who defines the man the president will become.

79 Smith, *The Presidents We Imagine*, 244.
80 Reedy, *The Twilight of the Presidency*, ix.

This is perhaps unsurprising because, as is so often suggested, the president acts, in many ways, as the nation's father. As is perhaps doubly unsurprising, it was George W. Bush's father who played the most significant role in his personal development. According to Renshon, although Bush spent most of his life in his (often absent) shadow, 'In George W.'s inner psychological world, it is quite clear his father ... looms large as an idealized object'.[81] However, even for a president who never knew his father (like Clinton), it is the complete *absence* of the paternal influence which can prove defining. As Renshon suggests, psychological literature stresses that

> weak identification with the father was associated with lower levels of moral development, and that boys from father-absent homes consistently scored lower than boys from father-present homes on a variety of indices of morality.[82]

I am not looking to establish Clinton's childhood as the defining explanation for his involvement with Monica Lewinsky, nor do I wish to suggest that a robust and cohesive understanding of all presidents can be achieved through such a method. It is merely an intriguing observation that scholarly works such as these appear to conform rigidly to a pattern established in Hollywood cinema: as Robin Wood suggests of Hollywood films in the Reagan era, the restoration of the father 'constitutes ... the dominant project, *ad infinitum* and *post nauseam*'.[83] Perhaps it is overstating the case to suggest the presidential psychobiography looks to 'restore' the father. Instead, it searches voraciously for him, placing him as a defining actor in the narrative of a future president even if, as was the case with Clinton, he was entirely absent. Indeed, as Juliet Mitchell argues, the father is such a dominant construct within our culture that 'he is present even in his absence.'[84] Such analyses conform closely to Freudian conceptions of the

81 Renshon, *In his father's shadow*, 54.

82 Stanley Renshon, *High Hopes: The Clinton Presidency and The Politics of Ambition* (New York: Nw York University Press, 1996), 168.

83 Wood, *Hollywood from Vietnam to Reagan ... and Beyond*, 152.

84 Juliet Mitchell, in *Women: The Longest Revolution Essays in Feminism, Literature and Psychoanalysis* (London: Virago, 1984), 231–2, quoted in Jonathan Rutherford, *Men's Silences: Predicaments in Masculinity* (London: Routledge, 1992), 113.

paternal bond, whereby it is the initially competitive, and subsequently identificatory, relationship to the father which wrenches the son away from the infantile attachment to his mother, and into society. To *become* president, it seems, requires a close identification with the father, but what kind of president the boy will become is determined by the degree of complexity within that relationship.

For example, although Kearns Goodwin gives ample demonstration of Johnson's intense bond with his mother, it was the movement towards his father as a pre-pubescent child which defined him: 'he listened to his father talk and, rejecting his mother's elocution lessons, adopted his father's crude, colourful, alive way of talking', which would prove a defining characteristic of his presidency.[85] This detachment from his mother triggered Johnson's suspicion of intellectuals.[86] Johnson's dreams established an intrinsic link between intellectualism and paralysis. He would often imagine himself as Woodrow Wilson, the president whose failure to cajole Congress into ratifying American membership of the League of Nations was swiftly followed by a paralysing stroke, and ultimately his death. As is indicative of pervasive attitudes towards the presidency, femininity was ultimately equated with weakness, and in this case, paralysis. It was Johnson's neurosis about his close affinity with his mother which drove him towards his father, and more conventionally masculine attributes.

In what is perhaps the defining real-world comparison to Bartlet in this particular case, Abraham Lincoln has been the subject of Strozier's detailed and expansive psychobiography. In a process of particular import to my analysis of the fictional president, Lincoln endured a significant struggle to liberate himself from the troublesome relationship he had with his father, and the guilt he experienced following his death (Lincoln could not bear to visit him even though he was dying). To exorcise this guilt and ill-feeling towards his biological father, Lincoln attempted to reinvent

85 Doris Kearns Goodwin, *Lyndon Johnson and The American Dream* (New York: Harper and Row, 1976), 34.

86 Ibid., 41–2.

himself in relation to the Founding Fathers.[87] According to Strozier, this psychological manoeuvre allowed Lincoln to obtain the requisite gravitas and sense of self to lead the United States through the collective trauma of the Civil War: 'As surrogate fathers in a psychological sense, the founders came to represent the integrity and authenticity so lacking in Lincoln's own sense of his biological father.'[88] Through this identification, 'Lincoln assumed a place in history which he quickly realized put him on a par with the founders.'[89] In Freudian terms, Lincoln triumphed over his biological father by reconstructing his superego in the guise of the Founding Fathers. Strozier's analysis of Lincoln is vital to my discussion of Bartlet's therapy: the similarities between Bartlet's psychological constitution and that of his real presidential predecessors suggest that *The West Wing* invites these comparisons. While it is widely thought that *The West Wing*'s popularity was because Bartlet was the president America *really* wanted, the programme appears keen to construct Bartlet as morally, intellectually, and psychologically worthy of such an honour. The therapeutic process by which Bartlet comes to this realisation will form the nucleus of my analysis.

However, it is crucial to maintain a sense of *The West Wing* within a history of audiovisual representation. Psychologising the president has become something of a preoccupation for Oliver Stone whose biopics, *Nixon* (1995) and *W.* (2008), put forward the notion that the presidencies of both Nixon and Bush Jr. were the result of troubled relationships with their parents, and traumas experienced in childhood. Like Bartlet, the Nixon of Stone's film is perceived to be driven by personal demons.[90] Through flashbacks, Stone develops a picture of Nixon's intense relationship with his pious mother, his cruel and dismissive father, and the traumas

87 Charles Strozier, *Lincoln's Quest for Union: A Psychological Portrait* (Philadelphia: Paul Dry Books, 2001) [2nd edn], 74.

88 Ibid.

89 Ibid., p. 87.

90 Richard Nixon is the only president definitively known to have undergone psychotherapy. For detailed analysis of his relationship with his psychotherapist, Dr Arnold Huitschnecker, see Anthony Summers and Robbyn Swan, *The Arrogance of Power: The Secret World of Richard Nixon* (London: Viking, 2000).

he experienced following the deaths of his brothers. Through this device, Stone suggests that Nixon's personal failings in office were the result of his difficult childhood. As suggested earlier, to pursue personal ends in public office is enormously problematic and, one might argue, the real-life Nixon and fictional Bartlet have much in common in this regard: where Nixon's seemingly unquenchable thirst for acceptance from the general public resulted in the calamity of Watergate (as his long-suffering wife Pat [Joan Allen] suggests, 'They'll never love you. No matter how many elections you win, they never will.'), Bartlet's desperation to attain the approval of his father leads to the obfuscation of his multiple sclerosis in his pursuit of the presidency, and the willingness to substitute moral clarity for political expediency whilst in office. As Henry Kissinger (Paul Sorvino) suggests of Nixon, 'Can you imagine what this man could have achieved if he had been loved?' Such a question could easily be levelled at President Bartlet.

While it has been important to establish the psychological investigation of Bartlet as merely a small part of a much larger scholarly and cinematic tradition, it is crucial to address this facet of *The West Wing* in relation to the representation of psychotherapy in television drama and, in more general terms, the presidency's relationship to television. It is perhaps unsurprising, given its penchant for the personal and intimate, that television has become somewhat preoccupied with representations of psychotherapy in recent years: Israeli programme *Be Tipul* (2005–8), and its American remake, *In Treatment* (2008–10), follow a psychotherapist through his weekly meetings with his patients. Of particular significance to *The West Wing* is a narrative which runs through both the Israeli and American versions: a fighter pilot seeks treatment after accidentally bombing a school while on a mission in the Middle East. Both narratives can be understood as attempting to process and understand some of the crimes committed in the battle against terrorism, issues which President Bartlet's therapy also looks to address.

The Sopranos attracted much critical attention for the ways in which it put its central character, Italian-American mobster Tony Soprano, through an intensive course of psychotherapy, as Tony attempted to reconcile the difficulties of managing two 'families': his biological family (wife and two children), and his Mafia friends and associates. Glen Creeber argues that

Tony's unwillingness to be confined by the strictures of the therapy sessions can be understood as an inevitable inability to confine what is essentially an expansive and spectacular cinematic creation (the 'gangster') within the private and personal world of television.[91] A similar process occurs in relation to President Bartlet's therapy sessions, albeit on a reduced scale. Bartlet makes plain his discomfort with the close analysis of his presidency in relation to his humanity, persistently challenging the therapist as to why he charges so much. Where the president may have previously enjoyed a status as a larger-than-life figure, allegedly god-like in his power to control events, when placed under the microscope of psychoanalysis, the mythological construction of the Commander in Chief does not stand up to scrutiny – it is perhaps difficult to accept that a president may be driven to triumph in personal battles rather than national and international ones. Indeed, as the ascent to the presidency may reveal the latent neuroses of the man behind it, so too has television slowly eroded the impression of the president as an omnipotent and infallible human being. Thomas Cronin and Michael Genovese, among others, suggest that television is the ultimate culprit for the overexposure of the presidency, resulting in a trivialisation of issues in American politics.[92] They identify the Clinton era as 'the moment when the distance between the president and the public evaporated forever.'[93] *The West Wing* has played a significant role in the erosion, with Bartlet's therapy sessions a particularly expressive example of this process.

The aesthetic conventions of television are significant. *The West Wing*'s visual style has been too rigidly defined by critics as preoccupied with slick, broad sweeps of the Steadicam through the corridors of power, employed in conjunction with a triumphantly patriotic orchestral score, developing an impression of the presidency as defined by a robust, forceful and dynamic conception of masculinity. These aspects of the programme's aesthetic strategies have been latched onto as indicative of its status as 'quality'

91 Glen Creeber, *Serial Television: Big Drama on the Small Screen* (London: British Film Institute, 2004), 103.

92 Cronin and Genovese, *The Paradoxes of the American Presidency*, 96–7.

93 Ibid.

television.[94] However, the stylistic choices adopted in the representation of Bartlet's therapy sessions speak more to the dynamics of regular television. It is telling that Creeber argues *The Sopranos*'s therapy sequences are reminiscent of a '"head-to-head" political interview', as *The West Wing*'s close-ups of Bartlet's contemplative face emphasise an intense interiority and level of emotion one more readily associates with soap opera, or the feminine mode of melodrama.[95] Indeed, Bartlet's therapy complicates the traditionally masculine conception of the presidency. The excavation of his psychology is emblematic of anxieties surrounding the presidency and its relationship with television: where the presidency is expansive and masculine in its conception, television is widely considered intimate and feminine. As Creeber suggests of *The Sopranos*, 'the therapy sessions ... force the viewer to take time out from the traditional attractions of the gangster genre ... the typically high-powered conventions of the genre are temporarily suspended'.[96] The investigation of Bartlet's psychology performs a similar function in *The West Wing*: it suspends the frantic nature of policy- and law-making, and pauses for a moment to develop a more human understanding of its fictional president, lending Bartlet a psychological depth absent in other representations of fictional presidents. This is a level of intimacy only really possible in television drama, as it is the form's '*gradual* excavation of character, desire, and perhaps even unconscious motivation' which enables this level of depth and complexity in the representation its president.[97]

94 For discussion and analysis of what constitutes 'quality' in American television drama, see Robert J. Thompson, *Television's Second Golden Age: From Hill Street Blues to ER* (New York: Syracuse University Press, 1997); Mark Jancovich and James Lyons, eds, *Quality Popular Television: Cult TV, the Industry and Fans* (London: British Film Institute, 2003); Janet McCabe and Kim Akass, eds, *Quality TV: Contemporary American Television and Beyond* (London: I.B. Tauris, 2007); Robin Nelson, *State of Play: Contemporary "High-End" TV Drama* (Manchester: Manchester University Press, 2007).

95 Creeber, *Serial Television*, 107.

96 Ibid.

97 Ibid., 108.

'Two Cathedrals' and The Flashback

The excavation of Bartlet's psyche does not, however, begin with his therapy sessions, but in the altogether more familiar form of the flashback. 'Two Cathedrals', the second season's finale, addresses the public exposure of Bartlet's multiple sclerosis and the sudden death of his private secretary and long-time friend Mrs Landingham (Kathryn Joosten). These events prompt the president to delve into his past in search of answers. *The West Wing* appears to suggest that Bartlet will only truly be a great president if he overcomes this scandal and, rather than step aside, runs for re-election out of the courage of his political convictions. As Cronin and Genovese suggest, 'Great presidents take risks ... effective presidential leadership is provided by those who follow their convictions and, at least on important issues, ignore middle-of-the-road pragmatism'.[98] Mrs Landingham, initially in flashback, and then in the rather literary form of a ghostly visitation, pushes Bartlet to stand up for what he believes.

Maureen Turim describes the flashback as the 'spontaneous recall of a memory image'.[99] This is certainly the case with Bartlet's flashbacks, whereby a close-up is followed by a fade to white, transporting the programme into the past. However, *The West Wing* adopts a peculiarly presidential twist: the flashbacks begin not merely through a close-up, as would be conventional, but through a close-up of Bartlet in profile, a familiar stylistic choice not only in the representation of Bartlet, but of presidents in general. This simple technique illustrates *The West Wing*'s careful negotiation of conventional aesthetic forms and its reverence for the presidency: the close-up is a familiar convention that signifies interiority, but Bartlet is framed in profile in order to reinforce his presidentiality.

The West Wing uses the flashback to illustrate the symmetry between past and present: the episode travels into the past to show the young Mrs Landingham demanding that the young Bartlet confront his father over the

98 Cronin and Genovese, *The Paradoxes of the American Presidency*, 78.

99 Maureen Turim, *Flashbacks in Film: Memory and History* (London: Routledge, 1989), 5.

issue of pay inequity between men and women at the private school which he attends. However, Bartlet recoils from the confrontation when his father slaps him for writing a newspaper editorial in which he criticises the librarian for excluding a number of controversial books from the shelves; as he writes in the article which so enrages his father, 'If you hide your ignorance, no-one will hit you and you'll never learn.' The irony, of course, is that the young Bartlet disguises his intelligence for fear of physical punishment. Indeed, as Freud suggests, the origins of guilt emerge from an initial fear of authority, which demand 'a renunciation of instinctual satisfactions', Bartlet retreating from an intellectual debate with his father primarily because he is afraid of the physical punishment that will inevitably follow.[100] Bartlet's father is overtly reminiscent of the Freudian primal father – formidable, terrifying, unreasonable – but Bartlet, even as an adult, still yearns for his approval. With his father now physically absent, but internalised in the form of his superego, Bartlet has, as Freud suggested, erected an internal authority, and renounces his instinct because of his fear of it.

This process reaches a hyperbolic zenith when, after Mrs Landingham's funeral in National Cathedral, Bartlet remains behind to confront God over his cruelty. It becomes apparent, however, that Bartlet's rage is directed as much at his own biological father as it is against the Holy Father. In psychoanalytic terms, it is difficult to differentiate between Bartlet's God and his father: as Freud suggests, 'the psychoanalysis of individual human beings ... teaches us with quite special insistence that the god for each of them is formed in the likeness of his father'.[101] Bartlet accuses God of exacting retribution for the president's dishonesty about his medical condition by killing Mrs Landingham in a random car accident, describing Him as a 'son of a bitch' and a 'feckless thug'. Despite his sins, Bartlet argues that he remains both a good man and a good president:

> 3.8 million new jobs, thirty million for conservation, bailed out Mexico, we're not fighting a war, I've raised three children ... Does that not get me out of the doghouse?

100 Freud, 'Civilisation and its Discontents', 319.
101 Freud, 'Totem and Taboo', 209.

The visual style of this sequence is typically grand, employing slow, considered tracking shots behind and alongside Bartlet as he strides up the aisle, emphasising the colossal scale of the cathedral (we are given an indication of the size of the building in an earlier scene in which Bartlet tells Charlie that the cathedral could accommodate the Washington Monument when laid on its side). It might be suggested that the size of the building is indicative of the enormous conflict raging between Bartlet and God, but when the flashbacks to the battles with his father are taken into account, it could be argued that this scene is also a re-enactment of Bartlet's Oedipal conflict, which has taken on a similarly awesome magnitude.

This reading is reinforced through the echoing of a flashback in which Bartlet's father demands that his son order his friends not to smoke in the school chapel: having challenged God for his vindictiveness, President Bartlet marches away from the altar, lights a cigarette, drops it, and crushes it beneath his shoe. This is the moment at which it becomes clear that Bartlet's rage is directed simultaneously at his biological father and his metaphysical one. Bartlet's furious dismissal of this paternal control – 'To hell with your punishments, to hell with you!' – could be interpreted as a riposte to his father's physical abuse. As it is spoken in Latin, and Bartlet's difficulties with his father appear to stem from his superior intelligence, this appears an appropriate reading. However, despite the provocative challenge to his two fathers in the cathedral, Bartlet still demonstrates his unwillingness to defy them altogether, as he punishes himself for his sins by refusing to stand for re-election. Indeed, in Freudian terms, Bartlet's superego (his father), here represented by the enormous cathedral, 'presses for punishment, since the continuance of the forbidden wishes cannot be concealed from the superego.'[102]

It is a discussion with the ghost of Mrs Landingham which pushes Bartlet to stand up for his beliefs, overcome the burdens of his superego and run for re-election. This relationship is demonstrated visually through a match-cut which shows the young Bartlet leaving his father's office having *not* confronted him over equal pay, and the older Bartlet emerging on the

102 Freud, 'Civilisation and its Discontents', 319.

other side, this time in the Oval Office, about to confront ultimately the decision whether to seek re-election. This scene, in which Bartlet seeks counsel from Mrs Landingham's ghost, constitutes his first 'therapy' session, albeit one in which his therapist is considerably more forthright than Dr Keyworth will be in later episodes (as Mrs Landingham asserts boldly, 'Your father was a prick who could never accept that he wasn't as smart as his brothers', employing language somewhat more colourful than might be ordinarily associated with psychotherapy). The literary nature of *The West Wing* is foregrounded explicitly in this sequence. Not only does the ghostly visitation recall Charles Dickens's *A Christmas Carol*, where Ebeneezer Scrooge comes to recognise his vindictiveness after being visited by three ghosts, but the unseasonal tropical storm which rages outside the White House can be seen either as straightforwardly indicative of the turmoil surrounding Bartlet's presidency following the revelation of his illness, or symbolically illustrative of Bartlet facing up to the simultaneous wrath of the Holy Father and his biological father. The fact that the patio door to the Oval Office keeps blowing open throughout the episode could be understood as the continued influence of Bartlet's superego, invading his presidency from the outside.

Recalling his earlier recounting of his achievements as president and father in the cathedral, Bartlet outlines with Mrs Landingham's ghost the plethora of problems still facing America: thirteen million children in poverty; 'forty-four million' Americans do not have health insurance; 'the number one cause of death for black men under thirty-five' is homicide; three million Americans in prison; five million Americans are drug addicts; a public education system that is falling apart. Bartlet's psyche channels Mrs Landingham's earlier demand that he confront his father, this time focusing on the possibility that he might not stand for re-election: 'If you don't do it because you think it's gonna be hard, or you think you're gonna lose, then God Jed, I don't even wanna know you.' This is followed by a cut to a close-up of Bartlet's face, his pensive expression accompanied by a rumble of thunder on the diegetic soundtrack. He then marches outside, through the Oval Office's patio door, allowing the driving rain to lash his face. The initial rumble of thunder might be understood as the rage of Bartlet's symbolic father that his son might dare to disobey him and seek re-election. The president's willingness to confront this awesome force by walking into the rain could therefore be indicative of his desire to overcome the power of his superego. At the subsequent press conference, Bartlet's decision is captured visually through a replication of the technique which accompanied the beginning of his flashbacks, the camera swooping around his head, and then moving into close profile. This mirroring of the flashback process perhaps gives a visual indication that the psychological process Bartlet has undergone in this episode has worked – because this shot is not followed by another flashback, perhaps Bartlet is no longer in awe of his superego, and more comfortable with standing up for what he believes. The profile shot, as suggested earlier, further reinforces his presidentiality, on this occasion demonstrating that he is perhaps no longer burdened by the psychological scars of the past. However, this confidence, indicated in visual and narrative terms, does not spell the end of Bartlet's battle with his (symbolic) father.

Bartlet's Therapy: 'The Two Bartlets', 'Night Five', 'Hartsfield's Landing'

Having seemingly overcome an initial fear of his superego, and decided to seek re-election despite the controversial disclosure of his multiple sclerosis, Bartlet's second campaign for the presidency is beset by the problems he initially faced in flashbacks. However, the debate now refocuses on Bartlet's refusal to emphasise his intellectualism as part of his campaign strategy. Bartlet's willingness to put his presidential ambitions ahead of personal conviction leads to a confrontation with Toby, who demands the president realign the message of his election campaign to incorporate the fruits of his academic education. However, Bartlet appears content to follow in the footsteps of John F. Kennedy, who once said of this very issue,

> There's no sense raising hell and then not being successful. There's no sense putting the office of the presidency on the line on an issue, and then being defeated.[103]

103 John F. Kennedy, quoted by William Doyle, *Inside the Oval Office: The White House Tapes from FDR to Clinton* (New York: Kodansha International, 1999), 97, in Renshon, *In his Father's Shadow*, 21.

Essentially, Bartlet does not want to challenge the anti-intellectual character of presidential campaigns for fear of appearing elitist, demonstrating that he is perhaps fearful of the punishment he endured as a young boy for being too smart. Bartlet is considerably more colourful in his language on this matter – 'There's no need to piss people off' – but the issue remains the same.

Toby confronts the president, provocatively suggesting that Bartlet's reluctance to speak with conviction stems from something primal; that his father was physically abusive towards him because the young Bartlet was smarter than him, 'but maybe if you get enough votes, win one more election' he will win his father's love and acceptance. As Volkan, Itzkowitz and Dod suggested of Nixon's psychology, 'the son with Oedipal problems always fears that his father will punish him, so he does the next worst thing – he punishes himself'.[104] As Mrs Landingham had done before him, Toby plays the therapist to Bartlet's patient, forcing him to confront his Oedipal issues. It is perhaps unsurprising that Toby would play such a role. As Rundle suggests, Toby has a stereotypical rabbinical look, and the association with Judaism, neurosis and psychotherapy has a long historical tradition in popular culture.[105] Bartlet rails against this interpretation of his psychosis, shouting at Toby, 'I don't know what the hell goes on in a Brooklyn shrink's office, but get it the hell out of my house.' Not only does this demonstrate Bartlet's discomfort with this kind of interpretation, but also speaks more widely to the anxiety surrounding the psychoanalysis of the president: as Bartlet suggests, it does not belong in the White House.

Seemingly, Bartlet's metaphorical confrontation with his father in the previous season has not seen the complete nullification of the power of his superego: his inability to resolve the issue continues to blight his ability to govern or campaign with the conviction and intellectualism that the position demands. The conclusion of the episode, however, introduces the battle that I believe to be intrinsic to an understanding of Bartlet's psychosis: between his own superego in the guise of his deceased father, and the

104 Volkan, Itzkowitz and Dod, *Richard Nixon*, 15.

105 Rundle, '*The West Wing*', 41.

wider concept of the cultural superego. As Freud suggested, the cultural superego 'is based on the impression left behind by the personalities of great leaders – men of overwhelming force of mind'.[106] As demonstrated by the previous section, through portraiture, framing and *mise-en-scène*, *The West Wing* constructs Bartlet in a variety of presidential poses as part of its critique of the Bush administration. Here, however, *The West Wing* reveals the psychological processes necessary to embody these formidable presidential ancestors. In this case, the cultural superego exerts a pressure on Bartlet's presidency similar to that of his own superego. This difficulty is captured visually as Toby leaves the Oval Office and switches off the television in the next room. Bartlet is left, captured in long shot, framed by the doorway, with the portrait of George Washington looming over his right shoulder. Small, isolated, weak, and caught between the diametrically opposed influences of his presidential forefathers and his own biological father, Bartlet is left beleaguered and uncertain as to which path to follow.

Following this confrontation with Toby, Bartlet endures four consecutive nights of sleeplessness, and is compelled to seek professional help. He ultimately confronts the essential conflict between his own superego and the cultural superego in 'Night Five', in which he undergoes his first session of psychotherapy. The episode gives the clearest articulation of Bartlet's psychosis, and further illustrates the burden of history hinted at in the previous episode. The opening scenes demonstrate this issue most vividly: Dr Keyworth arrives at the White House and Josh gives him a tour, attempting to maintain the secrecy of the president's therapy by treating Keyworth as merely another visitor. However, the tour ratchets up the psychological pressure on Bartlet by calling to attention the historical, international and cultural significance of the presidency: the communications bullpen, the Chief of Staff's office, the Oval Office and the residence have all been occupied by men held in the highest esteem, and great things have been achieved. Josh's identification of the HMS Resolute Desk which sits in the Oval Office cannot help but recall John F. Kennedy as, not only was he the first president to use it in the oval office, but it also became an iconic marker of his

106 Freud, 'Civilization and its Discontents', 335.

presidency when he was photographed by Stanley Tretick as he sat behind it, and his young son played underneath. All of this historical detail functions to emphasise the burdens of the past that Bartlet carries with him.

The unique position of the presidency is emphasised throughout the episode. Firstly, the problem of whether the president could ever admit to undergoing psychotherapy is addressed: Keyworth's presence in the White House is a fiercely guarded secret, particularly as Bartlet has already shown himself to be guilty of other human weaknesses (hiding his multiple sclerosis from the public, for example). It also confirms a certain suspicion of psychotherapy as a means of solving problems; the 'talking cure' is perceived to be distinctly unmasculine and, crucially, unpresidential. *The West Wing* suggests a similar problem: while it is vitally important that a president deals with these latent neuroses, how does he achieve this understanding given the widespread suspicion of self-inspection?

As Arnold Hutschnecker, Richard Nixon's psychotherapist, suggested,

> How strange ... that a man in public life would be allowed, even encouraged, to visit a heart specialist, say, but would be criticized for trying to understand the emotional undercurrent of his unconscious drives, fears, and conflicts, or possible neurotic hangups.[107]

Hutschnecker's observation is interesting with regard to my argument: the discomfort with the notion of a president undergoing psychotherapy stems primarily from an unwillingness to accept that the president is a man with human frailties and weaknesses, particularly one who wields such awesome power. This inability to see beneath the closely guarded veil of the presidency is emphasised when Josh says to Dr Keyworth during the tour, 'You're really seeing something here, Stanley. Tours don't go up to the second floor of the mansion.' Essentially, what Josh appears to be suggesting is that people do not bear witness to the private troubles of the man himself, and can therefore never really grasp the scale of the psychological burden that the president carries. The president's inability to be treated like an ordinary man is demonstrated by the initial investigations into

107 Arnold Hutschnecker, *The Drive for Power* (New York: M.Evans, 1974), 91.

Bartlet's sleeplessness – he attempted the most banal of remedies for his insomnia by taking a sleeping pill, but it did not take effect until a national security briefing the next morning. The suggestion that noise pollution (such as aeroplanes flying overhead) might be the cause is rebuffed with the assertion that 'Planes aren't allowed to fly over the White House.' Both of these examples demonstrate that diagnoses and solutions which would be appropriate for ordinary men are not suitable, or even possible, here.

Given his status as president, the explanation for Bartlet's sleeplessness is not straightforward. Keyworth focuses on the unique burden of the presidency, arguing that Bartlet will never be satisfied with his achievements because he is 'still trying to get his father to stop hitting him.' Keyworth goes on to cite Lincoln's achievements – 'Lincoln freed the slaves and won the Civil War' – before suggesting that, although he will most likely not be able to live up to this incredible legacy, Bartlet is not really trying because he is still engaged in a forlorn attempt to win the respect and admiration of his (now deceased) father. Essentially, despite his confrontation with his father/s in 'Two Cathedrals', Bartlet is still in thrall to his superego, renouncing his (political) instincts in fear of this internal authority. Keyworth points to Lincoln's demonstration of his political conviction as a possible presidential role model for Bartlet to follow, stating that

> Lincoln did what he thought was right even if it meant losing half the country. I think you don't do what you think is right if it means losing Michigan's electoral votes.

Bartlet is so fearful of displeasing his father that he is willing to compromise his political convictions. However, in order to fulfil the expectations of the presidency, it is essential that Bartlet is able to neutralise the influence of his superego, and refocus his attention on fulfilling the expectations of the *cultural* superego. This places Bartlet firmly within the genetic lineage of real presidents: as Lincoln had nullified the influence of his ineffectual and disappointing biological father, remaking himself in the guise of the idealised Founding Fathers, so too must Bartlet free himself from his Oedipal issues in order to become a great president.[108]

108 Strozier, *Lincoln's Quest for Union*, 74.

This reformulation of Bartlet's purpose as president is achieved visually at the conclusion of the episode. After Keyworth leaves, Bartlet walks over to his desk to retrieve a cigarette. He looks down at the photograph of his father which sits alongside the cigarette box. As Bartlet looks up from the picture, the camera tilts to reveal him gazing at the portrait of Lincoln hanging on the wall.

4.3 President Bartlet framed by the window in 'Night Five', season three, *The West Wing* (dir. Christopher Misiano, Warner Brothers Television, USA, 2002)

He lights the cigarette, ambles over to the window, the camera now positioned outside the room, framing him in one of the window panes, much like a presidential portrait (see Figure 4.3). In conjunction with the appearance of Washington's portrait at the conclusion of the previous episode, this brief sequence visually demonstrates Bartlet's movement away from his own superego towards the cultural superego, identifying the fulfilment of the expectations of the office as a suitable goal over the unachievable search for paternal approval. The portraits, according to Rundle, 'represent ... the external historical structures within which the characters work' and 'their "political unconscious"'.[109] As Toby suggests in the subsequent episode ('Hartsfield's Landing') as the two compete in a game of chess,

109 Rundle, '*The West Wing*', 59.

> You're not 'just folks', you're not 'plainspoken' … Make [this election] about heavyweight. You're a heavyweight, and you've been holding me up for too many rounds …

before knocking over his own king, letting it roll back and forth on the chessboard. The implication here is that Bartlet is a superior political and tactical mind, like Lincoln and Washington, and he should start behaving in such a manner. Toby's toppling of his own king is symbolic: to seize the opportunity and become a great president, Bartlet must expunge the influence of his father, whom he has constructed as a 'king' in his own mind despite his intellectual inferiority. The potential for greatness lies not in winning the approval of his deceased father, but in his ability to tap into the 'political unconscious' that exists all around him within the walls of the White House.

Bartlet's Therapy and the Assassination of Shareef: 'We Killed Yamamoto', 'Posse Comitatus' and 'Holy Night'

The West Wing employs a circular narrative as Bartlet comes to terms with his responsibility to the office of the presidency, and ultimately nullifies the influence of his own superego. The first Lincoln-esque decision Bartlet faces following his initial therapy session is whether to assassinate Qumari Defence Minister Abdul Shareef who, intelligence sources suggest, has been guilty of carrying out terrorist attacks on American interests abroad and plotting further atrocities on the United States' mainland. A year has passed since Mrs Landingham's death and Bartlet's initial confrontation with his superego in the cathedral, and now he returns to Mrs Landingham's grave, informing her that he has been undergoing psychotherapy while simultaneously wrestling with the mounting evidence against Shareef. The assistance of Dr Keyworth is shown to be redundant for the presidency in this situation, as it transcends Bartlet's humanity and becomes primarily about the execution of the powers of the office. Indeed, as Bartlet wrestles with his conscience, he says to Keyworth, 'If I tell you I intend to commit a crime, you are required by law to report it' (which calls to mind *The Sopranos*, in which Tony's therapist is under continual pressure to turn the other cheek when it comes to some of his more heinous acts). Bartlet continues to struggle with the decision, persisting with the impossible solution of Shareef standing trial in an American court, before eventually accepting the reality of the situation, and issuing the order for his assassination.[110]

Although the representation of this decision has been dealt with in the previous chapter section, and how lighting is employed to demonstrate Bartlet's shift away from his initial moral clarity into the murky, post-9/11 world of ethical ambiguity, there is a crucial, further point to be made about this sequence in relation to the president's psychology. He hangs his head, before moving behind the curtain, showing the outline of his profile in silhouette. As suggested previously, the profile shot has become a conventional means of connoting presidentiality, but the silhouetted profile generates a meaning far more specific: the real-life president most commonly represented in silhouette is, of course, Abraham Lincoln, whose distinctive top hat and beard lent themselves to such pictorial figuration. Bartlet is similarly represented here, further underlining the success of the process he underwent in his therapy sessions. His visual representation suggests he has moved towards a respect and understanding of the cultural superego, and a renewed determination to fulfil the legacy of past presidents rather than please his deceased father. In a manner of speaking, Bartlet *becomes* Lincoln, both through action and deed. As Cronin and Genovese suggest, Lincoln was driven by the doctrine of necessity, as he 'exercised both constitutional and extra-constitutional powers yet saved the union, and in doing so, he saw to it that the Constitution endured.'[111] Bartlet has undertaken a similar decision – most certainly extra-legal, but perpetrated to rescue the nation from far worse deeds – and has thereby triumphed over the indecision which so blighted his early presidency. He has come to accept that the cultural superego is the (not altogether benevolent) guide toward the fulfilment of the expectations of the presidency.

110 The situation reminds one of the assassination of Osama Bin Laden in 2011. While many had hoped he would return to the US to stand trial for the 9/11 attacks, this would apparently have proved far too politically difficult (perhaps because the evidence against him was rather tenuous, despite his admission he was responsible).

111 Cronin and Genovese, *The Paradoxes of the American Presidency*, 89.

The action appears to embolden Bartlet. In a later scene, he shakes off the accusations of anti-intellectualism levelled at him by Toby in earlier episodes to confront his presidential rival, Governor Robert Ritchie, over his ignorance of fundamental issues. He ultimately lays to rest the ghost of his father by beating a man with a similarly disdainful attitude towards his intellect: as he walks away from Ritchie after telling him of Simon's death, Bartlet tells him, 'In the future, if you're wondering, "Crime, boy, I don't know", is when I decided to really kick your ass.'

However, this is not to say that Bartlet, having ordered the assassination, has thereby erased his humanity. He undergoes a significant crisis of guilt and penitence over the assassination of Shareef, demonstrated in his final therapy session with Dr Keyworth. Lamenting his inability to address America's significant crisis in education and infant health, Bartlet accidentally utters the word 'airplane', when he meant to say 'education'. Keyworth quickly identifies that, in dreams, airplanes signify death, which may be interpreted as Bartlet's underlying sense of guilt surrounding Shareef's murder. Again, the weather plays a significant role in our understanding of the episode, as Washington, DC is overcome by an enormous blizzard; the airports are shut, and the staff at the White House are forced to hunker down for the evening. In response to this news, Bartlet makes a clumsy reference to Agatha Christie – 'Nobody be goin' nowhere, the bridge be washed out.' As Christie was known for writing murder mystery *whodunits*, this appears to be an appropriate reference to make with regard to Shareef's death, applying a sense of dramatic irony to the situation: Bartlet *knows* he has committed the crime, and is merely waiting for the discovery of his responsibility, and the retribution that will inevitably follow.

There is further doubling employed: Bartlet stands, contemplative, outside the Oval Office in the blizzard, much as he did during the freak tropical thunderstorm of the previous episode. Where before he was confronting his own superego, here he appears to be wrestling with the acceptance of his position within the wider, cultural superego. His imprisonment within the White House because of the snowstorm reinforces this impression – his uniquely presidential action to assassinate Shareef will position him forever within this lineage of American leaders. He will be, for eternity, part of the Oval Office, which lends the Agatha Christie reference further psychological weight – Bartlet's conscience certainly will not be able to escape, and the physical sense of confinement due to the blizzard reinforces this. This notion is rendered visually in the episode's concluding montage, which binds the disparate narrative strands together. Underscored by the diegetic performance of the melancholy Christmas carol, 'O Holy Night', the montage cuts between journalist Danny Concannon (Timothy Busfield) writing furiously at his computer about the Shareef assassination, C.J. tending to her goldfish, Bartlet's daughter Zoey and her boyfriend Jean-Paul leaving for Christmas vacation, Will Bailey working in his office, Josh and Leo answering telephone calls, and Toby and his father watching the carol singers. Interspersed within this action is a shot of Bartlet in the Oval Office, captured from distance and framed by the doorway, standing with hands on hips looking out of the window.

The president's motionlessness here has a different meaning than Shepherd's sturdiness in *The American President*, or Whitmore's powerlessness in *Independence Day*: here, it reinforces the state of melancholic contemplation Bartlet has been in throughout the episode. His stasis is remarkable given the generally intense and rapid nature of White House business in *The West Wing*. With the snowstorm having imprisoned him physically within the building, and Shareef's assassination consuming him psychologically, Bartlet has ultimately come to realise his position within the lineage of former presidents. This acceptance of his role is evidenced by his utterance to Zoey regarding the assassination: 'I did something a few months ago, and I'm sure I was right, and I'd do it again, but it's hard to live with.' As his dialogue suggests, this covert action has not erased his humanity, it has merely driven him to an acceptance that, rather than desperately searching for approval from his own *biological* father, he must work to fulfil the legacy handed down to him by the wider, cultural superego – the fathers from whom he must now seek endorsement are presidential, not biological.

***

This chapter began with the notion that scholarship about *The West Wing* has been too focused on the programme's early seasons, their relationship with the Clinton administration, and its visual style too rigidly defined as broad sweeps of the Steadicam through the corridors of power. While both suggestions are apt in relation to *The West Wing*'s early seasons, which represented the American political system as wholly benign with the righteous President Bartlet at the helm, the trauma of 9/11 resulted in an inevitable, but gradual, evolution of its visual style and its characterisation of the president. The adoption of more static framing, *chiaroscuro* lighting, and the handheld camera can be described as the aestheticisation of insecurity in the post-9/11 environment, offering an obvious counterpoint to the certainty of the Bush administration.

The changes in visual style and tone can be understood as a subtle critique of Bush's 'war on terror': where Bush's Manichean rhetoric constructed the battle against terrorism as a straightforward confrontation between good and evil, and therefore justified the extraordinary tactics adopted to combat the threat, *The West Wing* complicates the 'us' and 'them' dichotomy. It raises significant questions regarding the ability of the presidency to maintain control over this diffuse global environment, and determine the best course of action in such a convoluted situation. The 'war on terror' is morally ambiguous, and requires a leader of significant intellect and good conscience to ensure the United States remains a bastion of moral virtue. *The West Wing* clearly suggests that Bush is not that man: Governor Ritchie, Bartlet's challenger for the presidency and an obvious approximation of Bush, is populist, inarticulate and ignorant; Bartlet, who takes Washington, Theodore Roosevelt, Lincoln and Kennedy as his presidential guides, behaves in the conscientious manner a president should. The decisions Bartlet takes are not unproblematic; *The West Wing* merely suggests that the exercise of presidential power should be approached with due consideration and care.

However, constructing Bartlet in this manner is not a simple process. Because the programme is concerned with the president's humanity, it is vital that Bartlet resolve some of his internal conflicts to ensure the success of his presidency. Through psychological investigation, Bartlet is able to accept the flaws of his own biological father, thereby dismissing the remaining vestiges of this Oedipal conflict in order to fulfil the expectations of the presidential office handed down to him by his predecessors. This development is fundamental to *The West Wing*'s representation of presidential power, particularly its critique of the 'war on terror'. Seeing a president wrestle with his internal conflicts and their impact on his external actions offers a significant counterpoint to the perceived ruthlessness of presidential power practised during the Bush era. This level of proximity can only be achieved through the intimate medium of television: the employment of the close-up to capture Bartlet's interiority during therapy, and as a means of introducing flashbacks, allow a more personal impression of the president's doubts, concerns, and motives. By offering a window into the psyche of a *fictional* president, *The West Wing* enables Bartlet to fulfil a crucial role expected of the real president: as Cronin and Genovese note, 'The people, [Woodrow] Wilson suggested, should look to their presidents to promote the conscience of the nation.'[112]

During the Bush administration, when war crimes, human rights abuses and torture abounded, and the conscience of the nation was severely troubled, the fictional President Bartlet offered treatment for these psychological scars through psychotherapy. Given the immediate cultural reaction to 9/11, which was contemptuous of any attempt to contextualise the event, or administer therapeutic treatment to a traumatised nation (encapsulated by Mark Steyn's suggestion, in the days immediately following 9/11, that 'You can't begin "healing" until the guys have stopped firing'), *The West Wing* is atypical.[113] At a time when Bush constructed himself as a movie character – a hypermasculine cowboy at the edge of a wild and dangerous frontier – it is ironic that a fictional programme would be engaged in almost the opposite process.[114] *The West Wing* humanised President Bartlet, recognising that intensive self-examination is a vital process in order for a president to understand his responsibilities, fulfil the expectations of the office, and exercise power in an appropriate, and just, manner.

In essence, Bartlet provided a fictional antidote to Bush, who had 'been accused of being incurious and intellectually lazy', and preferred 'the world

112 Ibid., 68.

113 Mark Steyn, 'Fight Now, Love Later: The Awfulness of an Oprahesque Response', *National Review* (October 15th, 2001), 45, quoted in Faludi, *The Terror Dream*, 31.

114 For a discussion of the various ways in which President Bush constructed himself in this image, see Faludi, *The Terror Dream*, 189–214.

of action to that of self-contemplation.'[115] Indeed, it appears that Bush used the presidency to resolve his own Oedipal problems: he partially justified military action to remove Saddam Hussein because it would complete a job left undone by his father in Gulf War I, and also because Hussein 'tried to kill my dad.'[116] *The West Wing* argues that using the presidency to resolve personal difficulties is an inappropriate, even dangerous, use of its power; its responsibilities are far too significant for the pursuit of such trivial goals. In essence, *The West Wing* employs a therapeutic narrative to ease concerns regarding both Bartlet's character, and the character of the presidency as an institution, during a period of global turmoil.

115 Renshon, *In his father's shadow*, 116–17.

116 David Rennie, 'That man tried to kill my dad', *The Daily Telegraph*, September 28th, 2002, <http://www.telegraph.co.uk/news/worldnews/northamerica/usa/1408573/That-man-tried-to-kill-my-dad-says-Bush.html#>, accessed August 2012.

CHAPTER 5

Predicting Obama? Hollywood's Black Presidency and the Creation of a Stereotype

> Barack Obama's victory ... demonstrated, to the surprise of many Americans and much of the world, that we were ready to see a black man as president. Of course, we had seen several black presidents already, not in the real White House but in the virtual America of movies and television. The presidencies of James Earl Jones in *The Man* (1972), Morgan Freeman in *Deep Impact* (1998), Chris Rock in *Head of State* (2003) and Dennis Haysbert in *24* (2001–10) helped us imagine Mr Obama's transformative breakthrough before it occurred. In a modest way, they also hastened its arrival.[1]

> A cinema in which all black actors resembled Sidney Poitier might be as serious a cause for alarm as one in which they all resembled Stepin Fetchit. We should be equally suspicious of a naïve integrationism which simply inserts new heroes and heroines, this time drawn from the ranks of the oppressed.[2]

In *Head of State*, comedian Chris Rock plays Mays Gilliam, an alderman nominated hurriedly for president following the sudden death of the Democratic Party's candidate. As Election Day reaches its conclusion and ballots are counted, a radio announcer suggests, 'On current voting

1 Manohla Dargis and A.O. Scott, 'How the Movies Made a President', *The New York Times*, January 18th, 2009, <http://www.nytimes.com/2009/01/18/movies/18darg.html>, accessed June 2011.

2 Robert Stam and Louise Spence, 'Colonialism, Racism and Representation', *Screen* 24/2 (1983), 8.

trends, it's likely that for the first time in our history, a black man will become President of the United States of America.' This is followed by a high-angle crane shot of a tranquil suburban street. A manic rap song explodes onto the non-diegetic soundtrack to disturb this initial calm, and hordes of white people run from their houses, screaming to the heavens at the very *possibility* of a black president. Rock's film is a satirical take on the American political process, and its fundamental mistrust of what it perceives to be the hallmarks of African American identity and popular culture. Despite its triumphant ending, in which Gilliam is improbably elected, it cannot be viewed in the same terms as Barack Obama's 2008 election victory. Where Obama sought to heal the wounds that divide America along racial lines, Gilliam aggressively confronts white America with his blackness through recourse to tropes taken from hip-hop and gangsta rap, and emphasises his working-class roots to speak as a politician who identifies most closely with the disenfranchised and underprivileged. As Erica Edwards suggests, 'Mays Gilliam's campaign is a parody of the American presidency. ... Throughout the film, humor works to critique the ideology of the presidency as the province of white masculinity.'[3]

This parody is swiftly established at the film's beginning: *Head of State* opens with a sweeping aerial view of America's pastoral landscape, dissolving into a similarly elevated helicopter shot pivoting rightward to reveal Mount Rushmore, accompanied by a soothing, reverent score complete with clichéd orchestral swell upon the introduction of Presidents Washington, Jefferson, Roosevelt and Lincoln. Thus far, the film's opening would not appear incongruous if it were adopted as an alternative title sequence for *The West Wing*, the music and imagery achieving the appropriate level of benign patriotism one has come to associate with Aaron Sorkin's creation. However, there is an abrupt change of tone – a disembodied voice on the non-diegetic soundtrack interrupts the patriotic display, chanting 'One, two, three ... Hold up', demanding a halt to proceedings and a shift in focus. The camera then tilts downwards to reveal a black man performing

3 Erica R. Edwards, 'The Black President Hokum', *America Quarterly* 63/1 (March 2011), 43.

a hip-hop/R&B track, flanked on either side by white female dancers wearing bikini tops and hot pants patterned by the American flag. Rather like a Greek chorus, the performers outline the film's plot – 'an everyday man with a dream to be the Head of State'. The opening sequence suggests that African American culture and the predominantly white political establishment (embodied by the presidents on Mount Rushmore) are irreconcilable: *Head of State* suggests absolutely that there is a *black* America and a *white* America, separate and distinct.[4]

Head of State is not in keeping with the 'post-racial' rhetoric employed by Obama during his 2008 campaign, nor does it agree with his suggestion that America's Founding Fathers and past presidents hold the keys to the nation's apparently wholesome and tolerant soul. Certainly the thorny issue of race was never far from Obama's campaign but, as evidenced by his deft handling of the Jeremiah Wright controversy, Obama was able to defuse the anxieties of white America successfully enough to win a crucial 43% of their votes in 2008.[5] The same cannot be said for Mays Gilliam. *Head of State*, a confrontational piece of satire in the *Saturday Night Live* tradition, cannot be viewed through the prism of Obama's subsequent election. As a star, Chris Rock conforms to a longer tradition of black comedians-turned-actors, including Richard Pryor and Eddie Murphy, and *Head of State*'s satirical recourse to signifiers of African American culture recalls a longer cinematic history of blaxploitation and the 'New Jack' cycle of films that emerged in the early 1990s – *Boyz 'n the Hood* (John Singleton, 1991), *New Jack City* (Mario van Peebles, 1991) and *Menace II Society* (Albert Hughes and Allen Hughes, 1993).

4 This is further demonstrated at Gilliam's campaign headquarters, where portraits of Presidents Washington and Reagan are replaced with pictures of prominent African American musicians and sportsmen.

5 Obama's campaign became mired in controversy when comments made by his former pastor, Jeremiah Wright, were unearthed by the right-wing press. Wright was captured on camera excoriating the invasion of Iraq, and saying that 9/11 was an inevitable consequence of the United States' imperialistic behaviour in the Middle East. Obama successfully defused the controversy with his 'More Perfect Union' speech (March 18th, 2008).

However, cultural critics were quick to position *Head of State*, *Deep Impact*, *The Man* and television drama *24*, as omens of Obama's presidency. Articles addressing the notion that Hollywood 'predicted' a black president appeared in *The New York Times*, *The Huffington Post*, *The Times* and *The Guardian* in the period between Obama's election in November 2008, and his inauguration in January 2009. Some of the stars of these films and programmes were all too happy to have their names associated with Obama. Dennis Haysbert suggested that, by playing President Palmer in *24*, he 'helped prepare the way for Obama, opening the eyes of the American people [so] that they felt they could vote for a black president without triggering the apocalypse'.[6] Haysbert's statement here is particularly ironic, as Palmer spends the majority of his presidency in *24* attempting to avert nuclear catastrophe, terrorist attacks, and assassination attempts. Manohla Dargis and A.O. Scott expand the debate beyond the handful of fictional films and programmes that have featured a black president, positioning the phenomenon within the cinematic lineage of other black stars (Sidney Poitier), the archetype of the 'black father' (referencing the popularity of Bill Cosby), and the star image of Morgan Freeman.[7] They neglect to discuss the nuances of these texts, arriving at the conclusion that black heroism is alive and well in Hollywood films, and it is these fantasies which have prompted the election of a similarly heroic black leader.

Douglas Kellner's book *Cinema Wars* is primarily concerned with Hollywood's representations of 9/11 and 'war on terror', but the first chapter reserves special mention for the fictional black president and its relationship to Obama. Kellner quotes Haysbert's grandiose assertions of his performance's significance, conducts a perfunctory and superficial comparison between Obama and fictional Latino candidate Matt Santos from *The West Wing*, and highlights a handful of aspects of Morgan Freeman's star image and his associated popularity among cinema-goers. He goes on

6 John Harlow, 'Hollywood's warm-up act for Barack Obama', *The Times*, November 9th, 2008, <http://www.timesonline.co.uk/tol/news/world/us_and_americas/us_elections/article5114838.ece>, accessed June 2011.

7 Dargis and Scott, 'How the Movies Made a President', *The New York Times* (January 18th, 2009).

to cite Siegfried Kracauer as the inspiration for his 'diagnostic critique' of these films, a methodological approach that has been widely debunked, and has required significant qualification to reclaim its relevance. Written during World War II, Kracauer's *From Caligari To Hitler: A Psychological History of German Film* examines Weimar-era German cinema for harbingers of Nazism and Adolf Hitler's rise to power. As Kracauer suggests in his preface, 'It is my contention that through an analysis of the German films, deep psychological dispositions dominant in Germany from 1918 to 1933 can be exposed – dispositions which influenced the course of events during that time and which will have to be reckoned with in the post-Hitler era.'[8] The straightforwardness of Kracauer's and Kellner's assertions regarding film and its significance as historical artefact require significant qualification. Barry Salt succinctly summarises the pitfalls of such an approach: in his frenzied search for evidence of a collective psychological yearning for Hitler in German cinema, 'Kracauer suppresses information that spoils his case.'[9] In the introduction to the 2004 edition of the book, Leonardo Quaresima looks to contextualise Kracauer's methodology, but suggests that 'The future is not predictable in either sociological or futurological terms, and is therefore not an objective standard for a critic.'[10] In essence, history should not be read in reverse – it is cause-and-effect, not effect-and-cause. This problem is evident within discussions of the films and programmes that supposedly 'foresaw' Obama's presidency – in the thirst to position these texts as sociologically and politically significant harbingers of a real black presidency, critics viewed them in hermetic isolation from the rest of the actors' careers, elided the specificities of genre and its impact upon representation and, perhaps most egregiously of all, failed to acknowledge that African American masculine identity is not uncomplicatedly homogenous. For example, in what ways, other than the phenotypical fact of skin colour, is Barack Obama similar to Chris Rock or Morgan Freeman?

8 Siegfried Kracauer (1947), *From Caligari to Hitler: A Psychological History of the German Film* (Princeton, NJ: Princeton University Press, 2004), li.

9 Barry Salt, 'From Caligari to Who?', *Sight and Sound* 48 (1979), 123.

10 Leonardo Quaresima, 'Introduction to the 2004 Edition: Rereading Kracauer', in Kracauer, *From Caligari to Hitler*, xlii.

The failure to address these issues is perhaps indicative of the optimism that greeted Obama's candidacy and eventual victory. The palpable sense of seismic change, and the possibility that America had graduated into a 'post-racial' era has, with the rise of the Tea Party, and the racially inflected terms in which Obama is caricatured, largely evaporated.[11] In many ways, criticism of the fictional black presidency uncomplicatedly regurgitates much of the 'post-racial' rhetoric that Obama himself placed at the centre of his 2008 election campaign. The fact is, however, that neither Hollywood nor American politics had suddenly become 'post-racial'. The term itself invokes a problematic elision of racial issues which still persist, invoking a sense of colourblindness that attempts to will away the complexities of race relations in the United States. As Cornel West suggested, 'Post-racial means less racist on behalf of white voters, and that is progress, but post-racial ought not to mean black people disappearing as though there's no such thing as black people anymore, just human beings in the abstract.'[12] How can we be 'post-racial' in the most obvious sense of the term if we have not fully addressed issues of race? It might be argued, therefore, that the term 'post-racial' is designed, much like the fictional black presidency itself, to make white people feel better about themselves. It speaks to the desire to be seen as innocent, and blind to the realities of racial difference. As Mark Lawrence McPhail suggests of Obama's 'post-racial' rhetoric, 'It articulates

11 The Tea Party is an American political movement that advocates strict adherence to the US constitution, and massive reductions in government spending and taxes predicated upon dismantling the welfare state and reducing the tax burden on the wealthy. The movement is conservative, libertarian, populist and nostalgic, yearning for a supposedly more stable and benign past. Its definition of what constitutes 'American' is rather narrow, and looks to return the nation to its white, patriarchal, agrarian, heteronormative roots. Its influence on the Republican Party in the 2012 election cycle was demonstrated by the problematic campaign slogan: 'We are taking our country back', as though the people who possess it currently (led by Barack Obama) are somehow un-American.

12 Cornel West, interview, 'Cornel West Princeton Scholar and Pastor on Obama Win on CNN' (November 5th, 2008), quoted in Linda F. Selzer, 'Barack Obama, the 2008 Election, the New Cosmopolitanism Figuring the Black Body', *Multi-Ethnic Literature of the US* 35/4 (2010), 26.

well with white racial recovery narratives that silence serious discussions about race in [the United States].'[13] The term 'post-racial' looks to disavow race, to erase it from our view, to neutralise it. As McPhail and David A. Frank suggest of Obama's 2004 Democratic National Convention speech, Obama looked to erase the trauma of white racism rather than actually deal with its effects. The address revealed 'a troubling public expectation … that yearns for a denial of America's racial history as well as its contemporary consequences.'[14] I think this is true both of the films and television programmes featuring fictional black presidents, and the prematurely celebratory critiques that accompanied them during Obama's candidacy, and following his election. What has not been acknowledged is that, although these texts may be 'post-racial' in the sense that race is not the fundamental issue at stake, they are still irrevocably, manifestly and undeniably *racial*, and participate in generic, iconographic and stereotypical lineages of African Americans in films and television.

In this chapter, I will examine three examples of the fictional black presidency – President Tom Beck (Morgan Freeman) in *Deep Impact* (Mimi Leder, 1998), President Thomas Wilson (Danny Glover) in *2012* (Roland Emmerich, 2009), and President David Palmer (Dennis Haysbert) in the television drama *24* (Joel Surnow, 2001–10). Through *Deep Impact*, I will examine the black president as narrator – powerless but spiritually reassuring – and how his employment in the disaster genre participates in the desire for a post-apocalyptic, post-racial national recovery. I will discuss these issues in relation to *2012*, as well as indicating how Emmerich's film differs from *Deep Impact* in its construction of the post-9/11 presidency in a fully globalised world. My discussion of *24* will address the construction of the president as the inheritor of the Sidney Poitier stereotype of the acceptable and compliant African American man. I will examine the ideological implications of relocating conventional masculine power ordinarily

13 Mark Lawrence McPhail [with David A. Frank], 'Barack Obama's Address to the Democratic National Convention: Trauma, Compromise, Consilience, and the (Im) possibility of Racial Reconciliation, *Rhetoric and Public Affairs* 8/4 (2005), 583.

14 Ibid., 572.

associated with the presidency onto the white male hero (Jack Bauer) and the president's black wife. Do these texts constitute examples of a liberal nirvana within Hollywood's long tradition of marginalising and demonising African Americans, or do they instead operate in relation to pre-established stereotypes? I will address this question by exploring issues surrounding African American stardom in Hollywood, the representation of African American masculinity, and the conservative, pseudo-religious politics of the apocalypse/disaster genre, all of which function to construct a taxonomy of the fictional black presidency in film and television. In contrast to the critical attention thus far afforded these texts, it is essential to engage with their specificities, with particular attention paid to genre, iconography and stereotyping, and how these issues impact upon the representation of the president. It could be argued that, in the construction of the 'black president' stereotype, Hollywood draws upon a *specific* tradition in the representation of African Americans, reliant principally on the cultivation of a post-Civil Rights impression of black people as integrationist, non-threatening, compliant and amenable to white control (if not overt domination). Collectively, these films and television programmes demonstrate similarities that amount to a burgeoning stereotype of the black president, a phenomenon that demands excavation. By adopting a more appropriate critical framework than has been applied to these films and programmes previously, I will begin uncover the logic behind Hollywood's fictional black presidency.

***

There are two significant figures in the establishment of the black president stereotype – Sidney Poitier and Nelson Mandela. Donald Bogle's comprehensive excavation of black stereotypes highlights the plurality of African American identities in Hollywood film. His suggestion that black people in Hollywood film conform broadly to five stereotypes – subservient 'toms', comical 'coons', mixed-race (and therefore tragic) 'mulattoes', kind, caring, maternal 'mammies', and sexually aggressive, dangerous 'bucks' – is simultaneously invaluable and limiting (Freeman, Glover and Haysbert do not so readily conform to any one of these types in their roles as president). Of particular pertinence to the fictional presidency (and, it must be said, Obama's candidacy) is Bogle's work on the films of Sidney Poitier, and his appeal to white audiences. Poitier was the first African American 'star' in Hollywood, commanding enormous salaries and featuring in highly successful films. According to Bogle, Poitier was 'a black man who had met [white] standards' through his impeccable English, conservative dress and non-threatening asexuality.[15] Poitier 'lived out Hollywood's fantasies of the American black man', playing the black foil to a white compatriot in *Edge of the City* (Martin Ritt, 1957) and *The Defiant Ones* (Stanley Kramer, 1958), and enduring sexual neutralisation in *The Long Ships* (Jack Cardiff, 1964), *A Patch of Blue* (Guy Green, 1965) and *Guess Who's Coming to Dinner* (Stanley Kramer, 1967). Keith M. Harris suggests that Poitier became an 'exemplar and a figure of patriarchal masculinity, the breadwinner, the father, the husband; it is an image quite contrary to popular notions of black masculinity.'[16] However, his stardom was not entirely uncomplicated and, through Poitier's own autobiographical account, Harris explores some of the criticisms levelled at him. Black critics accused Poitier of complicity with white culture, derided him for his asexuality, and pilloried his characters' isolation from the black community.[17] In his famous roles in *Guess Who's Coming to Dinner*, *In the Heat of the Night* (Norman Jewison, 1967) and *To Sir, With Love* (James Clavell, 1967), Poitier portrays 'an outsider integrated into or integrating white communities, while simultaneously removed and isolated from the filmic black community.'[18] Poitier's characters were always 'saint like' in their construction, forced to endure an excessive amount of human suffering as

15 Donald Bogle, *Toms, Coons, Mulattoes, Mammies and Bucks: An Interpretive History of Blacks in American Films* [4th edn] (New York: Continuum, 2001), 175.

16 Keith M. Harris, *Boys, Boyz, Bois: An Ethics of Black Masculinity in Film and Popular Media* (Abingdon: Routledge, 2006), 54–5.

17 Ibid., 51.

18 Ibid., 60. Emerging in the same year, *Guess Who's Coming to Dinner*, *In the Heat of the Night*, and *To Sir, With Love* form part of Hollywood's delayed cultural response to the Civil Rights Movement.

a means of securing the white characters' ultimate salvation.[19] His image, Harris suggests, became 'the consciousness of the nation.'[20] Poitier is a significant figure in relation to the fictional black presidency – although he did not play a president himself during his long career (although he did play Nelson Mandela, an issue to which I will return later), his performances played a significant role in the establishment of a black stereotype – amenable, integrationist, non-threatening – which is crucial to the construction of the fictional black president.[21] Poitier is something of a father figure to contemporary African American stars, as evidenced by Denzel Washington's celebration of him upon receiving his 2002 Academy Award for Best Actor. In relation to the fictional presidency, therefore, I will argue that Poitier's star image continues to play a significant function in the presidential roles performed by Freeman, Glover and Haysbert, demonstrating that, when it comes to black stars, mainstream films and television programmes still function in the enormous shadow of Sidney Poitier.

However, a crucial facet of Sidney Poitier's star persona was his youth, whereas (in the cases of Freeman and Glover) the fictional black president is old, and therefore denied the dynamic, robust, active presidency of fictional white presidents in action/disaster films. Their age denotes simultaneous fragility and wisdom – while they are weak, they are also reassuring (advanced age is also crucial to the effacement of any potentially threatening sexuality, which has traditionally been a hallmark of Hollywood representation of African American men, from *The Birth of a Nation* to the blaxploitation cycle). Although it might not seem to be the case immediately, the figure of Nelson Mandela is crucial: all three actors who have portrayed fictional black presidents in the apocalyptic mode have also played South Africa's first black president (Glover in *Mandela* [Philip Saville, 1987], Freeman in *Invictus* [Clint Eastwood, 2009] and Haysbert in *Goodbye Bafana* [Bille August, 2007]). This is significant because what

19 Ibid., 62.

20 Ibid., 51.

21 It is worth noting that this stereotype was constructed to offer a counterpoint to the dominant representation of black men as aggressive and sexually threatening.

Mandela has come to symbolise in a Western political and representational context appears to transcend the traditional dichotomy of freedom fighter/terrorist. He now represents an uncomplicated moral righteousness, almost religious in his devotion to the causes of equality, tolerance and political and religious freedom. Despite his politically complicated past, Mandela's lengthy incarceration, subsequent triumphant release, and pivotal role in healing South Africa's apartheid-inflicted wounds in becoming the nation's first democratically elected president is Hollywood-like in its narrative structure; the story of a man who fought for what he believed to be right a cornerstone of Hollywood storytelling. Although he began his career as a young, aggressive Marxist firebrand with designs on dismantling white capitalist society, it was the complete *absence* of his image during his twenty-seven year imprisonment that allowed him, in Hollywood at least, to be reconstructed upon release as the elderly, wise and noble leader, his past rendered uncomplicated because, in terms of image at least, it did not exist. Indeed, widespread opposition to apartheid only really took hold in Western societies when the regime was in its death throes, with a cluster of Hollywood films representing the appalling treatment of black people in South Africa through the eyes of liberal whites – *Cry Freedom* (Richard Attenborough, 1987) and *A Dry White Season* (Euzhan Palcy, 1989) being two high-profile examples. Such a delayed cultural response allowed the comfortable elision of Mandela's more politically incendiary past, reconstructing him in the present as Hollywood's real-life 'black saint', the stereotype established by Sidney Poitier (who has also played Mandela, in *Mandela and De Klerk* [Joseph Sargent, 1997]). Mandela's construction raises significant issues in relation to the fictional black president – he is the ultimate real-life example of apparently straightforward reconciliation between blacks and whites, perhaps held in such high esteem because he renders *real* the Hollywood convention of the black man who suffers undeserved hardship and suffering, and comes to represent 'moral nobility'.[22] Mandela is so useful to mainstream Hollywood cinema because,

22 K. Anthony Appiah, '"No Bad Nigger": Blacks as the Ethical Principle in the Movies', in Marjorie Garber, Jann Matlock and Rebecca L. Walkowitz, eds, *Media Spectacles* (London: Routledge, 1993), 83.

as Anthony Appiah suggests of the black saint archetype, he speaks to the need for white people to be forgiven for their sins, 'seeking a black person who is not only admirable and lovable but who loves white people back'.[23]

The construction of Mandela and Poitier as 'black saints' prompts discussion of the 'black angel', a stereotype which has been frequently employed in recent Hollywood films. In films such as *The Green Mile* (Frank Darabont, 1999), *The Family Man* (Brent Ratner, 2000), and *The Legend of Bagger Vance* (Robert Redford, 2000), black actors portray characters with supernatural powers, using their paranormal gifts to better the lives of the white protagonists. Krin Gabbard suggests this phenomenon enables white filmmakers to 'create scenes of easy and unproblematic white/black reconciliation', and is 'most effective when racial, social, and cultural formations remain unmentioned and unquestioned.'[24] While it cannot be said that the constructions of Poitier and Mandela completely elide discussions of race, it must be noted that, in films at least, the black/white resolution is largely unproblematic – Mandela is a potent cultural symbol for Hollywood because, unlike Malcolm X, he favoured integrationist rather than separatist policies, advocating (after his release) harmonious coexistence with whites (it was this aspect of his politics that was most widely noted and celebrated in the Western media upon his death in December 2013). Moreover, the 'black angel' appears to operate as the logical extension of many of the noble, suffering servant roles played by Poitier in the 1950s and 1960s. Where those characters help their white companions see the goodness in themselves, these recent examples perform a similar, albeit more exaggerated, function. Appiah argues that the black saint operates within the Christian notion that 'suffering is ennobling' and, given that black Americans have suffered more than most due to state-sanctioned practices of slavery, segregation and violence, perhaps this is why 'blacks are represented as more effective at coping with misfortune and with dispensing

23 Ibid.

24 Krin Gabbard, *Black Magic: White Hollywood and African American Culture* (London: Rutgers University Press, 2004), 144.

soul-healing advice.'[25] This suggestion conforms to the popular conception of Mandela – having been enslaved and persecuted by his oppressors, he is in the best position to offer the reassuring counsel so desperately craved by the guilty whites.

This phenomenon is particularly pertinent in relation to the fictional black president and his function within the apocalyptic/disaster narrative: beset by natural forces beyond their control, Presidents Beck and Wilson, unlike the dynamic action heroes Presidents Whitmore (*Independence Day*) and Marshall (*Air Force One*), can only offer pseudo-religious words of comfort. While not explicitly angelic or supernatural, they certainly function in relation to a wider representational legacy of black characters that are spiritually insightful, existing apart from the wider black community, attempting harmonious reconciliation with their former white oppressors. In order to function as such, they must appear rather as disabled African American men did in the liberal, race 'message' films of the 1950s: 'weak, passive, dependent, vulnerable, persecuted, humble, and innocent ... sympathetic and not too threatening ... for contemporary white moviegoers'.[26] The emasculated position in which the fictional black president is placed allows the stereotype to operate comfortably within the generic confines of the post-Cold War disaster film. Where there is no individual 'hero' because there is no true 'villain', disaster films of the 1990s and 2000s (as they did in the 1970s) function more as ensemble pieces; the black president operating as the benign, spiritual healer of people, willing away a past blighted by racial tension and conflict.

Emotional and spiritual redemption has been a crucial thematic component of the disaster film since its inception. As Maurice Yacowar suggests, the 'basic point of the genre is that man must unite against calamity, that personal or social differences pale beside the assaulting forces in nature.'[27]

25 Appiah, '"No Bad Nigger"', 83; Gabbard, *Black Magic*, 166.

26 John Nickel, 'Disabling African American Men: Liberalism and Race Message Films', *Cinema Journal* 44/1 (2004), 32.

27 Maurice Yacowar, 'The Bug in the Rug: Notes on the Disaster Genre', in Barry Keith Grant, ed., *Film Genre: Theory and Criticism* (London: The Scarecrow Press, Inc., 1977), 99.

The pre-disaster world is often characterised by amorality and familial and societal dysfunction, but the arrival of the 'threat' erases what are conceived of as 'petty' differences (if such trifling demands such as gender and race equality can be dismissed as 'petty'), and inspires the characters to unite in an effort to overcome the impending catastrophe. As Nick Roddick argues, in their genocidal cleansing of all the complexities of modern living, and reassertion of a resolutely familial, patriarchal model, 'Disaster movies are "reactionary culture" *par excellence*.'[28] However, Yacowar and Roddick were writing of the 1970s disaster cycle, widely considered to be emblematic of the desire for conventional, strong white masculine leadership following the spasms of anxiety prompted by the disastrous management of the Vietnam War and the abuses of power in the Watergate scandal (*The Towering Inferno* [John Guillermin, 1974] and *Earthquake* [Mark Robson, 1974] for example). In the 1990s, the tropes of the disaster movie were realigned to articulate the 'instability and uncertainty' of the post-Cold War world.[29] While the genre continued to imagine catastrophe as somehow 'inevitable, total, inescapable, retributive and, finally therapeutic', the nature of the threat in the 1990s and 2000s altered fundamentally.[30] The cosmic and geological threats presented in *Deep Impact* (asteroids) and *2012* (earth crust displacement and solar hyperactivity) are indicative of this shift. Seemingly in keeping with environmental fears and the absence of an uncomplicated enemy in the shape of the Soviet Union, the genre tackles the threat of a global cataclysm, rendered natural, all-encompassing, and seemingly unstoppable. As with *Independence Day*, 'one detects the hunger for a "good war," which poses no moral problems, admits of no moral qualifications.'[31]

Of course, the 'good war' of the 1950s was vastly different from its 1990s counterpart – the post-Cold War context of the disaster movie demanded that this redemptive conflict be sought in arenas that would not challenge

28 Roddick, 'Only the stars survive: disaster movies in the seventies', 245.

29 King, *Spectacular Narratives*, 154.

30 Roddick, 'Only the stars survive: disaster movies in the seventies', 258.

31 Sontag, *Against Interpretation*, 219.

new global cooperation and harmony. Subsequently, 9/11 shifted the terrain by dissolving any ebullient optimism regarding America's place in world affairs. Growing understanding of climate change and its effects further altered the disaster movie's topography. Despite certain shifts in emphasis and tone, Despina Kakoudaki's suggestion of 1990s disaster films holds throughout the period – they articulate 'an insistent desire for a reunified, postracial, sublime point of view.'[32] It is these observations I will now go on to interrogate here in close analyses of *Deep Impact*, *2012* and *24*.

Deep Impact

Deep Impact is a disaster film that chronicles mankind's attempts to avert global apocalypse when an asteroid the size of New York City is discovered to be on a collision course with Earth.[33] As with earlier examples of the disaster genre, there is a large ensemble cast, and part of the pleasure of the film is guessing who will survive the impending threat. Adolescent Leo Biederman (Elijah Wood), amateur astronomer and inadvertent discoverer of the comet, must fight for his girlfriend (and later wife) Sarah Hotchner (Leelee Sobieski) to be granted passage into the underground caves specially constructed to ensure the continuity of America's way of life following the disaster. Journalist Jenny Lerner (Tea Leoni), who discovers the government's plan to combat the asteroid while investigating an alleged governmental sex scandal, spends the duration of the narrative attempting to reconcile herself with her parents' divorce and her father's subsequent re-marriage to a woman only two years her senior. In amongst this familial

32 Despina Kakoudaki, 'Spectacles of History: Race Relations, Melodrama, and the Science Fiction/Disaster Film', *Camera Obscura* 17/2 (2002), 144–5.

33 In *Deep Impact*, as in other 1990s global disaster films, 'America' appears to function synecdochically for 'mankind' – the cast of characters is a smorgasbord of race, class and ethnic difference, clearly designed to indicate the multicultural nature of the United States as emblematic of the diversity of all humanity.

angst, new allies America and Russia have constructed a spaceship named The Messiah (in one the film's numerous recourses to Christian narratives and iconographies), which, it is hoped, will deploy nuclear bombs to divert the comet from its present course. Geoff King discusses *Deep Impact* as having 'a classical narrative structure' that has more in common with 'the "women's film" or "weepie"' than the action heroics of other disaster movies of the period, particularly when compared to competing asteroid-themed blockbuster *Armageddon* (Michael Bay, 1998).[34] Stephen Keane describes *Deep Impact* as 'more of a disaster drama than a disaster movie.'[35] The narrative adopts a more melodramatic structure than one might expect from a disaster film, with the vast majority of the computer-generated spectacle kept back until the *denouement*. King argues that the 'real climax of the film, or at least a strong rival to the metropolitan apocalypse, is built up through a series of emotion-laden sacrifices focused around the most guaranteed of tear-jerking devices' (specifically, the handing over of the Hotchners' newborn baby to Leo and Sarah as they escape the approaching tsunami, and Jenny's donation of her survival space to colleague Beth and her young child).[36] *Deep Impact*'s relationship to melodrama is crucial to its representation of a black president – as Linda Williams argues, melodrama 'is the best example of American culture's (often hypocritical) attempt to construct itself as the locus of innocence and virtue'.[37]

Although not the protagonist, the narrative and emotional structures of *Deep Impact* are anchored by Morgan Freeman's President Beck who, despite featuring in only six scenes of a two-hour film, performs a pivotal function within the melodrama. Beck's introduction in the narrative is accompanied by serious doubts about the machinations of central government, and what exactly it is they are hiding. In conventional conspiracy thriller fashion, Jenny is followed by anonymous secret service agents, apprehended, bundled into a vehicle, and transported to an undisclosed location – in this case, not the generically familiar underground parking

34 King, *Spectacular Narratives*, 164–5.

35 Keane, *Disaster Movies*, 93.

36 King, *Spectacular Narratives*, 172.

37 Linda Williams, *Playing the Race Card: Melodramas of Black and White From Uncle Tom to O.J. Simpson* (Princeton, NJ: Princeton University Press, 2001), 17.

garage, but a similarly nondescript basement kitchen, which appears to be a storage facility for all manner of supplies and canned foodstuffs intended to sustain the survivors of the comet's impact. The movement of the camera here, following her progress through the space by creeping around corners and dodging food trolleys, renders the clandestine nature of the encounter explicit. As is conventional of the conspiracy thriller, Beck is initially framed as threatening, a medium shot at ground level of his shoes as they stride purposefully towards camera, his forceful movement punctuated by the sound of leather against the concrete floor. Flanked on either side by unidentified henchmen, his face obscured by darkness, the non-diegetic music tinged with ominous violins and militaristic drumbeats, Beck is constructed initially as the threatening black presence of numerous Hollywood films. Edwards suggests this sequence constructs the president initially as embodying 'a menacing racial blackness'.[38] Beck's attire, in conjunction with his anonymous henchmen, is reminiscent of the iconography associated with the gangster. Given the context in which *Deep Impact* was produced, with the various misdeeds perpetrated by President Clinton either common knowledge or on the verge of public disclosure, and the recycling of many of the tropes associated with the Hollywood conspiracy thriller, perhaps this construction has closer alignment with a broader suspicion of government officials (although the racial aspect certainly feeds into the general feeling of threat in this sequence).

However, I contend that when the president is revealed to be played by Morgan Freeman, this is instantly reassuring and, although the music continues to carry an ominous, conspiratorial edge, it is Freeman's performance here that neutralises these other aspects of the scene's construction. He appears stern, yet avuncular (and patronising): his arms are folded, and he addresses Jenny as 'young lady', conforming more closely to the construction of the president as father figure, and the Hollywood stereotype of the kindly, aged black father. As Philip Strick argues, 'The most predictable feature of this screen president is ... that he is played by Morgan Freeman. Mellow of voice, assuaging of gaze, even conciliatory of surname, Freeman has all the advantages when it comes to suggesting balance, reason and

38 Edwards, 'The Black President Hokum', 49.

acceptance.'[39] The pivot away from racial threat to reassuring presence in *Deep Impact* is corroborated by Freeman's wider career. As Appiah suggests, Freeman is the 'ultimate example of the black actor who goes from the bad nigger to the Saint', moving away from playing dangerous, violent pimp Fast Black in *Street Smart* (Jerry Schatzberg, 1987), towards more integrationist roles: the subservient chauffeur who helps an unthinkingly prejudiced old white woman realise the injustices of racial segregation in *Driving Miss Daisy* (Bruce Beresford, 1989); his cameo in *Bonfire of the Vanities* (Brian de Palma, 1990), in which his black judge lectures a multiracial audience about racial decency and justice; and the loyal, saintly Moor Saracen who assists Robin Hood in *Robin Hood: Prince of Thieves* (Kevin Reynolds, 1991). As Kakoudaki argues, Freeman is one of the few African American actors in Hollywood guaranteed to be unthreatening to a white, middle-class audience.[40] This is crucial not only in terms of Freeman's stardom (further placing him within a lineage of black actors stretching back to Sidney Poitier), but also to the conception of fictional black presidency. Unlike Chris Rock in *Head of State*, Freeman is a reassuring screen president to white audiences primarily because he is *not* confrontationally ethnicised – the roles for which he is most famous are compliant with structures of white dominance, and the soothing tones of his voice (for which he has become most renowned) carry a great deal of authority and gravitas.

This impression is further demonstrated by Beck's second appearance in the film. During a televised press conference, the president divulges the information he had for so long kept secret, and reveals the grave cosmic threat facing the human race. The dialogue here is hugely invested in its reassuring qualities, Beck opening his account by saying the issues are 'a bit complicated', reiterating that 'we get hit all the time by rocks and meteors … some the size of cars, some no bigger than your hand' and, 'rather like a billiard ball on a pool table', this gargantuan asteroid has been bumped into a path that will bring it into direct contact with Earth. The constant recourse to analogies reinforces this soothing tone, further constructing Beck as the

39 Philip Strick, '*Deep Impact*', *Sight and Sound* 8/7 (July 1998), 39.
40 Kakoudaki, 'Spectacles of History', 129.

kindly father, and the American people as the innocent, frightened children. Freeman has spent his career trading on the qualities of his voice by providing gentle narration for films such as *The Shawshank Redemption* (Frank Darabont, 1994), *Million Dollar Baby* (Clint Eastwood, 2004), *March of the Penguins* (Luc Jacquet, 2005) and *War of the Worlds* (Steven Spielberg, 2005), amongst others.[41] The representation of President Beck conforms to this aspect of Freeman's star persona. He functions rather like an expository narrator; the nature of the dialogue (in conjunction with the unique timbre and inflection of Freeman's voice) contributes to the warm, comforting tone of the film. The emphasis on *voice* is further demonstrated when, despite conducting a national, *televised* press conference that is broadcast across the country (on the enormous screen in Times Square, New York, in the Biederman family home, the homes of Jenny's mother and father, and watched by the crew of the Messiah) Beck seeks to reassure his audience through his voice – 'I can promise you this ... all of you, everyone in this room, and *everyone listening to my voice*, that at some point over the next ten months, all of us will entertain our worst fears and concerns.'[42] This is a curious choice of words, especially given the *visual* context in which President Beck is figured. But it is important for *Deep Impact*'s melodramatic tone and structure that its president is figured in this manner. Beck conforms to constructions of the president as the nation's benevolent old dad (like Presidents Eisenhower or Reagan, for example), while simultaneously drawing upon similar constructions of Freeman through his voice. The cut from an awestruck small child watching the big screen in Times Square to an image of Freeman/Beck on said screen reinforces this impression of the black president as both father and spiritual guide.

However, President Beck's function as narrator largely confines him to the White House, and significantly limits his agency and participation

41 The qualities of Freeman's voice have become such a significant facet of his star persona that, in the UK, an impersonator has been employed to offer voiceover narration to the "More Than" insurance advertisements, simultaneously parodying the preoccupation with Freeman's soothing tones, and profiting from its intrinsic gravitas.

42 My emphasis.

in the narrative – he *responds* to events with words, rather than *changes* them with actions. Unlike his white presidential counterparts in apocalyptic narratives (like Bill Pullman in *Independence Day*, for example), he plays no truly *active* role in the fight against the comet. Therefore, not only is Beck isolated in terms of physical space, the fact of his racial difference confines him more broadly within Hollywood stereotypes of the black man 'suffused with a passive, Christian imagery.'[43] When the Messiah fails to destroy the comet, Beck, still in his supportive paternalistic mould, is partially refigured within the tradition of the black preacher. This is in keeping with Freeman's star persona, most famously playing God in *Bruce Almighty* (Tom Shadyac, 2003), amongst other mystical and religious figures. As demonstrated earlier, it is not unusual for black Hollywood actors to be represented in this fashion.[44] Beck issues a sermon, bordering on a prayer, to the American people:

> I believe in God, I know a lot of you don't, but I still want to offer a prayer for our survival, mine included. Because I believe that God, whomever you hold that to be, hears all prayers, even if sometimes the answer is no. So may the Lord bless you, may the Lord keep you, may the Lord lift up his divine countenance upon you, and give you peace.

This sequence is accompanied by a warm, reverent, calming orchestral soundtrack, culminating in an orchestral swell, which underscores the emotional tenor of the scene, as well as reinforcing the religious flavour of Beck's speech. The slow track in on Freeman's face as he delivers the prayer/sermon reinforces the reassuring nature of his presence, the smooth glide of the camera gravitating towards the dulcet tones of his voice. The persistent cutaways to his image on television confirm his emotional proximity to the American people, while simultaneously reaffirming his ethereal, saintly appearance in their homes (television is a 'haunted medium', after all).[45] As Beck is never characterised outside of his duties as president, and appears

43 Tasker, *Spectacular Bodies*, 40.

44 Gabbard, *Black Magic*, 166.

45 Jeffrey Sconce, *Haunted Media: Electronic Presence From Telegraphy To Television* (Durham: Duke University Press, 2000).

to have no family or loved ones, his construction participates in the long tradition of the black angel being 'always outside history and culture.'[46] This strategy allows the film to disavow the specificities of Freeman's race, in turn conforming to a long tradition of black narrator figures that are in the film, but outside the action.[47]

With confinement comes passivity – in contrast with his first appearance, in which he strides confidently and dynamically, President Beck often appears still, contemplative, with the weight of the world on his shoulders. While this constructs the president as burdened with enormous responsibility, and reinforces Freeman's star persona as synonymous with meditative nobility, it also renders explicit his ultimate powerlessness. In one scene, he is shown standing, gazing out of the window, then sitting at his desk with his head in his hands, the sequence interspersed with news footage illustrating the breakdown of society in an orgy of looting and violence as the situation grows increasingly hopeless. This powerlessness is demonstrated by the spectacular failure of all his initiatives – not only does the Messiah (initially) fail to divert the comet, even inadvertently making the problem worse, the surface-to-air missiles that were humanity's last resort against the impending apocalypse fail to make the desired impact. Beck can only perform an expository role as these eventualities occur, giving precise information about where the comets will hit, and which cities will be destroyed in their wake. Having seemingly abandoned his preacher persona, Beck can only utter a fairly meaningless platitude – 'So that's it. Good luck to us all.'

However, humanity does ultimately triumph over the cosmic threat *despite* the president's physical powerlessness. In this regard, *Deep Impact* is in keeping with other disaster movies in which 'sufficient destruction is achieved to offer a cleansing or redeeming potential for the survivors.'[48] The film's final scene, following the destruction of America's eastern seaboard by the smaller comet, and the obliteration of the larger one through the

46 Gabbard, *Black Magic*, 166.

47 Ibid., 156; Harris, *Boys, Boyz, Bois*, 51.

48 King, *Spectacular Narratives*, 146.

benign implementation of nuclear weapons, confirms the therapeutic nature of this narrative, and draws together many of the strands I have explored in the conception of the fictional black president. Once again, President Beck delivers a national address, this time outside the Capitol Building, that potent symbol of American democracy, now under (re)construction. His faith seemingly restored after the spectacular destruction of the larger comet, he readopts his earlier role of narrator and preacher. His words are again descriptive, but infused with a patriotic and religious triumphalism. The tsunami which destroyed a significant proportion of the United States and, we are reliably informed, parts of Europe and Africa, appears to have functioned concurrently as a genocidal annihilation of the urban/modern United States (New York is destroyed), and a baptismal rebirth.[49] President Beck's sermon appears to suggest as much –

> Cities fall, but they are rebuilt, and heroes die, but they are remembered. We honour them in every brick we lay, with every field we sow, with every child we comfort, and teach to rejoice in what we have been *re-given*. Our planet, our home. So now, let us begin.

The fervour is both religious and nationally specific. Although he speaks more generally of 'our planet', the location is symbolically loaded with American national iconography – a soon-to-be completed, brand new Capitol Building, cleansed of its past sins, with a benevolent, pseudo-religious African American president at the helm. It is no accident, for example, that Africa and Europe were the continents that were destroyed by the comet – such narrative machinations enable the systematic erasure of America's past associations with slavery, and European domination of the developing world. This move enables the post-racial project of disavowing race as an issue, erasing its trauma, and manufacturing a 'new' nation innocent of the sins of racial domination and exploitation. *Deep Impact* appears to function in a similar fashion to network television's representation of African Americans which, as Herman Gray argues, 'consistently

49 Because the World Trade Centre rather improbably survives the impact, capitalism is left intact.

erase[s] the histories of conquest, slavery, isolation, and power inequalities, conflicts and struggles for justice and equality that are central features of US society.'[50] Through the representation of a black president, *Deep Impact* arguably goes further, offering the United States a second chance at racial equality and harmony. The formal construction of this sequence confirms this – once again, the camera tracks in slowly as President Beck delivers his rousing speech, ending in medium close-up, demonstrating both the gravitas and gravitational pull of Morgan Freeman's reassuring words and presence. The subsequent cut to a wide-angle long shot of the Capitol under construction (see Figure 5.1), with crowds cheering the president's words, unifies the nation in this benign, post-racial image.

The talk of collectivity – '*Our* planet, *our* home' – reaffirms this. This conclusion would appear to both confirm and extend Ella Shohat and Robert Stam's assertion regarding the appeal of interracial relationships in Hollywood cinema: such films 'touch something deep within the national unconscious, a historically conditioned longing for racial harmony.'[51] Beck's rhetoric calls to mind Obama's post-racial language in which he stated, 'There's not a Black America and a White America and Latino America and Asian America, there's the United States of America.'[52] Obama's vision of post-racial harmony has indeed been achieved in *Deep Impact*, but only following a baptismal global cataclysm, and only as long as racial difference is isolated and contained within the acceptable, paternalistic star persona of Morgan Freeman. In a similar vein to the characters played by Sidney Poitier, Freeman/Beck's compassionate, integrationist, asexual construction allows him, at a time of (inter)national crisis, to speak as 'the consciousness of the nation.'[53]

50 Herman Gray, *Watching Race: Television and the Struggle for 'Blackness'* (London: University of Minnesota, 1995), 85.

51 Ella Shohat and Robert Stam, *Unthinking Eurocentrism: Multiculturalism and the Media* (London: Routledge, 1994), 236.

52 Barack Obama, '2004 Democratic National Convention Keynote Address', <http://www.huffingtonpost.com/2008/03/18/obama-race-speech-read-th_n_92077.html>, accessed July 2011.

53 Harris, *Boys, Boyz, Bois*, 51.

5.1 President Beck (Morgan Freeman) addresses the crowds gathered at the Capitol Building (under reconstruction) in *Deep Impact* (dir. Mimi Leder, Paramount Pictures, USA, 1998)

In this regard, the final machinations of *Deep Impact*'s narrative are not entirely unproblematic. The reliance of the black president upon the ingenuity of a similarly aged but crucially *white* man, astronaut Spurgeon Tanner (Robert Duvall), who martyrs himself (and his fellow crew members) for the sake of the human race, is troubling. In similar generic Hollywood exercises, such as *Independence Day*, the white president is granted agency and dynamism in taking on the global threat. This is not to suggest, however, that *Deep Impact* is some straightforwardly racist tract that celebrates the black president as a wordsmith, but ultimately dismisses him as powerless. I would suggest that President Beck is *unable* to perform the role of dynamic action hero because of the generic and iconographic traditions in which he is placed, and that this generates an entirely different conception of presidential power. The positioning of the passive black character as reliant upon the masculine derring-do of a white partner is indicative of *Deep Impact*'s reliance upon the narrative processes of the interracial buddy movie, in which the black man's presence is employed to heighten the white buddy's heroism.[54] In this regard, it is difficult to view *Deep*

54 Jennifer Gillian, '"No One Knows You're Black!": *Six Degrees of Separation* and the Buddy Formula', *Cinema Journal* 40/3 (Spring 2001), 59.

Impact as a triumphant portent of Obama's post-racial candidacy primarily because, despite the film's supposed colourblindness, President Beck conforms to a significant number of African American stereotypes that are not altogether politically unproblematic. Despite Strick's suggestion that Freeman's 'presence sets such a tone of propriety that heroes seem to leap from the woodwork when he calls', and despite the noble, calm, reassuring, religious flavour of his characterisation, President Beck conforms to conventions of the disaster genre and representations of certain African American stereotypes, by functioning within *Deep Impact* as the benevolent, angelic black father figure for white America.[55]

2012

There are two crucial elements which differentiate *2012* from *Deep Impact*: it was produced *after* 9/11 and it acknowledges climate change as an immediate threat (captured also in Emmerich's *The Day After Tomorrow* [2004] and Al Gore's *An Inconvenient Truth* [2006]). These occurrences result in the film having a pessimistic outlook regarding mankind's ability to survive the threat. The film departs somewhat from the generic tropes of the disaster film, whereby 'any threat of annihilation usually recedes.'[56] Although the film is not as hopelessly pessimistic as its contemporary *The Road* (John Hillcoat, 2009), it goes further than most disaster movies in imagining an apocalypse of truly biblical proportions. Furthermore, it was released *after* the election of Barack Obama. The film cannot therefore be said to 'pre-empt' Obama, although it still has an interesting take on the fictional

---

The buddy movie is a crucial site of interest in relation to the representation of black men. From *The Defiant Ones*, starring Tony Curtis and Sidney Poitier, through *Lethal Weapon* (Richard Donner, 1987) and *Die Hard*, the black character is designed to reinforce the white character's purity and strength. I will explore this tradition later in relation to Jack Bauer and President Palmer in *24*.

55 Strick, '*Deep Impact*', 39.

56 King, *Spectacular Narratives*, 146.

black presidency, and presidential power in general, illustrating the pitfalls of reading film 'diagnostically'.

2012 is a fantastically preposterous piece of Hollywood cinema. The world is going to end, and this is revealed to be inevitable and unstoppable. In 2009, two scientists, Dr Adrian Helmsley (Chiwetel Ejiofor) and Dr Satnam Tsurutani (Jimi Mistry), discover a disturbing development. An overactive sun has caused Earth's crust to overheat and destabilise, which will trigger a cavalcade of catastrophes in 2012 – the eruption of the supervolcano beneath Yellowstone National Park generates an ash cloud stretching from coast to coast, the realignment of the tectonic plates beneath Los Angeles results in the city falling into the sea, the reversal of Earth's magnetic poles (the scientific term for which is 'Earth Crust Displacement') triggers seismic earthquakes and colossal tsunamis that ultimately submerge the majority of Earth's surface. President Thomas Wilson (Danny Glover) informs the rest of the G8's leaders in 2010, and plans are quickly set in motion to ensure the continuity of the human species. Billions of dollars are spent on the construction of arks in the mountains of China, rescuing those who are able to pay the exorbitant price of safety, while also preserving carefully selected examples of the finest human art and culture (for example, Leonardo da Vinci's *Mona Lisa* is saved from certain destruction).

As is always the case with the Emmerich brand of disaster film, the cataclysm is swift, brutal and uncompromising. Like *Independence Day*, *Godzilla* (1998) and *The Day After Tomorrow*, the threat arrives, and causes rapid and vast devastation, before the characters regroup and formulate a plan to counter it. As in *The Day After Tomorrow*, *2012*'s cataclysm arrives faster than was originally estimated by scientists – rather than at year's end as the Mayans prophesied, the events which will lead ultimately to the apocalypse occur halfway through 2012 (rendering the London Olympics a disaster, something that, like most prophecies, was predicted but never came to pass). Soon it becomes apparent that the human race has forty-eight hours to save itself. This precipitates a race against time for the select few to evacuate to the arks, leaving the ignorant billions behind to face inevitable death.[57]

57 It must be noted that a crucial facet of *2012*, like Emmerich's other disaster films and the genre in general, is the reconstitution of the nuclear family. This narrative

2012's representation of the presidency is in keeping with discourses surrounding the institution's decreased power and influence in the early 21st century. The botched response to 9/11, resultant intractable conflicts in Afghanistan and Iraq, and the difficulty in rescuing the American economy after the financial crisis of 2008 has led to a pervasive sense that the presidency, and the United States as a global power, is in terminal decline. It is then unsurprising, although unusual for this genre, that *2012* should recognise the United States as an important presence in a *global* community. Whereas post-Cold War buoyancy is illustrated by *Deep Impact*'s ham-fisted positioning of the United States as emblematic of all mankind, *2012* demonstrates, albeit rather unsubtly, the relative diffusion of global power in the post-9/11 period.[58] Although it is not particularly nuanced in its portrayal, globalisation is something that has clearly *happened* in *2012*: China's financial muscle and human resources are acknowledged, the wealth of oligarchs from Russia and the Middle East is significant to the construction of the arks, as is the importance of the United States' establishment of a consensus with her allies in Europe and beyond. However, the representation correlates also with the representation of African American masculinity and stardom demonstrated in *Deep Impact* – *2012* features a similarly iconic, aged African American star in Danny Glover as the President of the United States. He also functions as something of a narrational voice for the film, but his position as president is further complicated by the young African American scientist, Dr Helmsley, and the *inevitability* of the impending apocalypse. This one cannot be stopped, it must merely be survived.

---

trope is fulfilled by science-fiction writer and part-time limousine driver Jackson Curtis (John Cusack), who works out what is going on fast enough for him, his two children, estranged wife (Amanda Peet) and her new husband (Tom McCarthy) to hitch a ride to China with Russian billionaire Yuri Karpov (Zlatko Buric). Needless to say, the new husband is dispensed with by the film's end to ensure the successful re-establishment of the original family unit.

58 This might also have something to do with the increased significance of international territories as revenue streams for major Hollywood blockbusters, particularly with the important economic influence of China.

The president's powerlessness is established from the outset. His introduction, at the 2010 G8 summit in British Columbia, illustrates Glover's gravitas, but also his aged weakness. In terms of star persona, it seems Danny Glover has *always* been old – although he has played physical action heroes in films like *Predator 2* (Stephen Hopkins, 1990), he has more often played fathers or grandfathers, and is probably best known for playing Roger Murtaugh, a police officer nearing retirement, in the *Lethal Weapon* (1987–98) films. In response to the various bumps and scrapes his character endures, Murtaugh continually says, 'I'm too old for this shit.' This has become such a feature of his star persona that Glover sends up his own senescence in an Orange Mobile campaign, even uttering (minus the expletive) his most famous line. Tasker suggests that Murtaugh's advanced age is employed as a means of creating comedy out of his diminished potency, making fun of his ability to fire a gun accurately.[59] This construction feeds into Glover's portrayal of President Wilson – with a gravelly voice simultaneously suggesting weariness and experience, he announces 'The world as we know it will soon come to an end.' This establishes Wilson at the outset as a passive, expository figure, *to whom things happen*, rather than an active, dynamic agent within the film's narrative. Although he is discussing disability rather than frailty brought upon by age, Nickel's discussion regarding the humility, dependency, vulnerability and innocence of the African American characters in a post-war cycle of Hollywood films is useful in this regard. Their diminished potency rendered them sympathetic and unthreatening to predominantly white moviegoers.[60] This is true too of the fictional black president. In naming Glover's character President *Wilson*, one cannot help but recall the idealistic but similarly frail and ineffectual Woodrow Wilson, who failed to steer the United States into the League of Nations after World War I, spending the last eighteen months of his presidency partially incapacitated after a stroke. Therefore, through star persona and character naming, *2012* establishes a presidency characterised by fragility.

This is reinforced in a later scene in which Helmsley informs the president that the timetable to which they have been working is inaccurate, and

59 Tasker, *Spectacular Bodies*, 46.

60 Nickel, 'Disabling African American Men', 32.

the apocalypse will arrive sooner than expected. Here, Wilson is seated behind his Oval Office desk, the symbolic value of which would ordinarily connote presidential power and authority. However, the narrative events and formal composition of the sequence serve to undermine his power. His ignorance of the situation is reinforced by his passive, seated position, and his authority appears to be relocated to Helmsley, who is standing. Helmsley also encroaches on the framing of President Wilson, constricting him and making him appear smaller while seated. The top-down establishing shot of the Oval Office makes President Wilson appear insignificant, and this pattern is further established at the subsequent video conference with other G8 leaders. Wilson sits in the background, deferring all power to Helmsley who stands in the foreground and delivers his message. Upon arrival, President Wilson merely utters, 'Please continue, Adrian', sits down, and is thereby visually and narratively marginalised. Wilson does give the ultimate confirmation of the decision to move forward, but this feels like an afterthought given his visual construction and narrative participation up until this point. In this regard, *2012* shifts power, moral authority and knowledge from the old black president to the young black scientist.

This transferral of power is lent religious significance in a later scene, immediately prior to the evacuation of the White House. President Wilson, acknowledging the sudden irrelevance of his position, decides to remain behind, and forego his position on the ark. He seeks solace in prayer, retreating to the White House chapel where he has his final encounter with Dr Helmsley. The ominously darkened chapel bathed in white light emerging from the window lends the location an ethereal, ghostly, and spiritual sheen. It is here that Wilson expresses his desire to remain behind, and passes on the moral responsibility of the American presidency to Dr Helmsley. This is acknowledged through dialogue – 'It's a brave new world you're heading to. And a young scientist is going be worth twenty old politicians.' But it is also rendered visual, simultaneously corroborating the notion that Wilson is passing the baton onto Helmsley, while also feeding into discourses constructing the black character as spiritually attuned, potentially messianic. As the light pours in through the window and Wilson places his hands on Helmsley's shoulders, Wilson's head is captured in an almost transcendent glow (see Figure 5.2).

5.2 President Wilson (Danny Glover) passes the baton to Dr Adrian Helmsley (Chiwetel Ejiofor) in *2012* (dir. Roland Emmerich, Columbia Pictures, USA, 2009)

Wilson appears wraithlike, this shot prefiguring his inevitable death. The morality and sobriety necessary to execute the responsibility of the presidency is, therefore, passed on to Helmsley. This process is completed in a later scene in which Helmsley arrives at the airstrip to board Air Force One – the black limousine, an iconographic marker of the president's motorcade, pulls up, Helmsley steps out, and a cut to the reverse angle shows him walking towards the iconic aircraft. Although a power vacuum has been created as a result of Wilson's decision, *2012* employs non-representational signs – framing, lighting, iconographic markers – to shift presidential power from President Wilson to Dr Helmsley.

One way in which *2012* differs from *Deep Impact* is in its ambivalent relationship with Christianity – despite its employment of the Noah's Ark motif (something *Deep Impact* does too), there are various instances in which the film shows a dismissive attitude towards religion. Whereas earlier I argued that President Beck adopted the role of preacher as the apocalypse loomed, when President Wilson attempts to perform a similar function, he is undermined by the machinations of the narrative and many of the film's stylistic choices. I would hesitate to suggest this is part of a coherent critique of organised religion because *2012* is so bombastically unsubtle, but it is interesting in relation to the fictional black president and his relationship with other African American stereotypes.

Like President Beck, Wilson addresses the nation, fulfilling the expectations of the black preacher stereotype, and reinforcing Gabbard's notion that white Americans regard black people as highly spiritual and therefore more able to offer reassuring guidance.[61] The president is doing so, he says, 'for the last time' because 'catastrophe has struck our nation … has struck the world.' He looks to offer words of comfort and consolation. Like Beck, he is mediated through televisions across the country, including the iconic big screen in Times Square, his words accompanied by a tracking shot along a row of stricken citizens of all colours and creeds, including one New York police officer, which inevitably raises the palpable sense of American national unity following the 9/11 attacks. The camera cuts from New York, to Air Force One where Dr Helmsley is watching, to the cruise liner in the Pacific Ocean where Helmsley's father is, and finally to the airstrip in Las Vegas from which Jackson Curtis and his family are looking to escape. These leaps from temporal location to temporal location, unified by the weary timbre of Wilson's voice, emphasise that he is, like President Beck in *Deep Impact*, speaking *for* and *to* the nation. However, as soon as he begins to offer *religious* comfort – 'The lord is my shepherd, I shall …' – the communications technology that has been so crucial to the expansion of the American presidency in the past sixty years, fails him. The recourse to Christianity, the rhetorical haven for American presidents real and fictional, is shown in *2012* to offer no tangible safety. Emmerich appears to show utter contempt towards the notion that religion offers protection. Christ the Redeemer in Rio de Janeiro disintegrates. The Sistine Chapel crumbles, Michelangelo's The Creation of Adam splitting down the middle to violently divide God and man, and the entire edifice collapses, crushing the thousands of people who flocked there in search of religious consolation. Wilson's attempt to fulfil the role of preacher is shown to offer no reassurance in the way that President Beck does in *Deep Impact*, rendering *2012*'s attitude to the comforting nature of the black president/father/preacher stereotype to be one of utter disdain.

The ultimate human frailty of President Wilson is shown in a later sequence as the narrative gathers pace. Having remained behind, Wilson turns the White House into a sanctuary for the injured and homeless. He attempts to offer parental comfort to a little girl who has been separated

61 Gabbard, *Black Magic*, p. 166.

from her father, saying reassuringly, 'I'll find your daddy.' Unfortunately, Washington, DC is then struck by an enormous earthquake, and Wilson clings to an intravenous drip bag and witnesses the destruction of the Washington Monument. The look of terror on his face, coupled with the somewhat pathetic clutching onto the IV bag, and the camera framing him from a slightly elevated position, affirms Wilson's helplessness in the face of cataclysmic events: he is unable to find the girl's father, unable to save his citizens from certain death, unable to prevent the destruction of the city in which he lives, or the country he governs. Indeed, the very symbols of American democracy are crumbling in front of his eyes. In a final cruel joke, Wilson is crushed beneath the USS John F. Kennedy as it is catapulted along on the enormous tidal wave which swamps Washington, DC, obliterating the White House. The spectre of Kennedy, characterised as a vigorous, dynamic and forceful leader who exuded authority and control, memorialised in film and television as the president who averted the apocalypse through his handling of the Cuban Missile Crisis, crushes the ineffectual and hapless Wilson. However mocking *2012* may be of Wilson's powerlessness, the treatment of his character (in conjunction with the casting of Glover) conforms to a Hollywood tradition in which 'the victims are not damsels in distress but debilitated, defenceless, emasculated, and, for all practical purposes, feminized black men.'[62]

This scene confirms why it is somewhat inevitable that Danny Glover should play a president like Wilson – in action films (apart from *Predator 2*, perhaps), Glover's characters have always been characterised as old and physically vulnerable. As Ed Guerrero suggests of the infamous scene in *Lethal Weapon 2* (Richard Donner, 1989) in which Murtaugh is 'trapped in the business position on a toilet that is about to explode', Glover is placed in a position of subordination to the heroic, younger white male character.[63] This is roughly analogous to this point in *2012*, albeit not with the comic tone associated with the *Lethal Weapon* films. Facing down the inevitable

62 Nickel, 'Disabling African American Men', 39.

63 Ed Guerrero, 'The Black Image in Protective Custody: Hollywood's Biracial Buddy Films of the Eighties' in Manthia Diawara, ed., *Black American Cinema* (London: Routledge, 1993), 245.

apocalypse, Wilson is indeed 'caught in the business position' – he has abandoned the power he once had as president, and passed off the duty of saving humanity onto more heroic (though not necessarily white) characters. Being a black president during an apocalypse appears to be as difficult a plight as being trapped on a toilet which is about to explode – a vulnerable position to be sure, and one which relies on others to perform the acts of rescue. Despite *2012*'s supposedly 'post-racial' nature, the machinations of its narrative are dependent upon the racial stereotype which figures the African American male as morally noble and upstanding, but ultimately powerless to change the course of events.

While *2012* gives the decrepit President Wilson short shrift, the redistribution of presidential power to Dr Helmsley continues towards the film's climax. When one of the arks is deemed inoperative, a moral dilemma ensues – should they let the passengers onto one of the other ships or allow them to die? It is here that Helmsley takes on the *rhetorical* responsibilities of the American president. Transmitted by video link to the other arks, Helmsley introduces himself as 'scientific advisor to the late President Wilson.' He then calls upon the other heads of state to open the doors to the arks, arguing passionately, 'The moment we stop fighting for each other, that's the moment we lose our humanity. ... Everyone out there will have died in vain if we start our future with an act of cruelty.' To further labour the positioning of Helmsley within the presidential lineage, President Wilson's daughter, Laura (Thandie Newton), endorses his plea – 'If my father were here, he would open the gates.' The establishment of Helmsley's presidential heritage is therefore complete – in the new world, Dr Helmsley's morality is deemed worthy to follow in the footsteps of the similarly noble and wholesome President Wilson.

However, this process is again not entirely unproblematic. The figure of Dr Helmsley replicates many facets of the stereotype embodied by Presidents Wilson and Beck, established through the lineage of black Hollywood stars from Sidney Poitier through Morgan Freeman and Danny Glover. Like Poitier's characters, saintliness is Helmsley's defining characteristic.[64] Furthermore, Helmsley operates within a representational lineage

64 Harris, *Boys, Boyz, Bois*, 62.

of 'an exceptional African American character [who functions] as the conscience of white people.'[65] Helmsley appears to conform to Kakoudaki's assertion regarding black characters in positions of authority in disaster films as 'reviving previously lost "American" moral values.'[66] The transferral of power appears to reassert a much older disaster movie trope, which chronicles 'the transfer of power from the old, the incompetent and the corrupt to the new race of superheroes, brave, morally upright, and technologically brilliant.'[67] Helmsley's decisive role in *2012*'s *denouement* appears to corroborate Kakoudaki's assertion that the contemporary disaster film expresses 'an insistent desire for a reunified, postracial, sublime point of view.'[68]

Perhaps the adoption of these hackneyed disaster movie tropes enable *2012* to speak more specifically of its own cultural context. As crass and bombastic as it may be, *2012* is an excellent example of the problems with the Kracauer model of diagnostic film critique in assessing the cultural significance of the fictional black presidency. Emerging as it does *after* Obama's election victory, I contend that the figure of Dr Helmsley is at least partially *reflective* of President Obama, or at least potentially indicative of the resuscitation of the discourses surrounding basic human rights which suffered during the Bush administration – Obama issued an executive order to close Guantanamo Bay (although at the time of writing, it remains open), withdrew from the illegal 'dumb war' in Iraq, reached out initially to the Muslim world, and issued the decree that 'the United States does not torture'. Of course the divisiveness of partisan American politics, Obama's expansion of the war in Afghanistan, his use of drones to kill suspected terrorists without recourse to due process, and the revelations that the National Security Agency has radically expanded the state's surveillance of both US citizens and foreign nationals, has somewhat undermined this optimism (indeed, the continuities with the Bush administration are undeniable).

65 Kakoudaki, 'Spectacles of History', 136.

66 Ibid., 134.

67 Yacowar, 'The Bug in the Rug', 260.

68 Kakoudaki, 'Spectacles of History', 144–5.

However, the figure of Dr Helmsley speaks to the buoyancy of Obama's first year in office. Indeed, Helmsley bears a few superficial similarities to the real president – he is similarly youthful, optimistic, intellectual and, in this way, has far more in common with Obama than the decrepit and powerless Presidents Beck and Wilson. He is not framed through the prism of Christianity, but rather through the discourses of humanism: as he so passionately asserts, 'to be human means to care for each other, and civilisation means to work together to create a better life.' Emmerich is clearly fond of Obama, as his later film, *White House Down* (2013), features a black president (President James Sawyer, played by Jamie Foxx) with broad similarities to Helmsley, with particular emphasis placed on his ambivalence towards military intervention (I will discuss this example in more detail in the conclusion).

In effect, the global catastrophes in *Deep Impact* and *2012* enable both films to erase a complex past, and imagine a post-racial future; the calamities constitute a *tabula rasa* that enables the fictional societies to begin again. I suggest that the fictional black president sits at the nexus of this construction of the nation as innocent of its past sins – if the United States was benevolent and tolerant enough to elect a black leader, then her citizens deserve rescue from impending disaster. The presidents' blackness is therefore crucial. While critics may celebrate the 'post-racial' nature of these films, it is quite clear that they remain irrevocably racial: whether or not his race is explicitly acknowledged, the president's blackness serves a generic, iconographic and narrative purpose. The fictional black president exists not, as his white counterpart might, to rescue his citizens *physically* from the disaster, but to redeem them *spiritually* when the disaster comes. In this regard, the fictional black presidency mobilises a particular mode of munificent, spiritual black masculinity, embodied in the Hollywood tradition by figures such as Sidney Poitier and Nelson Mandela. The stereotype's positioning within the disaster genre continues Hollywood's overarching re-evaluation of presidential power in the post-Cold War and post-9/11 environments. I will now move on to examine the black president in relation to *24*, and its fictionalised representation of the 'war on terror'.

24: The African American President Leading the War on Terror

When *24* premiered in November 2001, just two months after the 9/11 atrocities, it immediately captured the cultural *zeitgeist*, garnering critical adoration and mainstream ratings success. It was considered narratively audacious (each episode is one hour played out in 'real time'), and stylistically groundbreaking (the use of handheld camera renders visual the immediacy of the real-time format, and the split-screen techniques which link all the numerous plot strands create a palpable sense of urgency). Coincidentally, it was also politically vital: although scripted and shot prior to 9/11, the first season chronicles an attempt on the president's life, part of the conspiracy involving the explosion of a passenger jet over American soil, immediately raising the spectre of the attacks on New York and Washington, DC. While the terrorists in the first season are firmly of the domestic variety, in later seasons *24* became a hyperbolic, fictional account of the 'war on terror', the US's campaign to combat terrorist organisations following the 9/11 attacks. It is this final aspect which is perhaps the most complex: while watching *24*, it is tempting to interpret it as state-sanctioned propaganda, working to justify the extraordinary measures taken by the Bush administration to combat terrorism. As Douglas L. Howard argues, '*24*, in all its violent glory, makes us believe that, if the terrorists are out there, something, everything, in fact, is being done to stop them and to keep us safe.'[69] Howard's observation is somewhat disturbing – can one read later seasons of *24* as propagandistic, constructing a terrorist threat so uncomplicatedly and straightforwardly malevolent that it *demands* such aggressive, often extra-legal, measures to combat it?

As suggested in the previous chapter, Bush's 'war on terror' was a campaign of dubious morality and legality. Whereas America's shift in policy direction towards Dick Cheney's 'Dark Side' is lamented by *The*

69 Douglas L. Howard, '"You're You're Going to Tell Me Everything You Know": Torture and Morality in Fox's *24*', in Stephen Peacock, ed., *Reading 24: TV Against the Clock* (London: I.B. Tauris, 2007), 142.

West Wing, *24* revels in it, reinforcing the Bush administration's construction of the terrorist threat as a pseudo-apocalyptic attack on the United States. As Stephen Prince suggests of *24*'s embrace of the extra-legal practices employed to combat terrorism, 'due process, civil rights, and the rule of law are impediments to getting the terrorists ... Desperate times call for emergency measures.'[70] As Anne Caldwell and Samuel A Chambers argue, the Bush administration constructed the response to 9/11 as a 'state of exception': 'a situation of crisis or emergency, wherein normal law is suspended.'[71] *24*'s popularity performed a significant function in the normalisation of this state of permanent crisis, 'offer[ing] viewers a representation of the "new world" that is, putatively, post-9/11 America and its "war on terror".'[72] Indeed, because each season chronicled a single day in which a grave terrorist threat against the United States must be (and, despite some 'collateral damage', is) thwarted, it could be argued *24* persistently reimagined and restaged 9/11 as a winnable battle against a defined enemy plucked from the nebulous 'threat environment' created by the Bush administration in the aftermath of the attacks. Unlike *The West Wing*, which offered a therapeutic response to the attacks, *24* 'constructs melodramas that mobilize the audience's desire for righteous vengeance and torture-as-payback for the crimes of 9/11.'[73] In concordance with the mainstream response to the terrorist attacks, *24* prescribed retributive violence as the best cure.

Despite this diagnosis and prescribed course of treatment, *24* reveals a consistent anxiety as to whether the president is capable of dealing with this threat. In *24*, the presidency is characterised by both moral and physical vulnerabilities, guilty of corruption (President Charles Logan supplies nerve gas to a Russian terrorist organisation in exchange for oil, and President Allison Taylor covers up Russian involvement in the assassination of the president of a fictional Islamic country), or victims of assassination

70 Stephen Prince, *Firestorm: American Film in the Age of Terrorism* (New York: Columbia University Press, 2009), 246.

71 Anne Caldwell and Samuel A Chambers, '*24* after 9/11: The American State of Exception', in Peacock, ed., *Reading 24*, 98.

72 Ibid., p. 97–8.

73 Prince, *Firestorm*, p. 239.

attempts successful and unsuccessful (the entire first season concerns an attempt on the life of presidential candidate Senator David Palmer, who is later assassinated after leaving office, President John Keeler is physically incapacitated following a terrorist attack on Air Force One, and President Wayne Palmer, brother of David, suffers brain damage after an attempt on his life by forces at work in his own administration). Seemingly mirroring Bush's frenetic scuttle across the country on 9/11, in *24* an equivalence is drawn between the president's body and the nation's – because the former is in consistent peril, so too is the country. As the programme is concerned with America's execution of the 'war on terror', the susceptibility of the presidency to corruption and death reveals the extent to which a post-9/11 angst regarding the rectitude and supremacy of its previously unchallenged symbols of power coursed through the veins of American popular culture.

Presiding over the execution of the initial phases of this 'war' in *24* is President David Palmer (Dennis Haysbert). In *24*'s fictional milieu, Palmer is the first African American to be elected president. Like *Deep Impact* and *2012*, the president is not the programme's main character or focus, but he still plays a significant narrative role – while still only a candidate for the presidency, Palmer is the target of an assassination attempt which provides the first season's central narrative drive and, newly elected in the second season, he faces the problem of how to respond to the threat of a terrorist nuclear bomb targeted at Los Angeles. Despite his character presiding over such crises, Haysbert argued that Palmer helped soften the electorate for the arrival of Obama.[74] This assertion demands unpacking. What does his status as an African American man say about *24*'s vision of the presidency in a post-9/11 context? How does the characterisation of Palmer conform to much older stereotypes of African American men, and is there any tension with the programme's representation of the presidency? Of particular import in *24* is the extent to which masculine agency and dynamism ordinarily associated with the president are displaced onto other characters, most notably the white, masculine action hero Jack Bauer (Kiefer Sutherland) and, more complicatedly, Palmer's black wife, Sherry

74 Dennis Haysbert, quoted by John Harlow, 'Hollywood's warm-up act for Barack Obama', *The Times* (November 9th, 2008).

(Penny Johnson). This places *24*'s representation of Palmer firmly within the interracial 'buddy' tradition, as well as the troubled history of mainstream film and television's representation of African American women, both of which demand further investigation and elucidation. Furthermore, these two displacements suggest that *24*'s representation of the 'war on terror' conforms to wider American culture which constructed 9/11 as the day that both '"changed America forever" and the event that prompted a repackaging of pre-existing constructs.'[75] Although younger than his fictional counterparts Presidents Beck and Wilson, Palmer's presidency appears to function within aspects of the stereotype of the fictional black presidency I have already discussed – he is isolated from the black community both visually and narratively, he is characterised by his passivity, and his blackness is crucial in *24*'s project of presenting the United States as a multicultural nation united against an implacable and unrelenting threat (in this case, however, the threat is not cosmic). These issues will form the basis of my discussion.

First, despite misgivings regarding such an approach, Haysbert's assertions regarding the character of Palmer and his relationship with Obama require analysis, particularly through the prism of post-racialism. Much like Obama during the 2008 campaign, *24* constructs Palmer as a unifying figure for the United States. As the head of his secret service detail asserts, 'If Palmer gets hit, the first African American with a real shot at the White House, it'll tear this country apart.' His adoring speechwriter gushes, 'I don't see many people stand by their principles the way you do, and I think our country will be a better place with you leading it.' Palmer's wife Sherry articulates the significance of Palmer's racial identity most plainly – 'You're the most important presidential candidate this country's had in a long time.' These statements reinforce the necessity of averting the attempt on his life: Palmer is the only man who can save America from itself. He embodies many of the characteristics demanded of post-Civil

75 Carmen R. Lugo-Lugo and Mary K. Bloodsworth-Lugo, 'Bare Biceps and American (In)Security: Post-9/11 Constructions of Safe(ty), Threat, and the First Black First Lady', *Women's Studies Quarterly* 39/1–2 (Spring/Summer 2011), 202.

Rights black leadership and the fictional black presidency – integrationist, appealing to a holistic American national identity, and providing an acceptable multicultural buttress for a system founded upon institutional white dominance. In *24*, it appears that the election of a black president, whether in fiction or reality, would constitute an instant disavowal of race as an issue, enabling structural racism to persist beneath the veneer of colourblind liberalism. Essentially, reform could be carried out without radically changing the system. Frank and McPhail argue that Obama's 2004 Democratic National Convention speech performed such a function through the employment of benign multicultural rhetoric, thereby 'eliminat[ing] any need for Americans to address the symbolic and social pathologies of white privilege and power.'[76] Obama's rhetoric, 'while stylistically appealing, nonetheless ignores the historical and social realities of American racism.'[77] The characterisation of Palmer conforms to such a construct, and corroborates Gray's assertions regarding the assimilationist nature of black characters in mainstream network television. Much as Obama's appeal to supposedly universal ideals of economic prosperity, religion, family values and personal liberty eliminated the specificities of the black American experience, the marginalisation of social and cultural difference in television 'consistently erase the histories of conquest, slavery, isolation, and power inequalities' suffered by blacks.[78] Like Presidents Beck, Wilson (and, perhaps, Obama), the phenotypical fact of Palmer's blackness is acknowledged in order to efface its meanings. As Gray suggests of the representation of the assimilationist African American on network television, 'blackness simply works to reaffirm, shore up, and police the cultural and moral boundaries of the existing racial order.'[79]

Palmer is viewed in such terms because he conforms to many of the characteristics of the integrationist African American man in mainstream film and television – despite plenty of evidence that the American justice

76 Frank and McPhail, 'Barack Obama's Address to the Democratic National Convention', 573.

77 Ibid., 583.

78 Gray, *Watching Race*, 85.

79 Ibid., 87.

system is disproportionately severe on African Americans, Palmer pleads with his son to 'Have a little faith in the system.' This compliance with the *status quo* is reaffirmed when Palmer is confronted by two threatening youths in an underground parking garage. When they ask 'What are you gonna do for me Mr President?', Palmer's response paraphrases the most famous lines from John F. Kennedy's inaugural address – 'See, that's the problem. You want everyone else to do the work. What are you going to do for yourself?' Added to the fact that he is the target of an assassination attempt on the day of the California Presidential Primary, the same event during which Bobby Kennedy was murdered in 1968, one develops the impression that Palmer is being constructed as an inheritor of the liberal Kennedy legacy. Not only does this position him firmly within the mainstream Civil Rights movement, it places Palmer in the history of the presidency. Indeed, where Obama sought to establish a link with the words of the Founding Fathers (if not the deeds) in order to expunge the realities of white racism, so the character of Palmer is placed within a lineage of American presidents that enables the evasion of his racial identity. As Frank and McPhail suggest, 'Obama's narrative ... embraced a vision of America grounded in the enlightened ideals of a social contract that espoused human equality, dignity, and justice regardless of race, class status, or ethnic origin.'[80] I doubt Haysbert intended his comments regarding the similarities between Palmer and Obama as an explication of the dominant culture's erasure of racial issues in order to reinforce benign white control over a multicultural society, but the strategies which constitute 'post-racialism' in electoral politics and mainstream visual media appear to conform to such a conception.

Because of Palmer's construction as America's potential unifier, his visual representation participates within the long history that represents African American men as compliant with the dominant (white) culture. Tall, conventionally attractive and always impeccably dressed whether playing the part of political campaigner, calm and authoritative leader of a nation

80 Frank and McPhail, 'Barack Obama's Address to the Democratic National Convention', 576.

on the brink of war, or father on a fishing trip with his son, Palmer is, like Obama and Poitier, 'the model integrationist hero'.[81] Palmer's relative youth in comparison to fictional presidential counterparts Beck and Wilson allows the character to operate more obviously within this stereotype – much like the young Nobel Prize-winning doctor seeking the approval of an upper middle-class white couple so he can marry their daughter in *Guess Who's Coming to Dinner*, so university-educated lawyer and former basketball star David Palmer must appear to be an *exceptional* African American in his pursuit of the presidency. Educated, intelligent, well-spoken, Palmer, like Poitier, never acts impulsively nor, as illustrated earlier, will he undermine or challenge a system characterised by white privilege. Such qualities are demonstrated consistently throughout *24*'s first two seasons – despite his vulnerable political position, Palmer continues to stand by hackneyed maxims such as 'Honesty is the best policy' and 'Do the right thing', and even risks political annihilation by revealing that his son accidentally killed his daughter's rapist seven years previously. His honesty, rather improbably, is rewarded by the electorate and he goes on to win the primary contest. But the question as to whether such candour on the part of a presidential candidate is a realistic depiction of American politics is not the one of most significance here. Rather, it is this characteristic which positions Palmer as the inheritor of a mantle handed down by Sidney Poitier; the African American character is 'governed by a code of decency, duty and moral intelligence', willing to sacrifice himself to preserve this impression.[82] In so doing Palmer is established as 'saint like', almost hyperbolically dignified, and the electorate's acceptance of his family's troubled past in turn ensures the salvation of the white majority. Overall, this aspect of *24*'s narrative ensures the acceptability of its black presidential candidate while simultaneously reinforcing the supposed colourblindness of the electorate.

However, there are other, more problematic, facets of Palmer's construction which position him within this representational lineage. As Tasker contends, 'Alongside Hollywood's construction of the black male as a sexual

81 Bogle, *Toms, Coons ...*, 175.
82 Ibid., 176.

threat, there exists an established tradition of representation in which the black man is suffused with a passive, Christian imagery.'[83] The manner in which *24* treats Palmer visually and narratively participates in this tradition, but this is rendered even more problematic by Palmer's status as 'The Leader of the Free World'. The programme's visual style largely reaffirms this notion – whereas *The West Wing*'s smooth, robust camera movement implies a sense of masculine agency, the combination of handheld and 'hidden' camera techniques in *24* suggest a lack of control over events, and render visual Palmer's generally reactive (rather than active) stance. While Bauer is subject to the same visual style, and a similar level of uncertainty as narrative events threaten to overtake him, his status as the protagonist imbues him with the skills required to overcome this sense of chaos, guided by a cast-iron conviction of the necessity of his actions, along with the requisite physical strength, tactical nous and capacity for improvisation. Palmer, because of his narrative position and his racial status, does not possess these characteristics. Some of his verbal responses to sudden occurrences reaffirm his passivity. The news report concerning the explosion of a passenger jet outside Los Angeles in the first season is met with a simple question and answer – 'Did you see this?' 'Yeah, it's horrible.' In the second season, when told that the plane carrying Bauer has crashed, Palmer can only utter, 'Oh God.' Unlike the terse responses of the white action hero president, whose decisive and forthright retorts reinforce the impression of dynamism and strength (I am thinking mainly of President Marshall in *Air Force One* bellowing 'Get off my plane!'), Palmer's language here is reactive rather than commanding, and implies a forlorn powerlessness. The tone here is not religious, but resigned. Like Beck and Wilson, he is ultimately reliant on more traditionally heroic saviours – in Palmer's case, mainly Jack Bauer – to perform the rescue of the nation state.

This inability to control events is most apparent when Palmer witnesses the nuclear detonation in the Mojave Desert from the safe confines of Air Force One. The camera whip-pans around to show Palmer sitting in his seat, his head bowed and hands clasped almost as if in prayer, figuring him as powerless and resigned. He moves to the other side of the plane, to

83 Tasker, *Spectacular Bodies*, 40.

witness the explosion from a seated position. Following this, there is a cut to the white heroes – George Mason (Xander Berkeley) makes the ultimate sacrifice by flying the plane until it explodes, and Jack Bauer parachutes to safety. These two characters demonstrate explicitly the kind of masculine agency and dynamism that Palmer so conspicuously lacks. As the sky lights up in the distance, Palmer, visibly troubled, breathes in sharply and looks away 'in a sombre moment of reflection.'[84] This sequence constructs Palmer strictly as a *witness* to events rather than an agent of them, ultimately reliant on white men to ensure the protection of the nation-state. Palmer even acknowledges his vulnerability in the face of such awesome forces when he quotes Lincoln – 'I don't claim to have controlled events, I confess plainly that events controlled me.' While this affirms Palmer's position within a lineage of great presidents, and affirms his straightforward honesty (a quality for which Lincoln too was famed), it places the fictional black president in a difficult position, merely corroborating many of the screen images of African American men as submissive and ineffectual, forced to relinquish power to more conventionally heroic white men.

Palmer's inability to manage events reaches hyperbolic heights towards the end of season two when his cabinet attempt to overthrow him because of his supposedly indecisive response to the terrorist threat. However, this element of *24*'s construction is not merely a further iteration of Palmer's powerlessness, because he is ultimately proved correct to have been cautious. It is here that *24* plays out *both* elements of the stereotype discussed earlier: Palmer is, first, the passive, suffering, noble, but marginalised, black man of post-war Hollywood and, ultimately, the conciliatory, forgiving, Mandela-esque saint, granted this designation because he has suffered at the hands of his oppressors, but maintained his dignity, strength and conviction.

The cabinet invokes the twenty-fifth amendment to the US constitution as legal justification for their action, a modification which was introduced, despite the ambiguity of the language, to ensure a smooth line of succession should the president become *physically* infirm or disabled. This again positions Palmer within the representational history of black men;

84 Daniel Herbert, 'Days and Hours of the Apocalypse: *24* and the Nuclear Narrative', in Peacock, ed., *Reading 24*, 90.

in particular, the suggestion that his hesitancy to declare war constitutes a *disability* conforms to a cycle of post-war and Civil Rights-era films which either represented the black character as physically disabled, or as subservient to an incapacitated white protagonist.[85] In the case of President Palmer, a refusal to act decisively (in this case, correctly so), and unleash the full force of the United States military upon her foes in the Middle East, is suggested to be a failure of conventional masculine and presidential leadership. Through the invocation of the twenty-fifth amendment, the absence of conventionally decisive, aggressive, militaristic masculinity in the presidency is put forward as evidence of a physical or mental disability.

Palmer's persistent, hopeless attempts to keep control over the actions of his wife, his family, the media, his staff and advisors, as well as combating the enemies external to this circle of power, are indicative of his impotence, and further substantiate the notion that the fictional black presidency is characterised by ultimate powerlessness. I suggest it is possible to equate the disabled black figure of post-war Hollywood cinema with the fictional black president at the turn of the twenty-first century, as here Palmer conforms to Nickel's observation of this stereotype as 'weak, passive, dependent, vulnerable, persecuted, humble, and innocent'.[86] Palmer may not be *physically* disabled (although he will be incapacitated by an assassination attempt at the conclusion of the second season, and in the videogame which plugs the narrative gap between seasons two and three, he recuperates in a wheelchair), but he is marginalised and debilitated by the visual and narrative choices of the programme. In what is dubbed 'The Trial of David Palmer', the president is not physically present in the room with his cabinet as they vote on the efficacy of his response to the terrorist threat. He is forced to communicate by video conference, distanced, isolated and unable to exert control over events.

85 Examples of this phenomenon include *Body and Soul* (Robert Rossen, 1947), *Home of the Brave* (Mark Robson, 1949), *Bright Victory* (Mark Robson, 1951), *To Kill a Mockingbird* (Robert Mulligan, 1962), *Nothing But a Man* (Michael Roemer, 1964), Sidney Poitier-starring *A Patch of Blue* (Guy Green, 1965), and *The Heart is a Lonely Hunter* (Robert Ellis Miller, 1968).

86 Nickel, 'Disabling African American Men', 32.

Palmer's isolation is indicative of what Guerrero describes as a 'strategy of containment' in mainstream film's representation of black characters.[87] This calls to mind the isolation of Presidents Beck and Wilson, confined to the White House, mediated through television screens, forcing them into a liminal space – isolated from the black community on the one hand, but not fully part of the dominant culture either. In *24*, this process is made even more explicit after Palmer is deposed, kept in a 'holding room' so he can no longer interfere in the political process. This represents merely the most extreme example of Palmer's isolation: throughout the second season, he is consistently positioned away from the hub of decision-making and, despite his persistent efforts to assert his status as Commander in Chief, he is often undermined by his subordinates who do not agree with his course of action. In a separate room from his advisors, framed through blinds and glass, President Palmer is *visually* marginalised, transforming his consistent reaffirmation of his powerful status into the desperate cries of an impotent man (see Figure 5.3).

5.3 President Palmer (Dennis Haysbert) is kept in isolation as his fate is decided in '4am–5am', season two, *24* (dir. Ian Toynton, Twentieth Century Fox Television, USA, 2003)

87 Guerrero, 'The Black Image in Protective Custody', 237.

Like the disabled black man of post-war Hollywood, Palmer continues to demonstrate his qualities of 'inner strength ... honor, integrity, grace, intelligence and ... dignity', despite his isolation and eventual humiliation.[88]

However, narratively, Palmer's cautiousness is proved to have been the correct approach, and this aspect of *24* completes the circle, positioning the president firmly within the stereotype of the amenable and conciliatory black man established by Poitier, and given more contemporaneous expression through mainstream representations of Nelson Mandela. Palmer's trust in Jack Bauer is justified, as the white masculine hero uses his strength and agency to prove the fraudulence of the evidence being used to justify military action. In the light of this evidence, those who challenged Palmer's presidential authority offer their resignations. In an act of astounding reconciliation, Palmer states forthrightly, 'I do not accept your resignations. We have a nation to heal, and you will all play a vital role in that healing process.' Here the black president is shown to be capable, as Poitier's characters were, of 'unproblematic black/white reconciliation', rendered all the more effective because 'racial, social and cultural formations remain unmentioned and unquestioned.'[89] In this regard, the characterisation of Palmer reinforces the notion that, in the representation of African Americans, 'underserved suffering in the American imagination can also ... represent moral nobility.'[90] However, the characterisation of Palmer moves beyond mere fulfilment of a Hollywood stereotype. Rather than confront the issues that drove his cabinet to depose him (his indecisiveness, his weakness and, concomitant with these characteristics I would argue, his blackness), he offers, like Obama and Mandela, a straightforward reconciliation. Through the colourblindness of post-racialism, and the Mandela-esque rhetoric of reconciliation, the black president reasserts control over the response to the terrorist threat. Paradoxically, however, this allows the established, white-dominated order to remain firmly in place.

88 Nickel, 'Disabling African American Men', 33.

89 Gabbard, *Black Magic*, 144.

90 Appiah, '"No Bad Nigger!"', 83.

***

In the absence of a conventionally militaristic, dynamic and masculine president, *24* performs acts of displacement to reinforce its representation of the United States as a strong nation-state, unified in its efforts to thwart the terrorist 'others'. One of these is the relocation of virile masculinity away from the president and onto the roguish white male hero, a shift roughly analogous to the generic machinations of the interracial buddy movie. Palmer's relationship with Jack Bauer is crucial to the president's construction. Bauer is unpredictable and uncompromising, willing to do almost anything to defeat the villains – he actively participates in torture, his tactics are often cruel and unusual and, crucially, he is himself able to withstand extraordinary levels of pain to keep his mission intact. He is, in effect, the action to Palmer's inaction. Bauer is exceptionally loyal to President Palmer and, despite being kept largely separate, the split-screen aesthetics and the wonders of mobile technology often unite the two men on screen. Their relationship bears many of the hallmarks of the interracial 'buddy' movie, particularly *Lethal Weapon* and its sequels: Bauer has to deal with the traumatic death of his wife; Palmer feels Bauer is the only man he can trust because of the conspiracies against him emanating from within his own government; Bauer saves Palmer's life in the first season; and Palmer bases the United States' response to the nuclear bomb on Bauer's ability to prove the veracity of the evidence. As in the interracial buddy film, the racial difference between the pair remains unacknowledged, positioning it squarely within a tradition that 'foregrounds race in order to efface it, thereby producing the illusion of successful integration and colourblindness in America.'[91] The buddy alliance, therefore, presents an uncomplicated image of integration, tolerance and multiculturalism, which allows racial tensions to evaporate almost instantly.

24 filters this tradition through its depiction of the 'war on terror'. As Cynthia J. Fuchs argues, 'The post-Vietnam popularity of buddy movies elaborates and builds on mythic wartime male camaraderie as a kind of last

91 Gillian, '"No One Knows You're Black!"', 47.

bastion against otherness.'[92] The bolstering of this construct proves crucial to *24*'s attitude to the 'war on terror', enabling the successful construction of Arab fundamentalists as the definitive 'others', while simultaneously marginalising women as damsels in distress, or terrorist sympathisers and colluders. The belated acceptance of African Americans within this construct of the benign nation-state has comparative examples from the real world. Jared Sexton argues the award of both major acting Oscars to black performers in 2002 represented 'a showcasing of racial liberalism and goodwill toward the nation's customary pariah ... courting the sentiments of generally unsympathetic black communities for then mounting military and police campaigns' in the response to 9/11.[93] It might be said, therefore, that the presence of a black president within an interracial 'buddy' relationship performs a similar function – providing timely fortification of the American nation as tolerant and multicultural, the unproblematic reconciliation of white and black at the very upper echelons of America's government and national security apparatus employed as a means of fighting the nation's external enemies (it is a model given further iteration in the action-comedy *White House Down*, which I will discuss in the conclusion). Although she is discussing straightforwardly apocalyptic films, Edwards' observation of the fictional black presidency is useful in this regard – when faced with a formidable challenge, whether it be a comet or a seemingly incessant terrorist threat, the president '*has* to be black in order to guarantee America's goodness, to reassure her innocence, and to reaffirm her claim to manifest destiny.'[94] I suggest that in order for this to ring true, the black president must be seen to cooperate directly with the conventional white hero in order to present a united front against America's adversaries.

As Tasker suggests, the black sidekick in the buddy action movie is 'there to marvel at the hero's achievements and to support him through

92 Cynthia J. Fuchs, 'The Buddy Politic', in Steven Cohan and Ina Rae Hark, eds, *Screening the Male: Exploring Masculinities in Hollywood Cinema* (London: Routledge, 1993), 197.

93 Jared Sexton, 'The Ruse of Engagement: Black Masculinity and the Cinema of Policing', *American Quarterly* 61/1 (2009), 45.

94 Edwards, 'The Black President Hokum', 52.

difficult situations. He operates as a supportive, sometimes almost fatherly figure.'[95] In *24*, this is most apparent when Palmer faces a tough decision to permit Bauer's murder in exchange for crucial information as to the whereabouts of the nuclear bomb. This conforms to the conventions of the buddy genre – Bauer must protect his black buddy Palmer at all costs because, in this case, he is the 'father of the nation'. Conversely, Palmer must provide emotional support for Bauer as he faces almost certain death in service of his country. As Gillian suggests, 'in the buddy relationship the black man's presence is supposed to heighten the white buddy's heroism.'[96] This notion is doubly reinforced in *24* because the black buddy is also the President of the United States. The split-screen technique enables this moment of bonding required within the interracial buddy genre.

As director Stephen Hopkins says of this visual strategy, 'there were so many phone calls in the script that these people would never share any screen-time together … I loved the idea of showing what people were saying on the phone but also what they didn't want other people to see'.[97] In the case of President Palmer, the thing he possibly does not want anyone else to see, but which confirms his position within the taxonomy of the feminised and vulnerable fictional black presidency, are his tears. Palmer cries as he is forced to accept the murder of Bauer to ensure the successful neutralisation of the nuclear weapon, a submission to emotion that simultaneously confirms the stoic heroism of the white male. Through this, *24* conforms to the conventions of the buddy genre very closely: the white hero is courageous and dispassionate, the black sidekick struggling to keep his emotions in check.

The interracial buddy relationship in *24* is reliant upon the construction of 'others'; in the case of *24*, the threat to America's national security is coded feminine. Fuchs suggests that the buddy genre excludes women, and this absence forces an 'overt condemnation of implicit and even explicit

95 Tasker, *Spectacular Bodies*, 44.

96 Gillian, '"No-One Knows You're Black!"', 59.

97 Stephen Hopkins, quoted in Michael Allen, 'Divided Interests: Split-Screen Aesthetics in *24*', in Peacock, ed., *Reading 24*, 39.

homoeroticism.'[98] I suggest that homoeroticism does not exist as such in *24*, because there is a definite *presence* of women, but their characterisation is along a very particular spectrum (they are all damsels in distress, obedient helpers to their male counterparts, or straightforward dastardly villains). Both Bauer and Palmer are victims of troublesome women – Bauer's extramarital affair with Nina Myers (Sarah Clarke) turns disastrous, as she reveals herself to be in cahoots with all manner of terrorist organisations and plots against the government. Palmer's campaign and presidency are complicated by the scheming of his wife, Sherry. The presence of bad women, who have betrayed their roles as subservient wives, daughters or assistants to the male heroes, enables the uncomplicated construction of aggressive, militaristic, patriarchal masculinity as *24*'s weapon of choice against these challenges to its supremacy.

I will address the representation of President Palmer's wife, Sherry, and how her characterisation as a manipulative, calculating, ruthless and dishonest individual (whom McCabe describes as the 'Lady Macbeth' of *24*) functions to reinforce the nobility, honesty and integrity of the fictional black president.[99] Concomitant with this, her characterisation conforms to a tradition that represents African American women as a grave threat to the dominant masculine order. As Edwards suggests of *Head of State*, the construction of the fictional black presidency appears to have merely traded 'a racist presidency for a sexist and heterosexist one.'[100] Sherry is shown to have gone to extraordinary lengths to ensure Palmer rises through the political ranks – she suppressed the fact that her son accidentally killed her daughter's rapist because of the damage it would do to Palmer's presidential ambitions. When it becomes apparent that she no longer has Palmer's full trust, she attempts to orchestrate an affair between him and his chief speechwriter, ensuring she continues to have influence over his decisions. Although she always asserts that her actions

98 Fuchs, 'The Buddy Politic', 196.

99 Janet McCabe, 'Damsels in Distress: Female Narrative Authority and Knowledge in *24*', in Peacock, ed., *Reading 24*, 158.

100 Edwards, 'The Black President Hokum', 45.

are in Palmer's own best interests, once she becomes embroiled with the oil company looking to guarantee a war in the Middle East to boost profits, such pleas of justification become rapidly meaningless.

She possesses many of the characteristics of the 'Jezebel' stereotype, which K. Sue Jewell suggests is ordinarily 'a fair-complexioned African American female, who possesses features that are considered European. Thin lips, long straight hair, slender nose, thin figure and fair complexion are the physical characteristics that make up this image, which conforms more to the American standard of beauty than [the mammy stereotype].'[101] Yanick St. Jean and Joe R. Feagin suggest that the Jezebel stereotype depicts 'African American women as violators of all things moral in a society of morally upright whites.'[102] Coupled with the possibility that she will become First Lady of the United States, a position which, as discussed in Chapter 3, has recently carried its own set of anxieties regarding female involvement in the determinedly 'masculine' institution of the presidency, the character of Sherry is a necessary site of concern for *24*. There is an interesting duality at work within the construction of the African American female – while the qualities of aggressiveness, decisiveness and individuality are the province of the white male and therefore untenable when possessed by a black female, there is the simultaneous coding of her as a sexually alluring temptress, which presents its own challenges to the dominant order. With these issues in mind, I will now examine the programme's constant need to contain Sherry, while also employing her duplicity and manipulation in order to maintain the rectitude of President Palmer.

Jewell argues that the privileged class's construction of African American women with conventionally masculine characteristics renders them a 'challenge to the authority and privilege of ... those who occupy the highest position on this hierarchy, the privileged white male.'[103] These

101 K. Sue Jewell, *From Mammy to Miss America and Beyond: Cultural Images & The Shaping of US Social Policy* (London: Routledge, 1993), 36.

102 Yanick St. Jean and Joe. R. Feagin, *Double Burden: Black Women and Everyday Racism* (New York: M.E. Sharpe, 1998), p. 9, quoted in Lugo-Lugo and Bloodsworth-Lugo, 'Bare Biceps and American (In)Security', 205.

103 Jewell, *From Mammy to Miss America*, 36.

qualities are 'exaggerated and defined negatively when they are associated with images that symbolize African American women.'[104] Dominant mainstream culture appears to demand the black female, if she is visible at all, conform to the 'mammy' stereotype – unthreatening, nurturing, determinedly not sexual, and sometimes comical. Although significantly less hyperbolic, a similar anxiety appears to hover around Michelle Obama whom, as a black American woman in a position of power, is 'expected to embody – and to behave in service to the image of – the Mammy. To the extent that Obama does not fit this stereotype, she is rendered unsafe and threatening – uncontained by her "proper role".'[105] Carmen Lugo-Lugo and Mary Bloodsworth-Lugo contextualise this uncertainty surrounding Michelle Obama through the prism of post-9/11 constructions of safety and threat. When she speaks out about issues that directly concern the black community, she is perceived to be violating her role as maternal First Lady.[106] Her responsibility is to be unconditionally loyal to the white family (the country) and, when she agitates at the boundaries of this construct, this leads to her caricaturing as a militant black woman. The infamous and controversial July 2008 cover of *The New Yorker*, featuring caricatures of the future President and First Lady as traditionally dressed (full-length robes and headdress) Muslim and radicalised, gun-toting Black Panther respectively, parodies the fear-mongering, right-wing misrepresentations of the Obamas in the run-up to the 2008 election. It also demonstrates the way in which Michelle Obama was imagined by some sections of the American press and electorate as a dangerous 'other', and a threat to mainstream society.

What further complicates matters is Michelle Obama's sexual appeal, which moves her away from the safe and contained 'Mammy' stereotype towards the problematic 'Jezebel'. Obama was the subject of a great deal

104 Ibid., 47.

105 Lugo-Lugo and Bloodsworth-Lugo, 'Bare Biceps and American (In)Security', 212.

106 It must be noted, however, that Michelle Obama is also celebrated, in the United Kingdom as well as the United States, as a fashion icon. This suggests she conforms to the taste-maker model of First Lady established by Jackie Kennedy in the early 1960s.

of controversy regarding her choice of sleeveless dresses that revealed her significantly sculpted biceps. This was problematic because it confirmed her simultaneous feminine sexual allure, and masculine physical strength. Obama's alleged physical power has even been parodied in *The Simpsons*, where she arrives in Springfield in a helicopter to deliver a speech. As she readies to depart, the soldiers who have accompanied her are unable to open the hatch to the helicopter. Obama steps in and, showing her caricatured, muscular upper arms, wrenches the door open using only brute force. These examples from *The New Yorker* and *The Simpsons* corroborate Lugo-Lugo and Bloodsworth-Lugo's suggestion that 'The representation of Michelle Obama ... reflects not only the fears of mainstream US society about black militancy in a post-9/11 world but also *generalized fears about a black woman not conforming to expectations in a world where threats must be contained*.'[107] A similar process occurs in the characterisation of Sherry Palmer, and this is reflected by her treatment both visually and narratively in *24*.

Over the course of the first season, Sherry is involved in a clandestine operation to prevent her husband from revealing to the world that their son, Keith, was responsible for the death of their daughter's rapist. As Palmer discovers her involvement in this cover-up, she slowly begins to be marginalised. This happens as early as the first episode, where Palmer, having had an angry conversation with a journalist about the incident, walks out onto the balcony. He does not respond to Sherry's questions regarding the content of the telephone call and, closing the patio door behind him, physically shuts her out. Later, once Palmer has discovered the full extent of her involvement in the cover-up, he confronts her. However, there is a significant discrepancy between Palmer's words and the visual composition of the sequence. The camera is positioned behind Sherry when she enters the hotel room. She is dressed in a luxurious hotel bathrobe, a towel wrapped around her head, blowing on her newly painted fingers. Although Palmer is now aware of the truth, he is still visually figured as powerless, shown from a distance, and contained by the frame of the door,

107 Lugo-Lugo and Bloodsworth-Lugo, 'Bare Biceps and American (In)Security', 215. My emphasis.

appearing small and isolated. Sherry motivates camera movement as she strides towards Palmer's desk, but when Palmer stands and moves back towards her, there is a conspicuous absence of similar movement. Sherry shows herself to be more aware, and comfortable, with the complexities of electoral politics, suggesting her ambition is the reason Palmer married her. Palmer shoots back, 'I married you because I love you.' This recourse to a sentimental response reinforces not only Palmer's obvious discomfort with what obtaining power entails, but also begins the process of exposing the treachery of the black woman which exists beneath her sexually alluring veneer. This process is confirmed by the final shot in the sequence where Palmer ignores Sherry's pleas, removes her freshly manicured hand from the door handle, and leaves the room.

Later, Sherry confirms Palmer's worst suspicions when she destroys what she thinks is the evidence that confirms Keith's guilt. In this sequence, Sherry is framed initially in medium-long-shot, sitting with her feet up on the couch. Her costuming illustrates further her sexual appeal – she wears a sleeveless dress (like Michelle Obama), with further emblems of power and sexuality conveyed through her high heels, deep red lipstick and opulent pearl necklace. This confirms Sherry's fulfilment of the Jezebel stereotype, as 'it garners fascination at the same time as it poses threat.'[108] Palmer confronts her and reveals the tape that she destroyed was a fake, planted as a moral test to see the lengths to which she was willing to go in order to preserve her (and Palmer's) designs on power. Her ruthlessness is confirmed when, in tight close-up, she says, 'I will do anything to protect my family. Anything. Does that make me a bad person?' Palmer's reaction again conforms to the representation of the black man through the prism of passive, Christian imagery – his reaction to Sherry's treachery is largely calm, although his eyes glisten as though on the edge of tears, and he bows his head, closes his eyes, and clasps his hands together as if in prayer. He even admits to being heart-broken, demonstrating a willingness to express his emotions, not something ordinarily associated with a tough, virile and masculine leader. By contrast, Sherry glares at her husband, defiant and

108 Ibid., 214.

unemotional. Her representation here is in keeping with the stereotype of the African American woman demonstrating conventionally masculine traits of aggressiveness, decisiveness and independence. Although Palmer's reaction to the revelation is more decisive than is usual for him (he immediately calls a press conference), the contrasting impressions of the two characters affirms what might be termed as a reversal of gender roles, complicated by the issue of race.

Unfortunately for Sherry, this characterisation of the African American woman is far too problematic for *24*'s overall valorisation of masculine power and authority to proceed unchecked. In order for the passive African American man to be elected president, the aggressive black woman with similar designs on power has to be contained and, ultimately, eliminated – Palmer separates from Sherry at the end of the season, telling her forthrightly, 'You've lost touch with what it is to be a parent, a friend, a wife.' In her relentless pursuit of power, Sherry has failed to fulfil what is expected of her as a black woman – she has compromised the nature of the political process and presidency by not adequately performing the role of nurturing wife and mother. As Edwards suggests of *Head of State*, black women need to be policed 'either into the normative, nuclear family or literally [taken] out of the picture altogether.'[109] In a similar, albeit more extreme, fashion to the anxiety surrounding Michelle Obama, Sherry is deemed to be 'unsafe and threatening' to the presidency and the nation, and she must be removed.[110] Sherry's expulsion from the narrative (and with it the possibility of her becoming First Lady) corroborates Lugo-Lugo and Bloodsworth-Lugo's suggestion that 'for post-9/11 Americans, there is nothing safe about the black female body situated within the highest office of the United States, for such a body invokes "the racial images"' that are so 'threatening [to] the meaning of whiteness and of the United States as a "white republic".'[111] In order for Palmer to fulfil the Poitier stereotype of amenable and compliant black man who will reconcile uncomplicatedly

109 Edwards, 'The Black President Hokum', 46.

110 Lugo-Lugo and Bloodsworth-Lugo, 'Bare Biceps and American (In)Security', 214.

111 Ibid., 215.

with dominant white culture to become president, the threat to this order must be neutralised. Sherry returns, almost manipulating her way back into Palmer's affections in season two, but she is thwarted. Indeed, her later threat to national security is even more explicit, as she inveigles her way into a conspiracy to destroy Palmer's administration with the ostensible mission of undermining said coup. Her proximity to power again proves too problematic and she is removed. Her threat is dealt with ultimately when she is killed in the third season.

Therefore, despite the perceived cultural necessity for the president to be married, as it offers the most compelling evidence of a reassuring, conventional heterosexuality, *24* appears to suggest that if the choice is between *no* First Lady, or a manipulative, calculating, threatening *black* First Lady, the former is preferable. It is telling that the other two fictional black presidents discussed in this chapter do not have visible wives – Beck never acknowledges the presence of a spouse (she might be glimpsed in the film's final shot standing behind him at the podium, although her identity is never actually revealed), and Wilson's wife is deceased. It appears that, in order for the fictional black president to operate as an extension of the amenable, compliant, docile, non-threatening stereotype established by Poitier's characters, the presence of a black female cannot be tolerated. As James Snead argued, 'in *all* Hollywood film portrayals of blacks … the political is never far from the sexual, for it is both as a political and as a sexual threat that … black skin appears on screen.'[112] In *24*, the political threat is neutralised by the fictional black president's compliance with dominant white culture. The sexual threat is displaced onto the black woman, where it is addressed, confronted and ultimately contained.

***

To conclude, I must return to the beginning. I took as my original hypothesis the idea that the fictional black presidency does not function as a portent of the Obama presidency. Instead, I have demonstrated that it operates

112 James Snead, *White Screens, Black Images* (New York: Routledge, 1994), 8, quoted in Sexton, 'The Ruse of Engagement', 52.

within Hollywood's fairly rigid ideological parameters in its representation of African American men – in order to appear unthreatening to white audiences, the fictional black president must appear reassuring and familiar, within a recognisable star persona, and within an iconographic tradition of the black character as wholesome, saintly and integrationist, characteristics established in Hollywood cinema by the stardom of Sidney Poitier. Harris's succinct summary of the appeal of Poitier to white audiences appears to corroborate the appeal of this particular mode of fictional black presidency – Poitier was 'the model integrationist hero. ... his characters were tame; never did they act impulsively, nor were they threats to the system. They were amenable and pliant. And finally, they were non-funky, almost sexless and sterile.'[113] To paraphrase Harris here, Freeman's, Haysbert's and Glover's black presidents are the perfect dream for white liberals anxious to demonstrate their tolerance by having a 'coloured man' in the White House. Their blackness is not emphasised, although it is crucial to their construction. The fictional presidencies of Glover and Freeman appear to demonstrate a contemporary extension of what Bogle described as the 'Era of Tan', whereby 1980s Hollywood 'sanded down ... all ethnic edges ... so that while [the stars] *looked* black, everything about them seemed expressed in a white cultural context'.[114] So refuting the claim put forward at the beginning of this chapter that the fictional black presidency might be indicative of Hollywood beating the 'post-racial' nature of Obama's candidacy to the punch, I contend that this invisibility of race actually replicates many of Hollywood's problematic representations of African Americans – always saintly, always isolated, present to ease the conscience of the white majority that, despite the sins of the fathers, they are worthy of rescue and redemption. In imagining a fictional black presidency within these iconographic parameters perhaps there is the danger, as Gabbard suggests, that 'the fantasy of apolitical, enchanted blacks saving white heroes

113 Harris, *Boys, Boyz, Bois*, 175.

114 Bogle, *Toms, Coons ...*, 268.

may actually stand as an obstacle to structural change, reassuring white audiences that there is nothing wrong with the old racial hierarchies.'[115]

The heralding of Obama's election in 2008 as the dawn of a new 'post-racial' age in American politics has proved troublingly premature, as evidenced by the resurgence of the far right. If anything, Obama's presidency has served to reignite the embers of racial intolerance and fear, albeit under new terms of anxiety (Obama is by turns a socialist, a fascist, a foreigner and a Muslim, all of which are supposedly 'un-American', and therefore 'other' to mainstream America). While his re-election in 2012 suggests these forces are not as powerful as they once were, their continued influence on American politics and society is undeniable. Therefore, the problem seems to be with the *term* 'post-racial'. Rather than speaking of a comprehensive working through of issues of racial difference and identity, the term in fact demonstrates the *disavowal* of race as an issue. Obama's conciliatory rhetoric is certainly indicative of this notion, and it could be suggested that Hollywood's strategies of unacknowledged black integration performs a similar function. However, the assimilation of racial difference has created new problems and constructed new stereotypes. As Stam and Spence suggest, these can be just as pernicious and problematic as the overtly racist caricatures of African Americans, as they elide the specificities of the African American experience to create supposedly positive images which render black characters as complicit with a culture that has oppressed them for centuries. As the president is the most potent symbol of America, representing a *black* president manufactures a tolerant and multicultural society without having to deal with the circumstances that engendered such a racist, unequal and intolerant culture in the first place. The pernicious demonisation of blacks in visual culture has contributed to this intolerance, and to the systemic oppression of those who are not part of a white, heteronormative ideal. To compensate for this, stereotypes such as the fictional black president have been created. However, these constructs have been established on terms that are deemed hegemonically acceptable – black sexuality, the black exercise of political power, and a

115 Gabbard, *Black Magic*, 175.

fictional black president with the dynamism and assertiveness of a white leader, are still not possible. The structural issues that created a racist culture have not been dealt with; only its combustibility has been neutralised. It still exists, beneath an acceptable veneer, and this chapter has demonstrated the ways in which racial stereotypes continue to be extended and expanded to include black people in advanced positions in society while simultaneously containing them within certain stereotypical parameters to ensure a comforting rearticulation of dominant power relations. In essence, the fictional black president is useful because it puts 'the race issue' back in its box, to project the fantasy image of a tolerant and multicultural society.

Therefore, what I have demonstrated is that the fictional black president was not immaculately conceived. He is the progeny of a variety of iconographic, generic and representational traditions within Hollywood film and television, the inevitable and logical extension of what is now a long and complex history of African Americans on screen. He variously embodies the archetypes of the passive and integrationist black man established by Sidney Poitier, the saint/angel/preacher figure perpetuated throughout the 1990s and into the new century, and the black figure of authority (policemen and detectives, roles played on numerous occasions by Freeman, Glover and Haysbert amongst others). In terms of real world references, the fictional black president conforms largely to the Hollywood construction of Nelson Mandela as conciliatory, avuncular and grandfatherly, willing to forgive and forget the racially divided past while simultaneously bolstering existing, white-dominated power structures. Like Hollywood's representation of blackness in general, the fictional black president 'may be constructed as marginal' within these narratives, but he 'has a *symbolic centrality*.'[116] The archetype exists to make predominantly white middle class Western audiences feel better about themselves, his preacher persona forgiving them their sins, while also reasserting the United States' best image of itself as a bastion of innocence and virtue. If 'Poitier's integrationist image had been an instrument, along with the social problem film genre, promoting the film industry's liberal ideals', then I would argue that the

116 Tasker, *Spectacular Bodies*, 37.

fictional black presidency performs a similar function.[117] The enthusiasm following Obama's remarkable election victories is understandable, but the fictional black president did not predict the future; the archetype is merely the concluding punctuating mark to a tradition that stretches back into Hollywood's past.

117 Thomas Cripps, *Making Movies Black: The Hollywood Message Movies from World War II to the Civil Rights Era* (New York: Oxford University Press, 1993), 284–94, quoted in Harris, *Boys, Boyz, Bois*, 62.

CHAPTER 6

'Having it Allen': Motherhood, Family and the Female Presidency in *Commander in Chief*

> One of the great lessons of [Hillary Clinton's] campaign is the continued and accepted role of sexism in American life, particularly in the media ... It isn't just Hillary Clinton who needs to learn a lesson from this primary season – it's all the people who crossed the line, and all the women and men who let them get away with it.[1]

Despite being a highly successful lawyer and Yale graduate, a two-term senator for one of the US's most populous states (New York), and redefining the role of the First Lady to incorporate a more active role in policy during her husband's eight years in office, Hillary Clinton's campaign for the Democratic presidential nomination in 2008 was hindered by the refusal by substantial proportions of the media and the electorate to countenance the possibility of a female president. As Susan J. Carroll argues, female candidates for elected office, particularly one so rigidly defined around traditional conceptions of masculinity such as the presidency, struggle to counter stereotypes of women as being unqualified for the job (despite often possessing more experience than their male opponents, as Clinton did over Obama), not sufficiently tough, and too emotional.[2] It has been suggested that Clinton's failure to secure the nomination stemmed from

1 Katie Couric, quoted by Danny Shea, 'Katie Couric: Sexist Media Hurt Hillary Clinton's Chances', *The Huffington Post*, June 19th, 2008, <http://www.huffingtonpost.com/2008/06/11/katie-couric-sexist-media_n_106595.html>, accessed August 2013.

2 Susan J. Carroll, 'Reflections on Gender and Hillary Clinton's Election Campaign: The Good, The Bad, and the Misogynic', *Politics and Gender* 5 (2009), 6–9.

her failure to make an emotional connection with voters, and placing too much emphasis on her experience for the position in a year that the *status quo* was under significant duress, resulting from the ongoing conflicts in Iraq and Afghanistan, and the collapsing economy. As Carroll notes, 'the Clinton campaign got trapped into emphasizing experience in an election where voters were hungry for change.'[3] However, it could also be argued this strategy was adopted precisely in order to counter the pervasive tendency in mainstream media to fall back on stereotypical assumptions about female candidates as being too weak or too emotional to lead. Because Clinton had spent considerable effort in cultivating an image of herself as strong and in control, when she *did* reveal more of her emotions prior to the New Hampshire primary contest, shedding a few tears while speaking of her passion for public service and her desire to lead the United States out of troubled times, this was not dismissed as weakness but rather as 'calculating', 'inauthentic', and indicative of her raw ambition.[4]

There was a tendency in the media to refer to her informally as 'Hillary' rather than 'Senator Clinton', which played a significant role in infantilising her, reducing her claim to power and authority, and delegitimising her bid for the nomination.[5] Furthermore, she was subjected to outright misogyny while on the campaign trail, confronted with placards held by men featuring slogans such as 'Iron My Shirts!' and Clinton-branded nutcrackers sold at the nation's airports. Newspeople frequently and unthinkingly equated their dislike of her with her status as a woman, describing her voice as shrill and unpleasant, one commentator admitting to 'involuntarily crossing his legs' every time he saw Clinton on television.[6] Despite all the supposed

3 Ibid., 8.

4 Ibid., 13.

5 Joseph E. Uscinski and Lilly J. Goren, 'What's in a Name? Coverage of Senator Hillary Clinton during the 2008 Democratic Primary', *Political Research Quarterly* 64/4 (2011), 887.

6 Ryan Chiachiere, 'Tucker Carlson on Clinton: "'[W]hen she comes on television, I involuntarily cross my legs"', *Media Matters for America*, July 18th, 2007, <http://mediamatters.org/research/2007/07/18/tucker-carlson-on-clinton-when-she-comes-on-tel/139362>, accessed July 2013.

progress that had been made by the second-wave feminist movement since the 1960s and 1970s, Clinton was still defined negatively by her association with that era. As explored in Chapter 3, Clinton had symbolised 'all that was wrong with the '60s' during her husband's first term in office.[7] Although nearly two decades had elapsed since then, the examples I have highlighted here demonstrate that, when she ran for president in 2008, Clinton continued to be viewed as 'a stereotypical (and negative) representation of second wave feminism'.[8]

Lori Cox Han and Caroline Heldman argue that Clinton's pursuit of the Democratic nomination demonstrated that it proved impossible to imagine a woman – the traditional 'caregiver' in American society – in a role that required her to become a 'protector', a conventionally male position associated with fatherhood, leadership and heroism in battle.[9] The presidency and masculinity remained discursively linked. As Linda Horwitz and Holly Swyers suggest,

> American history is still told as a story of 'Founding Fathers', and the idea of a patriarch as a president has a firm hold in the American imagination. The result is that the notion of what a president should look like, of what is presidential, is fundamentally masculine.[10]

Clinton tried to 'wear masculinist ideology', casting herself in the role of protector through an advertising campaign designed to position herself as the most experienced candidate in the race for the Democratic nomination.[11] The televised advertisement, dubbed the '3am' campaign, featured a series of children asleep in their beds in suburban, middle-class homes. Voters were asked to imagine the president taking a phone call in

7 Parry-Giles, 'Mediating Hillary Rodham Clinton', 207.

8 Uscinski and Goren, 'What's in a Name?', 885–6.

9 Lori Cox Han and Caroline Heldman, *Rethinking Madam President: Are We Ready For a Woman in the White House?* (Boulder: Lynne Rienner Publishers, 2007), 27.

10 Linda Horwitz and Holly Swyers, 'Why Are All The Presidents Men?: Televisual Presidents and Patriarchy', in Lilly Goren, ed., *You've Come a Long Way, Baby: Women, Politics and Popular Culture* (Lexington: University Press of Kentucky, 2009), 119.

11 Cox Han and Heldman, *Rethinking Madam President*, 21.

the middle of the night that might have serious national security implications.[12] The voiceover narration asked, 'Who do you want answering the phone?', suggesting that Clinton's experience, knowledge, toughness, decisiveness and intellectual acuity (all part of the 'traditionally masculine schema') made her the ideal candidate for the job.[13] Rather than *redefine* the conception of the presidency, therefore, Clinton attempted to operate within its narrow parameters. However, 'because masculinity is an exclusively male prerogative', and the presidency 'is soaked to the bone in masculinist ideology', it proved impossible.[14] Coupled with Obama's extraordinary rise to prominence, capturing the imagination with seductive messages of hope and change, Clinton missed out on the nomination. It appears that the postfeminist discourses in popular culture that both explored and questioned the possibility that women could 'have it all' (a successful career *and* a successful family life) reached its ultimate match with the presidency:

> Given prevailing cultural notions of gender role delineation in the household, it is difficult to envision women as the head of the household and, thus, difficult to imagine a woman as the symbolic head of the national household. The caretaker role is simply not presidential. The misfit between being a woman and protector is seen in the paucity of such roles in popular culture.[15]

Therefore, Clinton's failure to secure the nomination in 2008 can be partially contextualised by the perpetuation and continued significance of a series of stereotypes of women in popular culture, particularly the persistent suggestion that a successful woman is necessarily a domestic one: as Julie Levinson suggests, 'In Hollywood movies, success for women generally goes hand-in-hand with marrying and mothering well.'[16] While women may be accepted in many other professional positions, Clinton's case

12 Ibid.
13 Ibid.
14 Ibid., 24.
15 Ibid., 27.
16 Julie Levinson, *The American Success Myth on Film* (Basingstoke: Palgrave Macmillan, 2012), 111.

demonstrates that, if professional success is the sole aim, they may only play the supporting role.

This chapter is intended as a demonstration of the enormous extent to which, in fiction as much as in reality, the conceptualisation of the presidency is preoccupied with patriarchal masculinity; as diverse and multifaceted as representations of the president have become since the early 1990s, what is considered 'presidential' continues to coalesce around particular, highly conservative formulations of race, class and, in the case of this chapter, gender. Hillary Clinton's treatment in the press in 2008 is indicative of a wider tendency within a culture that struggles to create images of powerful women that are not rearticulations of misogynistic stereotypes, or somewhat sentimentalised explorations of the difficulties of managing the duties of being a wife, a mother and a highly capable professional. While Chapters 3 and 5 addressed popular cultural anxiety surrounding the increased proximity of women to the presidency in both the pre- and post-9/11 periods, this chapter will explore how the possibility that a woman might actually become president has manifested itself in the popular imagination. Focusing primarily on *Commander in Chief*, a television drama which featured President Mackenzie Allen (Geena Davis), an Independent, non-partisan vice president who ascends to the highest office when the president dies, this chapter will explore the programme's inability to separate the president's domestic and professional lives, how it struggles to establish a distinctive visual language to represent female leadership, and how issues surrounding feminine 'care-giving' and masculine 'protecting' are negotiated.

The limited work that has been done on the female president in film and television, and *Commander in Chief* in particular, perpetuates many of the same problems in writing about representations of presidents more generally: namely, a refusal to engage with the programme as an audio-visual text with a particular representational, iconographic and generic history. There has been a tendency to view *Commander in Chief* as *evidence* that the United States is not ready for a female president, rather than a programme that exists in a more complex relationship with the political culture it represents and the televisual traditions from which it is drawn. Indeed, *Commander in Chief* has much more in common with the workplace sitcom or dramedy that features a woman in the lead role, like *The Mary Tyler Moore Show* (1970–77), *Murphy Brown* (1988–98) or *Ally McBeal* (1997–2002), all of which have been considered as cultural expressions of the achievements and problems of the second-wave feminist movement, than it has with other presidential fiction. Where *The West Wing* placed significant emphasis on policy, *Commander in Chief* sets out to address the means by which the president negotiates her job and her domestic responsibilities, a significant element of third-wave or 'post-'feminism. This chapter will place *Commander in Chief* in its specific context, examining its relationship to both second- and third-wave feminisms and, concomitantly, how it operates in relation to representations of women in film and television in the 1990s and 2000s. It will place particular emphasis on the means by which the programme carves a space for Allen within a traditionally hypermasculine schema, how it negotiates the apparent conflict between Allen's professional life and her domestic life and, finally, the difficulty the programme has in reconciling this with its representation of Allen's husband, Rod Calloway (Kyle Secor). I will explore these issues through close attention to narrative and character construction, as well as camera movement, editing and framing. Through this I will establish whether *Commander in Chief* is able to represent female political power while remaining simultaneously wedded to a conventional preoccupation with female domesticity. Essentially, does *Commander in Chief* operate within the masculinised presidential schema I have interrogated throughout this book, or is there room within mainstream representation for something genuinely feminine (even femin*ist*) in the representation of women presidents?

***

There are not a vast number of precursors to *Commander in Chief*. However, there are a few significant examples that require further exploration here, not least because they operate within a longer history of representation of women in film and television, as well as forming the basis for contemporary incarnations of the female president.

Kisses for My President (Curtis Bernhardt, 1964) is an important antecedent, not only because Polly Bergen, who plays President McCloud, returned to the White House as President Allen's mother in *Commander in Chief*. More significantly, both film and later television drama foreground the domestic issues that arise from female presidencies, in particular the inadequacies felt by the 'First Gentleman'. In *Kisses for My President*, this role is played by the put-upon, downtrodden Fred MacMurray (playing Thad McCloud) who, in *Double Indemnity* (Billy Wilder, 1944), and *There's Always Tomorrow* (Douglas Sirk, 1956), portrayed feminised American males who are no longer the masters of their domain. Indeed, one might view *Kisses for My President* as a more hyperbolic example of the subtler men-in-crisis films from the previous decade like *There's Always Tomorrow*, *The Man in the Grey Flannel Suit* (Nunnally Johnson, 1956), *Bigger than Life* (Nicholas Ray, 1956), and *The Wrong Man* (Alfred Hitchcock, 1956) in which, as Bruzzi argues, 'the breadwinner patriarch, the supposedly hegemonic male of 1950s America, is shown not to be as content and secure as might be expected, but conversely, to be miserable, desperate and insecure.'[17] This insecurity is rendered literal in *Kisses for My President*, where Thad is put in a position previously unimaginable in the annals of American history and politics; as Lilly Goren notes, rather than focus upon the historic shift that sees a woman in the Oval Office for the first time, the film focuses upon 'the awkward situations in which First Gentleman McCloud finds himself and the comedic twists and turns he faces as he tries to fit into what is clearly presented as a woman's place.'[18] Moreover, the president is shown to be incapable of managing her job and her family life simultaneously: her two children descend into delinquency, and Thad is nearly seduced by an old girlfriend (a *femme fatale* in feathers and furs). Entirely uncomfortable with this situation, *Kisses for My President* resolves itself when the president becomes pregnant and resigns (why exactly this is necessary is not clear, other than a broad assumption

17 Stella Bruzzi, *Men's Cinema: Masculinity and Mise-en-Scène in Hollywood* (Edinburgh: Edinburgh University Press, 2013), 40.

18 Lilly J. Goren, 'Fact or Fiction: The Reality of Race and Gender in Reaching the White House', in Justin S. Vaughan and Lilly J. Goren, eds, *Women and the White House: Gender, Popular Culture and Presidential Politics* (Lexington: University Press of Kentucky, 2013), 107.

that pregnant women are far too delicate to work in any capacity, let alone in a position as stressful and demanding as US president). This eventuality reasserts the virility of her husband, and restores the president to her 'proper' role as mother, thereby reuniting the family. The film's restoration of 'social order' corroborates Molly Haskell's suggestion that, in mainstream Hollywood, 'women suffer because of their professional status' and the suffering only ends 'once the main female character recognizes the repercussions of her devotion to work and is restored to her putatively proper place.'[19] Released the year after the publication of Betty Friedan's *The Feminine Mystique* (1963) and the passage of the Equal Pay Act, it is possible to view *Kisses for My President* as representative of a culture on the cusp of major change, although the film still clings desperately to the *status quo*: its conclusion is a reactionary reinforcement of hegemonic power relations between men and women, taking women's liberation to its 'logical conclusion' and showing it to be an entirely unworkable and undesirable state of affairs. Whereas throughout this book I have shown examples of male presidents who succeed in resolving the tensions between being an ordinary man and President of the United States, the conclusion of *Kisses for My President* lays down an important marker for representations of female leaders: the conflict between being a heterosexual, married woman with children, and being president, is shown to be impossible to reconcile. One thing has to be sacrificed for the other.

This is an issue explored at some length in *24*. In the final two seasons, President Allison Taylor picks up the mantle from her predecessors and becomes a victim of terrorist attacks, conspiracies within her own government, and has to be rescued and protected by Jack Bauer. As suggested in the previous chapter, *24*'s representation of presidential power is indicative of a wider concern surrounding the physical vulnerability and powerlessness of the position in the post-9/11 environment. The 'protector' role is deemed no longer available to the president, and it is arguable that *24*'s representation of a female president represents the logical

19 Molly Haskell, *From Reverence to Rape: The Treatment of Women in the Movies* (Chicago: University of Chicago Press, 1987), 112.

conclusion to a programme that has been preoccupied with reinforcing traditional conceptions of race and gender. As with the representation of villainous Sherry Palmer, *24* shows itself to be profoundly uncomfortable with authoritative women, clearly preferring the 'damsel in distress' (a role which Taylor fulfils in the programme's seventh season, as she is rescued by Bauer after an invasion of the White House itself). At the conclusion of the seventh season, it becomes apparent that Taylor's daughter Olivia (Sprague Grayden), who has been acting as her chief of staff, is guilty of political treachery and murder. Taylor now has to make a literal choice between her presidency and her duties as a mother; ultimately, she places her constitutional responsibility to the nation above her individual needs, and this means Olivia must go to prison. Her husband suggests it is her professional ambition that has cost their family so dearly, and that she is responsible for the death of their son (killed by malevolent forces at work in her own government) and Olivia's misdeeds. As Taylor comes to realise the implications of this, she picks up a framed photograph of her previously complete family and cries. She states, 'I've lost my family, I've lost everyone' because of her job. She made the only choice she could have in the situation, but she is punished for it. This rehearses a fairly common trope in Hollywood cinema, whereby a woman who pursues a career in addition to looking after her children fails to juggle the competing demands, and is damned for being a 'bad mother'. Essentially, Taylor has violated the expectations of her gender, and is penalised for her ambition. It is telling that, despite being made forty years apart, with *Kisses for My President* produced on the cusp of the second-wave feminist movement and *24* a long way after it, they are both preoccupied with the irreconcilability of being president and being a wife and mother.

Aside from these two examples, there are very few other female presidents in fiction.[20] The female *vice* president is slightly more commonplace in

20 Indeed, the only other ones are distinctly unremarkable: Patty Duke played the president in sitcom *Hail to the Chief* (1985), which lasted only seven episodes. The other examples are long-forgotten science-fiction *Project Moonbase* (1953), or satirical comedy *Whoops Apocalypse* (1986), in which Loretta Swit from the television series *M*A*S*H* portrayed the fictional leader who succeeds a president who is an actual

popular culture, perhaps indicative of the fact that there *have* been female vice-presidential candidates (Geraldine Ferraro in 1984 and Sarah Palin in 2008) or, as is perhaps more likely, reflective of a tendency to cast the female character in the 'supportive' role proximate to, but rarely holding, real power: Kathryn Bennett (Glenn Close) in *Air Force One* (discussed in Chapter 3), Laine Hanson (Joan Allen) in *The Contender* (Rod Lurie, 2000) and, most recently, Selina Meyer (Julia Louis-Dreyfus) in *Veep* (Armando Iannucci, 2012–). All three, however, evince certain representational problematics: Bennett is largely defined by her emotional reaction to violence and, despite her constitutional responsibility to fulfil the duties of president while Marshall is incapacitated, she consistently acquiesces to him; *The Contender* is not particularly interested in what a female vice president would actually be like, as its primary focus is on Hanson's confirmation hearings, which are dogged by accusations of her sexual impropriety as a young college student; and Meyer, harnessing Louis-Dreyfus's considerable comedic skills, is something of a buffoon. However, it is clear this has little to do with her gender specifically and more to do with the preposterousness of contemporary politics (in keeping with Iannucci's *The Thick Of It* [2005– 12] and film version *In the Loop* [2009]). Moreover, although Meyer, and Hanson in *The Contender*, are the protagonists of their respective stories, neither is able to exert real control over any situation without the intervention of men (the latter is very much focused on the dramatic potential of this situation, the former plays it for laughs). The popular cultural tendency to place a woman in the vice-presidential role appears to be 'symptomatic of a cultural anxiety toward empowered professional/managerial women': they may hold symbolic power, but they should always be answerable to a man.[21]

---

circus clown. In keeping with this level of absurdity, *Iron Sky* (2012) features a female president (Stephanie Paul) seeking reelection when Nazis, who have been hiding on the moon since 1945, capture Washington, DC. The president here is a fairly blunt parody of Sarah Palin, presumably intended as a comedic vision of what might have happened had she ever ascended to the Oval Office.

21 Levinson, *The American Success Myth in Film*, 122.

***

Commander in Chief represents the most expansive, elaborate representation of a female US president in audiovisual fiction to date. As with the fictional black presidents that preceded Obama's presidency, the absence of a compelling real-world referent results in a construction that inevitably reverts to representational, iconographic and narrative traditions drawn from earlier films and television programmes. In advance of the close textual analysis of *Commander in Chief*, I will explore some of the literature that has dealt with this subject, particularly mainstream film and television's persistent exploration of the supposed tensions between a woman's professional ambitions and her domestic duties.

Produced in the mid-2000s, *Commander in Chief* can be broadly said to operate within a relatively long period of Western culture and intellectual thought defined (not unproblematically) as 'postfeminist'. Joel Gwynne and Nadine Muller are keen to enforce the distinction between 'post-feminism' and 'postfeminism', with the former defined as a temporal marker (literally 'after' feminism), and the latter more akin to a cultural sensibility.[22] It is clear, however, that the term means different things to different people, and can, according to Gwynne and Muller, 'represent both a repudiation and an affirmation of feminist politics, depending on how it is deployed within a certain cultural context.'[23] I will sketch the evolution of the term here. In its most benign form, postfeminism refigured feminism as a personal choice rather than a radical movement looking to effect structural change; in its most pernicious, it blamed feminism itself, not patriarchy, for women's supposed 'unhappiness'. Angela McRobbie's suggestion – that 'postfeminism' is a problematic term because it puts forward the incorrect notion that the battle for equality has been achieved and therefore discards feminism as obsolete – is an instructive one, particularly given the term's

22 Joel Gwynne and Nadine Muller, 'Introduction', in Gwynne and Muller, eds, *Postfeminism and Contemporary Hollywood Cinema* (Basingstoke: Palgrave Macmillan, 2013), 2.

23 Ibid.

origins within the conservative rearticulation of the aims of the second-wave feminist movement in the 1980s.[24]

This is a fundamental aspect of Susan Faludi's *Backlash*, which argues that the conservative media in the 1980s repositioned the women's movement itself as the source of female anxiety: the backlash suggested 'women were unhappy because they were too free; their liberation had denied them marriage and motherhood.'[25] This theme was manifest in numerous Hollywood films throughout the 1980s: rather than challenge the sexist, patriarchal nature of the workplace as in *9-to-5* (Colin Higgins, 1980), suddenly women were looking to escape it altogether, as demonstrated by films like *Baby Boom* (Charles Shyer, 1987) and *Broadcast News* (James L. Brooks, 1987). As Levinson argues of this cycle,

> the popular culture response to the incursion of women into the workplace and the elite professions was, by the evidence of Hollywood movies, a sort of ideological retrenchment; most of the films of that era that deal with highly placed professional women end up endorsing gender essentialism and reinscribing women's place in the home.[26]

Mainstream cinema's repudiation of feminism manifested itself most infamously through the refiguration of the unmarried, childless, independent career woman as psychopathic adulteress in the notorious *Fatal Attraction* (Adrian Lyne, 1987), casting the traditional model of femininity (the dutiful and subservient homebody) as the ideal.[27] More negotiated representations of the supposed dichotomy between feminism and femininity were addressed in two films later in the decade: as Charlotte Brunsdon suggests of *Working Girl* (Mike Nichols, 1988) and *Pretty Woman* (Garry Marshall, 1990), the female protagonists' combination of traditional (pre-feminist)

24 Angela McRobbie, 'Postfeminism and Popular Culture: Bridget Jones and the New Gender Regime', in Diane Negra and Yvonne Tasker, eds, *Interrogating Postfeminism: Gender and the Politics of Popular Culture* (Durham: Duke University Press, 2007), quoted in Gwynne and Muller, 'Introduction', 2.

25 Faludi, *Backlash*, 141.

26 Julie Levinson, *The American Success Myth on Film*, 118.

27 Faludi, *Backlash*, 147–52.

femininity in appearance and behaviour towards men, with feminist desire for career advancement, equality and independence, was indicative of an approach that came to be labelled as 'postfeminist'.[28] Indeed, as Yvonne Tasker and Diane Negra suggest, it is precisely this double-bind between the celebration of the advances of second-wave feminism, and anxieties surrounding the movement's consequences, that constitute the somewhat contradictory nature of postfeminism.[29] Although it was produced in the mid-2000s, *Commander in Chief*'s representation of the presidency almost inevitably becomes embroiled in a similar struggle between second- and third-wave feminisms that will be explored later.

Ally McBeal is a key example of postfeminist American television drama of the 1990s and early 2000s, as it chronicles the attempts of the eponymous young lawyer (Calista Flockhart) to 'have it all': a fulfilling career, a loving husband (which, unlike President Allen, Ally does not quite achieve by the end of the programme), and children. Unlike the earlier *Murphy Brown*, which suggested that 'professional success and personal happiness were mutually exclusive', *Ally McBeal* recognised this difficulty without dismissing it as impossible.[30] Although it was written about in popular discourses as a 'backlash' text, and a 'postfeminist' text (in the sense that it disavowed the importance of second-wave feminism), Rachel Moseley and Jacinda Reid put forward the compelling notion that the programme's central project was to reject totalising conceptualisations of 'femininity' and 'feminism' in order to 'address the new conditions of women's lives' as a result of second-wave feminism.[31] However, despite chronicling and taking seriously McBeal's attempt to 'have it all', it is

28 Charlotte Brunsdon, *Screen Tastes: Soap Opera to Satellite Dishes* (London: Routledge, 1997), in Karen Boyle, 'Feminism Without Men: Feminist media studies in a post-feminist age', in Charlotte Brunsdon and Lynn Spigel, eds, *Feminist Television Criticism* [2nd edn] (Maidenhead: Open University Press, 2008), 177.

29 Yvonne Tasker and Diane Negra, eds, *Interrogating Postfeminism: Gender and the politics of popular culture* (Durham: Duke University Press, 2007), 4.

30 Rachel Moseley and Jacinda Reid, '"Having it Ally": Popular Television (Post-) Feminism', *Feminist Media Studies* 2/2 (2002), 247.

31 Ibid.

telling that, ultimately, she fails in the pursuit of this ideal, confirming Hannah Hamad's suggestion that '"having it all" is an anachronism of postfeminist femininity – because postfeminist culture has long averred that women cannot'.[32]

The suggestions of Hamad, Moseley and Reid are most instructive in relation to *Commander in Chief* because it remains concerned precisely with the possibility of 'having it all'. The American presidency perhaps represents a unique case in this pursuit because, as I suggested in relation to *The American President*, the president both lives and works in the White House, and domestic and professional lives are necessarily very closely associated. The demarcation enforced by *Murphy Brown* would be, for President Allen, impossible; indeed, the proximity of the supposedly 'separate spheres' may in fact be desirable. The life of a US president, with both domestic and professional activities housed under the same roof, could be viewed as roughly analogous to the eroding distinctions between work and home being enjoyed and/or suffered by millions of people in the early twenty-first century, where 'the growth in home working and of the home office as a feature of domesticity for many workers suggests a continuing blurring of these spaces and of the gendered roles supported by compartmentalisation of working and domestic lives.'[33]

However, despite these shifts in wider culture and society, as the treatment of Hillary Clinton attests, gender roles and spheres in the White House continue to be rigidly enforced. As explored in Chapter 3, it was her involvement in the 'masculine' sphere of government policy early in her husband's first term as president that made Clinton so unpopular with the American people. Perhaps as a result of this, when her husband became president in 2009, Harvard- and Princeton-educated lawyer Michelle Obama suggested her most important job was now 'mom in chief' to

32 Hannah Hamad, 'Hollywood Fatherhood: Paternal Postfeminism in Contemporary Hollywood Cinema', in Gwynne and Muller, eds, *Postfeminism and Contemporary Hollywood Cinema*, 102.

33 Yvonne Tasker, 'Practically Perfect People: Postfeminism, Masculinity and Male Parenting in Contemporary Hollywood Cinema', in Murray Pomerance, ed., *A Family Affair: Cinema Calls Home* (London: Wallflower Press, 2008), 183.

their daughters, Sasha and Malia, seemingly acknowledging that politics and family life continue to operate in separate spheres.[34] Carving a space for herself as a spokesperson for national health and well-being, Michelle Obama has remained consistently (and significantly) more popular than her husband throughout his presidency. Reinforcing traditional conceptualisations of First Lady and President (broadly in line with conventional gender roles), Michelle is the care-giver (almost becoming the nation's 'mom' through her commitment to better nutrition), Barack the protector. While clearly President Obama is not an *absent* father, the expectations of the presidency dictate that he be responsible for the protection of the nation, rather than only his two daughters (although of course these two issues are closely related, as demonstrated by films such as *First Daughter* [Forest Whitaker, 2004] and *Chasing Liberty* [Andy Cadiff, 2004], in which the post-9/11 desire for simultaneous freedom and security is played out in the conflict between the over-protective president and his rebellious, independently minded daughter). So while the professional and domestic lives of the US president might be uniquely *physically* intertwined, they remain *discursively* and irretrievably separate. In everyday life outside the White House, there might be the possibility of 'Having it Ally' but, despite amenable conditions, is it likely that someone can be wife, mother, and President of the United States, and 'Have it Allen'? How *Commander in Chief* attempts to negotiate these issues will form the basis of the rest of this chapter.

***

Commander in Chief gives itself a problem from the outset, acquiescing to the pervasive discourses surrounding the inherent legitimacy of the patriarchal presidency by not *electing* Allen to the presidency but having her *ascend* to it following the death of President Teddy Bridges (Will Lyman). Much of the existing criticism of the programme focuses primarily on this

34 'Michelle Obama describes duty as mother-in-chief', *USA Today*, August 4th, 2008, <http://usatoday30.usatoday.com/news/politics/election2008/2008-08-04-michelle-obama_N.htm>, accessed November 2013.

issue.[35] However, I contend that the first two episodes of the programme are somewhat more complicated, as they attempt to carve a space for a female president within this traditionally patriarchal schema, and negotiate Allen's expected subservience to the will of her male predecessor.

Indeed, because Allen is an Independent and therefore not necessarily beholden to the ideological vision the Republican Bridges had for the country, she has to fight to be seen as legitimate (despite her constitutional prerogative to assume the presidency). *Commander in Chief* makes it plain that this question is bound up wither her gender: despite being a former member of Congress, university chancellor and Vice President of the United States, her main rival for the presidency, Speaker of the House Nathan Templeton (Donald Sutherland) dismisses her as a 'schoolteacher' (a traditionally feminine role), and seriously questions whether a woman would be able to handle the post-9/11 world, particularly in thorny negotiations with Middle Eastern countries who would supposedly be unwilling 'to follow the edicts of a woman'. However, Templeton places particular emphasis on the size, scope and significance of presidential power; that you must want to be president because 'you want the power to control the universe.' The pieties and platitudes Allen offers in response to the question – that she wants to help people and make a difference – are dismissed by Templeton perhaps largely because they smack of the feminine roles of mothering and care-giving, and are therefore decidedly unpresidential. Allen's determination to rescue a Nigerian woman, Oria Madula, from being stoned to death for committing adultery indicates to Templeton that she would use the power of the presidency to intervene in issues irrelevant to the United States' interests (as if women's rights are of trifling concern). In essence, Templeton argues that Allen *cannot be* presidential because she is a woman, not only because this would represent a significant change to a position defined by its close, historical alignment with traditional, patriarchal masculinity, but also because, as a woman, she is incapable of exercising presidential power in a manner necessary and appropriate to ensure the protection and reputation of the nation at a time of international turmoil.

35 Horwitz and Swyers, 'Why Are All The Presidents Men?', 125.

The extent to which Allen remains beholden to the patriarchal establishment, and how she negotiates the legacy bequeathed by her deceased predecessor, is a fundamental aspect of *Commander in Chief*. The subservience of a powerful woman to a male mentor or role model is a common trope in mainstream film and television. As Kate Waits argues of Hollywood's 'warrior woman' archetype (a role with which Geena Davis is associated through films like *Cutthroat Island* [Renny Harlin, 1995] and *The Long Kiss Goodnight* [Renny Harlin, 1996]), the character is often created by, and therefore deferential towards, a sometimes-absent male authority figure.[36] In *Tomb Raider* (Simon West, 2000), *Charlie's Angels* (the TV series [1976–81] and the later films [McG, 2000 & 2003]) and *Kill Bill* (Quentin Tarantino, 2003), this enacts itself through recourse to violence and aggression, but the relationship between male mentor and female protégé is a compelling one in relation to *Commander in Chief* and the spectre of the deceased president. When Bridges asks Allen to resign on his deathbed, he says Templeton 'shares [his] vision and supports [his] will' in a way that Allen, as an Independent, will not. At Bridges' funeral, Templeton's eulogy concludes with a call for the nation to pray for the new president 'to answer the clarion call of Teddy Bridges. For it is only through [her] deeds that his genius can be fulfilled for us all.' Essentially, Templeton demands Allen deny herself any agency in the most powerful position in the world in order to act merely as a breathing cypher for the deceased, male (and therefore legitimate) president. Initially, Allen appears to have a conflicted relationship with this requirement: although she tells her cabinet that the common link between them is the deceased president who brought them together to serve the country, she later announces to the wider public that she will not simply fulfil the legacy of the man she has succeeded, but will continue the legacy of a nation. The irony of this is obvious – although Allen correctly identifies The White House as the symbolic home of American democracy and home to the *presidency* and

36 Kate Waites, 'Babes in boots: Hollywood's oxymoronic warrior woman', in Suzanne Ferriss and Mallory Young, eds, *Chick flicks: Contemporary women at the movies* (London: Routledge, 2008), 205.

not the *president*, it is a place and a history inextricably linked to traditional conceptions of masculinity.

Allen is clearly indebted to the symbolic value of this patriarchal past. In this regard, she performs a similar move to the female hero in Hollywood cinema who, as Tasker suggests, 'may be represented as identified with the father, in search of authority and, sometimes reconciliation with authority.'[37] Given the masculine character of the presidency, Allen *has* to identify, be identified, and reconcile with her symbolic fathers (both her immediate predecessor and those that came before him): she quotes Harry Truman in her speech, and later names an executive order introducing interest-free college loans in exchange for teaching service after Bridges (even though he wanted to spend the money on a manned mission to Mars, a more conventionally 'masculine' pursuit). However, the programme seeks a negotiated position, and attempts to transcend these rigid definitions: *Commander in Chief* is keen to position Allen as the inheritor of a patriarchal role, but who will not merely submit to its demands. Her first speech as president is cross-cut with images of American military forces successfully rescuing Madula (something that Templeton implies Bridges is unlikely to have done). In this regard, *Commander in Chief* establishes itself early on as primarily concerned with maintaining a conservative vision of the United States as a benign superpower, but finding a way of expanding this vision to show women directly involved in the maintenance of this image. This is referred to in a later episode in a rather mawkish fashion, when Allen's press secretary Kelly (Ever Carradine) states that, in rescuing Madula, the president was not acting as a 'representative of women, but a representative of the human race.' *Commander in Chief* is engaged in a project here to include women within the parameters of a position previously defined by its masculine character. Unlike *The West Wing*, which consistently positioned 'women's issues' as outside the

37 Yvonne Tasker, *Working Girls: Gender and Sexuality in Popular Cinema* (London: Routledge, 1998), 69.

necessary, pragmatic business of the nation state, *Commander in Chief* sets out early on to change this dynamic.[38]

However, *Commander in Chief* does not achieve this straightforwardly, and this tension is no more visibly evident than in a narrative arc, played out over two episodes, in which the president contends with a threat of nuclear war from North Korea, precipitated by an American submarine running aground perilously close to hostile territory. These two episodes of *Commander in Chief* represent the programme's best opportunity to offer an image of a female president in the role of 'protector'. Allen's attempt to negotiate a truce with a nuclear power is obviously intended to recall the Cuban Missile Crisis which, when represented in film and television, consistently positions President Kennedy as the protective father to a nation of frightened children.[39] In this regard, Allen's similar prevention of conflict is clearly designed to further reinforce the notion that she belongs in a position that has been constructed around supposedly 'masculine' characteristics of toughness, decisiveness, rectitude and tactical nous. However, while ostensibly Allen leads with similar courage and decisive strength to President Kennedy, in her own conflict with the military over how best to handle the situation, it becomes apparent that *Commander in Chief* struggles to sustain the impression that a woman can operate independently within the masculine schema of the presidency. Firstly, Allen suddenly becomes reliant on male 'helpers' in the execution of her foreign policy: she brings in Templeton who, although throughout the series is constructed as Allen's arch-enemy and greatest threat to her leadership, happens to be an expert on the region and a close friend of the Chinese ambassador (without whose help the United States will most likely go to war), as well as depending on her Chief of Staff Jim Gardener (Harry Lennix) to issue her military advisors with a dressing down when they continually obfuscate, divert attention and challenge her authority.

38 Parry-Giles and Parry-Giles, *The Prime-Time Presidency*, 54–86.

39 This is particularly true of *Thirteen Days* (Roger Donaldson, 2000), where Kennedy is frequently shown pondering the best course of action in relation to Cuba by looking at, and fearing for, young children.

As Rod says to Jim, 'Someone has to talk to the generals', but the programme appears to decree that it cannot be Allen: *Commander in Chief* perpetuates mainstream culture and society's profound discomfort with assertions of female power.

This uneasiness reveals itself quite clearly in the programme's *mise-en-scène*. Although Steadicam is employed reasonably often (although not as a defining stylistic characteristic as in *The West Wing*) it is consistent in its framing of Allen in a two-shot with a man, usually either her chief of staff or her husband (see Figure 6.1).

6.1 President Allen (Geena Davis) strides down the corridor alongside her husband (Kyle Secor) in 'Sub Enchanted Evening', season one, *Commander in Chief* (dir. Jesse Bochco, Touchstone Television, USA, 2006)

In *The West Wing*, if flanked by advisors, Bartlet was most often framed centrally, or at the front of a larger entourage. In Chapter 3, I argued that President Whitmore's weakness of leadership in the initial phases of *Independence Day* manifested itself in the camera positioning and framing choices, consistently placing him in two-shot. It is apparent that *Commander in Chief* has made a similar move, although perhaps not as an intentional slight on Allen's leadership skills, but more as a reflection of the uncertainty regarding the appropriate *modus operandi* now that a woman is in power. Bruzzi suggests that the Steadicam is not innately masculine, but can, in certain contexts and in conjunction with other stylistic elements, be indicative of a strident, in-control masculinity.[40] However, the infrequent, somewhat confused, employment of this stylistic choice in *Commander in Chief* suggests that the equation of slick, robust forward momentum with masculinity is not one that is easily abandoned. On the one occasion during the North Korean crisis in which Allen is framed as the dominant force in a Steadicam shot through the West Wing, showing her make steady, determined and unwavering progress toward the Oval Office, the visual display of power is undercut by a joke: like the schoolteacher of whom Templeton was so dismissive, Allen gently rebukes her assistant, Vince (Anthony Azizi), for running in the corridor. This is a strategy the programme has employed consistently, whereby any anxiety about Allen's displays of power, or shifts in protocol now there is a female president, is neutralised through humour (it is particularly notable in the episode in which she dances with the Russian president, and her staff fret over whether she is 'leading' or not). It seems that the Steadicam 'power walk', rendered culturally significant by *The West Wing*, cannot be uncomplicatedly replicated with a woman in charge.

Commander in Chief is considerably more reliant upon medium shots, two-shots, tighter angles and rapid cutting in the creation of its visual style. The impact this has on the impression of female presidential power is telling: when Allen is discussing the nuclear crisis with her advisors in the Cabinet Room, the speed of the editing never allows her to command the space, as the shot changes from Allen, to Templeton, to Gardner, to her other advisors, and back to her, with barely a pause for breath. The framing consistently boxes her in, with an advisor on one side, or with her husband and Chief of Staff looming over her from behind (see Figure 6.2).

40 Bruzzi, *Men's Cinema*, 166–7.

6.2 President Allen is surrounded by her advisors as she considers action against North Korea in 'No Nukes is Good Nukes', season one, *Commander in Chief* (dir. Jesse Bochco, Touchstone Television, USA, 2006)

Tellingly, on two occasions when she issues a direct order (first to chastise the military for not informing her of the incursion into North Korean territory, and secondly to action the plan to rescue the sailors) the camera cuts to long-shot, almost recoiling from a display of presidential power. While Allen consistently plays with spaces within the White House in order to control situations on what she deems as 'her' territory (choosing to deliver the State of the Union address from the Oval Office when it is ordinarily staged in the Capitol Building, or shifting the handling of the North Korea crisis from the Situation Room to the Cabinet Room), the programme's visual choices do not reflect her authority and command, and these assertions of power are often done so quietly. For example, rather than rebuke the military in the Situation Room, as Bartlet does frequently in *The West Wing*, she asks them for a quiet word in the corridor outside. While her leadership is always firm, she is consistently caught between the 'masculine' demands of her job (particularly the need to be authoritative and aggressive, which sometimes includes raising your voice, something Bartlet does often), and her femininity. Mainstream film and television since the 1980s often demonstrates significant discomfort with demonstrations of female power. Either the successful career woman is demonised for being overly authoritative and ambitious (like Katharine Parker [Sigourney Weaver] in *Working Girl* or, more recently, Miranda Priestly [Meryl Streep] in *The Devil Wears Prada* [David Frankel, 2006], both of whom are deemed to have made bad choices by valorising their careers over personal happiness), or, in the case of the 'new *femme fatale*' in films like *Basic Instinct* (Paul Verhoeven, 1992), *The Last Seduction* (John Dahl, 1994), *Disclosure* (Barry Levinson, 1994) and *Presumed Innocent* (Alan J. Pakula, 1990), the powerful woman is presented as murderous, and therefore threatening to the patriarchal order.[41] Because of this pernicious heritage, displays of power that would be open to a man in these situations are not available to Allen.

Even when the crisis is finally resolved peacefully, and Allen stages a press conference, the camera is still never positioned centrally, in the usual convention, but always off-kilter, at an angle to the left or right. As explored in the previous chapters concerning male presidents, this kind of framing is usually employed to indicate there is power lacking, as in *The American President*, *Independence Day* or the later seasons of *The West Wing*. As explored in Chapter 4, Bartlet's diminished power in later seasons of the programme revealed itself in the adoption of more traditional techniques of editing and framing. While it is clear *Commander in Chief* has progressive credentials, and is not deliberately attempting to represent Allen as weak, it has not developed the visual language to render female power through *mise-en-scène* particularly effectively. It is almost as though the 'separate spheres' ideology that decrees men be protectors and women care-givers has manifested itself stylistically: the Steadicam belongs primarily to male power, and *Commander in Chief* has not developed an alternative means to represent female power in a similarly dynamic fashion.

The involvement of Templeton in the negotiations with the Chinese are most problematic in the representation of Allen's leadership. It might be argued that Allen's willingness to listen to other learned parties (particularly when they are her enemies) demonstrates a more mature attitude to foreign affairs (traditionally viewed as solely the president's domain). However,

41 Levinson, *The American Success Myth on Film*, 122.

visually, Templeton's presence alongside Allen does not look appropriate in comparison with other representations of presidential power: while it could be argued Allen is doing a sensible thing by bringing in an expert, it might also be suggested that such a manoeuvre demonstrates that she is not strong or decisive enough to do this on her own. The masculine schema of the presidency decrees that, in this situation, Allen needs a man to hold her hand and tell her what to do. The framing choices reinforce this impression: in the Cabinet Room, from which she handles the crisis and issues most of her orders, she is consistently positioned alongside Templeton as *equally* powerful agents in negotiations. Templeton sits next to her on the sofa when she speaks with the Chinese ambassador. Templeton's presence is not solely for support: the negotiation is clearly a two-hander, as he takes over in outlining a potential deal with the Chinese for the use of their marine rescue equipment. The final image of the scene, a medium shot, shows Templeton and Allen facing each other in the Oval Office, Templeton dismissing Allen's concerns about the deal they have made, Allen tempering some of Templeton's more bellicose rhetoric. Conventional gender roles – the man as bullish and strident, the woman as a conciliatory, tempering influence on the man – are reinforced. Later, when Allen confronts the North Korean ambassador in the Oval Office, she is physically 'backed up' by Jim Gardener and National Security Advisor Anthony Prado (Alex Fernandez). As Horowitz and Swyers suggest of *Commander in Chief*, 'the general idea is that a female president is only viable when she is backed by men.'[42] While the programme may have set out initially to counter the notion that 'women are less prepared than men for the role of commander in chief and less able than men to handle the military, national security, and foreign affairs', in its representation of a national security crisis it ultimately perpetuates this stereotype.[43] Allen is not allowed to fulfil the role of sole 'protector' of the nation: her femininity, it seems, excludes her from playing this role on her own.

42 Horowitz and Swyers, 'Why are all the presidents men?', 125.

43 Carroll, 'Reflections on Gender and Hillary Clinton's Election Campaign', 9.

Why might this be the case? It is worth pondering the context in which the programme was produced. Faludi argued in *The Terror Dream* that post-9/11 American culture was deeply invested in 'the denigration of capable women, the magnification of manly men, the heightened call for domesticity, the search for and sanctification of helpless girls', implicating women's independence in the nation's failure to protect itself.[44] George W. Bush's leadership of the United States' 'war on terror', as discussed in Chapter 4, consistently recalled images of the cowboy at the edge of a wild and dangerous frontier. There is very little room for powerful women in this construct, as they are required to fulfil the roles of helpless protectees. *Commander in Chief*'s somewhat hesitant view of Allen's power might be indicative of this environment. The behaviour of the men who surround Allen throughout these two episodes comes across very much in this fashion, with Jim asking Rod whether the president has eaten or slept, also stepping in to defend the president against the military and national security advisors ('You have the president's orders, I haven't heard her change them'). Allen needs male support to lead effectively. This is a dynamic that only emerges in *The West Wing* when Bartlet's multiple sclerosis worsens in the final three seasons, and he increasingly has to be 'handled' by his wife and chief of staff (following Leo's heart attack this role is fulfilled by a woman, former press secretary C.J. Cregg). *Commander in Chief* seems considerably more at ease in the domestic realm. I will now proceed to examine this facet of its construction.

***

As Justin Vaughan and Stacy Michaelson note of *Commander in Chief*, 'the show portrays President Allen striving to be both a good president and a good mother; she puts in long days and still tries to make it home for dinner at night.'[45] It is the attempt to fulfil the competing duties of the

44 Faludi, *The Terror Dream*, 14.

45 Justin S. Vaughn and Stacy Michaelson, 'It's a Man's World: Masculinity in Pop Culture Portrayals of the President', in Vaughn and Goren, eds, *Women and the White House*, 153.

postfeminist woman that is of central concern in *Commander in Chief*. As creator Rod Lurie suggested, the focus on familial issues was a means of distinguishing itself from the more 'arcane' *West Wing*, but, given that this is a programme featuring a female president, this choice has political consequences.[46]

Several presidents have sought to humanise themselves for the electorate by having pictures taken with their children in the Oval Office (most famously, John F. Kennedy, and more recently, Barack Obama). This is clearly done to suggest that they are capable of being attentive fathers as well as good leaders; that one's professional life and domestic life can be managed simultaneously. However, in *Commander in Chief*, the practical difficulty of this is manifest and, like *Kisses for My President*, it consistently suggests that Allen's presidency is disruptive to her family life. Some of the direct and indirect consequences of Allen's job include the following: the disappearance of her daughter Becca's (Caitlin Wachs) diary and the possibility that embarrassing revelations regarding her abilities as a mother will surface, her son Horace (Matt Lanter) struggling academically at school, Becca's boyfriend's secret attempt to film them having sex in order to boast to his friends that he had slept with the president's daughter, as well as myriad concerns regarding the children's nutrition and behaviour in and out of school (this is not to mention the difficulties she has with her husband, which will be explored later).

For Allen, motherhood and the protection of children is the frequent motivating factor behind her decisions. In this regard, *Commander in Chief* conforms to a pattern established in action films like *Aliens* (James Cameron, 1986), *Terminator 2: Judgment Day* (James Cameron, 1991) and, more recently, *Kill Bill*, in which the female action hero's violent acts are justified as a necessary part of her parental or quasi-parental role.[47] Within Davis's career, the most apt comparison to be made is with *The Long Kiss Goodnight*, in which she plays housewife and mother Samantha Caine suffering from amnesia who, following a car accident, begins to

46 Rod Lurie, quoted by Cox Han and Heldman, *Rethinking Madam President*, 34–5.
47 Waites, 'Babes in boots', 205.

recall her past life as a CIA-trained assassin named 'Charley'. Although the film indulges in the pleasurable spectacle of 'Charley' employing all manner of sophisticated weaponry and colourful language, the two personas are ultimately deemed irreconcilable, and the *denouement* is primarily concerned with Charley/Samantha rescuing her daughter, and restoring Samantha to her 'proper' role in the home. It seems a similar move occurs in *Commander in Chief*, whereby despite exercising the awesome power of the presidency, Allen's ultimate motives and drive are always towards the homestead and her offspring. However, in keeping with its inheritance from other postfeminist television drama, the reconciliation between work and home is often the source of significant tension, with the space of the Oval Office playing a crucial role.

In episode five, while dealing with a terrorist threat against an elementary school (a further illustration of the post-9/11 environment in which all other concerns took a back seat to the protection of the nation's children), Allen's youngest child, Amy (Jasmine Jessica Anthony), comes to visit her mother in the Oval Office, but the president is too busy to attend to her.[48] Later, when Allen discovers her national security team have tortured a terror suspect in direct contravention of her orders, she fires the Attorney General. Allen walks across the Oval Office carpet (which features a giant presidential seal) barefoot, and picks up Amy's toy gun. Framed in the Oval Office window, Allen is pictured crying. Most obviously, this recalls the devastating conclusion of *Stella Dallas* (King Vidor, 1937), in which the eponymous protagonist (Barbara Stanwyck), realising that her continued presence in her daughter Laurel's life is proving detrimental to her happiness, can only stand in the rain and watch through the window as Laurel marries a wealthy socialite. *Commander in Chief* uses a similarly heightened melodramatic register, adapting this familiar image through the perpetuation of a trope of postfeminist television drama: while Allen is inside the building, meaning there is the *possibility* conflict can be resolved, the emphasis here is on the president's *struggle* to fulfil the duties she has to her job and the responsibilities she has to her children. Indeed, in an

48 Faludi, *The Terror Dream*, 207.

earlier episode (another that deals with Allen's moves to protect children), the conclusion has the camera crane up to show a top-down view of the Oval Office with her daughter asleep next to her husband on the sofa (see Figure 6.3).

6.3 President Allen recovers at the end of the day with her husband and young daughter in the Oval Office in 'First Strike', season one, *Commander in Chief* (dir. Jesse Bochco, Touchstone Television, USA, 2006)

The presidential seal looms large, dominating the middle of the image, offering the symbolic suggestion that the job is overwhelming Allen's domestic life, coming between herself and her family. Unlike earlier postfeminist workplace dramas like *Murphy Brown*, enforcing the distinction between the career and family is not the intention here. In correlation with Moseley and Read's discussion of *Ally McBeal*, *Commander in Chief* shows Allen's personal and professional lives to be highly integrated, and the desire to hold them together is a site of significant struggle.[49] In saving so many other people's children in these two episodes, Allen acknowledges she has neglected her own, as confirmed by her tears.

49 Moseley and Read, '"Having it Ally"', 232.

The programme's preoccupation with the domestic ramifications of Allen's presidency is consistent. While she enjoys many political triumphs, including avoiding nuclear war, rescuing children from terrorist attacks, navigating the complex issues of state's rights, surviving the publication of a tell-all memoir about her term as vice president, managing the closure of a naval base, and neutralising a bomb threat against Air Force One, *Commander in Chief* often concludes its episodes in the domestic sphere, Allen saying goodnight to her children, getting into bed with her husband, or eating cookies with her mother and chatting about her (usually extraordinary) day at work. It is clear that 'Having it Allen' means being reminded that the president is also a wife, mother and daughter: her feminine domesticity must be frequently reaffirmed in order to prevent her from becoming the dominant woman of the workplace so often depicted as dangerous or threatening in mainstream film and television. However, this strategy somewhat undercuts her preceding exertions of power: at the conclusion of the double episode in which Allen prevents a nuclear confrontation with North Korea, she goes to the residence to read her youngest daughter a bedtime story (taking back the reins from her older son who had been fulfilling this duty while she was working), to find her mother has baked cookies. Allen admits to her mother that 'it was a rush, being the most powerful person on Earth, it was a helluva rush' (as though it is something of which to be slightly embarrassed), before her mother jokes, 'You may not want to mention "the most powerful person on Earth" part your husband.' As Haskell suggested, 'a movie heroine could action the same power and career drives as a man only if, at the climax, they took second place to the sacred love of a man.'[50] It is clear that *Commander in Chief* has somewhat adapted this formulation to incorporate wider domestic concerns, but retained its essence: Allen can absolutely fulfil the role of president, as long as she, and we, are reminded of her familial roles and, more specifically, that she is able to *disguise* her displays of power for the sake of retaining a semblance of traditional gender roles within her marriage.

50 Haskell, *From Reverence to Rape*, 4.

In relation to this, in its desire to represent a positive image of a postfeminist woman struggling (but just about managing) to fulfil her duties as president, wife and mother, *Commander in Chief* has some trouble in constructing an appropriate role for Allen's husband, Rod, 'The First Gentleman'. While it shows itself capable of reconciling Allen with her male forebears, and carves out a place for a female president within this masculine institution, it fails spectacularly to find a similar role for a man in a traditionally 'feminine' position. In the second episode, Allen arrives at the breakfast table, her husband Rod already sitting down with the children. She notices Amy eating a doughnut, and challenges her regarding the nutritional value of her breakfast, before handing her an apple. Allen chastises her other children, not her husband, for allowing this to happen. There is no doubt the scene is played for humour, an impression reinforced by the light-hearted orchestral score, but Rod remains silent throughout the exchange, absolving himself of any responsibility for his child's nutrition. This follows Allen's discovery of a half-eaten chocolate dessert next to Amy's bedside when she returns to the residence to say goodnight to her family: Allen chuckles somewhat exasperatedly, before sighing and appearing concerned, presumably about the effect her demanding job is having on her child. Both examples demonstrate that Rod is not fulfilling his parental duties, failing to provide adequate support to his wife. This seems curious, given that mainstream cinema and television has grown comfortable with representing fathers as willing, and highly capable, carers for children. What is it about being the husband of the President of the United States that alters this formulation?

Films which featured capable fathers were initially figured as part of the 'backlash' against feminism, where men were required to fulfil both parental roles after their wives had 'abandoned' them, a prominent example of this cycle being *Kramer vs Kramer* (Robert Benton, 1979).[51] These films were indicative of a culture aggressively responding to feminist calls for men to be more involved in childcare and family life, not to exist merely as distant, authoritarian breadwinners. This led to the development of a

51 Bruzzi, *Bringing Up Daddy*, 107–14.

negotiated image of the father as both protector *and* nurturer, the incorporation of a domestic component into the construct of idealised masculinity occurring as part of a re-evaluation of the purpose of men in a post-Cold War, postfeminist, post-industrial environment. As Jeffords argued, stars like Arnold Schwarzenegger, who had previously been defined by his 'hard body' and violent aggressiveness, was refigured as a softer, more caring, paternalistic figure able to care for children in films like *Kindergarten Cop* and *Terminator 2*, even giving birth to a baby in *Junior* (Ivan Reitman, 1994).[52] Citing films such as *Signs* (M. Night Shyamalan, 2002), *Minority Report* (Steven Spielberg, 2002) and *The Pursuit of Happyness* (Gabriele Muccino, 2006), Hamad argues 'the currency of fatherhood as a defining component of ideal masculinity has emerged as a dominant cultural trope of postfeminism' in the early 2000s.[53] As noted by a variety of critics, these cultural demonstrations of capable, idealised, occasionally unconventional fatherhood can be read as emblematic of patriarchy's attempt to beat feminism at its own game; as Tania Modleski argues, 'men ultimately deal with the threat of female power by incorporating it'.[54]

Then why does Rod Calloway in *Commander in Chief* spectacularly fail where so many others have succeeded? The examples discussed by Modleski, Jeffords and Hamad are indicative of an attempt in Hollywood to generate images of men in which the sought-after participation in family life is necessarily contingent upon the newly sensitive and attentive male being given the simultaneous chance to fulfil more traditional roles: provide for, protect and/or rescue his children from harm. It is the driving force behind Chris Gardner's (Will Smith) search for employment as a stockbroker in *The Pursuit of Happyness*; defending the homestead against alien invaders preoccupies the thoughts and actions of Graham Hess (Mel Gibson) in *Signs*; the failure to protect his son is the source of John Anderton's (Tom Cruise) angst in *Minority Report*. Indeed, while 'families provide[d] both

52 Jeffords, 'The Big Switch', 199.

53 Hamad, 'Hollywood Fatherhood', 99.

54 Tania Modleski, *Feminism without Women: Culture and Criticism in a 'Postfeminist' Age* (London: Routledge, 1991), 7.

the motivation for and the resolution of changing masculine heroisms' in the aftermath of the Cold War, it was still a role predicated on a traditional equation of fatherhood with protection: while Schwarzenegger may have become the sensitive, paternal robot in *Terminator 2*, his main job is still to save John Connor from the malevolent T-1000 (Robert Patrick).[55] It is clear that, as First Gentleman, Rod cannot fulfil these roles: he lives in the most heavily guarded building in the world, and his wife is, as the president, *de facto* head of the household. He may still sit at the head of the dining table, but to all intents and purposes, he has been emasculated.

While Allen was vice president, Rod was her chief of staff, a conventionally highly masculine position, involved in pursuing her agenda by strong-arming members of Congress, challenging the president, and being a tough advocate for this programme while she, as the public face of the operation, remained genteel and accommodating. Allen recognises the difficulty of maintaining this relationship when she becomes president – 'I can't have it seem like my husband is running the country.' However, the programme struggles to position Rod in the traditional 'First Lady' role without revealing certain anxieties. Firstly, *Commander in Chief*'s desperation to make light of this supposedly absurd situation in fact demonstrates its hesitancy: Rod's initial encounters with his new duties are underscored with a jaunty soundtrack (as though the very notion of a 'First Gentleman' is inherently humorous), highlighting his discomfort immediately when he sees his offices: 'Woah ... it's very pink.' While Rod is keen to maintain his influence on policy, his chief of staff is keen to reinforce to him that his role is a ceremonial one, consistently emphasising that Hillary Clinton's attempts to make the position more political were hugely problematic, unpopular, and therefore, wrong: she refused to be involved with the White House's food menus ('Mrs Clinton shunned that, made the staff guess. That didn't go over very well.'), put her offices in the West Wing ('I think staying here like a traditional First Lady is a splendid idea.'), and had a larger staff than usual ('Mrs Clinton had twenty. That didn't go over very well.'). As shown by the misogynistic tenor of her coverage in her bid for the Democratic nomination in 2008, Clinton has

55 Jeffords, 'The Big Switch', 200.

been consistently lambasted for attempting to shift the gender dynamics of the presidency. Her attempts to refashion the role of First Lady as a political position rather than only a ceremonial one by asserting her own agenda independent of her husband's was not received entirely favourably.[56] Indeed, as Parry-Giles and Parry-Giles note, opinions of her changed significantly over the course of her husband's two terms in office: Clinton went from being deeply unpopular in his first term when she was viewed as an aggressive feminist, but was more accepted by the wider public when her husband's sexual improprieties became public and she was recast in the more conventional role of the wronged woman who was nevertheless 'standing by her man'.[57] Within the American presidency, *Commander in Chief* makes clear that gender roles need to be rigidly enforced because changes to tradition are vehemently opposed.

But this presents a problem for the programme, as it shows itself to be entirely incapable of simply allowing Rod to fulfil the 'traditional' role. He consistently agitates for a larger influence on policy, stating that if this is not possible, then 'this isn't gonna work, professionally ... or personally.' It is clear that Rod's anxiety stems from his inability to fulfil the 'protector' role within the presidential schema: that position is now necessarily his wife's. Rod's insecurity perhaps speaks more widely to the resurgence of traditional hypermasculinity in the years following 9/11, where calls for a restoration of the male breadwinner model and a return to conventional domesticity dominated the popular cultural realm. The fact he no longer embodies this image appears to cause significant concern for Rod: as Barbara Ehrenreich noted, 'breadwinning was so completely aligned with mature heterosexual masculinity in the 1950s and 1960s that men who failed to achieve the role were considered to be either "not fully adult or not fully masculine"'.[58] So obsessed is Hollywood with the notion of the male breadwinner that Rod's refusal to 'just' be a dad is remarkably similar to that of Charlie Hinton (Eddie Murphy) in *Daddy Day Care* (Steve Carr, 2003) who, handed sole responsibility for looking after his children when he loses his job and his

56 Burrell, 'The Clintons and Gender Politics', 240.

57 Parry-Giles and Parry-Giles, 'Mediating Hillary Rodham Clinton', 205–26.

58 Barbara Ehrenreich, quoted by Peberdy, *Masculinity and Film Performance*, 128.

successful lawyer wife returns to work, laments his plight and yearns for the days when he used to be 'a big shot'. However, he transforms the family home into a business offering care for the children of working parents, thus neutralising any anxiety surrounding his breadwinning capabilities. As Tasker suggests of the film, 'The scene of childcare becomes manageable or pleasurable only when it is transformed into a site of paid labour, a process that points to a significant cultural anxiety around constructing a suitably masculine form of male parenting. Thus the transformation of Charlie's relationship with his son does not take place until the home has become a workplace.'[59] However, because Rod lives in the White House and has particular responsibilities despite his protestations to the contrary, this option is obviously not open to him, again emphasising the unique nature of the demarcated gender roles within the presidency.

However, the programme remains preoccupied with the restoration of this traditional image, even rehearsing a confrontation between father and son that is much more closely aligned with the 1950s. Horace's conflict with Rod about the extent to which Rod is being denigrated by Horace's classmates at school because of his supposedly feminised position explicitly recalls Jim Stark's frustration with his apron-wearing dad in *Rebel Without a Cause* (Nicolas Ray, 1955): Horace tells his father he is embarrassed by him, that his friends at school think he is a 'wimp'.[60] *Commander in Chief* resolves this tension in a much more straightforward fashion than Ray's film, however; Horace is ultimately placated because his father pursues the more traditionally masculine role as commissioner for a major baseball team. The move to provide traditional reinforcement to the father's masculinity when handed the role of care-giver is fairly typical of Hollywood films: in *Cheaper by the Dozen* (Shawn Levy, 2003), Tom Baker (Steve Martin) is required to take on primary responsibility for his twelve children when his wife, Kate (Bonnie Hunt), goes on tour marketing her new book. Tom is able to retain a semblance of his former manhood by staying on as coach for the baseball team; as Tasker argues, 'his association with the masculine

59 Tasker, 'Practically Perfect People', 181.
60 Bruzzi, *Bringing Up Daddy*, 50–6.

world of sports functions to guarantee his gender identity and to underline the specificity of what he brings as a male parent.'[61] It is clear that, in order to resolve Horace's anxiety about his father's manhood, *Commander in Chief* resorts to a similar manoeuvre. As press secretary Kelly says, it must be 'every boy's dream' to have a father in such a position (the corollary of this is that having a mother who is President of the United States is not the source of a comparable level of pride, perhaps largely because of the feminised position in which it places the father).

However, again Rod's status as the presidential spouse means a move that would be open to other characters in mainstream films and television is rendered impossible here. Because being baseball commissioner would result in Rod having to live away from the White House and mean further disruption of the traditional image of the 'presidential family', *Commander in Chief* has to solve a further narrative conundrum: Rod is ultimately made a 'senior advisor' to the president (and here the narrative machinations mercifully cease). It is precisely the kind of negotiated settlement which *Commander in Chief* consistently seeks: Rod is now neither proximate enough to the president to raise questions about him encroaching on her authority, nor so distant as to generate anxieties about his masculine identity. So concerned is the programme with constructing an authentically 'postfeminist' president (good mother, good president), it falls back on very stereotypical anxieties surrounding the feminisation of men as a result of changes brought about by second-wave feminism.

***

Commander in Chief was cancelled after eighteen episodes. The final five were never aired, and nor have they ever resurfaced on a home viewing format. By coincidence, the final episode broadcast, 'Unfinished Business', chronicles Allen's attempt to pass the Equal Rights Amendment, a proposed alteration to the US constitution that would guarantee equal rights for women. Although *Commander in Chief* spends the majority of its episodes attempting to reconcile Allen's femininity with the masculine

61 Tasker, 'Practically Perfect People', 182–3.

schema of the presidency, the final episode looks to once again find a space for second-wave feminism in mainstream American politics, pitching the battle between those who think the battle for equality has already been won (third-wave or 'post'-feminism), and those who believe there is still some way to go. In this regard, it looks to disentangle itself from a postfeminist discourse which, as Tasker and Negra argue, 'draws on and sustains an invented social memory of feminist language as inevitably shrill, bellicose, and parsimonious.'[62] The myth that feminist protesters burned their braziers is referenced early in the episode, and the attempt to reposition feminism as an acceptable, mainstream ideology to be pursued within the bounds of American politics, is rendered explicit in an exchange between Allen's mother and eldest daughter, Becca. When Becca dismisses the relevance of the debate to her own interests, stating that she is 'no feminist', her grandmother asks her, 'So you don't believe women should have equal rights to men?' When she responds, 'Of course', her grandmother, almost as a riposte to the discourses of postfeminism, states, 'Then might I suggest you look up the definition of the word "feminist"!'

It is clear that this episode of *Commander in Chief* somewhat deviates from its original project of placing Allen as the inheritor of a masculine mantle: whereas earlier she is shown watching archive footage of inaugural addresses from Kennedy and Reagan, in preparing to make her case to the nation for the ERA's passage, she watches archive footage of Alice Paul, Gloria Steinem and Betty Friedan. Allen challenges the amendment's detractors, particularly Florida Senate Majority Leader Christine Chambers (Sarah Clarke), whom she convinces would not have received her university degree, and therefore achieved the position she has, without the victories of second-wave feminism (specifically, an amendment to the 1965 Education Acts stating that nobody could be excluded from any education programme on the basis of their sex). Finally, crucially, Rod appears comfortable in the supportive role of spouse, spending the episode organising time for a journalist to interview the president's family about domestic life in the

62 Yvonne Tasker and Diane Negra, 'Introduction: Feminist Politics and Postfeminist Culture', in Tasker and Negra, eds, *Interrogating Postfeminism*, 3.

White House. The episode concludes with a town hall debate between Allen and Templeton in which the president defends the aims of the ERA passionately: 'If not us, who? If not now, when?' Templeton is, unsurprisingly, dismissive of the attempt to pass the amendment, describing it as a 'suffragette's agenda', a bill 'pulled out of the waste basket of history', and that Allen's presidency confirms it as 'obsolete'. *Commander in Chief* clearly positions itself *against* the patriarchal establishment's dismissive attitude towards legislated equality, but because it has consistently looked to place Allen within mainstream presidential politics (and therefore as the inheritor of a male legacy), her attempts to pass the ERA appear as though she is staging a second-wave feminist insurgency. Like *The West Wing*, which consistently positioned 'women's issues' as outside the practical bounds of politics, Allen is warned that she is battling forces she cannot defeat: as her political advisor Dickie tells her, 'You've reached a point in your presidency where people view you as the president, not a female president. [The ERA] is just not worth it.' Perhaps it was not, because the episode would prove to be *Commander in Chief*'s last.

'Unfinished Business' is an interesting episode of *Commander in Chief* not least because of its conclusion, where Allen emerges from the debate to greet the public outside. It is one of the only occasions in the programme that Allen has been shown as a president engaging with the public, rather than immediately retreating to her 'natural' domestic realm at the end of the day. This move is signalled as the camera pulls out to reveal the large crowd waiting to greet her, a similar visual strategy employed at the conclusion of *The American President* to signal the reconciliation of President Shepherd's twin identities as a man and the president. In this scene, she is definitively The President of the United States: not wife, mother and *only then* president. Although the possibilities of this are never realised, again it is intriguing to ponder the context from which it emerged. As Faludi argues, after 9/11, the United States began to purge feminist discourse from the national culture, looking instead to reinstall highly traditional images of men as aggressive, independent warriors and women as domestic homebodies.[63] For a mainstream network television drama to put a feminist agenda

63 Faludi, *The Terror Dream*, 14.

so clearly on the table presents an obvious challenge to this reactionary formulation (although perhaps the show's producers knew their days were numbered, as Allen's doubts about whether she will get another opportunity to pass the amendment are voiced explicitly, indicative diegetically of the struggles she will face running for re-election, and non-diegetically of the threats to the programme's future). It is examples such as this that reveal *Commander in Chief* to be a considerably richer representation of a fictional female president than the scholarship addressing it suggests, and it would have been interesting to see the programme realise its attempt to pass the Equal Rights Amendment. Given the dominance of patriarchal conceptualisations of the presidency, it is revealing that it was never given the opportunity to do so.

As demonstrated in this chapter, *Commander in Chief* offers a vivid example of the ways in which the fictional presidency continues to operate around very conservative formulations of gender. Allen is constructed as a highly capable, intelligent and tactically astute leader: she is able to outmanoeuvre her political enemies consistently, as well as protect the United States from harm. It is the programme *itself* that struggles to provide the visual and narrative means to demonstrate that power. She is often boxed in visually, and narrative elements that view her presidency as unwelcome and disruptive dominate proceedings: not only the villainous Templeton but, more problematically, the disgruntled, emasculated husband and the embarrassed, misbehaving children. Rather than an indictment of Allen's competence, *Commander in Chief*'s conservatism is indicative perhaps of the wider unwillingness to disturb the traditional formulations of the presidency working in conjunction with its close alliance to other mainstream television drama that features a female protagonist. The example of *Commander in Chief* demonstrates that the female presidency is very much the 'unfinished business' of presidential fiction. While Clinton's bid for the White House in 2008 made substantial 'cracks in the glass ceiling', *Commander in Chief* remains a somewhat isolated example in the imaginary this book has explored.

CONCLUSION

Old Constructs in a New Era: The White House Invasion Narrative and the Return of Abraham Lincoln

This book has offered a broad account of the forms and functions of the American presidency in mainstream cinema and television in the last two decades, demonstrating the myriad ways in which Hollywood's presidency is as much about Hollywood history as it is about American history. I began with the suggestion that, to understand fully the constitution of the presidency in cinema and television, one needed to pay close attention to the formal constitution of the texts in which the institution is represented: through discussion of the generic, iconographic and narrative frameworks in which the president is positioned, and by paying close attention to the manner in which the president is figured through aesthetic strategies (camera movement, lighting, editing techniques, framing), one can begin to unpick the ideological ramifications of these representations. Does Hollywood's presidency look to reinforce, critique, question, or destabilise dominant constructions of the 'real' president?

My approach has been greatly informed by analyses of Hollywood cinema that suggest mainstream film is broadly predicated on the maintenance of dominant political and economic power structures in American society. Although I have problems with such approaches because they tend to ignore the pleasures offered to audiences by mainstream Hollywood cinema, there is no doubt that the texts themselves (unsurprisingly, perhaps) offer reinforcement to mainstream values and dominant power structures. This book has demonstrated the ways in which mainstream cinema and television have reacted to the seismic geopolitical shifts that have taken place over the past two decades, and how the representation of the president has changed in accordance with these. Since 1992, the presidency has changed enormously: it shrank in ambition and scope in the Clinton years, expanded beyond all reasonable limits during the Bush administration, and, in the Obama years has, in domestic affairs, become hamstrung by a bitter, partisan battle for control over the American government. Writing from the perspective of the first half of Obama's second term, the United States is perhaps also realising its diminished ability to influence global politics, evidenced by the prevarications over military intervention in Syria in September 2013, and the apparently impotent response to Russia's invasion of the Crimea in February 2014 (although many would suggest, in both cases, that the unwillingness to rush into military intervention was a wiser course). In October 2013, the protracted argument between Democrats and Republicans over the future of the federal budget resulted in a government shutdown, diminishing the status of the United States globally, and casting serious doubts over its economic future. This was followed closely by the botched rollout of Obama's signature reforms of the healthcare system, which threatened to undermine his second term entirely, and bring his difficult tenure to a protractedly ignominious close. Given this period of turmoil and change, this book has argued that the proliferation of fictional presidencies in film and television during this period has provided crucial support to the myth that the president is an omnipotent but benevolent leader (a construct that has formed the basis of the institution's conception since its founding). I have also argued that the constant rearticulation of this myth is psychologically *necessary* given its manifest fragility. However, while I will not challenge the suggestion that film and television plays a role in reiterating dominant ideologies, I am more interested in the structure of the relationship between the texts I have discussed, and the messages they might disseminate regarding American political power. This conclusion will ruminate on some of these ideas, while also offering potential future avenues that may be explored.

I began with the suggestion that the representation of the president in the contemporary period can be characterised by its diversity. This is certainly true – the president has been represented in numerous Hollywood genres (action, comedy, thriller, science-fiction, disaster) and a variety of narratives (romantic, comedic, parodic, dramatic). What all these examples demonstrate is that Hollywood's presidency does not reflect the institution as it really *is* or *was*, but what it is hoped to be, and how different contexts impact upon what brand of leadership is sought. In this sense, the scholarly work that dismisses the representation of the presidency in film and television as historically inaccurate, or even anti-historical, wholly misses the point. However, the diversity that has characterised the past two decades of presidential fiction disguises how conservative the institution's representation actually is. All of them pivot around a handful of important notions: ordinarily conceived of as the nation's father, the president fulfils a psychological and mythological function, and is constructed from a variety of sources. These have tended to be (but are not exclusively) visual – portraiture, photography, documentary film, cinema, television, news footage. Representations of the president – whether interpretations of real-life leaders or fictional creations – are largely regressive, governed by a desire to reinforce dominant conceptions of the office. Almost without exception, they posit old, mythologised models of presidential leadership as solutions for the dissatisfaction felt with the present incumbent.

Chapters 3 and 4 suggest film and television offered critiques of Clinton and Bush, but they invariably conclude with nostalgic yearning for previous commanders in chief, filtered through their generic, iconographic and narrative parameters: *Dave* wants the president to be a combination of Jefferson Smith and Franklin Roosevelt; through *mise-en-scène*, set design, and characterisation, *The American President* longs for John F. Kennedy, and a return to a time when being president was 'easier'; *Independence Day* yearns for the simplicity of a Cold War narrative and presidency; *Air Force One* wants Harrison Ford and Ronald Reagan, not Bill Clinton; *The West Wing* celebrates Washington, Lincoln, Kennedy and Theodore Roosevelt as appropriate models of leadership. Indeed, while I suggest *The West Wing*'s aesthetic and narrative choices render it a fairly explicit critique of the Bush administration, it is still dependent upon mythological constructions of the American president to provide its evaluation of contemporary politics.

Indeed, representations of the fictional black president and female president occupy an important place in the overall narrative of this book: the other chapters have addressed presidents who are white, middle-class, masculine figures that, by and large, conform to pre-existing constructions of the president. The fictional black presidency also repackages old constructs: despite the fact that there was no real-life precursor to the fictional black presidency, its representation is still a reformulation of stereotypes of black men. *Deep Impact*, *24* and *2012* revert to images of black masculinity associated with passivity, pseudo-Christian spiritualism and confinement. The notion that Hollywood 'predicted' Obama's presidency is a fallacy. The conception of the presidency as a religious leader is reinforced by these texts, but this operates alongside the reaffirmation of the stereotype of the compliant black man that has been a mainstay of Hollywood cinema since the 1960s.

As demonstrated by *Commander in Chief*, the fictional female presidency also inevitably resorts to representations of women drawn from wider popular culture: President Mackenzie Allen is a tough, competent leader, but she is not Hillary Clinton. Typically for a programme produced in the postfeminist period, the dramatic struggle at the heart of *Commander in Chief* is Allen's attempt to juggle her competing roles as wife, mother and President of the United States. It is not shown to be impossible, but the female presidency is constructed as a disruptive force in the everyday business of the nation state and the normal functioning of the traditional nuclear family: while the programme successfully carves a space for Allen in the masculine schema of the presidency, it struggles ultimately to see this project through as she becomes increasingly dependent on male 'helpers', her husband rebels against his diminished status as 'First Gentleman', and her children struggle with the adjustment, either developing bad eating habits resulting from no proper oversight of their behaviour, or becoming embroiled in scandal and controversy. *Commander in Chief*'s failure to secure a second season is perhaps less indicative of an unwillingness to view women as competent and capable leaders, and more to do with how entrenched the patriarchal, masculine conception of the presidency really is. The female presidency is conceivable as an idea, but it is ultimately too disruptive.

The fictional presidencies that depart from the traditional, white, patriarchal conception of the office indicate precisely the power of this original conception: in *Deep Impact*, *24* and *Commander in Chief*, the president is dependent on the white, male rescuer or mentor to provide essential support to the nation. Despite the supposed 'progressiveness' of these representations, they in fact perpetuate discourses regarding white male power and heroism in the United States. Overall, the presidential myth satisfies the need to believe that the nation's leader is extraordinary: a hero who will defend and protect his people, provide moral guidance and comfort. As demonstrated by the success of Ronald Reagan's presidency, it does not much matter whether this construct is based on fictions, as long as the story being told is a reassuring one. The president, in essence, symbolises the hopes and anxieties of the United States, and his representation in cinema and television visualises these concerns. While there are different models of the leader at work in these texts – spiritual leader or macho man, childlike innocent or intellectual heavyweight – as a collective they demonstrate the desire for a paternal leader, predicated on the desire for 'a daddy, a king, a god, a hero [to] carry that lance and that sword into the field and fight for us.'[1]

As demonstrated by my Freudian analyses of *The West Wing*, the presidents that came before continue to have a profound impact upon the conception of the office, and its more recent occupants: they remain father figures for their successors, and to the nation as a whole. If this idealisation were based solely on an understanding of the historical record, it would be easily dismissed as irrational, but the presidency is an emotional institution. The legacies of certain former presidents have been idealised to the point where the mere mention of their names conjures vivid imagery of heroism – Washington defeated the British and founded the free and democratic United States; Lincoln freed the slaves and ended the Civil War; Franklin Roosevelt restored prosperity after the Great Depression and won World War II; Kennedy saved the world from nuclear apocalypse. The 'real' man behind these images is either rendered insignificant, or he is disavowed in the service of the myth – Roosevelt and Kennedy were both philanderers, Lincoln was a depressive, Washington had false teeth made

1 Robin Lakoff, quoted in Maureen Dowd, 'Of Knights and Presidents: Race of Mythic Proportions', *New York Times*, October 10th, 1992, 1, archived at <http://www.nytimes.com/1992/10/10/us/1992-campaign-political-memo-knights-presidents-race-mythic-proportions.html?pagewanted=all&src=pm>, accessed September 2012.

from hippopotamus ivory. These men have been memorialised in marble, portraiture and celluloid as almost omnipotent, messianic figures, but they were only human. These disavowals and displacements are necessary to maintain the myth of the president – the all-powerful, all-knowing, strong, caring leader of a global superpower.

***

I would like to end with some brief analyses of more recent examples of how the myth of the presidency continues to be visited in Hollywood cinema, and how it conforms to the constructs I have discussed throughout this project. I will first examine the resurgence of nostalgia for Abraham Lincoln as indicative of a desire for heroic leadership in a period of economic turmoil through a discussion of *Abraham Lincoln: Vampire Hunter* (Timur Bekmambetov, 2012), before moving to examine White House invasion films *Olympus Has Fallen* (Antoine Fuqua, 2013) and *White House Down* (Roland Emmerich, 2013) as suggestive of the presidency's continued symbolic significance in the contemporary period despite its manifest fragility since 9/11 and the collapse of the economy.

As its title suggests, *Abraham Lincoln: Vampire Hunter* has a casual relationship with the historical record. It rewrites Lincoln's origin story to propose that it was the murder of his mother by a vampire, and his subsequent realisation that a race of vampires sought to take over the United States, that drove him to presidential success in later life. As suggested in a review of the film, 'Abraham Lincoln (as played by Benjamin Walker) isn't merely an earnest young Illinois striver who learns vampires are real and spends his life fighting them, both personally and politically ... he's a superpowered warrior-god with highly advanced axe-fu skills.'[2] This sentence neatly summarises the difficulty *Vampire Hunter* has reconciling its historical subject matter with its generic conventions: its refusal to abandon the historical record altogether results in some problematic narrative machinations. Not only did the vampires fight on the side of the

2 Tasha Robinson, '*Abraham Lincoln: Vampire Hunter*', <http://www.avclub.com/articles/abraham-lincoln-vampire-hunter,81607/>, accessed September 2012.

Confederacy (which itself is politically awkward, especially given that sensitivities surrounding the outcome of the Civil War persist to this day), it suggests they did so to ensure that slavery was not outlawed, because the slaves provided their sustenance. This supernatural explanation entirely displaces the argument that the Confederacy sought to maintain slavery for economic purposes, and becomes, like many fictionalisations of the presidency, a straightforward battle between good and evil.

However, these recourses to generic convention generate issues of interest in relation to this book despite their ideologically problematic implications. Hollywood has performed an important role in the maintenance of the Lincoln myth: *Abraham Lincoln* (D.W. Griffith, 1930), *Young Mr Lincoln* (John Ford, 1939), and *Abe Lincoln in Illinois* (John Cromwell, 1940) all locate the origin of Lincoln's greatness in his formative years: his rugged, backwoods upbringing imbued him with the supposedly 'American' values of self-reliance, honesty, and hard work, qualities which rendered his presidency *extra*-ordinary. *Vampire Hunter* conforms to this myth, but presents the notion that Lincoln was somewhat feeble in his early life. While he was committed to avenging his mother's death, he lacked the inherent fighting abilities necessary to achieve this aim. To become great, Lincoln had to first prove himself a man in the most traditional sense: a strong, tough, aggressive warrior. Indeed, the film recycles a trope common in representations of the presidency in the last two decades: a successful president must possess the characteristics associated with traditional manhood, and display these abilities in battle (as shown in *Independence Day* and *Air Force One*).

In order to attain these qualities, Lincoln retreats to the woods, and is taught by his mentor, Henry Sturges (Dominic Cooper), how to fight and use weapons against the vampires. In this sense, *Vampire Hunter* has less in common with the sober, serious, biographical treatments of Lincoln's life mentioned previously, and is more akin to a particular sub-genre of Hollywood action film in which men are shown to harness, or rediscover, their supposedly inherent masculine strength through combat training. This is ordinarily achieved through a montage, in which the central character rapidly develops agility, muscular potency, or masters the use of weaponry: the most famous examples of this are *Rocky* (John G. Avildsen, 1976) and its sequels (1979, 1982, 1985, 1990, 2006), *The Empire Strikes Back* (Irvin Kirshner, 1980), *The Karate Kid* (John G. Avildsen, 1984), and *Bloodsport* (Newt Arnold, 1988) in which the male protagonist demonstrates extraordinary levels of endurance, commitment and strength to develop the abilities necessary to triumph in battle (whether it is sport, intergalactic warfare, or simply to confront school bullies). While the convention has continued in more recent films like *The Matrix* (The Wachowskis, 1999), *Batman Begins* (Christopher Nolan, 2005), and *Wanted* (Timur Bekmambetov, 2008), it is perhaps most readily associated with the 1980s and the Reagan era.

As suggested in Chapter 3, Hollywood cinema of this period was deeply invested in the restoration of traditional masculinity after the perceived weakening of America's body politic in the 1970s following defeat in Vietnam and the presidency of Jimmy Carter. The training montage, where the male body is transformed from weak to strong, is the cinematic embodiment of a process the American national character was perceived to have undergone in the Reagan era: the callow and fragile protagonist only 'becomes a man' through physical training, feats of endurance, and combat. There is always firm emphasis on the display of strength through formal techniques: in *Rocky IV* (Sylvester Stallone, 1985), Rocky (Sylvester Stallone) is shown lifting boulders and pulling sleds at a rural cabin retreat (reinforcing all manner of American myths, from the ingenuity and self-reliance of the frontiersman, to Lincoln's own log-cabin origins), with close-ups of his sweaty, muscular torso illustrating his physical exertion. *Vampire Hunter* is similarly unsubtle, but its formal technique of choice is its excessive use of slow-motion to illustrate Lincoln's agility and skill in battle. In both cases, the formal technique is employed to display feats considered inherently masculine.

The representation of Lincoln 'becoming a man' is inevitably complicated by its historical subject, and past representations of the president: as suggested in Chapter 2, Hollywood's recycling of the Lincoln myth in the Depression era was indicative of a nostalgic yearning for a leader associated with wholesome character and honest endeavour at a time of profound national self-doubt. One might interpret the current Lincoln nostalgia in similar terms: Steven Spielberg's more traditional *Lincoln* (2012) represents the president as an extraordinary individual able to defeat the reactionary forces in Congress to pass the thirteenth amendment to abolish slavery just a few months before his assassination (in this sense, Spielberg's film reiterates mythological conceptions of the martyred Lincoln as an American Jesus Christ, further indulging his own interest in messianic figures as shown in *E.T.: The Extra-Terrestrial* [1982] and *Schindler's List* [1993]). Spielberg's film, and Daniel Day-Lewis's justifiably lauded portrayal of Lincoln, perpetuate the old notion of historical change being dependent upon the actions of great men, providing stark contrast with the manner in which contemporary American politics is conducted.

Often described as a history lesson, the considerably more dialogue-heavy *Lincoln* is actually just as nostalgic as *Vampire Hunter*, but perhaps for slightly different reasons. In the film, Lincoln's triumph in passing the thirteenth amendment somewhat against the odds is shown as a victory for humanity, and the promise of a better future for the United States (touchingly, if slightly ham-fistedly, enacted as Thaddeus Stevens [Tommy Lee Jones] climbs into bed at the film's conclusion, and shows the amendment to his black partner). *Lincoln* serves as a reminder that, at a time when the American democratic process is mired in partisan gridlock, there was once a time when the system functioned as it was supposed to. While biopics and historical films such as this are often troubling because their nostalgia tends to shut down further discussion of the ways in which racial intolerance, inequality and prejudice persist (a tendency of which director Steve McQueen was obviously aware when he accepted the 2014 Best Picture award for *12 Years a Slave*, stating that, despite all the progress that has been made, there are still millions of people across the world who live in slavery), *Lincoln* is designed and executed as a reminder that the President of the United States was once capable of great things, of securing sweeping change, and of righting wrongs. The effect of Lincoln's assassination at the film's conclusion is clear: it lends the film's triumph an elegiac quality. Intentionally or not, it appears to suggest such radical, progressive change, and the people with the abilities to achieve it, lie firmly in the past.

Taken together, perhaps *Vampire Hunter* and *Lincoln* suggest that current political ructions and economic turmoil have inspired a similar look to heroes of the past for comfort and inspiration. However, while *Lincoln* yearns for a more effective democratic process and a benign, saintly leader to preside over it, *Vampire Hunter*'s expression of desire for an *action hero* to lead the United States suggests there continues to be, as there was in the Reagan era, a longing for a conventional masculine presence to fight for American interests and confront the nation's enemies. As with all the films and television programmes discussed in this book, the complex intersection of generic convention and historical record results in the construction of a presidency that reinforces aspects of American mythology: *Abraham Lincoln: Vampire Hunter* is undeniably nostalgic but, unlike *Lincoln*, it draws its inspiration not from the historical record (with which it has a tenuous relationship), but from Hollywood's own history. The Lincoln portrayed in *Vampire Hunter* is not the conflicted depressive read about in history books, but comprised of Henry Fonda in *Young Mr Lincoln*, and Hollywood action heroes of the past three decades.

It is clear that a historian would have little use for *Vampire Hunter* as an interpretation of the past, but the film says a lot about Hollywood's representation of the presidency, and mainstream cinema and television's role in maintaining dominant mythological conceptions of the institution. While it is certainly not incorrect to approach *Abraham Lincoln: Vampire Hunter* through a comparison with the 'real' Lincoln and his representation, or suggest that representations of the president reflect the moment in which they were produced, the relationship between text and historical context is more complicated. Representing Lincoln as an action hero suggests a number of things, most of which have nothing to do with the 'real' Lincoln. Any pretence towards historical accuracy and verisimilitude is superseded by a desire to reinforce the presidential myth: there remains the desire for a presidential strongman in a period in which the dominant attitude towards politicians and presidents appears to be one of cynicism and disdain, and that such a representation performs a psychological function, simplifying complex issues (The Civil War), providing comforting explanations (the supernatural element effaces troublesome historical truths) and, through the nostalgic, idealised representation of a former president, delivers an uncomplicated model of heroism in an environment defined by its complexity.

The appearance of *Abraham Lincoln: Vampire Hunter* in 2012 cannot be a coincidence: the bitter campaign for the presidency between Barack

Obama and Mitt Romney was met with widespread disenchantment with the political process. Following the election, the American political system appears to be at a crossroads: almost bankrupted by unfunded tax cuts and military interventions in foreign lands during the Bush administration, and rapidly being overtaken as the world's largest economy by China, the presidency is struggling to maintain a grasp on its former power. The myths Barack Obama invoked in 2008 – American exceptionalism, individualism, and the images of Abraham Lincoln, Martin Luther King Jr., and John F. Kennedy – may have encouraged the belief that, perhaps, some of the idealised constructions of American presidents that Hollywood has given us may be achieved in reality. The economic crisis, war in Afghanistan, climate change, and a Republican Party intent only on the destruction of its opponents and a return to power, have put paid to any such fanciful hopes. As during the Great Depression, Lincoln's reassuring, mythologised image has resurfaced amid turmoil. The overt display of muscular masculinity in *Vampire Hunter* appears to confirm the notion that 'there is an inextricable link between the fate of masculinity and that of the nation'; in essence, crises require a reversion to a traditionally masculine president.[3] *Vampire Hunter*'s appearance affirms my suggestion that Hollywood's presidency is cyclical, founded upon a handful of core concepts, designed to reinforce governing ideologies regarding American national identity.

***

The notion that there is an important connection between 'the fate of masculinity and that of the nation' is rendered in particularly hyperbolic fashion by two films released in 2013 that concern terrorist invasions of the White House. *Olympus Has Fallen* and *White House Down* witness the invasion and destruction of the symbolic home of American democracy (by North Koreans in the former, and a ragtag bunch of war veterans, survivalists and disgruntled secret service agents in the latter). In both films, there is the capture or attempted capture of the president: in *Olympus*

3 Susanne Kord and Elisabeth Krimmer, *Contemporary Hollywood Masculinities: Gender, Genre, and Politics* (New York: Palgrave Macmillan, 2011), 6.

Has Fallen, President Asher (Aaron Eckhardt) spends the majority of the film as a hostage requiring rescue by disgraced former Secret Service Agent Mike Banning (Gerard Butler), while *White House Down*'s President Sawyer (Jamie Foxx) proves himself slightly more capable of evading the terrorists' clutches and joins forces with Capitol Police Officer John Cale (Channing Tatum), who just happens to find himself in the White House when the attack occurs. Although many critics cite the films' near simultaneous release as pure coincidence, noting other examples of similarly themed Hollywood blockbusters produced in close proximity to each other (a large volcano threatens a densely populated area in *Dante's Peak* [Roger Donaldson, 1997] and *Volcano* [Mick Jackson, 1997], and an asteroid threatens the existence of mankind in *Deep Impact* and *Armageddon*), there is perhaps something potentially more revealing at work regarding the contemporary anxieties of the United States, her ability to defend itself against her enemies, and whether the presidency is capable of fulfilling its role as protector and defender of the nation.

While mainstream cinema has shown the president in peril in a variety of films – the threat of assassination forms the basis of a few fictional movies since World War II, including *Suddenly* (1954), *The Manchurian Candidate*, *Executive Action* and *In the Line of Fire* – the narrative device becomes pervasive in the years following 9/11 and the success of *24*, in which, as explored in Chapter 5, plots to kill the president were constant (and frequently successful). *The Sentinel* (Clark Johnson, 2006), *Shooter* (Antoine Fuqua, 2007) and *Vantage Point* (Pete Travis, 2008) all concern plots to kill the President of the United States. In all three, however, the president is something of a non-entity: in *The Sentinel*, President Ballentine (David Rasche) is important to the narrative only because Secret Service Agent Pete Garrison (Michael Douglas) is having an affair with his wife, Sarah (Kim Basinger). This forms the basis of a plot to frame Garrison for the president's death. Indeed, the film is self-conscious enough to acknowledge that the man is important and powerful in a primarily symbolic sense: when asked to change his schedule because of the threats against him, the president refuses to do so because it would undermine the symbolic potency of the office. In *Vantage Point*, President Ashton (William Hurt) is bland enough to be replaced by a lookalike when the plot to kill him becomes apparent. In both instances, we learn very little of the president's character or his ideology: in *The Sentinel*, there is vague mention of the urgency of ratifying the Kyoto Protocol, and in *Vantage Point* Ashton is in Salamanca to coordinate an international effort against terrorism. While both films acknowledge the president's physical vulnerability and suggest the people protecting him may be unable to prevent his death (both feature corrupt forces within the Secret Service), the desire to protect him stems primarily from the fact that the death of the nation's leader is potentially traumatic. There is little sense that anyone has any particular love or affection for the man himself.

Olympus Has Fallen and *White House Down* feature more well-rounded chief executives and, like *24*, offer further iterations of popular culture's propensity for restaging 9/11 and the 'war on terror' as a winnable battle confined to a single day, rather than the open-ended conflict with which we continue to deal. It is clear that both films operate as part of a small number of post-9/11 films that offer fantasies of wish-fulfilment: in this realm, the individual hero *can* triumph over the terrorist threat, evidencing a desire to recapture the initiative and reassert a semblance of control that was lost on September 11th, 2001, and in the calamitous events that have followed. Indeed, it is possible to read both films as hyper-violent revenge fantasies staged within the symbolic home of American democracy. In this regard, while they clearly belong in the broad generic category of the action-adventure film, they also operate quite obviously within the conventions of the 'home invasion' narrative which has been somewhat resurgent in the years following 9/11, perhaps indicative of the contemporaneous discursive recalibration of the United States as a 'homeland' in need of defence.

As James Morrison argues, 'home invasion' narratives have been an aspect of American cinema since D.W. Griffith's *The Lonely Villa* (1909) (which largely established the sub-genre's conventions), but have reemerged in a variety of genres since 2001: as domestic melodrama like *The Glass House* (Daniel Sackheim, 2001), *Panic Room* (David Fincher, 2002), *Hostage* (Florent-Emilio Siri, 2005) and *Firewall* (Richard Loncraine, 2006); as action cinema like *Collateral Damage* (Andrew Davis, 2002) and *Cellular* (David R. Ellis, 2004); and horror films such as *Cold Creek Manor* (Mike Figgis, 2003), *Saw* (James Wan, 2004) and *When a Stranger Calls* (Simon

West, 2006).[4] Further examples released since the publication of Morrison's article in 2008 include horror films *The Strangers* (Bryan Bertino, 2008) and *The Purge* (James DeMonaco, 2013), both of which witness white middle-class homes subjected to invasion by unwanted intruders. While Morrison does not posit the cycle as indicative of American insecurity in this period, Hamad suggests the films, particularly those featuring patriarchal heroes defending the homestead like *Signs*, *Hostage* and *Firewall*, 'emerged congruent with a masculinist post-9/11 cultural logic of protecting the family homestead.'[5]

To view *Olympus Has Fallen* and *White House Down* as part of this 'home invasion' cycle is instructive: both take the sense of post-9/11 national vulnerability and simultaneously hyperbolise and universalise the thematic concerns of the 'home invasion' film. Indeed, as Morrison suggests, the recent examples of the sub-genre have removed the class dimensions that dominated its earlier conceptions, to be replaced by a generalised concern for the protection of the family: 'the invading others' of the recent cycle 'stand in for a heady range of threats, representing both locally disenfranchised parties seeking violent restitution or contingent or arbitrary alien powers that personify the postmodern condition as such.'[6] It is clear that *Olympus Has Fallen* and *White House Down* both operate within this conception of the contemporary home invasion film as they feature 'locally disenfranchised parties' and 'arbitrary alien powers' but, because they concern the president's physical well-being and symbolic significance, they potentially have more to say regarding the vulnerability of the nation in a more diffuse and complex post-9/11 threat environment. This book has argued throughout that the President of the United States effectively symbolises the nation as a whole, so what does it say about the psychological state of that nation if the leader's home is under threat of destruction and his physical body faces the prospect of violent death?

4 James Morrison, 'Hostages and Houseguests: Class and Family in the New Screen Gothic', in Pomerance, ed., *A Family Affair*, 189.

5 Hamad, 'Hollywood Fatherhood', 110.

6 Morrison, 'Hostages and Houseguests', 192–3.

However, as is typical of the disaster genre, following scenes of audacious destruction and violence, both films ultimately offer reassurance. As Morrison suggests of the contemporary home invasion film, any doubt or contradiction regarding the family unit is expunged by the triumphant conclusion: 'In their diagnoses, the postmodern family is doing just fine, or would be, if it were not constantly beset by forces from without.'[7] I suggest these two films put forward the idea that the *nation* would be doing 'just fine' if it were not subject to a consistent barrage from its enemies, but the invasion offers the opportunity for violent catharsis, the reestablishment of the potency of the presidency and, concomitantly, the swift and uncomplicated restoration of its control and authority over the state and the world. Indeed, as Melani McAlister has said of the hostage rescue action sub-genre, 'the uncertain and messy outcomes of real-life hostage and terrorist situations [are] reimagined in the simpler language of defined threat and unambiguous victory'.[8] It might be suggested, therefore, that both films disavow the complexity of the origins of terrorist actions and the responses to them in order to provide a feel-good restoration of the United States as a benign superpower.

By the conclusion of *Olympus Has Fallen*, for example, the devastation wrought by the North Korean invaders' destruction of the White House has begun to be cleared, the trauma neutralised and the nation's wounds healed: we see the partially destroyed Washington Monument being rebuilt, President Asher delivering a typically patriotic speech, arguing the nation has been granted an opportunity for renewal and rebirth as a result of the successful defeat of the invaders. These words are accompanied by the American flag being raised outside the White House (after it had been shot to pieces and thrown off the roof by terrorists). In this sense, the restoration of nationhood is purely symbolic: because the president has been returned to his rightful place, the United States can breathe more easily; its leader, and therefore the country and the values for which it stands, have been

7 Ibid., 190.

8 Melani McAlister, 'A Cultural History of the War Without End', *The Journal of American History* 89/2 (2002), 451.

deemed worthy of rescue and preservation. *White House Down* completes its project with President Sawyer indulging his favourite pastime – flying past The Lincoln Memorial in Marine One, the presidential helicopter. Lincoln has played a crucial role throughout (it is Lincoln's gold pocket-watch that prevents Sawyer's death by a terrorist's bullet as he keeps it in his jacket pocket) and, by association with The Great Emancipator, Sawyer is deemed similarly worthy of rescue as a potent symbol of the supposedly American values of freedom and democracy. By restaging the 'war on terror' as a winnable battle over the course of a single day, *Olympus Has Fallen* and *White House Down* revisit the nightmarish imagery of 9/11 and the possibility of the destruction of the United States' most potent symbols, before restoring the presidency to its 'rightful' position, reaffirming the nation's ability to face down its enemies and emerge victorious.

In both films, it is clear that while the presidency still has enormous symbolic value, its power to control the universe has been diminished. President Asher in *Olympus Has Fallen* spends the vast majority of the film incapacitated by his captors, while President Sawyer in *White House Down* proves himself incompetent in handling the weaponry required to ensure the defeat of the terrorists, mishandling a rocket launcher during a daring car chase around the White House lawn. Unlike *Independence Day* and *Air Force One*, where the president takes control of the situation, ensuring the preservation and defence of himself and the nation over which he presides, Presidents Asher and Sawyer are considerably more reliant upon others: as in *24*, the protection of the president's life and the ultimate restitution of social order falls to the heroic white males Cale and Banning, both of whom prove willing to go beyond the bounds of the reasonable, the proportionate, even the possible, to ensure the protection of the nation's leader. Indeed, the contrast is rendered particularly stark in *White House Down*, where the bespectacled (and, therefore, in Hollywood terms, intellectual) Sawyer relies upon the muscle-bound Cale's abilities to escape from harm. In this sense, both films demonstrate the extent to which the action genre in Hollywood continues to owe a great debt to *Die Hard* and *Lethal Weapon*. Like McClane and Riggs, Cale and Banning operate far enough outside the establishment so as not to allow their power to be restricted by the established bureaucracy, but remain proximate enough to be easily identified as defenders of the *status quo*.

***

Olympus Has Fallen and *White House Down* provide particularly expressive recent examples of the argument that has been developed throughout this book: Hollywood has played, and continues to play, a crucial role in upholding the presidential myth, in increasingly extreme fashion. While some of the films and programmes discussed have offered critiques of power, they still posit the notion that there is an *ideal* for which the president must strive. In this regard, the presidency is a myth that has been constructed as much in Hollywood, CA as it has in Washington, DC. As demonstrated by the presidencies of Ronald Reagan, John F. Kennedy, and Barack Obama, the techniques Hollywood has employed in the preservation of this myth have proved crucial in the increasingly imagistic nature of the election campaign. But the increased scrutiny of the presidency by the mass media has also partially undermined its mythological dimensions. The myth has also come under immense strain because the presidency has demonstrated its limitations in the more diffuse geopolitical environment of the past twenty years. To combat this, Hollywood has stepped into the breach to offer models of leadership constructed from a variety of sources. There can be no doubt that past occupants provide a rich vein of material for fictional presidents, but this book has demonstrated the extent to which Hollywood's generic, iconographic and narrative frameworks, aesthetic strategies and star system have significant influence upon them too. In this environment, it seems the presidential myth is no longer strong enough to stand on its own, and requires assistance from the realm of Hollywood fantasy. As the relationship between the people and the presidency has become more intimate, so the people have been forced to confront the reality that the office is inevitably occupied by people with human frailties and foibles. However, the myth of the presidency has not entirely disappeared. If anything, mainstream film and television have somewhat overcompensated for this perceived 'lack', as the attempts in the past twenty years to reinforce dominant constructions of the President of the United States have become more feverish and outlandish. One wonders where the archetype might go from here, but it would be foolish to doubt Hollywood's capacity to reinvent and repackage the president for new eras, new anxieties and new constructs.

Bibliography

Adorno, Theodor, and Max Horkheimer [1944], *Dialectic of Enlightenment* (London: Verso, 1979).

Allen, Michael, 'Divided Interests: Split-Screen Aesthetics in *24*', in Peacock, ed., *Reading 24*, 35–47.

Allen, Robert C., and Annette Hill, eds, *The Television Studies Reader* (London: Routledge, 2004), 373–88.

Ang, Ien, 'Melodramatic Identifications: Television Fiction and Women's Fantasy', in Brunsdon and Spigel, eds, *Feminist Television Criticism*, 235–46.

Alter, Jonathan, *The Promise: President Obama – Year One* (London: Simon & Schuster, 2010).

Altman, Rick, *Film/Genre* (London: British Film Institute, 1999).

Anderson, Benedict, *Imagined Communities: Reflections on the Origin and Spread of Nationalism* (London: Verso, 2006).

Appiah, K. Anthony, '"No Bad Nigger": Blacks as the Ethical Principle in the Movies', in Garber, Matlock and Walkowitz, eds, *Media Spectacles*, 77–90.

Arroyo, José, ed., *Action/Spectacle Cinema: A Sight and Sound Reader* (London: British Film Institute, 2000).

Aslan, Reza, 'Foreword', in Birkenstein, Froula and Randell, eds, *Reframing 9/11*, xi–xiii.

Auslander, Philip, *Liveness: Performance in a Mediatized Culture* [2nd edn] (London: Routledge, 2008).

Auster, Albert, 'All in the Family: The Kennedy Saga and Television', *Journal of Popular Film and Television* 19/3 (1991), 128–37.

Baehr, Helen, and Gillian Dyer, eds, *Boxed In: Women and Television* (London: Pandora, 1987).

Barber, James David, *The Presidential Character: Predicting Performance in the White House* [4th edn] (Upper Saddle River, NJ: Prentice Hall, 1992).

Barger, Harold M., *The Impossible Presidency* (Glenview: Scott, Foresman, 1984).

——, 'The Incredible Shrinking Image: From Cold War to Globalist Presidency', in Eksterowicz and Hastedt, eds, *The Post-Cold War Presidency*, 57–80.

Barker, Adam, 'Cries and Whispers', *Sight and Sound* 1/10 (1992), 10–11.

Barthes, Roland [1957], *Mythologies* (London: Grafton Books, 1973).

Baudrillard, Jean, *America* [translated Chris Turner] (London: Verso, 1988).

——, *The Gulf War Did Not Take Place* [translated by Paul Patton] (Bloomington: Indiana University Press, 1995).

——, *Simulacra and Simulation* [translated by Sheila Faria Glaser] (Ann Arbor: The University of Michigan Press, 1994).

Beail, Linda, and Rhondy Kinney Longworth, 'Puritan or Pit Bull: The Framing of Female Candidates at the National Level', in Vaughn and Goren, eds, *Women and the White House*, 25–48.

Beavers, Staci, '*The West Wing* as a Pedagogical Tool: Using Drama to Examine American Politics and Media Perceptions of Our Political System', in Rollins and O'Connor, eds, *The West Wing*, 175–86.

Bell, Daniel, 'The End of American Exceptionalism', *National Affairs* 41 (Fall 1975).

——, *The End of Ideology: On the Exhaustion of Political Ideas in the Fifties* (Cambridge, MA and London: Harvard University Press, 1988).

Benjamin, Walter [1936], *The Work of Art in the Age of Mechanical Reproduction* (London: Penguin Books, 2008).

——, [1974], 'On the Concept of History', *Gesammelten Schriften* 1/2, archived in English at <http://www.arts.yorku.ca/soci/barent/wp-content/uploads/2008/10/benjamin-concept_of_history1.pdf> accessed May 2010.

Benyon, John, *Masculinities and Culture* (Buckingham: Open University Press, 2002).

Bergman, Andrew, *We're in the Money: Depression America and its Films* (New York: New York University Press, 1971).

Bingham, Dennis, *Acting Male: Masculinities in the Films of James Stewart, Jack Nicholson, and Clint Eastwood* (New Brunswick, NJ: Rutgers University Press, 1994).

——, 'Oliver Stone's *Nixon* and the Unmanning of the Self-Made Man', in Lehman, ed., *Masculinity*, 257–78.

Birkenstein, Jeff, Anna Froula and Karen Randell, eds, *Reframing 9/11: Film, Popular Culture and the 'War on Terror'* (London: Continuum, 2010).

——, 'Introduction', in Birkenstein, Froula and Randell, eds, *Reframing 9/11*, 1–8.

Biskind, Peter, *Seeing is Believing: or How Hollywood Taught us to Stop Worrying and Love the 50s* (London: Bloomsbury, 2001).

Blake, David Haven, 'Hollywood, Impersonation, and Presidential Celebrity in the 1990s', in Rollins and O'Connor, eds, *Hollywood's White House*, 320–32.

Bogle, Donald, *Toms, Coons, Mulattoes, Mammies and Bucks: An Interpretive History of Blacks in American Films* [4th edn] (New York: Continuum, 2001).

Boorstin, Daniel J., *The Genius of American Politics* (Chicago: The University of Chicago Press, 1964).

——, *The Image, or What Happened to the American Dream* (London: Weidenfeld and Nicolson, 1961).

——, *The Image: A Guide to Pseudo-Events in America* (Atheneum: New York, 1985).

Borrelli, Stephen A., 'Finding the Third Way: Bill Clinton, the DLC, and the Democratic Platform of 1992', *The Journal of Policy History* 13/4 (2001), 429–62.

Bovenschen, Simone, 'Is There a Feminine Aesthetic?', *New German Critique* 10 (Winter 1977), 111–37.

Boyle, Karen, 'Feminism Without Men: Feminist media studies in a post-feminist age', in Brunsdon and Spiegel, eds, *Feminist Television Criticism*, 174–90.

Bradby, David, Louis James and Bernard Sharratt, eds, *Performance and politics in popular drama* (Cambridge: University of Cambridge Press, 1980).

Brady, Sara, *Performance, Politics, and the War on Terror* (London: Palgrave Macmillan, 2012).

Brigance, Linda, 'For One Brief Shining Moment: Choosing to Remember Camelot', *Studies in Popular Culture* 25 (2003), <http://pcasacas.org/SiPC/25.3/Brigance.htm> accessed November 2010.

Brinkley, Alan, *Liberalism and its Discontents* (London: Harvard University Press, 2000).

Britton, Andrew, 'Blissing Out: The Politics of Reaganite Entertainment', *Movie* 31/32 (1986), 1–42, reprinted in Grant, ed., *Britton on Film*, 97–154.

——, 'Sideshows: Hollywood in Vietnam', in Grant, ed., *Britton on Film*, 74–96.

Brown, Jeffrey, 'Gender and the Action Heroine: Hard Bodies and The Point of No Return', *Cinema Journal* 35 (Spring 1996), 52–71.

Brown, Thomas, *JFK: History of an Image* (London: I.B. Tauris & Co Ltd, 1988).

Brunsdon, Charlotte, *Screen Tastes: Soap Opera to Satellite Dishes* (London: Routledge, 1997).

——, and Lynn Spigel, eds, *Feminist Television Criticism: A Reader* [2nd edn] (Maidenhead: Open University Press, 2008).

Bruzzi, Stella, *Bringing Up Daddy: Fatherhood and Masculinity in Post-War Hollywood* (London: British Film Institute, 2005).

——, *Men's Cinema: Masculinity and Mise-en-scène in Hollywood* (Edinburgh: Edinburgh University Press, 2013).

——, 'Men's Cinema', in Gibbs and Pye, eds, *Close-Up 03*, 143–222.

——, *New Documentary: A Critical Introduction* (London: Routledge, 2000).

——, *New Documentary: A Critical Introduction* [2nd edn] (London: Routledge, 2006).

Burgoyne, Robert, *Film Nation: Hollywood Looks at US History* (Minneapolis: University of Minnesota Press, 2010).

——, 'Modernism and the Narrative of Nation in *JFK*', in Sobchack, ed., *The Persistence of History*, 113–24.

Burrell, Barbara, 'The Clintons and Gender Politics', in Schier, ed., *The Postmodern Presidency*, 238–54.

Cahiers du Cinéma editors, 'John Ford's *Young Mr Lincoln*', in Nichols, ed., *Movies and Methods*, 493–529.

Caldwell, Anne, and Samuel A Chambers, '*24* after 9/11: The American State of Exception', in Peacock, ed., *Reading 24*, 97–108.

Carnes, Mark C., ed., *Past imperfect: History according to the movies* (New York: Henry Holt, 1995).

Carney, Raymond, *American Vision: The Films of Frank Capra* (Cambridge: University of Cambridge Press, 1986).

Carr, E.H. [1961], *What is History?* (Basingstoke: Palgrave, 2001).

Carroll, Susan J., 'Reflections on Gender and Hillary Clinton's Election Campaign: The Good, The Bad, and the Misogynic', *Politics and Gender* 5 (2009), 1–20.

Caughie, John, *Edge of Darkness* (London: British Film Institute, 2007).

Chollet, Derek and James Goldgeier, *America Between the Wars: From 11/9 to 9/11 – The Misunderstood Years Between the Fall of the Berlin Wall and the Start of the War on Terror* (New York: Public Affairs, 2008).

Christensen, Terry, *Reel Politics: American Political Movies from Birth of a Nation to Platoon* (Oxford: Basil Blackwell, 1987).

Christensen, Terry, and Peter J. Haas, *Projecting Politics: Political Messages in American Films* (M.E. Sharpe, 2005).

Clare, Anthony, *On Men: Masculinity in Crisis* (London: Chatto and Windus, 2000).

Cohan, Steven, and Ina Rae Hark, eds, *Screening the Male: Exploring Masculinities in Hollywood Cinema* (London: Routledge, 1993).

Collins, Jim, Hilary Radner and Ava Preacher Collins, eds, *Film Theory Goes to the Movies* (London: Routledge, 1993).

Combs, James, ed., *Movies and Politics: The Dynamic Relationship* (New York and London: Garland Publishing, 1993).

Comolli, Jean-Louis and Jean Narboni, 'Cinema/Ideology/Criticism', in Nichols, ed., *Movies and Methods I*, 22–30.

Cook, David A., *Lost Illusions: American Cinema in the shadow of Watergate and Vietnam 1970–1979* (Berkeley: University of California Press, 2000).

Cox Han, Lori and Caroline Heldman, eds, *Rethinking Madam President: Are We Ready For a Woman in the White House?* (Boulder: Lynne Rienner Publishers, 2007).

Coyne, Michael, *Hollywood Goes to Washington: American Politics on Screen* (London: Reaktion Books Limited, 2008).

Crawley, Melissa, *Mr Sorkin Goes to Washington: Shaping the President on Television's The West Wing* (London: McFarland and Company, Inc., 2006).

——, 'Television', in Matviko, ed., *The American President in Popular Culture*, pp. 183–98.

Creeber, Glen, *Serial Television: Big Drama on the Small Screen* (London: British Film Institute, 2004).
——, *The Singing Detective* (London: British Film Institute, 2007).
Cripps, Thomas, *Making Movies Black: The Hollywood Message Movies from World War II to the Civil Rights Era* (New York: Oxford University Press, 1993).
Cronin, Thomas, *The State of the Presidency* [2nd edn] (Boston: Little, Brown, 1980).
Cronin, Thomas, and Michael A. Genovese, *The Paradoxes of the American Presidency* [2nd edn] (New York: Oxford University Press, 1998).
Crowther, Bruce, *Hollywood Faction: Reality and Myth in the Movies* (Bromley: Columbus Books, 1984).
Cull, Nicholas J., 'Kennedy on Film', *Film International* 6 (2003), 16–19.
D'Acci, Julie, 'Television, Representation and Gender', in Allen and Hill, eds, *The Television Studies Reader* (London: Routledge, 2004), 373–88.
Davies, Philip, ed., *Representing and Imagining America* (Keele: Keele University Press, 1996).
Davies, Philip John, and Paul Wells, eds, *American film and politics from Reagan to Bush Jr* (Manchester: Manchester University Press, 2002).
Davies, Philip John, 'Hollywood in Elections and Elections in Hollywood', in Davies and Wells, eds, *American film and politics from Reagan to Bush Jr*, 43–64.
——, 'The Media and US Politics', in Peele *et al.*, eds, *Developments in American Politics 3* (Basingstoke: Macmillan, 1998).
——, and Brian Neve, *Cinema Politics and Society in America* (Manchester: Manchester University Press, 1987).
Davis, Vincent, ed., *The Post-Imperial Presidency* (New Brunswick: Transaction Books, 1980).
de Tocqueville, Alexis [1835/40], *Democracy in America* (New York: Harper Collins, 2000).
Debord, Guy, *The Society of the Spectacle* [translated by Donald Nicholson-Smith] (New York: Zone Books, 1994).
Denton, Robert E., Jr., and Rachel L. Holloway, *The Clinton Presidency: Images, Issues and Communication Strategies* (London: Praeger, 1996).
Denton, Robert E., Jr., ed., *The 2008 Presidential Campaign: A Communication Perspective* (Plymouth: Rowman and Littlefield Publishers, 2009).
Diawara, Manthia, ed., *Black American Cinema* (London: Routledge, 1993).
Dickenson, Ben, *Hollywood's New Radicalism: War, Globalisation and the Movies from Reagan to George W. Bush* (London: I.B. Tauris, 2006).
Dixon, Wheeler Winston, ed., *Film and Television after 9/11* (Carbondale: Southern Illinois University Press, 2004).

Doherty, Thomas, 'Movie-Star Presidents', in Lewis, ed., *The End of Cinema as we know it*, 150–57.

Dow, Bonnie J., *Prime-Time Feminism: Television, Media Culture, and the Women's Movement Since 1970* (Philadelphia: University of Pennsylvania Press, 1996).

Doyle, William, *Inside the Oval Office: The White House Tapes from FDR to Clinton* (New York: Kodansha International, 1999).

Duffy, Michael, and Dan Goodgame, *Marching in Place: The Status Quo Presidency of George Bush* (New York: Simon and Schuster, 1992).

Dyer, Richard, *The Matter of Images: Essays on Representations* (London: Routledge, 1993).

——, *The Matter of Images: Essays on Representations* [2nd edn] (London: Routledge, 2002).

——, *Only Entertainment* [2nd edn] (London: Routledge, 2002).

——, *Stars* (London: British Film Institute, 1998).

Easthope, Anthony, *What a Man's Gotta Do: The Masculine Myth in Popular Culture* (Winchester: Unwin Hyman, 1990).

Eberwein, Robert, ed., *Acting for America: Movie Stars of the 1980s* (London: Rutgers University Press, 2010).

Edelman, Murray, *Constructing the Political Spectacle* (Chicago: University of Chicago Press, 1995).

——, *From Art to Politics: How Artistic Creations Shape Political Conceptions* (Chicago: University of Chicago Press, 1995).

Edgerton, Gary R., and Jeffrey P. Jones, eds, *The Essential HBO Reader* (Lexington: The University Press of Kentucky, 2008).

Edgerton, Gary R., and Peter C. Rollins, eds, *Television Histories: Shaping Collective Memory in the Media Age* (Lexington: The University Press of Kentucky, 2001).

Edwards, Erica R., 'The Black President Hokum', *America Quarterly* 63/1 (2011), 33–59.

Elder, Harris J., 'The Kennedys', in Rollins, ed., *The Columbia Companion to American History on Film*, 169–74.

Ellis, John, *Visible Fictions: Cinema/Television/Video* [rev. edn] (New York: Routledge, 1992).

Elsaesser, Thomas, 'The Pathos of Failure: American Films in the 1970s', in Thomas Elsaesser, Alexander Horwath and Noel King, eds, *The Last Great American Picture Show*, 279–92.

——, Alexander Horwath and Noel King, eds, *The Last Great American Picture Show: New Hollywood Cinema in the 1970s* (Amsterdam: Amsterdam University Press, 2004).

Engelhardt, Tom, *The End of Victory Culture: Cold War and the Disillusioning of a Generation* (New York: Basic Books, 1995).

Eksterowicz, Anthony J. and Glenn P. Hastedt, eds, *The Post-Cold War Presidency* (Lanham: Rowman and Littlefield, 1999).

Ezell, Pamela, 'The Sincere Sorkin White House, or, the Importance of Seeming Earnest', in Rollins and O'Connor, eds, *The West Wing*, 159–74.

Faludi, Susan, *Backlash: The Undeclared War Against Women* (London: Vintage, 1992).

——, *Stiffed: The Betrayal of Modern Man* (London: Vintage, 2000).

——, *The Terror Dream: Myth and Misogyny in an Insecure America* (New York: Picador, 2008).

Featherstone, Mike, and Andrew Wernick, eds, *Images of Aging: Cultural Representations of Later Life* (London: Routledge, 1995).

Feeney, Mark, *Nixon at the Movies: a Book about Belief* (Chicago: University of Chicago Press, 2004).

Ferrara, Alessandro, *Modernity and Authenticity: A Study of the Social and Ethical Thought of Jean-Jacques Rousseau* (Albany: State University of New York, 1993).

Ferriss, Suzanne, and Mallory Young, eds, *Chick flicks: Contemporary women at the movies* (London: Routledge, 2008).

——, 'Introduction', in Ferriss and Young, eds, *Chick Flicks*, 1–25.

Fisher, Walter R., 'Reaffirmation and Subversion of the American Dream', *Quarterly Journal of Speech* 59 (1973), 160–67.

——, 'Romantic Democracy, Ronald Reagan, and Presidential Heroes', *Western Journal of Communication* 46 (1982), 299–310.

Frame, Gregory, '"The Real Thing": Election Campaigns and the Question of Authenticity in American Film and Television', *Journal of American Studies* 50/3 (August 2016), 755-77.

——, 'The Leader of the Free World? Representing the declining presidency in television drama', in Kaklamanidou and Tally, eds, *Politics and Politicians in Contemporary US Television*, 61-74.

Frank, David. A., and Mark Lawrence McPhail, 'Barack Obama's Address to the Democratic National Convention: Trauma, Compromise, Consilience, and the (Im)possibility of Racial Reconciliation', *Rhetoric and Public Affairs* 8/4 (2005), 571–93.

Frasure, Lorrie, 'The Burden of Jeckyll and Hyde: Barack Obama, Racial Identity and Black Political Behavior', in Gillespie, ed., *Whose Black Politics?*, 133–54.

Freda, Isabelle, '*Survivors* in *The West Wing*': 9/11 and the United States of Emergency', in Winston Dixon, ed., *Film and Television After 9/11*, 226–44.

Freud, Sigmund [1913], 'Totem and Taboo', *The Origins of Religion: Totem and Taboo, Moses and Monotheism and Other Works*, Albert Dickson, ed., (London: Penguin Books, 1990).

—— [1923], 'The Ego and the Id', *On Metapsychology*, Angela Richards, ed., (London: Penguin Books, 1991).

—— [1930], 'Civilisation and its Discontents', *Civilization, Society and Religion*, Albert Dickson, ed. (London: Penguin Books, 1991).

Friedman, Lester D., ed., *Unspeakable Images: Ethnicity and the American Cinema* (Chicago: University of Illinois Press, 1991), 308–28.

Fuchs, Cynthia J., 'The Buddy Politic', in Cohan and Hark, eds, *Screening the Male*, 194–212.

Fukuyama, Francis, 'The End of History?', *The National Interest* 16 (1989).

——, *The End of History and The Last Man* (London: Penguin Books, 1992).

Gabbard, Krin, *Black Magic: White Hollywood and African American Culture* (London: Rutgers University Press, 2004).

Gans-Boriskin, Rachel, and Russ Tisinger, 'The Bushlet Administration: Terrorism and War on *The West Wing*', *The Journal of American Culture* 28/1 (2005), 100–13.

Garber, Marjorie, Jann Matlock and Rebecca L. Walkowitz, eds, *Media Spectacles* (London: Routledge, 1993).

Gehring, Wes D., 'Pushing the Capra Envelope: *Hero*', *Journal of Popular Film and Television* 23 (1995), 36–43.

Gianos, Phillip L., *Politics and Politicians in American Film* (Greenwood Press, 1999).

Gibbs, John and Douglas Pye, eds, *Close-Up 03* (London: Wallflower Press, 2009).

Giglio, Ernest, *Here's Looking at You: Hollywood Film and Politics* (New York: Peter Lang, 2005).

Gillespie, Andra, ed., *Whose Black Politics?: Cases in Post-Racial Black Leadership* (Abingdon: Routledge, 2010).

Gillian, Jennifer, '"No One Knows You're Black!": *Six Degrees of Separation* and the Buddy Formula', *Cinema Journal* 40/3 (2001), 47–68.

Girgus, Sam B., *Hollywood Renaissance: The Cinema of Democracy in the Era of Ford, Capra, and Kazan* (Cambridge: University of Cambridge Press, 1998).

Glass, Loren, 'After the Phallus', *American Imago* 58/2 (2001), 545–66.

——, 'Publicizing the President's Privates', *Postmodern Culture* 9/3 (1999).

Goren, Lilly, 'Fact or Fiction: The Reality of Race and Gender in Reaching the White House', in Vaughan and Goren, eds, *Women and the White House*, 97–120.

——, ed., *You've Come a Long Way, Baby: Women, Politics and Popular Culture* (Lexington: University Press of Kentucky, 2009).

Grant, Barry Keith, ed., *Auteurs and Authorship: A Film Reader* (Oxford: Blackwell Publishing, 2008).

——, ed., *Britton on Film: The Complete Film Criticism of Andrew Britton* (Detroit: Wayne State University Press, 2009).

——, ed., *Film Genre: Theory and Criticism* (London: The Scarecrow Press, Inc., 1977).

Graubard, Stephen, *The Presidents: The Transformation of The American Presidency from Theodore Roosevelt to George W. Bush* (London: Penguin Books, 2006).

Gray, Herman, *Watching Race: Television and the Struggle for 'Blackness'* (London: University of Minnesota Press, 1995).

Gray, Jonathan, Jeffrey P. Jones and Ethan Thompson, eds, *Satire TV: Politics and Comedy in the Post-Network Era* (New York: New York University Press, 2009).

Green, Philip, *Cracks in the Pedestal: Ideology and Gender in Hollywood* (Amherst: University of Massachusetts Press, 1998).

Greenstein, Fred I., 'Change and Continuity in the Modern Presidency', in King, ed., *The New American Political System* (Washington, DC: American Enterprise Institute, 1978), 45–86.

Greven, David, *Manhood in Hollywood from Bush to Bush* (Austin: University of Texas Press, 2009).

Gross, Larry, 'Big and Loud', in Arroyo, ed., *Action/Spectacle Cinema*, 3–9.

Guerrero, Ed, 'The Black Image in Protective Custody: Hollywood's Biracial Buddy Films of the Eighties', in Diawara, ed., *Black American Cinema*, 237–46.

Gwynne, Joel, and Nadine Muller, 'Introduction', in Gwynne and Muller, eds, *Postfeminism and Contemporary Hollywood Cinema*, 1–10.

——, eds, *Postfeminism and Contemporary Hollywood Cinema* (Basingstoke: Palgrave Macmillan, 2013.

Halliday, Fred, *Shocked and Awed: How the War on Terror and Jihad Have Changed the English Language* (London: I.B. Tauris, 2011).

Hamad, Hannah, 'Hollywood Fatherhood: Paternal Postfeminism in Contemporary Hollywood Cinema', in Gwynne and Muller, eds, *Postfeminism and Contemporary Hollywood Cinema*, 99–115.

Hampton, Howard, 'See How They Run', *Film Comment* 44/5 (September/October 2008), 30–4.

Hampton-Reeves, Stuart, and Carol Chillington Rutter, *The Henry VI Plays* (Manchester: Manchester University Press, 2006).

Harris, Keith M., *Boys, Boyz, Bois: An Ethics of Black Masculinity in Film and Popular Media* (Abingdon: Routledge, 2006).

Hart, John, 'The Presidency in the 1990s', in Peele *et al.*, eds, *Developments in American Politics 2* (Basingstoke: Macmillan, 1994).

Hart, Roderick P., *Seducing America: How Television Charms the Modern Voter* (Oxford: Oxford University Press, 1994).

——, and Bartholomew H. Sparrow, eds, *Politics, Discourse and American Society: New Agendas* (Oxford: Rowman and Littlefield, 2001).

Haskell, Molly, *From Reverence to Rape: The Treatment of Women in the Movies* (Chicago: University of Chicago Press, 1987).

Hastedt, Glenn P., ed., *The Post-Cold War Presidency* (Oxford: Rowman and Littlefield Publishers, 1999).
Hearn, Jeff, 'Imaging the Aging of Men', in Featherstone and Wernick, eds, *Images of Aging*, 97–115.
Hellman, John, *The Kennedy Obsession: The American Myth of JFK* (New York: Columbia University Press, 1977).
Herbert, Daniel, 'Days and Hours of the Apocalypse: *24* and the Nuclear Narrative', in Peacock, ed., *Reading 24*, 85–96.
Hersh, Seymour M., *The Dark Side of Camelot* (New York: Back Bay Books, 1997).
Hicks, Heather S., 'Hoodoo Economics: White Men's Work and Black Men's Magic in Contemporary American Film', *Camera Obscura* 18/2 (2003), 27–55.
Hjort, Mette and Scott Mackenzie, eds, *Cinema and Nation* (London: Routledge, 2000).
Hoberman, J., '*Nashville* contra *Jaws*', in Thomas Elsaesser, Alexander Horwath and Noel King, eds, *The Last Great American Picture Show*, 195–222.
——, 'Under the Rainbow', *Sight and Sound* 9/1 (1999), 14–16.
——, 'When Dr No Met Dr Strangelove', *Sight and Sound* 3/12 (1993), 16–21.
Hofstadter, Richard, *The Paranoid Style in American Politics and Other Essays* (London: Jonathan Cape, 1966).
Hollern Harvey, Diane, 'The Public's View of Clinton', in Schier, ed., *The Postmodern Presidency*, 124–42.
Hollows, Joanne and Mark Jancovich, *Approaches to Popular Film* (Manchester: Manchester University Press, 1995).
Holmund, Chris, *Impossible Bodies: Femininity and Masculinity at the Movies* (London: Routledge, 2002).
Horwitz, Linda, and Holly Swyers, 'Why Are All The Presidents Men?: Televisual Presidents and Patriarchy', in Goren, ed., *You've Come a Long Way, Baby*, 115–36.
Howard, Douglas, '"You're You're Going to Tell Me Everything You Know": Torture and Morality in Fox's *24*', in Peacock, ed., *Reading 24*, 133–45.
Hunt, Darnell M., ed., *Channeling Blackness: Studies on Television and Race in America* (New York: Oxford University Press, 2005).
Hutschnecker, Arnold, *The Drive for Power* (New York: M.Evans, 1974).
Jackson, Martin A., 'Abraham Lincoln', in Rollins, ed., *The Columbia Companion to American History on Film*, 175–9.
Jackson, Richard, *Writing the War on Terrorism: Language, Politics and Counter-Terrorism* (Manchester: Manchester University Press, 2005).
Jameson, Frederic, 'Periodizing the 60s', in Sayres *et al.*, eds, *The 60s Without Apology*, 178–209.
——, *Postmodernism or, The Cultural Logic of Late Capitalism* (London: Verso, 1991).

Jamieson, Kathleen Hall, *Packaging the Presidency: A History and Criticism of Presidential Campaign Advertising* (Oxford: Oxford University Press, 1984).

Jancovich, Mark, *Rational Fears: American Horror in the 1950s* (Manchester: Manchester University Press, 1996).

Jancovich, Mark, and James Lyons, eds, *Quality Popular Television: Cult TV, the Industry and Fans* (London: British Film Institute, 2003).

Jeffers McDonald, Tamar, *Romantic Comedy: Boy Meets Girl Meets Genre* (London: Wallflower Press, 2007).

Jeffords, Susan, 'The Big Switch: Hollywood Masculinity in the Nineties', in Collins, Radner and Collins, eds, *Film Theory Goes to the Movies*, 196–208.

——, *Hard Bodies: Hollywood Masculinity in the Reagan Era* (New Brunswick, NJ: Rutgers University Press, 1994).

——, *The Remasculinization of America: Gender and the Vietnam War* (Bloomington: Indiana University Press, 1989).

Jewell, K. Sue., *From Mammy to Miss America and Beyond: Cultural Images and the Shaping of US Social Policy* (London: Routledge, 1993).

Jhally, Sut, and Justin Lewis, 'White Responses: The Emergence of "Enlightened" Racism', in Hunt, ed., *Channeling Blackness*, 74–88.

Johnston, Claire, 'Women's Cinema as Counter-Cinema', in Grant, ed., *Auteurs and Authorship*, 119–26.

Jones, Jeffrey P., 'With all Due Respect: Satirizing Presidents from *Saturday Night Live* to *Lil' Bush*', in Gray, Jones and Thompson, eds, *Satire TV*, 37–63.

Judis, John B., 'The Great Awakening', *The New Republic* 41 (February 1993).

Kakoudaki, Despina, 'Spectacles of History: Race Relations, Melodrama, and the Science Fiction/Disaster Film', *Camera Obscura* 17/2 (2002), 108–53.

Kaklamanidou, Betty and Margaret J. Tally, eds, *Politics and Politicians in Contemporary US Television: Washington as Fiction* (Abingdon: Routledge, 2017).

Kann, M., 'Manhood, Immortality and Politics During the American Founding', *The Journal of Men's Studies* 5 (1996) <http://www.thefreelibrary.com/Manhood,+immortality,+and+politics+during+the+American+founding.-a019095214>, accessed October 2010.

Kantorowicz, Ernst (1957), *The King's Two Bodies: A Study in Medieval Political Theology* (Princeton, NJ: Princeton University Press, 1997).

Kaplan, E. Ann, *Trauma Culture: The Politics of Terror and Loss in Media and Literature* (New Brunswick, NJ: Rutgers University Press, 2005).

Keane, Stephen, *Disaster Movies: The Cinema of Catastrophe* (London: Wallflower Press, 2001).

Kearns Goodwin, Doris, *Lyndon Johnson and the American Dream* (New York: Harper & Row, 1976).

Keathley, Christian, 'Trapped in the Affection Image: Hollywood's Post Traumatic Cycle' (1970–1976)', in Thomas Elsaesser, Alexander Horwath and Noel King, eds, *The Last Great American Picture Show*, 293–308.

Kelley, Beverly Merrill, 'Populism in *Mr Smith Goes to Washington*', in Kelley, Pitney, Smith and Gooch, eds, *Reelpolitik*, 7–24.

——, John. J. Pitney Jr., Craig R. Smith and Herbert E. Gooch III, eds, *Reelpolitik: Political Ideologies in 30s and 40s Films* (Westport, CT: Praeger, 1998).

Kellner, Douglas, *Cinema Wars: Hollywood Film and Politics in the Bush-Cheney Era* (Chichester: Wiley-Blackwell, 2010).

——, 'Film, Politics and Ideology: Toward a Multiperspectival Film Theory', in Combs, ed., *Movies and Politics*, 55–92.

Kendrick, James, 'Representing the Unrepresentable: 9/11 on Film and Television', in Rollins and O'Connor, eds, *Why We Fought*, 511–28.

Kennedy, John Fitzgerald [1956], *Profiles in Courage* (New York: Harper Collins, 2003).

—— [1940], *Why England Slept* (Westport: Greenwood Press, 1961).

Kennedy, Rose Fitzgerald, *Times to Remember* (Pan Books: London, 1975).

Keyishian, Harry, *Screening Politics: The Politician in American Movies* (Scarecrow Press, 2006).

Kimmel, Michael, *Manhood in America: A Cultural History* (New York: Free Press, 1996).

King, Anthony, ed., *The New American Political System* (Washington, DC: American Enterprise Institute, 1978).

King, Claire Sisco, *Washed in Blood: Male Sacrifice, Trauma and the Cinema* (New Brunswick, NJ: Rutgers University Press, 2011).

King, Geoff, *Spectacular Narratives: Hollywood in the Age of the Blockbuster* (London: I.B. Tauris, 2000).

——, ed., *The Spectacle of the Real: From Hollywood to 'Reality' TV and Beyond* (Bristol: Intellect, 2005).

Klein, Joe, *The Natural: The Misunderstood Presidency of Bill Clinton* (London: Hodder and Stoughton, 2002).

Knee, Adam, 'Harrison Ford: A Well-Tempered Machismo', Eberwein, ed., *Acting for America*, 160–79.

Knock, Thomas J., 'History with Lightning: The Forgotten Film *Wilson* (1944)', in Rollins, ed., *Hollywood as Historian*, 88–108.

Kord, Susanne, and Elisabeth Krimmer, *Contemporary Hollywood Masculinities: Gender, Genre, and Politics* (New York: Palgrave Macmillan, 2011).

Kracauer, Siegfried, *From Caligari to Hitler: A Psychological History of the German Film* (London: Princeton University Press, 2004).

Krauthammer, Charles, 'The Unipolar Moment', *Foreign Affairs* 70/1 (1990/91), 23–33.

Langford, Barry, *Post-Classical Hollywood: Film Industry, Style and Ideology Since 1945* (Edinburgh: Edinburgh University Press, 2010).

Langston, Thomas, *With Reverence and Contempt: How Americans Think About Their President* (Baltimore: John Hopkins University Press, 1995).

Lawrence, John Shelton, 'The 100 Million$ Men: President Action/Adventure Heroes of *Independence Day* (1996) and *Air Force One* (1997)', in Rollins and O'Connor, eds, *Hollywood's White House*, 223–33.

Leff, Leonard. J. and Jerold Simmons, '*Wilson*: Hollywood Propaganda for World Peace', *Historical Journal of Film, Radio and Television* 3/1 (1983), 3–18.

Lehmann, Chris, 'The Feel-Good Presidency: The Psuedo-Politics of *The West Wing*', in Rollins and O'Connor, eds, *The West Wing*, 213–21.

Lehman, Peter, ed., *Masculinity: Bodies, Movies, Culture* (London: Routledge, 2001).

Lev, Peter, ed., *The Fifties: Transforming the Screen 1950–1959* (Berkeley: University of California Press, 2003).

Levine, Lawrence, 'Hollywood's Washington: Film Images of National Politics During the Great Depression', *Prospect* 10 (1985), 169–85.

——, *The Unpredictable Past* (Oxford: Oxford University Press, 1993).

Levine, Myron A., 'Myth and Reality in the Hollywood Campaign Film: *Primary Colors* (1998) and *The War Room* (1994)', in Rollins and O'Connor, eds, *Hollywood's White House*, 288–308.

——, '*The West Wing* (NBC) and The West Wing (D.C.): Myth and Reality in Television's Portrayal of the White House', in Rollins and O'Connor, eds, *The West Wing*, 42–62.

Levinson, Julie, *The American Success Myth on Film* (Basingstoke: Palgrave Macmillan, 2012).

Lewis, Jon (ed.) *The End of Cinema as we know it: American Film in the Nineties* (London: Pluto Press, 2002).

Lichtenfeld, Eric, *Action Speaks Louder: Violence, Spectacle and the American Action Movie* (Middletown: Wesleyan University Press, 2007).

Lindholm, Charles, and John A. Hall, 'Frank Capra Meets John Doe: Anti-Politics in American National Identity', in Hjort and MacKenzie, eds, *Cinema and Nation*, 34–42.

Lipschutz, Ronnie D., *Cold War Fantasies: Film, Fiction and Foreign Policy* Lanham: Rowman & Littlefield Publishers, Inc., 2001).

Lugo-Lugo, Carmen R., and Mary K. Bloodsworth-Lugo, 'Bare Biceps and American (In)Security: Post-9/11 Constructions of Safe(ty), Threat, and the First Black First Lady', *Women's Studies Quarterly* 39/1–2 (2011), 200–17.

Macinnes, John, *The End of Masculinity* (Buckingham: Open University Press, 1998).

Mackey-Kallis, Susan, *Oliver Stone's America: 'Dreaming the Myth Outward'* (Oxford: Westview, 1996).

Macnab, Geoffrey, '*Air Force One*', in Arroyo, ed., *Action/Spectacle Cinema*, 250–2.

MacNeil, Robert, *The People Machine: The Influence of Television on American Politics* (London: Eyre & Spottiswoode, 1970).

Malin, Brenton J., *American Masculinity Under Clinton: Popular Media and the Nineties 'Crisis of Masculinity'* (New York: Peter Lang, 2005).

Maltby, Richard, *Harmless Entertainment: Hollywood and the ideology of consensus* (London: Scarecrow, 1983).

Marcus, Daniel, *Happy Days and Wonder Years: The Fifties and Sixties in Contemporary Cultural Politics* (New Brunswick, NJ: Rutgers University Press, 2004).

——, 'Profiles in Courage: Televisual History on the New Frontier', in Edgerton and Rollins, eds, *Television Histories*, 79–99.

Marcus, Greil, *The Manchurian Candidate* (London: British Film Institute, 2002).

Marshall, Kingsley, 'Oliver Stone's Improbable *W.*', in Morgan, ed., *Presidents in the Movies*, 177–91.

Mason, Robert, '"If You're Disgusted with Us, I Don't Blame You": Television and American Politics Today', in Singh, ed., *American Politics and Society Today*, 80–100.

Matthews, Nicole, *Comic politics: Gender in Hollywood comedy after the new right* (Manchester: Manchester University Press, 2000).

Matviko, John, 'Television Satire and the Presidency: The Case of *Saturday Night Live*', in Rollins and O'Connor, eds, *Hollywood's White House*, 333–48.

——, ed., *The American President in Popular Culture* (Greenwood Press, 2005).

May, Ernest R., and Philip D. Zelikow, eds, *The Kennedy Tapes: Inside the White House During the Cuban Missile Crisis* (New York: The Miller Center of Public Affairs, 2002).

May, Lary, *The Big Tomorrow: Hollywood and the Politics of the American Way* (London: University of Chicago Press, 2000).

Mayer, Jane, *The Dark Side: The Inside Story on How the War on Terror Turned into a War on American Ideals* (New York: Random House, 2008).

McAlister, Melani, 'A Cultural History of the War Without End', *The Journal of American History* 89/2 (September 2002), 439–56.

McCabe, Janet, 'Damsels in Distress: Female Narrative Authority and Knowledge in *24*', in Peacock, ed., *Reading 24*, 149–61.

——, *The West Wing* (Detroit: Wayne State University Press, 2013).

——, and Kim Akass, eds, *Quality TV: Contemporary American Television and Beyond* (London: I.B. Tauris, 2007).

McCormick, James M., 'Clinton and Foreign Policy: Some Legacies for a New Century', in Schier, ed., *The Postmodern Presidency*, 61–82.

McCrisken, Trevor, *American Exceptionalism and the Legacy of Vietnam: American Foreign Policy since 1974* (Basingstoke: Palgrave Macmillan, 2003).

——, and Andrew Pepper, *American History and Contemporary Hollywood Film* (Edinburgh: Edinburgh University Press, 2005).

McGregor, Alex, 'This Old House', *American Cinematographer* 76/11 (1995), 83–6.

McIlwain, Charlton, 'Leadership, Legitimacy, and Public Perceptions of Barack Obama', in Gillespie, ed., *Whose Black Politics?*, 155–72.

McPhail, Mark Lawrence, and David A. Frank, 'Barack Obama's Address to the Democratic National Convention: Trauma, Compromise, Consilience, and the (Im) possibility of Racial Reconciliation, *Rhetoric and Public Affairs* 8/4 (2005), 571–93.

Mickelson, Sig, *From Whistle Stop to Sound Bite: Four Decades of Politics and Television* (London: Praeger, 1989).

Miroff, Bruce, 'Courting the Public: Bill Clinton's Postmodern Education', in Schier, ed., *The Postmodern Presidency*, 106–23.

——, 'From "Midcentury" to *Fin-de-Siecle*: The Exhaustion of the Presidential Image', *Rhetoric and Public Affairs* 1 (1998), 185–99.

——, *Icons of Democracy: American Leaders as Heroes, Aristocrats, Dissenters, and Democrats* (New York: Harper Collins, 1993).

——, 'The Presidency and the Public: Leadership as Spectacle', in Nelson, ed., *The Presidency and the Political System*, 299–322.

Mitchell, Juliet, *Women: The Longest Revolution Essays in Feminism, Literature and Psychoanalysis* (London: Virago, 1984).

Modleski, Tania, *Feminism without Women: Culture and Criticism in a 'Postfeminist' Age* (London: Routledge, 1991).

Monsell, Thomas, *Nixon on stage and screen: the thirty-seventh president as depicted in films, television, plays and opera* (Jefferson: McFarland, 1998).

Morgan, Iwan W., 'Introduction', in Morgan, ed., *Presidents in the Movies*, 1–25.

——, ed., *Presidents in the Movies: American History and Politics on Screen* (New York: Palgrave Macmillan, 2011).

Morreale, Joanne, 'Playing Politics: Mythical Portraiture in Presidential Campaign Film,' *Visual Communication Quarterly* 3/1 (1996), 8–12.

——, *The Presidential Campaign Film: A Critical History* (Westport: Praeger, 1996).

——, '*Tanner '88*', in Edgerton and Jones, eds, *The Essential HBO Reader*, 103–15.

Morrison, James, 'Hostages and Houseguests: Class and Family in the New Screen Gothic', in Pomerance, ed., *A Family Affair*, 189–201.

Moseley, Rachel, and Jacinda Reid, '"Having it Ally": Popular Television (Post-Feminism', *Feminist Media Studies* 2/2 (2002), 231–49.

Murphy, John M., 'The Heroic Tradition in Presidential Rhetoric', *Rhetoric and Public Affairs* 3 (2000), 466–70.

Muscio, Giuliana, *Hollywood's New Deal* (Philadelphia: Temple University Press, 1997).

Nadel, Alan, *Flatlining on the Field of Dreams: Cultural Narratives in the Films of President Reagan's America* (New Brunswick: Rutgers University Press, 1997).

Neale, Steve, 'The big romance or something wild', *Screen* 33:3 (Autumn 1992), 284–99.

Nel, Philip, 'Obamafiction for Children: Imagining the 44th President', *Children's Literature Association Quarterly* 35/4 (2010), 334–56.

Nelson, Michael, ed., *The Presidency and the Political System* [5th edn] (Washington, DC: C.Q. Press, 1998).

Nelson, Robin, *State of Play: Contemporary 'High-End' TV Drama* (Manchester: Manchester University Press, 2007).

Neustadt, Richard, *Presidential Power and The Modern Presidents* (New York: The Free Press, 1980).

Neve, Brian, *Film and Politics in America: A Social Tradition* (London: Routledge, 1992).

——, 'Frames of Presidential and Candidate Politics in American Films of the 1990s', *The Public* 7/2 (2000), 19–32.

——, 'HUAC, The Blacklist, and The Decline of Social Cinema', in Lev, ed., *The Fifties*, pp. 65–86.

——, '"The Picture Man": The Cinematic Strife of Theodore Roosevelt', in Morgan, ed., *Presidents in the Movies*, 65–86.

Newcomb, Horace, ed., *Television: The Critical View* [5th edn] (Oxford: Oxford University Press, 1994).

Newcomb, Horace, and Paul Hirsch, 'Television as Cultural Forum', in Newcomb, ed., *Television: The Critical View*, 503–15.

——, 'Television as a Cultural Forum: Implications for Research', in Rowland and Watkins, eds, *Interpreting Television*, 58–73.

Nichols, Bill, ed., *Movies and Methods: An Anthology* (London: University of California Press, 1976).

Nichols, David K., *The Myth of the Modern Presidency* (University Park: The Pennsylvania State University Press, 1994).

Nickel, John, 'Disabling African American Men: Liberalism and Race Message Films', *Cinema Journal* 44/1 (2004), 25–48.

Nixon, Richard, *Seize the Moment: America's Challenge in a One-Superpower World* (New York: Simon and Schuster, 1994).

Norton, Anne, *Republic of Signs: Liberal Theory and American Popular Culture* (Chicago: University of Chicago Press, 1993).
Obama, Barack [2006], *The Audacity of Hope: Thoughts on Reclaiming the American Dream* (Edinburgh: Canongate Books, 2007).
—— [1995, *Dreams From My Father: A Story of Race and Inheritance* (Edinburgh: Canongate Books, 2007).
O'Donnell, Victoria, 'Science Fiction Films and Cold War Anxiety', in Lev, ed., *The Fifties*, 169–96.
Oppenheimer, Jean, 'The Halls of Power', *American Cinematographer* 81/10 (2000), 74–83.
Orman, John, *Comparing Presidential Behavior: Carter, Reagan and The Macho Presidential Style* (New York: Greenwood Press, 1987).
Orvell, Miles, *The Real Thing: Imitation and Authenticity in American Culture 1880–1940* (Chapel Hill and London: University of North Carolina Press, 1989).
Osborne-Thompson, Heather, 'Tracing the "Fake" Candidate in American Television Comedy', in Gray, Jones and Thompson, eds, *Satire TV*, 64–81.
Parry-Giles, Shawn J., 'Mediating Hillary Rodham Clinton: Television News Practices and Image-Making in the Postmodern Age', *Critical Studies in Communication* 17/2 (2000), 205–26.
——, 'Political Authenticity, Television News, and Hillary Rodham Clinton', in Hart and Sparrow, eds, *Politics, Discourse and American Society*, 211–27.
——, and Trevor Parry-Giles, 'Meta-Imaging, *The War Room*, and the Hyperreality of US Politics', *Journal of Communication* (1999), 28–45.
——, *Constructing Clinton: Hyperreality and Presidential Image-Making in Postmodern Politics* (New York: Peter Lang, 2002).
Parry-Giles, Trevor and Shawn J. Parry-Giles, *The Prime-Time Presidency: The West Wing and US Nationalism* (Chicago: University of Illinois Press, 2006).
Peacock, Stephen, ed., *Reading 24: TV Against the Clock* (London: I.B. Tauris, 2007).
Peberdy, Donna, *Masculinity and Film Performance: Male Angst in Contemporary Cinema* (New York: Palgrave Macmillan, 2011).
Peele, Gillian, Christopher J. Bailey, Bruce Cain and B. Guy Peters, eds, *Developments in American Politics 3* (Basingstoke: Macmillan, 1998).
——, eds, *Developments in American Politics 2* (Basingstoke: Macmillan, 1994).
Peretti, Burton W., *The Leading Man: Hollywood and the Presidential Image* (New Brunswick: Rutgers University Press, 2012).
Petric, Vlada, 'Two Lincoln Assassinations by DW Griffith', *Quarterly Review of Film Studies* (1978), 347–69.

Phalen, Patricia F., Jennie Kim and Julia Osellame, 'Imagined Presidencies: The Representation of Political Power in Television Fiction', *The Journal of Popular Culture* 45/3 (2012), 532–50.

Philpott, Simon, and David Mutimer, 'Inscribing the American Body Politic: Martin Sheen and Two American Decades', *Geopolitics* 10/2 (2005), 335–55.

Pipolo, Tony, 'Hero or Demagogue?: Images of Lincoln in American Film', *Cineaste* 35/1 (2009), 14–26.

Pitney, John J., Jr., 'Fascism in *Gabriel over the White House*', in Kelley, Pitney, Smith and Gooch, eds, *Reelpolitik*, 45–60.

Podhoretz, John, 'The Liberal Imagination', in Rollins and O'Connor, eds, *The West Wing*, 222–31.

Pomerance, Murray, ed., *A Family Affair: Cinema Calls Home* (London: Wallflower Press, 2008).

Pompper, Donnalyn, '*The West Wing*: White House Narratives That Journalism Can't Tell', in Rollins and O'Connor, eds, *The West Wing*, 17–31.

Powers, Stephen, David J. Rothman and Stanley Rothman, *Hollywood's America: Social and Political Themes in Motion Pictures* (Oxford: Westview, 1996).

Prince, Stephen, *Firestorm: American Film in the Age of Terrorism* (New York: Columbia University Press, 2009).

Purse, Lisa, *Contemporary Action Cinema* (Edinburgh: Edinburgh University Press, 2011).

Quart, Leonard, and Albert Auster, *American Film and Society Since 1945* [3rd edn] (London: Praeger, 2002).

Randell, Karen, '"It was Like a Movie": The Impossibility of Representation in Oliver Stone's *World Trade Center*', in Birkenstein, Froula and Randell, eds, *Reframing 9/11*, 141–52.

Ranney, Austin, *Channels of Power: The Impact of Television on American Politics* (New York: Basic Books, 1983).

Raphael, Timothy, *The President Electric: Ronald Reagan and The Politics of Performance* (University of Michigan Press: 2009).

Redfield, Marc, *The Rhetoric of Terror: Reflections on 9/11 and the War on Terror* (New York: Fordham University Press, 2009).

Reedy, George E., *The Twilight of the Presidency: From Johnson to Reagan* (New York: New American Library, 1987).

Reeves, Thomas C., *A Question of Character: A Life of John F. Kennedy* (New York: Crown Forum Publishing, 1991).

Renshon, Stanley A., *High Hopes: The Clinton Presidency and the Politics of Ambition* (London: New York University Press, 1996).

——, *In His Father's Shadow: The Transformations of George W. Bush* (Basingstoke: Palgrave Macmillan, 2004).

Richards, Jeffrey, 'Frank Capra and The Cinema of Populism', in Nichols, ed., *Movies and Methods*, 65–77.

Richardson Hayton, Heather, 'The King's Two Bodies: Identity and Office in Sorkin's *West Wing*', in Rollins and O'Connor, eds, *The West Wing*, 63–79.

Rochelle, Warren G., 'The Literary Presidency', *Presidential Studies Quarterly* 29/2 (1999), 407–20.

Roddick, Nick, 'Only the stars survive: disaster movies in the seventies', in Bradby, James and Sharratt, eds, *Performance and politics in popular drama*, 243–71.

Roffman, Peter and Jim Purdy, *The Hollywood Social Problem Film: Madness, Despair and Politics from the Depression to the Fifties* (Bloomington: Indiana University Press, 1981).

Rogin, Michael, *Independence Day: Or How I Learned to Stop Worrying and Love the Enola Gay* (London: British Film Institute, 1998).

——, *Ronald Reagan, The Movie: And Other Episodes in Political Demonology* (Berkeley and Los Angeles: University of California Press, 1987).

Rollins, Peter C., 'Introduction', in Rollins, ed., *Hollywood as Historian*, 1–8.

——, 'The Presidency After World War II', in Rollins, ed., *The Columbia Companion to American History on Film*, 402–8.

——, ed., *The Columbia Companion to American History on Film* (New York: Columbia University Press, 2003).

——, ed., *Hollywood as Historian: American Film in a Cultural Context* (Lexington: University of Kentucky Press, 1983).

——, and John E. O'Connor, eds, 'Introduction', in Rollins and O'Connor, eds, *Hollywood's White House*, 1–16.

——, 'Introduction: *The West Wing*, The American Presidency as Television Drama', in Rollins and O'Connor, eds, *The West Wing*, 1–13.

Rollins, Peter C., and O'Connor, John E. (eds), *Hollywood's White House: The American Presidency in Film and History* (Lexington: University of Kentucky Press, 2003).

——, eds, *The West Wing: The American Presidency as Television Drama* (Syracuse: Syracuse University Press, 2003).

——, eds, *Why We Fought: America's Wars in Film and History* (Lexington: University Press of Kentucky, 2008).

Roosevelt, Theodore [1899], *The Strenuous Life: Essays and Addresses* (New York: Cosimo, 2006).

——, *Roosevelt, His Life, Meaning and Messages* (New York: Current Literature Publishing, 1919).

Roper, Jon, *The American Presidents: Heroic Leadership from Kennedy to Clinton* (Edinburgh: Edinburgh University Press, 2000).

Rose, Richard, *The Postmodern President: George Bush Meets the World* [2nd edn] (Chatham, NJ: Chatham House Publishers, 1991).

Rosenstone, Robert A., *Revisioning History: Film and Construction of a new Past* (Princeton, NJ: Princeton University Press, 1994).

Rossinow, Doug, *The Politics of Authenticity: Liberalism, Christianity, and the New Left in America* (New York: Columbia University Press, 1998).

Rossiter, Clinton, *The American Presidency* [2nd edn] (London: Hart-Davis, 1960).

Rostron, Allen, 'Mr Carter Goes to Washington', *Journal of Popular Film and Television* 25/2 (1997), 57–67.

Rowland, Willard D., and Bruce Watkins, eds, *Interpreting Television: Current Research Perspectives* (London: Sage, 1984).

Rundle, Guy, *The West Wing* (BFI Television Classics), unpublished manuscript, 2011.

Rutenburg, Jeannie, 'Television Fantasy, Political Reality, and Pop Culture in Aaron Sorkin's *The West Wing*', *Film International* 6 (2003), 10–15.

Rutherford, Jonathan, *Men's Silences: Predicaments in Masculinity* (London: Routledge, 1992).

Ryan, Michael, and Douglas Kellner, *Camera Politica: the Politics and Ideology of Contemporary Hollywood Film* (Bloomington: Indiana University press, 1988).

St. Jean, Yanick and Joe R. Feagin, *Double Burden: Black Women and Everyday Racism* (New York: M.E. Sharpe, 1998).

Salt, Barry, 'From Caligari to Who?', *Sight and Sound* 48 (1979), 119–23.

Sarris, Andrew, *Politics and Cinema* (New York: Columbia University Press, 1978).

Sayres, Sohnya, Anders Stephanson, Stanely Aronowitz and Frederic Jameson, eds, *The 60s Without Apology* (Minneapolis: University of Minnesota Press, 1984).

Schier, Steven E., 'A Unique Presidency', in Schier, ed., *The Postmodern Presidency*, 1–16.

——, ed., *The Postmodern Presidency: Bill Clinton's Legacy in US Politics* (Pittsburgh: University of Pittsburgh Press, 2000).

Schlesinger Jr., Arthur, *The Imperial Presidency* (London: Andre Deutsch Limited, 1974).

Schroeder, Alan, *Presidential Debates: Forty Years of High-Risk TV* (New York: Columbia University Press, 2000).

Schwartz, Barry, 'The Character of Washington: A Study in Republican Culture', *American Quarterly* 38 (1986), 202–22.

Sconce, Jeffrey, *Haunted Media: Electronic Presence From Telegraphy To Television* (Durham: Duke University Press, 2000).

Scott, Ian, *American Politics in Hollywood Film* (Edinburgh: Edinburgh University Press, 2000).

——, *American Politics in Hollywood Film* [2nd edn] (Edinburgh: Edinburgh University Press, 2011).

——, 'Mr Innocence Goes to Washington: Hollywood and the Mythology of American Politics', in Davies, ed., *Representing and Imagining America*, 232–39.

——, 'Transition: The Making of Screen Presidents', in Morgan, ed., *Presidents in the Movies*, 27–44.

Selzer, Linda F., 'Barack Obama, the 2008 Election, and the New Cosmopolitanism Figuring the Black Body', *Multi-Ethnic Literature of the US* 35/4 (2010), 15–37.

Sexton, Jared, 'The Ruse of Engagement: Black Masculinity and the Cinema of Policing', *American Quarterly* 61/1 (2009), 35–63.

Shapiro, Jerome F., *Atomic Bomb Cinema* (London: Routledge, 2002).

Shaw, Marc E., and Elwood Watson, 'Obama's Masculinities: A Landscape of Essential Contradictions', in Watson and Shaw, eds, *Performing American Masculinities*, 134–52.

Shaw, Tony, *Hollywood's Cold War* (Edinburgh: Edinburgh University Press, 2007).

Shohat, Ella, and Robert Stam, *Unthinking Eurocentrism: Multiculturalism in the Media* (London: Routledge, 1994).

Shull, Michael S., 'Franklin and Eleanor Roosevelt', in Rollins, ed., *The Columbia Companion to American History on Film*, 184–90.

Silberstein, Sandra, *War of Words: Language, Politics and 9/11* (London: Routledge, 2002).

Simon, Art, *Dangerous Knowledge: The JFK Assassination in Art and Film* (Philadelphia: Temple University Press, 1996).

Singh, Robert, ed., *American Politics and Society Today* (Cambridge: Polity Press, 2002).

Skirrow, Gillian, 'Women/Acting/Power', in Baehr and Dyer, eds, *Boxed In*, 164–83.

Smith, Carol R., 'Gender and family values in the Clinton presidency and 1990s Hollywood film', in Davies and Wells, eds, *American Film and Politics from Reagan to Bush Jr.*, 77–88.

Smith, Gavin, 'The Dark Side', *Sight and Sound* 6/3 (1996), 6–9.

Smith, Jeff, *The Presidents We Imagine: Two Centuries of the White House Fictions on the Page, on the Stage, Onscreen and Online* (Madison: University of Wisconsin Press, 2009).

Smith, Kathy, 'Reframing Fantasy: September 11 and the Global Audience', in King, ed., *The Spectacle of the Real*, 59–70.

Smoodin, Eric, '"Compulsory" Viewing for Every Citizen: *Mr Smith* and The Rhetoric of Reception', *Cinema Journal* 35/2 (1996), 3–23.

Snead, James, *White Screens, Black Images* (New York: Routledge, 1994).

Sobchack, Vivian, ed., *The Persistence of History: Cinema, Television and the Modern Event* (London: Routledge, 1996).

Sontag, Susan, *Against Interpretation* (London: Vintage, 2001).

Spigel, Lynn, 'Entertainment Wars: Television Culture After 9/11', *American Quarterly* 56/2 (2004), 235–70.

Stam, Robert, and Louise Spence, 'Colonialism, Racism and Representation', *Screen* 24/2 (1983), 2–20.

Stephanopoulous, George, *All Too Human: A Political Education* (London: Little, Brown and Company, 1999).

Stoakes, Geoff, 'JFK, Vietnam and the Public Mind', in Davies, ed., *Representing and Imagining America,* 200–9.

Stoddart, Scott F., 'Film', in Matviko, ed., *The American President in Popular Culture,* 155–70.

Stokes, Melvyn, 'D.W. Griffith's *Abraham Lincoln*', in Morgan, ed., *Presidents in the Movies,* 45–61.

Strick, Philip, '*Deep Impact*', *Sight and Sound* 8/7 (1998), 39–40.

Stringer, Julian, ed., *Movie Blockbusters* (London: Routledge, 2003).

Strozier, Charles B., *Lincoln's Quest for Union: A Psychological Portrait* [2nd edn] (Philadelphia: Paul Dry Books, 2001).

Stuckey, Mary E., and Shannon Wabshall, 'Sex, Lies and Presidential Leadership: Interpretations of the Office', *Presidential Studies Quarterly* 30 (2000), 514–33.

Summers, Anthony, and Robbyn Swan, *The Arrogance of Power: The Secret World of Richard Nixon* (London: Viking, 2000).

Tasker, Yvonne, 'Dumb Movies for Dumb People: Masculinity, the body, and the voice in contemporary action cinema', in Cohan and Park, eds, *Screening the Male,* 230–44.

——, 'Practically Perfect People: Postfeminism, Masculinity and Male Parenting n Contemporary Hollywood Cinema', in Pomerance, ed., *A Family Affair,* 175–87.

——, *Spectacular Bodies: Gender, Genre and the Action Cinema* (London: Routledge, 1993).

——, *Working Girls: Gender and Sexuality in Popular Cinema* (London: Routledge, 1998).

Tasker, Yvonne, and Diane Negra, eds, *Interrogating Postfeminism: Gender and the politics of popular culture* (Durham: Duke University Press, 2007).

——, 'Introduction: Feminist Politics and Postfeminist Culture', in Tasker and Negra, eds, *Interrogating Postfeminism,* 1–26.

Taubin, Amy, 'Playing it Straight', *Sight and Sound* (August 1996), 6–8.

Thimsen, A. Freya, 'Populist Celebrity in the Election Campaigns of Jesse Ventura and Arnold Schwarzenegger', *The Velvet Light Trap* 65 (2010), 44–57.

Thomson, David, 'The Decade When Movies Mattered', in Thomas Elsaesser, Alexander Horwath and Noel King, eds, *The Last Great American Picture Show,* 73–82.

Thompson, Robert J., *Television's Second Golden Age: From Hill Street Blues to ER* (New York: Syracuse University Press, 1997).

Timmerman, David M., '1992 Presidential Candidate Films: The Contrasting Narratives of George Bush and Bill Clinton', *Presidential Studies Quarterly* 26/2 (1996), 364–73.

Toplin, Robert Brent, *History by Hollywood: the use and abuse of the American past* (Urbana: University of Illinois Press, 1996).

——, *Reel History: In Defense of Hollywood* (University Press of Kansas, 2002).

——, ed., *Oliver Stone's USA: Film, History and Controversy* (Lawrence: University press of Kansas, 2000).

Traube, Elizabeth G., *Dreaming Identities: Class, Gender, and Generation in 1980s Hollywood Movies* (Boulder: Westview Press, 1992).

Turim, Maureen, *Flashbacks in Film: Memory and History* (London: Routledge, 1989).

Tulis, Jeffrey, *The Rhetorical Presidency* (Princeton, NJ: Princeton University Press, 1987).

Uscinski, Joseph E., 'Gendering the Presidency without Gender in the Presidency', in Vaughn and Goren, eds, *Women and the White House*, pp. 121–34.

——, and Lilly J. Goren, 'What's in a Name? Coverage of Senator Hillary Clinton during the 2008 Democratic Primary', *Political Research Quarterly* 64/4 (2011), 884–96.

Vaughn, Justin S., and Lilly J. Goren, eds, *Women and the White House: Gender, Popular Culture and Presidential Politics* (Lexington: University Press of Kentucky, 2013).

Vaughn, Justin S., and Stacy Michaelson, 'It's a Man's World: Masculinity in Pop Culture Portrayals of the President', in Vaughn and Goren, eds, *Women and the White House*, 135–59.

Vest, Jason P., 'From *The American President* to *The West Wing*: A Scriptwriter's Perspective', in Rollins and O'Connor, eds, *The West Wing*, 136–56.

Volkan, Vamik D., Norman Itzkowitz and Andrew W. Dod, *Richard Nixon: A Psychobiography* (New York: Columbia University Press, 1997).

Waites, Kate, 'Babes in boots: Hollywood's oxymoronic warrior woman', in Ferriss and Young, eds, *Chick flicks*, 204–20.

Walker, Martin, 'Clinton's Hollywood', *Sight and Sound* (September 1993), 13–14.

Walzer, Judith B., 'Yes, Ms. President?', *Dissent* (Winter 2009), 101–4.

Watson, Elwood and Marc E. Shaw, eds, *Performing American Masculinities: The 21st-Century Man in Popular Culture* (Bloomington: Indiana University Press, 2011).

Waxman, Sharon, 'Inside *The West Wing*'s New World', in Rollins and O'Connor, eds, *The West Wing*, 203–12.

Webster, Duncan, *Looka Yonder! The imaginary America of populist culture* (London: Routledge, 1988).

Whaley, Donald M., 'Richard Nixon', in Rollins, ed., *The Columbia Companion to American History on Film*, 180–83.

Wheeler, Mark, 'Darryl F. Zanuck's *Wilson*', in Morgan, ed., *Presidents in the Movies*, 87–104.

White, Hayden, 'The Modernist Event', in Sobchack, ed., *The Persistence of History*, 17–38.

White, Mark, 'The Cinematic Kennedy: *Thirteen Days* and The Burnishing of an Image', in Morgan, ed., *Presidents in the Movies*, 131–50.

White, Theodore H., *America in Search of Itself: The Making of the President 1956–80* (London: Jonathan Cape, 1983).

——, *In Search of History: A Personal Adventure* (London: Jonathan Cape, 1978).

Wiegman, Robyn, 'Black Bodies/American Commodities: Gender, Race, and the Bourgeois Ideal in Contemporary Film', in Friedman, ed., *Unspeakable Images*, 308–28.

Wildavsky, Aaron, ed., *The Beleaguered Presidency* (New Brunswick: Transaction Publishers, 1991).

Williams, Linda, *Playing the Race Card: Melodramas of Black and White From Uncle Tom to O.J. Simpson* (Princeton, NJ: Princeton University Press, 2001).

Williams, Raymond, *Marxism and Literature* (Oxford: Oxford University Press, 1977).

Wills, Garry, *The Kennedy Imprisonment: A Meditation on Power* (Boston: Little Brown and Company, 1981).

——, *Reagan's America: Innocents at Home* (London: Heinemann, 1988).

Winston Dixon, Wheeler, ed., *Film and Television After 9/11* (Carbondale: Southern Illinois University Press, 2004).

Wood, Robin, *Hollywood from Vietnam to Reagan ... and Beyond* (New York: Columbia University Press, 2003).

Yacowar, Maurice, 'The Bug in the Rug: Notes on the Disaster Genre', in Grant, ed., *Film Genre*, 90–107.

Newspaper/Magazine Articles

'Barack Obama's First Year in the White House – Photo Gallery', *Time Magazine*, archived online at <http://www.time.com/time/photogallery/0,29307,1946919_2011502,00.html> accessed August 2010.

Chiachere, Ryan, 'Tucker Carlson on Clinton: '"[W]hen she comes on television, I involuntarily cross my legs"', *Media Matters for America* (July 18th, 2007), <http://mediamatters.org/research/2007/07/18/tucker-carlson-on-clinton-when-she-comes-on-tel/139362>, accessed July 2013.

Dargis, Manohla, and A.O. Scott, 'How the Movies Made a President', *The New York Times* (January 18th, 2009), <http://www.nytimes.com/2009/01/18/movies/18darg.html>, accessed June 2011.

Dowd, Maureen, 'Of Knights and Presidents: Race of Mythic Proportions', *New York Times* (October 10th, 1992), 1.

Drew, Robert, 'A President to Remember: In the Company of John F. Kennedy', <http://www.drewassociates.net/Main/synopsislong.html>, accessed December 2011.

Ellwood, Mark, 'Yes, Barack Obama can lead with great style', *The New York Daily News* (November 5th, 2008), <http://www.nydailynews.com/lifestyle/fashion/2008/11/06/2008-11-06_yes_barack_obama_can_lead_with_great_sty.html>, accessed August 2010.

Harlow, John, 'Hollywood's warm-up act for Barack Obama', *The Times* (November 9th, 2008), <http://www.timesonline.co.uk/tol/news/world/us_and_americas/us_elections/article5114838.ece>, accessed June 2011.

Harnden, Toby, 'Barack Obama is JFK heir, says Kennedy aide' (October 12th, 2007), archived at <http://www.telegraph.co.uk/news/worldnews/1565992/Barack-Obama-is-JFK-heir-says-Kennedy-aide.html>, accessed August 2010.

Harris, Paul, 'Cult TV mogul angers Kennedy scholars with "sexy" life of JFK', *The Observer* (February 21st, 2010), p. 9.

Mailer, Norman, 'Superman Comes to the Supermarket', *Esquire* (November 1960), <http://www.esquire.com/features/superman-supermarket>, accessed August 2010.

'Martin Sheen shares worldview on *Charlie Rose*' (October 14th, 2002), archived at <http://martinsheen.net/id110.html>, accessed August 2012.

Mars-Jones, Adam, 'Get Me Out of Here', *The Independent* (September 11th, 1997), <http://www.independent.co.uk/arts-entertainment/get-me-out-of-here-1238525.html>, accessed April 2010.

'Michelle Obama describes duty as mother-in-chief', *USA Today* (August 4th, 2008), <http://usatoday30.usatoday.com/news/politics/election2008/2008-08-04-michelle-obama_N.htm>, accessed November 2013.

'Moviefone Poll Suggests Voters Want Nation Run By Fictional Idiots', <http://gawker.com/5068639/moviefone-poll-suggests-voters-want-nation-run-by-fictional-idiot-presidents>, accessed June 2012.

'Reagan Gets Idea from *Rambo* For Next Time', *The Los Angeles Times* (July 1st, 1985), <http://articles.latimes.com/1985-07-01/news/mn-10009_1_hostage>, accessed August 2012.

Rees-Mogg, William, 'Barack Obama – a John Kennedy for Our Times', *The Times* (18 February 2008), <http://www.timesonline.co.uk/tol/comment/columnists/william_rees_mogg/article3386292.ece>, accessed August 2010.

Reid, Tim, 'Obama savours his own White House Camelot in photo homage to Kennedy', *The Times* (Septmeber 3rd, 2009), <http://www.timesonline.co.uk/tol/news/world/us_and_americas/article6819237.ece>, accessed August 2010.

Rennie, David, 'That man tried to kill my dad', *The Daily Telegraph* (September 28th, 2002), <http://www.telegraph.co.uk/news/worldnews/northamerica/usa/1408573/That-man-tried-to-kill-my-dad-says-Bush.html#>, accessed August 2012.

Rich, Frank, 'Why Has He Fallen Short?', *The New York Review of Books* (July 22nd, 2010), <http://www.nybooks.com/articles/archives/2010/aug/19/why-has-he-fallen-short/?pagination=false>, accessed August 2010.

Robinson, Tasha, '*Abraham Lincoln: Vampire Hunter*', <http://www.avclub.com/articles/abraham-lincoln-vampire-hunter,81607/>, accessed September 2012.

Ryan, Josiah, '"This was a whitelash": Van Jones' take on the election results' (November 9th, 2016), <http://edition.cnn.com/2016/11/09/politics/van-jones-results-disappointment-cnntv/index.html>, accessed September 2017.

Shea, Danny, 'Katie Couric: Sexist Media Hurt Hillary Clinton's Chances', *The Huffington Post* (June 19th, 2008), <http://www.huffingtonpost.com/2008/06/11/katie-couric-sexist-media_n_106595.html>, accessed August 2013.

Sherwell, Phillip, 'Barack Obama "the new Jack Kennedy"', *The Telegraph* (January 14th, 2007), <http://www.telegraph.co.uk/news/worldnews/1539486/Barack-Obama-the-new-Jack-Kennedy.html>, accessed August 2010.

Sontag, Susan, 'The Talk of the Town', *The New Yorker* (September 24th, 2001), <http://www.newyorker.com/archive/2001/09/24/010924ta_talk_wtc>, accessed August 2012.

Steyn, Mark, 'Fight Now, Love Later: The Awfulness of an Oprahesque Response', *National Review* (October 15th, 2001).

Stolworthy, Jacob, 'Donald Trump presidency sparks rise in *The West Wing* viewership', *The Independent* (16th February 2017), <http://www.independent.co.uk/arts-entertainment/tv/news/donald-trump-the-west-wing-where-to-watch-aaron-sorkin-a7583516.html>, accessed March 2017.

Žižek, Slavoj, 'On 9/11, New Yorkers faced fire in the minds of men', *The Guardian* (September 11th, 2006), <http://www.guardian.co.uk/commentisfree/2006/sep/11/comment.september11>, accessed August 2012.

Speeches [Archived Online]

George W. Bush, State of the Union address, January 29th, 2002 <http://edition.cnn.com/2002/ALLPOLITICS/01/29/bush.speech.txt/>, accessed August 2012.

George W. Bush, address to joint session of Congress, September 20th, 2001 <http://edition.cnn.com/2001/US/09/20/gen.bush.transcript/>, accessed August 2012.

George W. Bush, 'US 'Will Hunt Down And Punish' Terrorists, Bush Says' (September 11th, 2001), <http://www.defense.gov/news/newsarticle.aspx?id=44914>, accessed August 2012.

Dick Cheney, 'Interview on *Meet the Press*', September 16th, 2001 <http://www.freerepublic.com/focus/f-news/525111/posts>, accessed August 2012.

John F. Kennedy, Inaugural Address, January 20th, 1961, <http://www.bartleby.com/124/pres56.html>, accessed November 2010.

Barack Obama, '2004 Democratic National Convention Keynote Address', <http://www.huffingtonpost.com/2008/03/18/obama-race-speech-read-th_n_92077.html>, accessed July 2011.

Index